THE TOP 30 THINGS YOU NEED TO KNOW FOR TOP SCORES IN MATH LEVEL 2

1. FRACTIONS

Make sure you know how to simplify fractions because answers are generally presented in simplest form. Be able to find the least common denominator of two or more fractions. Know how to multiply and divide fractions as well as use mixed numbers and improper fractions. Be comfortable solving fraction problems that involve variables.

See Chapter 4.

2. PERCENTAGES

Be able to convert between percents, decimals, and fractions. Be able to recognize the meaning of terminology used in percentage problems in order to solve for an unknown.

See Chapter 4.

3. EXPONENTS

Familiarize yourself with the exponential notation and know how to apply the rules of exponents, particularly to simplify an expression containing multiple exponents. Avoid common mistakes with exponents, such as incorrectly addressing negative exponents or multiplying exponents when they should be added. Be aware of rational exponents as well as variables in exponents.

See Chapter 4.

4. REAL NUMBERS

Be able to relate the different types of real numbers, and which groups are subsets of other groups. Know the properties of real numbers, including the properties of addition and multiplication. Be able to apply the distributive property. Review absolute value to know:

- what it means
- how it is represented in symbolic form
- how to solve problems involving absolute value

See Chapter 4.

5. RADICALS

Know how to find roots of real numbers. Be aware that some problems two solutions. Know how to:

- identify the principal square root
- use the product and quotient properties of radicals

- determine the simplest radical form
- rationalize a denominator containing a radical for both square roots and cube roots
- use a conjugate, especially when the denominator contains a binomial radical expression

See Chapter 4.

6. POLYNOMIALS

Know how to add, subtract, multiply, and factor polynomials. Be familiar with the products of special polynomials, such as $(a + b)^2$, $(a - b)^2$, and $(a + b)(a - b)$. Be able to recognize perfect square trinomials and the difference of perfect squares.

See Chapter 4.

7. QUADRATIC EQUATIONS

Know the meaning of each term in the Quadratic Formula. Be able to:

- choose the answer that lists the roots of the quadratic equation
- determine the nature of the roots of a quadratic equation without actually solving for them
- use the discriminant to decide if there are two real rational roots, two real irrational roots, one real root, or no roots

See Chapter 4.

8. INEQUALITIES

Know the Transitive Property of Inequality as well as the addition and multiplication properties. Inequalities questions may involve conjunctions or disjunctions, as well as absolute values. Be prepared to relate a solution to a graph.

See Chapter 4 and Chapter 6.

9. RATIONAL EXPRESSIONS

Know how to simplify rational expressions and solve equations involving rational expressions. Be familiar with the special products studied with polynomials. Be able to multiply, divide, add, and subtract rational expressions.

See Chapter 4.

10. SYSTEMS

Review simultaneous equations and equivalent systems. Be able to solve systems by substitution or linear combination. Distinguish between the three possible solution sets: one solution, no solution, and infinitely many solutions. Be familiar with word problems with two unknowns. Know how to set up a system and solve it to find the answer.

See Chapter 4.

11. THREE-DIMENSIONAL FIGURES

Study the terminology relating to polyhedra: faces, edges, vertices, or bases. Be able to distinguish among and calculate volume, surface area, and lateral surface area. Review the area formulas for various shapes, such as rectangles, triangles, parallelograms, trapezoids, and circles. Know the characteristics of prisms, cylinders, pyramids, cones, and spheres. Be able to find the ordered triple that describes the vertex of a figure graphed in three dimensions.

See Chapter 5.

12. COORDINATE GEOMETRY—LINES

Understand plane rectangular coordinate systems. Know how to:

- name the ordered pair describing a point
- find the midpoint of a line segment
- determine the distance between two points

Know how to use these skills to describe a figure, such as finding the area of a parallelogram given a graph.

Be able to find the slope of a line and distinguish between positive and negative slopes. Know that parallel lines have the same slope and perpendicular lines have slopes that are opposite reciprocals. Be able to:

- recognize linear equations in slope-intercept form, point-slope form, and standard form
- determine the x and y intercepts given information about a line

See Chapter 6.

13. COORDINATE GEOMETRY—CURVED GRAPHS

Review the standard form for the equation of a circle. Be able to find the x and y intercepts from a given equation or to determine the equation given the center and radius of a circle.

Know the standard form for the equation of a parabola and be able to identify the vertex. Be able to determine whether the vertex is a maximum or a minimum value.

Study the properties of an ellipse and know the standard form for an equation of an ellipse. Be able to find the equation from provided foci of an ellipse and the length of the major axis.

Be able to recognize a hyperbola on a graph and know the standard form for an equation of a hyperbola. Know how to identify the two asymptotes that intersect at the center of the hyperbola.

See Chapter 6.

14. POLAR COORDINATES

Be familiar with the polar coordinate system and the relationships use to convert between polar coordinates and rectangular coordina able to rename points between the polar and rectangular coordinate s

See Chapter 6.

15. TRIGONOMETRY

Know the sine, cosine, and tangent trigonometric ratios for an angle. Be able to determine the length of a side of a triangle from a given angle. Know the reciprocal functions of secant, cosecant, and cotangent. Recognize the cofunction identities and be able to use them to solve for unknown values. Know how to use inverse functions, including the arcsine, arccosine, and arctangent.

Familiarize yourself with special right triangles. Also know the trigonometric identities, be able to convert to radian measure, and be prepared to use the laws of sines and cosines. Review the double angle formulas for sine, cosine, and tangent.

See Chapter 7.

16. INTRODUCTION TO FUNCTIONS

Review function notation and know how to determine the domain and range for a given function. Be able to differentiate between linear functions and quadratic functions as well as even and odd functions. Know how to use the vertical line test to determine if a graph represents a function or a relation. Familiarize yourself with graphs of common functions, such as an identity function, constant function, absolute value function, squaring function, and cubing function.

See Chapter 8.

17. WORKING WITH FUNCTIONS

Be able to recognize and evaluate the following types of functions:

- composition functions
- identity functions
- zero functions
- constant functions
- quadratic function
- inverse functions
- rational functions
- polynomial functions (especially first-degree and second-degree polynomial functions and the properties of their graphs)

Be able to determine if a function is decreasing, increasing, or constant.

See Chapter 8.

18. SPECIAL FUNCTIONS

Practice working with the following types of special functions:

- exponential functions: recognize the graphs and know how to determine if two exponential functions are the same
- logarithmic functions: know how to evaluate logarithms and inverses of logarithmic functions; review common logarithmic functions
- trigonometric functions: be able to relate trigonometric relationships to their graphs, and recognize such graphs as that of sine and cosine
- periodic functions: be able to decide if a function is periodic and iden-

tify a graph of a periodic function
- piecewise functions: be able to attribute a graph to a piecewise function
- recursive functions: know how to identify a specific term in a given sequence; the Fibonacci Sequence is an example of this type of special function
- parametric functions: be able to recognize the graph of a parametric function and to determine its domain

See Chapter 8.

19. MEASURES OF CENTRAL TENDENCY

Be able to determine a measure of central tendency, including mean, median, and mode. Understand how a change in data will affect each measure of central tendency. Know how to calculate the standard deviation and to find the range of data along with the interquartile range.

See Chapter 9.

20. DATA INTERPRETATION

Know how to interpret data presented in histograms, pie charts, frequency distributions, bar graphs, and other displays. Review how information is provided in each type of display.

Be able to evaluate a set of data and determine which type of model best fits the data. Make sure you are familiar with linear, quadratic, and exponential models.

See Chapter 9.

21. PROBABILITY

Be able to identify a sample space and an event, and then use this information to calculate the probability of dependent and independent events.

See Chapter 9.

22. INVENTED OPERATIONS AND "IN TERMS OF" PROBLEMS

Familiarize yourself with invented operations, which are mathematical problems that show a symbol, unfamiliar but defined for you, that represents a made-up mathematical operation. Know how to use the definition to solve for a given variable, and to solve for more than one unknown variable.

See Chapter 10.

23. RATIO AND PROPORTION

Familiarize yourself with solving straightforward proportions in which you cross multiply to solve for an unknown. Understand how to set up these proportions for diagrams and word problems.

See Chapter 10.

24. COMPLEX NUMBERS

Review the form of a complex number and know how to perform mathematical operations on complex numbers, including operations that involve absolute value. Understand how to find the complex conjugate of a denominator to simplify a quotient.

See Chapter 10.

25. COUNTING PROBLEMS

Study the Fundamental Counting Principle and be able to recognize mutually exclusive events. Know how to determine the number of possible combinations and how to use a factorial to solve problems involving permutations.

See Chapter 10.

26. NUMBER THEORY AND LOGIC

Be comfortable with the properties of positive and negative numbers, prime numbers, integers, and odd and even numbers. Be able to evaluate various even/odd combinations of two numbers and draw a conclusion about the result of an operation performed on the numbers.
    Review conditional statements, inverses, and contrapositives.

See Chapter 10.

27. MATRICES

Understand how to identify the value of variables within a matrix that is set equal to another matrix or to the determinant. Know how to find the sum or product of two matrices.

See Chapter 10.

28. SEQUENCES AND SERIES

Review the difference between finite and infinite sequences. Be able to compare arithmetic and geometric sequences. Know how to choose the nth term in a specific sequence or to find a common ratio given two terms in a sequence.
    Understand how series are related to sequences. Be able to find the sum of a finite arithmetic sequence, a finite geometric sequence, or an infinite geometric sequence. Study the appropriate formulas for each task.

See Chapter 10.

29. VECTORS

Know what a vector is and how it is described. Review resultants and norms.

See Chapter 10.

30. LIMITS

Review the meaning of a limit and how limits are indicated by symbols. Know how to find the limit of a function $f(x)$ as x approaches a given value or infinity.

See Chapter 10.

McGRAW-HILL's

SAT

SUBJECT TEST

MATH LEVEL 2

McGRAW-HILL's

SAT
SUBJECT TEST
MATH LEVEL 2

Third Edition

John J. Diehl

Editor
Mathematics Department
Hinsdale Central High School
Hinsdale, IL

Christine E. Joyce

New York / Chicago / San Francisco / Lisbon / London / Madrid / Mexico City
Milan / New Delhi / San Juan / Seoul / Singapore / Sydney / Toronto

McGRAW-HILL's SAT Subject Test: Math Level 2, Third edition

Copyright © 2012, 2009, 2006 by The McGraw-Hill Companies, Inc. All rights reserved. Printed in the United States of America. Except as permitted under the United States Copyright Act of 1976, no part of this publication may be reproduced or distributed in any form or by any means, or stored in a database or retrieval system, without the prior written permission of the publisher.

4 5 6 7 8 9 10 11 12 13   QVS/QVS   4 3 2 1 0 9 8 7 6 5 4

Book-alone version:
ISBN 978-0-07-176367-7
MHID 0-07-176367-8

Book–CD set:
ISBN: 978-0-07-176370-7
MHID: 0-07-176370-8

E-book:
ISBN: 978-0-07-176366-0
MHID: 0-07-176366-X

Printed and bound by Quad/Graphics.

McGraw-Hill books are available at special quantity discounts to use as premiums and sales promotions, or for use in corporate training programs. To contact a representative, please e-mail us at bulksales@ mcgraw-hill.com.

SAT is a registered trademark of the College Entrance Examination Board, which was not involved in the production of, and does not endorse, this product.

To

My colleagues at Canton High School, an incredibly dedicated bunch of teachers;
Mr. Martin Badoian, whose passion for teaching and drive toward excellence are contagious;
John and my family, whose support sustained me through endless hours of writing.

—Christine E. Joyce

CONTENTS

PART I: ABOUT THE SAT MATH LEVEL 2 TEST / 1

Chapter 1: **Test Basics / 3**
About the Math Level 2 Test / 3
When to Take the Test / 4
The Level 1 vs. Level 2 Test / 5
Scoring / 6
How to Use This Book / 6

Chapter 2: **Calculator Tips / 7**
On the Day of the Test / 8

Chapter 3: **Diagnostic Test / 9**
Answer Sheet for the Diagnostic Test / 11
Diagnostic Test Questions / 14
Answer Key / 27
Answers and Solutions / 27
Diagnose Your Strengths and Weaknesses / 35

PART II: MATH REVIEW / 37

Chapter 4: **Algebra / 39**
Evaluating Expressions / 41
Fractions / 41
Percentages / 46
Exponents / 47
Real Numbers / 52
Absolute Value / 56
Radical Expressions / 57
Polynomials / 60
Quadratic Equations / 64
Inequalities / 68
Rational Expressions / 71
Systems / 74
Binomial Theorem / 79

Chapter 5: **Solid Geometry / 81**
Vocabulary for Polyhedra / 82
Review of Area Formulas / 83
Prisms / 84
Cylinders / 87
Pyramids / 88
Cones / 90
Spheres / 92
Volume Ratio of Similar Figures / 93
Coordinates in Three Dimensions / 94

Chapter 6: Coordinate Geometry / 96
Plotting Points / 97
Midpoint / 99
Distance / 99
Slope / 101
Slope of Parallel and Perpendicular Lines / 102
Equations of Lines / 102
Circles / 106
Parabolas / 108
Ellipses / 111
Hyperbolas / 112
Graphing Inequalities / 114
Graphing Absolute Value / 115
Symmetry / 116
Transformations / 117
Polar Coordinates / 118

Chapter 7: Trigonometry / 120
Right Triangle Trigonometry / 121
Relationships Among Trigonometric Ratios / 123
Special Right Triangles / 127
Trigonometric Identities / 128
Radian Measure / 129
Law of Cosines / 130
Law of Sines / 131
Trigonometric Equations / 133
Double Angle Formulas / 134

Chapter 8: Functions / 136
Function Notation / 137
Functions vs. Relations / 140
Composition of Functions / 143
Determining the Maximum or Minimum / 144
The Roots of a Quadratic Function / 146
Inverse Functions / 147
Rational Functions / 149
Higher-Degree Polynomial Functions / 150
Exponential Functions / 154
Logarithmic Functions / 155
Trigonometric Functions / 159
Inverse Trigonometric Functions / 163
Periodic Functions / 165
Piecewise Functions / 167
Recursive Functions / 168
Parametric Functions / 169

Chapter 9: Data Analysis, Statistics, and Probability / 171
Mean, Median, Mode / 172

Range / 173

Interquartile Range / 174

Standard Deviation / 174

Data Interpretation / 175

Regression / 177

Probability / 181

Chapter 10: Numbers and Operations / 184

Invented Operations / 185

"In Terms of" Problems / 186

Ratio and Proportion / 186

Complex Numbers / 187

Counting Problems / 189

Number Theory / 191

Logic / 192

Matrices / 194

Sequences / 197

Series / 199

Vectors / 201

Limits / 202

PART III: EIGHT PRACTICE TESTS / 205

Practice Test 1 / 207

Answer Sheet for Practice Test 1 / 209

Practice Test 1 Questions / 212

Answer Key / 223

Answers and Solutions / 223

Diagnose Your Strengths and Weaknesses / 231

Practice Test 2 / 233

Answer Sheet for Practice Test 2 / 235

Practice Test 2 Questions / 238

Answer Key / 249

Answers and Solutions / 249

Diagnose Your Strengths and Weaknesses / 255

Practice Test 3 / 257

Answer Sheet for Practice Test 3 / 259

Practice Test 3 Questions / 262

Answer Key / 271

Answers and Solutions / 271

Diagnose Your Strengths and Weaknesses / 279

Practice Test 4 / 281

Answer Sheet for Practice Test 4 / 283

Practice Test 4 Questions / 286

Answer Key / 297

Answers and Solutions / 297

Diagnose Your Strengths and Weaknesses / 303

Practice Test 5 / 305

    Answer Sheet for Practice Test 5 / 307

    Practice Test 5 Questions / 310

    Answer Key / 321

    Answers and Solutions / 321

    Diagnose Your Strengths and Weaknesses / 327

Practice Test 6 / 329

    Answer Sheet for Practice Test 6 / 331

    Practice Test 6 Questions / 334

    Answer Key / 345

    Answers and Solutions / 345

    Diagnose Your Strengths and Weaknesses / 351

Practice Test 7 / 353

    Answer Sheet for Practice Test 7 / 355

    Practice Test 7 Questions / 358

    Answer Key / 369

    Answers and Solutions / 369

    Diagnose Your Strengths and Weaknesses / 375

Practice Test 8 / 377

    Answer Sheet for Practice Test 8 / 379

    Practice Test 8 Questions / 382

    Answer Key / 393

    Answers and Solutions / 393

    Diagnose Your Strengths and Weaknesses / 399

PART I

ABOUT THE SAT MATH LEVEL 2 TEST

CHAPTER 1
TEST BASICS

ABOUT THE MATH LEVEL 2 TEST

The SAT Math Level 2 test is one of the Subject Tests offered by the College Board. It tests your knowledge of high school math concepts and differs from the SAT, which tests your math *aptitude*. The test consists of 50 multiple-choice questions and is one hour long.

The SAT Subject Tests (formerly known as the SAT II tests or Achievement Tests) are the lesser-known counterpart to the SAT, offered by the same organization—the College Board. However, whereas the SAT tests general verbal, writing, and mathematical reasoning skills, the SAT Subject Tests cover specific knowledge in a wide variety of subjects, including English, Mathematics, History, Science, and Foreign Languages. SAT Subject Tests are only one hour long, significantly shorter than the SAT, and you can take up to three tests during any one test administration day. You can choose which SAT Subject Tests to take and how many to take on test day, but you cannot register for both the SAT and Subject Tests on the same test day.

The Math Level 2 test covers the topics shown in the pie chart below.

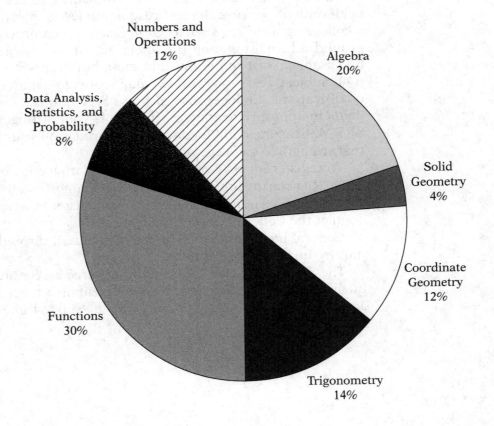

The Math Level 2 test is designed to test a student's math knowledge, ability to apply concepts, and higher-order thinking. Students are not expected to know every topic covered on the test.

When determining which SAT Subject Tests to take and when to take them, consult your high school guidance counselor and pick up a copy of the "Taking the SAT Subject Tests" bulletin published by the College Board. Research the admissions policies of colleges to which you are considering applying to determine their SAT Subject Test requirements and the average scores students receive. Also, visit the College Board's website at www.collegeboard.com to learn more about what tests are offered.

Use this book to become familiar with the content, organization, and level of difficulty of the Math Level 2 test. Knowing what to expect on the day of the test will allow you to do your best.

WHEN TO TAKE THE TEST

The Math Level 2 test is recommended for students who have completed *more than* 3 years of college-preparatory mathematics. Most students taking the Level 2 test have studied 2 years of algebra, 1 year of geometry, and 1 year of precalculus (elementary functions) and/or trigonometry. Many students take the math Subject Tests at the end of their junior year or at the beginning of their senior year.

Colleges look at SAT Subject Test scores to see a student's academic achievement because the test results are less subjective than other parts of a college application, such as GPA, teacher recommendations, student background information, and the interview. Many colleges require at least one SAT Subject Test score for admission, but even schools that do not require SAT Subject Tests may review your scores to get an overall picture of your qualifications. Colleges may also use SAT Subject Test scores to enroll students in appropriate courses. If math is your strongest subject, then a high SAT Math score, combined with good grades on your transcript, can convey that strength to a college or university.

To register for SAT Subject Tests, pick up a copy of the *Registration Bulletin*, "Registering for the SAT: SAT Reasoning Test, SAT Subject Tests" from your guidance counselor. You can also register at www.collegeboard.com or contact the College Board directly by mail.

General inquiries can be directed via email through the Web site's email inquiry form, or by telephone.

The SAT Math Level 2 test is administered six Saturdays (or Sunday if you qualify because of religious beliefs) each year in October, November, December, January, May, and June. Students may take up to three SAT Subject Tests per test day.

THE LEVEL 1 VS. LEVEL 2 TEST

As mentioned, the Math Level 2 test is recommended for students who have completed *more than* 3 years of college-preparatory mathematics. The Math Level 1 test is recommended for students who have completed 3 years of college-preparatory mathematics. Most students taking the Level 1 test have studied 2 years of algebra and 1 year of geometry.

Typically, students who have received A or B grades in precalculus and trigonometry elect to take the Level 2 test. If you have taken more than 3 years of high school math and are enrolled in a precalculus or calculus program, don't assume that taking the Level 1 test guarantees a higher score. Many of the topics on the Level 1 test will be concepts studied years ago.

Although the topics covered on the two tests overlap somewhat, they differ as shown in the table below. The College Board gives an approximate outline of the mathematics covered on each test as follows:

Topic	Level 1 Test	Level 2 Test
Algebra and Functions	38–42%	48–52%
Plane Euclidean Geometry	18–22%	—
Three-dimensional Geometry	4–6%	4–6%
Coordinate Geometry	8–12%	10–14%
Trigonometry	6–8%	12–16%
Data Analysis, Statistics, and Probability	8–12%	8–12%
Number and Operations	10–14%	10–14%

Overall, the Level 2 test focuses on more advanced content in each area. As shown in the table, the Level 2 test does not directly cover Plane Euclidean Geometry, although Plane Euclidean Geometry concepts may be applied in other types of questions. Number and Operations was formerly known as Miscellaneous.

This book provides a detailed review of all the areas covered on the Math Level 2 test. More advanced topics that are covered only on the Level 2 test are denoted by an asterisk (*) in the topics list at the beginning of each of the math review chapters.

SCORING

The scoring of the Math Level 2 test is based on a 200–800-point scale, similar to that of the math and verbal sections of the SAT. You receive one point for each correct answer and lose one quarter of a point for each incorrect answer. You do not lose any points for omitting a question. In addition to your scaled score, your score report shows a percentile ranking indicating the percentage of students scoring below your score. Because there are considerable differences between the Math Level 1 and Level 2 tests, your score on one is not an accurate indicator of your score on the other.

Score reports are mailed, at no charge, approximately 5 weeks after the test day. Score reports are available approximately 3 weeks after the test day for free at www.collegeboard.com. Just as with the SAT, you can choose up to four college/scholarship program codes to which to send your scores, and the College Board will send a cumulative report of all of your SAT and SAT Subject Test scores to these programs. Additional score reports can be requested, for a fee, online or by telephone.

HOW TO USE THIS BOOK

- **Become familiar with the SAT Math Level 2 test.** Review Chapters 1 and 2 to become familiar with the Level 2 test and the guidelines for calculator usage.

- **Identify the subject matter that you need to review.** Complete the diagnostic test in Chapter 3 and evaluate your score. Identify your areas of weakness and focus your test preparation on these areas.

- **Study smart.** Focus your studying on areas that will benefit you. Strengthen your ability to answer the types of questions that appear on the test by reviewing Chapters 4–10 as necessary, beginning with your weaker areas. Work through each of the questions in the chapters in which you are weak. Skim the other chapters as needed and work through problems that are not clear to you.

- **Practice your test-taking skills and pacing.** Complete the practice tests under actual test-like conditions. Evaluate your score, and again, review your areas of weakness.

CHAPTER 2
CALCULATOR TIPS

The SAT Math Level 2 test requires the use of a scientific or graphing calculator. The Math Level 1 and Level 2 tests are actually the only Subject Tests for which calculators are allowed. It is not necessary to use a calculator to solve every problem on the test. In fact, there is no advantage to using a calculator for 35–45% of the Level 2 test questions. That means a calculator is helpful for solving approximately 55–65% of the Level 2 test questions.

It is critical to know how and when to use your calculator effectively . . . and how and when to NOT use your calculator. For some problems, using a calculator may actually take longer than solving the problem by hand. Knowing how to operate your calculator properly will affect your test score, so practice using your calculator when completing the practice tests in this book.

The Level 2 test is created with the understanding that most students know how to use a graphing calculator. Although you have a choice of using either a scientific or a graphing calculator, **choose a graphing calculator.** A graphing calculator provides much more functionality (as long as you know how to use it properly!). A graphing calculator is an advantage when solving many problems related to coordinate geometry and functions.

Remember to make sure your calculator is working properly before your test day. Become comfortable with using it and familiar with the common operations. Because calculator policies are ever changing, refer to www.collegeboard.com for the latest information. According to the College Board, the following types of calculators are NOT allowed on the test:

- calculators with QWERTY (typewriter-like) keypads
- calculators that contain electronic dictionaries
- calculators with paper tape or printers
- calculators that "talk" or make noise
- calculators that require an electrical outlet
- cell-phone calculators
- pocket organizers or personal digital assistants
- hand-held minicomputers, powerbooks, or laptop computers
- electronic writing pads or pen-input/stylus-driven devices (such as a Palm Pilot).

There are a few rules to calculator usage on the SAT Subject Tests. Of course, you may not share your calculator with another student during the test. Doing so may result in dismissal from the test. If your calculator has a large or raised display that can be seen by other test takers, the test supervisor has the right to assign you to an appropriate seat, presumably not in the line of sight of other students. Calculators may not be on your desk during other SAT Subject Tests, aside from the Math Level 1 and Level 2 tests. If your calculator malfunctions during the test, and you don't have a backup or extra batteries, you can either choose to continue the test without a calculator or choose to cancel your test score. You must cancel the score before leaving the test center. If you leave the test center, you must cancel your scores for all subject tests taken on that date.

When choosing what calculator to use for the test make sure your calculator performs the following functions:

- squaring a number
- raising a number to a power other than 2 (usually the {^} button)
- taking the square root of a number
- taking the cube root of a number (or, in other words, raising a number to the $\frac{1}{3}$ power)
- sine, cosine, and tangent
- $\sin^{-1}$, $\cos^{-1}$, $\tan^{-1}$
- can be set to both degree mode and radian mode

Also know where the π button and the parentheses buttons are, and understand the difference between the subtraction symbol and the negative sign.

Because programmable calculators are allowed on the SAT Math test, some students may frantically program their calculator with commonly used math formulas and facts, such as: distance, the quadratic formula, midpoint, slope, circumference, area, volume, surface area, lateral surface area, the trigonometric ratios, trigonometric identities, the Pythagorean Theorem, combinations, permutations, and nth terms of geometric/arithmetic sequences. Of course, if you do not truly understand these math facts and when to use them, you end up wasting significant time scrolling through your calculator searching for them.

ON THE DAY OF THE TEST

- Make sure your calculator works! (Putting new batteries in your calculator will provide you with peace of mind.)
- Bring a backup calculator and extra batteries to the test center.

CHAPTER 3

DIAGNOSTIC TEST

To prepare for the Math Level 2 test most effectively, you should identify where your skills are weak. Then, focus on improving your skills in these areas. (Of course, also becoming stronger in your strong areas will only help your score!) Use the results of the diagnostic test to prioritize areas in which you need further preparation.

The following diagnostic test resembles the format, number of questions, and level of difficulty of the actual Math Level 2 test. It incorporates questions in the following seven areas:

1. Algebra
2. Solid Geometry
3. Coordinate Geometry
4. Trigonometry
5. Functions
6. Data Analysis, Statistics, and Probability
7. Numbers and Operations

When you are finished with the test, determine your score and carefully read the answer solutions for the questions you answered incorrectly. Identify your weak areas by determining the areas in which you made the most errors. Review these chapters of the book first. Then, as time permits, go back and review your stronger areas.

Allow 1 hour to take the diagnostic test. Time yourself and work uninterrupted. If you run out of time, take note of where you ended after 1 hour and continue until you have tried all 50 questions. To truly identify your weak areas, you need to complete the test. Remember that you lose $\frac{1}{4}$ of a point for each incorrect answer. Because of this penalty, do not guess on a question unless you can eliminate one or more of the answers. Your score is calculated using the following formula:

$$\text{Number of correct answers} - \frac{1}{4} \text{ (Number of incorrect answers)}$$

The diagnostic test will be an accurate reflection of how you'll do on the Level 2 test if you treat it as the actual examination. Here are some hints on how to take the test under conditions similar to the actual test day:

- Complete the test in one sitting.
- Time yourself.
- Use a scientific or graphing calculator. Remember that a calculator may be useful in solving about 55–65% of the test questions and is not needed for about 35–45% of the test.
- Tear out your answer sheet and fill in the ovals just as you would on the actual test day.
- Become familiar with the directions to the test and the reference information provided. You'll save time on the actual test day by already being familiar with this information.

DIAGNOSTIC TEST

MATH LEVEL 2

ANSWER SHEET

Tear out this answer sheet and use it to complete the practice test. Determine the BEST answer for each question. Then, fill in the appropriate oval using a No. 2 pencil.

1. (A) (B) (C) (D) (E)	21. (A) (B) (C) (D) (E)	41. (A) (B) (C) (D) (E)
2. (A) (B) (C) (D) (E)	22. (A) (B) (C) (D) (E)	42. (A) (B) (C) (D) (E)
3. (A) (B) (C) (D) (E)	23. (A) (B) (C) (D) (E)	43. (A) (B) (C) (D) (E)
4. (A) (B) (C) (D) (E)	24. (A) (B) (C) (D) (E)	44. (A) (B) (C) (D) (E)
5. (A) (B) (C) (D) (E)	25. (A) (B) (C) (D) (E)	45. (A) (B) (C) (D) (E)
6. (A) (B) (C) (D) (E)	26. (A) (B) (C) (D) (E)	46. (A) (B) (C) (D) (E)
7. (A) (B) (C) (D) (E)	27. (A) (B) (C) (D) (E)	47. (A) (B) (C) (D) (E)
8. (A) (B) (C) (D) (E)	28. (A) (B) (C) (D) (E)	48. (A) (B) (C) (D) (E)
9. (A) (B) (C) (D) (E)	29. (A) (B) (C) (D) (E)	49. (A) (B) (C) (D) (E)
10. (A) (B) (C) (D) (E)	30. (A) (B) (C) (D) (E)	50. (A) (B) (C) (D) (E)
11. (A) (B) (C) (D) (E)	31. (A) (B) (C) (D) (E)	
12. (A) (B) (C) (D) (E)	32. (A) (B) (C) (D) (E)	
13. (A) (B) (C) (D) (E)	33. (A) (B) (C) (D) (E)	
14. (A) (B) (C) (D) (E)	34. (A) (B) (C) (D) (E)	
15. (A) (B) (C) (D) (E)	35. (A) (B) (C) (D) (E)	
16. (A) (B) (C) (D) (E)	36. (A) (B) (C) (D) (E)	
17. (A) (B) (C) (D) (E)	37. (A) (B) (C) (D) (E)	
18. (A) (B) (C) (D) (E)	38. (A) (B) (C) (D) (E)	
19. (A) (B) (C) (D) (E)	39. (A) (B) (C) (D) (E)	
20. (A) (B) (C) (D) (E)	40. (A) (B) (C) (D) (E)	

DIAGNOSTIC TEST

Time: 60 minutes

Directions: Select the BEST answer for each of the 50 multiple-choice questions. If the exact solution is not one of the five choices, select the answer that is the best approximation. Then, fill in the appropriate oval on the answer sheet.

Notes:

1. A calculator will be needed to answer some of the questions on the test. Scientific, programmable, and graphing calculators are permitted. It is up to you to determine when and when not to use your calculator.

2. Angles on the Level 2 test are measured in degrees and radians. You need to decide whether your calculator should be set to degree mode or radian mode for a particular question.

3. Figures are drawn as accurately as possible and are intended to help solve some of the test problems. If a figure is not drawn to scale, this will be stated in the problem. All figures lie in a plane unless the problem indicates otherwise.

4. Unless otherwise stated, the domain of a function f is assumed to be the set of real numbers x for which the value of the function, $f(x)$, is a real number.

5. Reference information that may be useful in answering some of the test questions can be found below.

Reference Information	
Right circular cone with radius r and height h:	Volume $= \dfrac{1}{3}\pi r^2 h$
Right circular cone with circumference of base c and slant height ℓ:	Lateral area $= \dfrac{1}{2}c\ell$
Sphere with radius r:	Volume $= \dfrac{4}{3}\pi r^3$ Surface area $= 4\pi r^2$
Pyramid with base area B and height h:	Volume $= \dfrac{1}{3}Bh$

GO ON TO THE NEXT PAGE

DIAGNOSTIC TEST QUESTIONS

1. $c^{-1}\left(\dfrac{1}{a}+\dfrac{1}{b}\right)=$

   (A) $\dfrac{2}{c}$

   (B) $c\,\dfrac{a+b}{ab}$

   (C) $\dfrac{a+b}{abc}$

   (D) $-c\,\dfrac{a+b}{abc}$

   (E) $\dfrac{1}{abc}$

2. $(x+y+3)(x+y-3)=$

   (A) $x^2+y^2-3^2$
   (B) $(x+y)^2+6(x+y)+9$
   (C) $(x+y)^2+6(x+y)$
   (D) $(x+y)^2-9$
   (E) $x^2+2xy+y^2+3^2$

3. If $2^x=5$, $5^x=$
   (A) 2
   (B) 2.32
   (C) 11.61
   (D) 41.97
   (E) 25

4. If $\sqrt{7x}=6.24$, then what is the value of x?
   (A) 38.94
   (B) 5.56
   (C) 30.94
   (D) 2.36
   (E) 6.49

5. If E and F are different points in a plane, then the set of all points in this plane the sum of whose distances from E and F is constant is

   (A) a square
   (B) a circle
   (C) a parabola
   (D) a hyperbola
   (E) an ellipse

GO ON TO THE NEXT PAGE

6. Assuming cos and sec are defined, $\cos(4\theta)\sec(4\theta) =$

USE THIS SPACE AS SCRATCH PAPER

 (A) 4
 (B) −1
 (C) 1
 (D) 0
 (E) $\cot 4\theta$

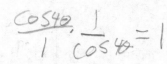

7. What is the equation of a line that contains the point $(-5, 2)$ and is parallel to the y-axis and perpendicular to the x-axis?

 (A) $y = -\dfrac{2}{5}x$

 (B) $y = -5$

 (C) $y = x + 2$

 (D) $x = -5$

 (E) $y = 2$

8. What is the distance in space between the points $A(-2, 1, 3)$ and $B(3, 4, -1)$?

 (A) $5\sqrt{2}$

 (B) $3\sqrt{2}$

 (C) $\sqrt{34}$

 (D) $\sqrt{41}$

 (E) 10

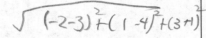

9. $\sin\dfrac{\pi}{2} =$

 (A) $\sin 4\pi$

 (B) $\sin 3\dfrac{\pi}{2}$

 (C) $\cos 2\pi$

 (D) $\sin -\dfrac{\pi}{2}$

 (E) $\cos \pi$

10. If 1 and −4 are both roots of a given polynomial, then which of the following must be a factor of the polynomial?

 (A) $x + 1$
 (B) $x^2 - 3x - 4$
 (C) $x^2 + 3x - 4$
 (D) $x - 4$
 (E) $x^2 - 1$

GO ON TO THE NEXT PAGE

11. Figure 1 shows one cycle of the graph of $y = \sin 2x$ for $0 \leq x < \pi$. What are the coordinates of the point where the maximum value of the function occurs on this interval?

    (A) $\left(\dfrac{\pi}{4}, \pi\right)$

    (B) $\left(\dfrac{\pi}{4}, 1\right)$

    (C) $\left(\dfrac{\pi}{2}, \pi\right)$

    (D) $\left(\dfrac{\pi}{2}, 1\right)$

    (E) $\left(\dfrac{\pi}{3}, 2\right)$

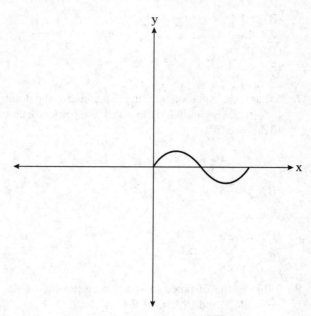

Figure 1

12. In Figure 2, $r \sin \theta =$
    (A) x
    (B) y
    (C) r
    (D) $\dfrac{y}{r}$
    (E) $\dfrac{ry}{x}$

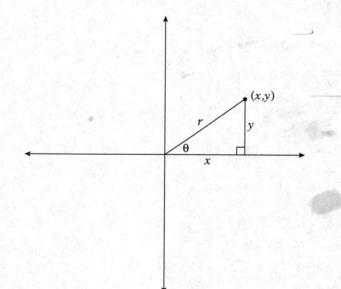

Figure 2

13. If $f(x) = 4x - 1$ and $f\left(g(6)\right) = -\dfrac{1}{3}$, then $g(x)$ could equal which of the following?

    (A) $\dfrac{1}{x}$

    (B) x^2

    (C) $\dfrac{x}{6}$

    (D) $-\dfrac{x}{18}$

    (E) $\dfrac{2}{x}$

GO ON TO THE NEXT PAGE

14. At a distance of 50 feet from a flagpole, the angle from the ground to the top of the flagpole is 42°. Assuming the flagpole is perpendicular to the ground, what is its height?

(A) 75 ft
(B) 56 ft
(C) 37 ft
(D) 33 ft
(E) 45 ft

15. If $f(x) = \sqrt{x-4}$ and $g(x) = x^3 + 1$, then $g(f(12)) =$

(A) 9
(B) $16\sqrt{2} + 1$
(C) $5\sqrt{69}$
(D) $2\sqrt{2}$
(E) $8\sqrt{2} + 1$

16. What is the domain of the function defined by $f(x) = \sqrt[3]{4x^2 - 1}$?

(A) $-\dfrac{1}{2} \le x \le \dfrac{1}{2}$

(B) $-\dfrac{1}{2} \le x$ or $x \ge \dfrac{1}{2}$

(C) $x \ge \dfrac{1}{2}$

(D) $x \ge 0$

(E) All real numbers

17. The half-life of a radioactive substance is 9 years. If 40 grams of the substance exist initially, how much will remain after 23.5 years?

(A) 0.077 grams
(B) 244.30 grams
(C) 6.11 grams
(D) 2.49 grams
(E) 6.55 grams

18. Which of the following could be a quadratic equation with integral coefficients having roots $3 + i$ and $3 - i$?

(A) $x^2 + 9x - 10 = 0$

(B) $x^2 - 6x + 10 = 0$

(C) $x^2 - 9x + 8 = 0$

(D) $x^2 - 9 = 0$

(E) $x^2 + 9x - 8 = 0$

GO ON TO THE NEXT PAGE

19. If $f(x) = \dfrac{x^2 - 25}{x - 5}$, what value does the function approach as x approaches 5?

    (A) 5
    (B) 10
    (C) 0
    (D) 11
    (E) Undefined

20. Figure 3 shows the graph of $y = f(x)$. Which of the following could be the graph of $y = |f(x)|$?

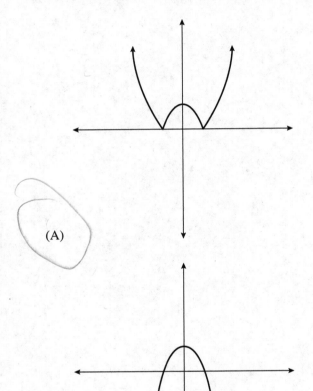

    (A)

    (B)

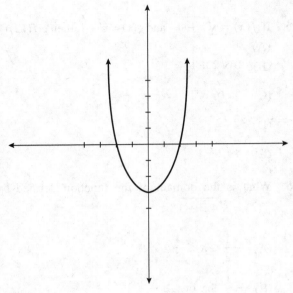

Figure 3

GO ON TO THE NEXT PAGE

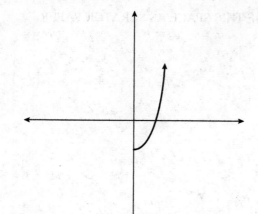

(C)

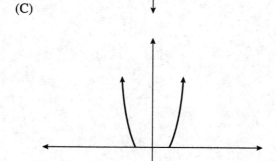

(D)

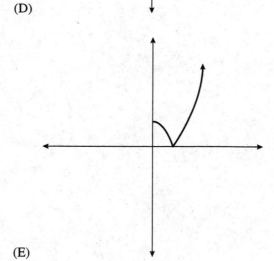

(E)

21. What is the equation, in standard form, of the hyperbola having foci at $(0, 4)$ and $(6, 4)$ and vertices $(1, 4)$ and $(5, 4)$?

(A) $\dfrac{(x-3)^2}{4} - \dfrac{(y-4)^2}{9} = 1$

(B) $\dfrac{(x-3)^2}{5} - \dfrac{(y-4)^2}{4} = 1$

(C) $\dfrac{(x-3)^2}{4} - \dfrac{(y-4)^2}{5} = 1$

(D) $\dfrac{(y-4)^2}{5} - \dfrac{(x-3)^2}{4} = 1$

(E) $\dfrac{(x-3)^2}{5} - \dfrac{(y-4)^2}{9} = 1$

22. In how many ways can the letters of the word NUMBER be arranged using all of the letters?

(A) 16
(B) 24
(C) 120
(D) 720
(E) 5,040

23. The second term of a geometric sequence is 6 and the 5th term is $\dfrac{81}{4}$. What is the common ratio of the sequence?

(A) $\dfrac{3}{2}$

(B) $\dfrac{27}{8}$

(C) $\dfrac{19}{4}$

(D) $\dfrac{2}{3}$

(E) $3\sqrt{\dfrac{6}{4}}$

24. If $x^2 - 5x + 1 = (x - a)^2 + c$, then what is the value of c?

    USE THIS SPACE AS SCRATCH PAPER

    (A) $-\dfrac{29}{4}$

    (B) $-\dfrac{21}{4}$

    (C) $-\dfrac{5}{2}$

    (D) $-\dfrac{25}{4}$

    (E) 1

    $x^2 - 2ax + a^2 + c$

    $\dfrac{5}{2}, \dfrac{5}{2} = \dfrac{25}{4}$

25. Solve $3x - 5\sqrt{x} - 2 = 0$

    (A) $\left\{\dfrac{1}{9}, 4\right\}$

    (B) $\left\{\dfrac{1}{9}\right\}$

    (C) $\{4\}$

    (D) $\left\{\dfrac{1}{9}, -4\right\}$

    (E) $\{-4\}$

    $3x - 5\sqrt{x} = 2$

26. If $16^{2-x} = 8^{8-x}$, then $x =$

    (A) 16

    (B) -16

    (C) -3

    (D) 32

    (E) 8

27. If $f(x) = 4x + 1$ and $g(x) = x^2 - 3x + 1$, then $(f + g)(-2) =$

    (A) 8

    (B) -7

    (C) -8

    (D) 4

    (E) 3

    $x^2 - x + 2$

    $(x - 2)(2x +$

    $4 \quad 4 \quad -1$

28. $(2x - 1)^5 =$

    (A) $32x^5 + 80x^4 + 80x^3 + 40x^2 + 10x + 1$

    (B) $32x^5 - 80x^4 + 80x^3 - 40x^2 + 10x - 1$

    (C) $(2x - 1)(8x^3 - 12x^2 + 6x - 1)$

    (D) $32x^5 - 1$

    (E) $x^5 - 5x^4 + 10x^3 - 10x^2 + 5x - 1$

GO ON TO THE NEXT PAGE

$4x^2 - 4x + 1$

29. How many different chords can be drawn from 8 distinct points on a circle?

    (A) 48
    (B) 7
    (C) 8
    (D) 16
    (E) 28

30. The diagonals of a rhombus measure 24 and 18 inches. What is the measure of the larger angle of the rhombus?

    (A) 73.7°
    (B) 53.1°
    (C) 145°
    (D) 120°
    (E) 106.3°

31. The first three terms of an arithmetic sequence are $3n$, $6n - 2$, and $8n + 1$ where n is any real number. What is the value of the fourth term of the sequence?

    (A) 41
    (B) 56
    (C) 54
    (D) 58
    (E) 14

32. Which of the following is NOT a factor of $x^4 - 3x^3 - 11x^2 + 3x + 10$?

    (A) $x + 1$
    (B) $x - 1$
    (C) $x + 2$
    (D) $x - 2$
    (E) $x - 5$

33. $f(x) = ax^2 + bx + c$ for all real numbers x. If $f(0) = -1, f(1) = 3$, and $f(2) = 5$, then what is $f(x)$?

    (A) $2x^2 + 2x - 1$

    (B) $-x^2 + 5x - 1$

    (C) $x^2 + 3x - 1$

    (D) $x^2 + 4x - 1$

    (E) $-2x^2 + 6x - 1$

GO ON TO THE NEXT PAGE

34. If $\left(\sqrt{a}\sqrt{b}\right)^4 = 10b^2$ and a and b are nonzero real numbers, then which of the following could equal a?

    (A) $\sqrt{10}$
    (B) 0.1
    (C) 10
    (D) $\sqrt[4]{10}$
    (E) −10

35. In a class of 25 students, 80% are passing the class with a grade of C or better. If two students are randomly selected from the class, what is the probability that neither student is passing with a grade of C or better?

    (A) 0.03
    (B) 0.20
    (C) 0.08
    (D) 0.63
    (E) 0.64

36. If, for all real numbers x, $f(4x - 8) = 2x - 2$, then $f(x)$ could equal which of the following?

    (A) $\dfrac{1}{4}x$

    (B) $4x - 4$

    (C) $\dfrac{1}{2}x + 2$

    (D) $\dfrac{1}{2}x - 2$

    (E) $2x - 4$

37. If $f(x) = 2x^3 + 6$, then what is $f^{-1}(-10)$?

    (A) 1.26
    (B) −2
    (C) −7.08
    (D) −2.52
    (E) 2.83

38. What are the intercepts of the circle given by the equation $(x + 3)^2 + (y - 3)^2 = 9$?

    (A) $(-3, 3)$
    (B) $(0, 3)$
    (C) $(0, \pm 3), (\pm 3, 0)$
    (D) $(0, 3), (-3, 0)$
    (E) $(0, -3), (3, 0)$

GO ON TO THE NEXT PAGE

39. If $11x - 2y = -4$ and $x^2 - y = 1$, then what is the value of y, assuming $y \geq 0$?

(A) $\dfrac{3}{4}$

(B) 35

(C) 6

(D) $\dfrac{1}{2}$

(E) 8

40. The height of a right circular cone is twice its diameter. If the volume of the cone is 6, what is the length of its diameter?

(A) 1.42
(B) 1.56
(C) 1.79
(D) 2.25
(E) 3.39

41. If $f_{n+1} = f_{n-1} - 2f_n$ for $n = 2, 3, 4, \ldots$ and $f_1 = 2$ and $f_2 = 6$, then what is f_4?

(A) 6
(B) −10
(C) −62
(D) 26
(E) −14

42. A line has parametric equations $x = 4t + 1$ and $y = -3 + 2t$, given t is the parameter. What is the y-intercept of the line?

(A) −3
(B) 3
(C) $-\dfrac{7}{2}$
(D) $\dfrac{1}{2}$
(E) $-\dfrac{1}{3}$

GO ON TO THE NEXT PAGE

43. The mean age of 21 students in a biology class was 16.20 years. When a new student enrolled in the class, the mean age increased to 16.27 years. What was the age of the new student?

(A) 16.3
(B) 15.5
(C) 16.5
(D) 18
(E) 17.7

44. In how many ways can 12 people be divided into two groups if one group has 8 people and the other has 4?

(A) 40,320
(B) 495
(C) 60
(D) 1,485
(E) 11,880

45. Given θ is in the first quadrant, if $\sec \theta = \dfrac{5}{3}$, what is the value of $\sin 2\theta$?

(A) 0.80
(B) 0.48
(C) 0.96
(D) 0.60
(E) -0.28

46. The graph of $f(x) = |x|$ is translated 5 units down, 1 unit left, and reflected over the x-axis. If the resulting graph represents $g(x)$, then $g(-4) =$

(A) 2
(B) -2
(C) 4
(D) 1
(E) 8

47. If each score in a set of scores is decreased by 2, which of the following would be true statements?

I. The mean is decreased by 2.
II. The mean is unchanged.
III. The standard deviation is decreased by 2.
IV. The standard deviation is unchanged.

(A) I only
(B) III only
(C) I and III only
(D) II and IV only
(E) I and IV only

48. $\triangle ABC$ has sides measuring 4, 13, and 16 inches. What is the measure of its largest angle?

    (A) 46.9°
    (B) 120°
    (C) 139.9°
    (D) 133.1°
    (E) 135°

49. $|4 + 2i| =$

    (A) 6
    (B) 2
    (C) $2\sqrt{5}$
    (D) $2\sqrt{3}$
    (E) 20

50. In $\triangle ABC$ in Figure 4, $\dfrac{\cos B \sin A}{\sec A} =$

    (A) $\dfrac{a^2}{c^2}$

    (B) $\dfrac{a^2}{b}$

    (C) $\dfrac{a^3}{c^3}$

    (D) $\dfrac{ab^2}{c^3}$

    (E) $\dfrac{a^2 b}{c^3}$

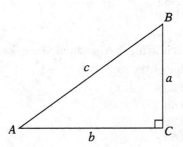

Figure 4

![img] **DIAGNOSE YOUR STRENGTHS AND WEAKNESSES**

Check the number of each question answered correctly and "X" the number of each question answered incorrectly.

Algebra	1	2	3	4	24	25	26	28	34	39	Total Number Correct
10 questions											

Solid Geometry	8	40	Total Number Correct
2 questions			

Coordinate Geometry	5	7	12	21	38	46	Total Number Correct
6 questions							

Trigonometry	6	9	14	30	45	48	50	Total Number Correct
7 questions								

Functions	10	11	13	15	16	17	18	20	27	32	33	36	37	41	42	Total Number Correct
15 questions																

Data Analysis, Statistics, and Probability	35	43	44	47	Total Number Correct
4 questions					

Numbers and Operations	19	22	23	29	31	49	Total Number Correct
6 questions							

Number of correct answers $-\frac{1}{4}$ (Number of incorrect answers) = Your raw score

_____ $-\frac{1}{4}$ (_____) =

Compare your raw score with the approximate SAT Math Test score below:

	Raw Score	SAT Math Approximate Score
Excellent	43–50	770–800
Very Good	33–43	670–770
Good	27–33	620–670
Above Average	21–27	570–620
Average	11–21	500–570
Below Average	< 11	<500

PART II
MATH REVIEW

CHAPTER 4
ALGEBRA

This chapter provides a review of basic algebraic principles. On the Level 2 test, 48–52% of the questions relate to algebra and functions. That translates to about 20% of the test questions relating specifically to algebra and about 30% to functions. In reality, however, algebra is needed to answer nearly all of the questions on the test including coordinate geometry, solid geometry, and, especially, functions. The pie chart shows approximately how much of the Level 2 test is related directly to algebra.

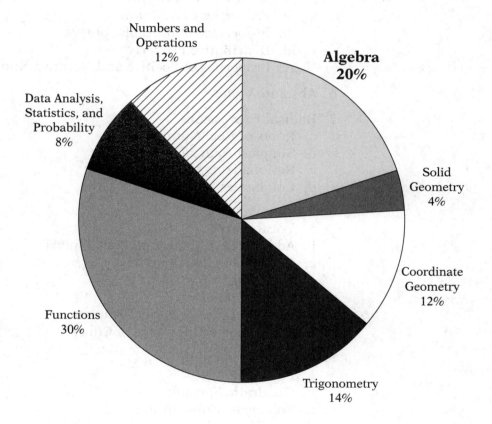

A wide variety of algebraic topics are covered in this chapter as an overall review of basic algebraic concepts. The topics are:

1. Evaluating Expressions

2. Fractions
   a. Simplifying Fractions
   b. Least Common Denominator
   c. Multiplying Fractions
   d. Using Mixed Numbers and Improper Fractions
   e. Variables in the Denominator

3. Percentages
   a. Converting Percentages to Decimals
   b. Converting Fractions to Percentages
   c. Percentage Problems

4. Exponents
   a. Properties of Exponents
       i. Rules of Exponents
   b. Common Mistakes with Exponents
   c. Rational Exponents
   d. Negative Exponents
   e. Variables in an Exponent

5. Real Numbers
   a. Vocabulary
   b. Properties of Real Numbers
       i. Properties of Addition
       ii. Properties of Multiplication
       iii. Distributive Property
       iv. Properties of Positive and Negative Numbers

6. Absolute Value

7. Radical Expressions
   a. Roots of Real Numbers
   b. Simplest Radical Form
   c. Rationalizing the Denominator
   d. Conjugates

8. Polynomials
   a. Vocabulary
   b. Adding and Subtracting Polynomials
   c. Multiplying Polynomials
   d. Factoring
       i. Trinomials
       ii. Difference of Perfect Squares
       iii. Sum and Difference of Cubes

9. Quadratic Equations
   a. Factoring
   b. Quadratic Formula
   c. Solving by Substitution
   d. The Discriminant
   e. Equations with Radicals

10. Inequalities
   a. Transitive Property of Inequality
   b. Addition and Multiplication Properties
   c. "And" vs. "Or"
   d. Inequalities with Absolute Value

11. Rational Expressions
   a. Simplifying Rational Expressions
   b. Multiplying and Dividing Rational Expressions
   c. Adding and Subtracting Rational Expressions
   d. Solving Equations with Rational Expressions

12. Systems
    a. Solving by Substitution
    b. Solving by Linear Combination
    c. No Solution vs. Infinite Solutions
    d. Word Problems with Systems

13. *Binomial Theorem

EVALUATING EXPRESSIONS

Problems asking you to evaluate an expression represent the easiest of the algebra questions on the Math Level 2 test. To answer this type of question, simply substitute the value given for the variable.

EXAMPLE:

If $x = n^3$ and $n = \dfrac{1}{2}y$, then find the value of x when $y = 4$.

Substitute $y = 4$ into the second equation to get $n = \dfrac{1}{2}(4) = 2$.

Now substitute $n = 2$ into the first equation to get $x = 2^3 = 8$.

The correct answer is 8.

FRACTIONS

Simplifying Fractions

Fractions are in simplest form when the numerator and denominator have no common factor other than 1. To simplify a fraction, factor both the numerator and denominator.

Don't cancel terms that are not common factors. Below is a common mistake:

$$\frac{x^2 - 4}{8} \neq \frac{x^2}{2}.$$

$x^2 - 4$ and 8 do not have a common factor, so this expression is already in simplest form.

EXAMPLE:

Simplify $\dfrac{(3x + 12)}{(3x + 3y)}$.

$= \dfrac{3(x + 4)}{3(x + y)}$ Factor the numerator and denominator. 3 is a common factor.

$= \dfrac{(x + 4)}{(x + y)} x \neq -y$ (This restriction is important because you cannot divide by zero!)   (*Answer*)

---

*Denotes concepts that are on the Level 2 test only.

Least Common Denominator

The least common denominator (LCD) of two or more fractions is the least common multiple (LCM) of their denominators. To find the LCD:

1. Factor each denominator completely and write as the product of prime factors. (Factor trees are usually used for this.)

2. Take the greatest power of each prime factor.

3. Find the product of these factors.

EXAMPLE:

Find the LCD of $\dfrac{1}{4}$ and $\dfrac{7}{30}$.

$4 = 2 \times 2 = 2^2.$ $30 = 2 \times 3 \times 5.$

The greatest power of 2 is 2^2. The greatest power of 3 is 3, and the greatest power of 5 is 5.

$2^2 \times 3 \times 5 = 60.$

60 is the LCD.   (*Answer*)

The least common denominator is helpful when adding and subtracting fractions.

$$\frac{1}{4} + \frac{7}{30} = \frac{15}{60} + \frac{14}{60} = \frac{29}{60}.$$

The least common denominator is also used when simplifying complex fractions. A **complex fraction** is a fraction whose numerator or denominator contains one or more fractions. Find the LCD of the simple fractions and multiply the numerator and denominator of the complex fraction by it.

EXAMPLE:

Simplify $\dfrac{\dfrac{5}{x}}{\left(\dfrac{1}{x} - 5x\right)}.$

We first start by finding a common denominator for the expression in the numerator, which is x. This gives us:

$$= \frac{\dfrac{5}{x}}{\left(\dfrac{1}{x} - \dfrac{5x^2}{x}\right)} = \frac{\dfrac{5}{x}}{\left(\dfrac{1 - 5x^2}{x}\right)}.$$

$$= \frac{5}{x} \times \left(\frac{x}{1 - 5x^2}\right)$$

$$= \frac{5}{(1 - 5x^2)}.$$

Multiplying Fractions

To multiply fractions, simply multiply straight across. $\dfrac{a}{b} \times \dfrac{c}{d} = \dfrac{ac}{bd}$.

E X A M P L E :

Simplify $\dfrac{2}{5} \times \dfrac{3}{6} \times \dfrac{4}{7}$.

$= \dfrac{2 \times 3 \times 4}{5 \times 6 \times 7}$.

$= \dfrac{24}{210}$.   Divide by a common
                  factor to simplify.

$= \dfrac{4}{35}$.   (*Answer*)

You can also simplify the fractions before multiplying to save time.

E X A M P L E :

$\dfrac{2}{5} \times \dfrac{3}{6} \times \dfrac{4}{7} = \dfrac{1}{5} \times \dfrac{1}{1} \times \dfrac{4}{7}$.   Remove the common factors of 2 and 3.

$= \dfrac{1 \times 1 \times 4}{5 \times 1 \times 7}$.

$= \dfrac{4}{35}$.

To divide by a fraction, multiply by its reciprocal. $\dfrac{a}{b} \div \dfrac{c}{d} = \dfrac{a}{b} \times \dfrac{d}{c}$. This is known as the Division Rule for Fractions. Of course, b, c, and d cannot equal zero because you cannot divide by zero.

E X A M P L E :

Simplify $18 \div \dfrac{6}{11}$.

$= 18 \times \dfrac{11}{6}$.

$= 3 \times \dfrac{11}{1}$.   Divide through by a common factor of 6.

$= \dfrac{3 \times 11}{1} = 33$.   (*Answer*)

Using Mixed Numbers and Improper Fractions

A mixed number represents the sum of an integer and a fraction.

$3\dfrac{1}{4} = 3 + \dfrac{1}{4}$

In fractional form: $3\dfrac{1}{4} = \dfrac{4 \times 3 + 1}{4} = \dfrac{13}{4}$.

When $3\dfrac{1}{4}$ is written as the fraction $\dfrac{13}{4}$, it is called an **improper fraction.**

Improper fractions are fractions whose numerator is greater than the denominator. It is often easier to change mixed numerals to improper fractions when simplifying an expression.

EXAMPLE:

Simplify $8\dfrac{2}{3} \div \dfrac{1}{6}$.

$= \dfrac{3 \times 8 + 2}{3} = \dfrac{24 + 2}{3} = \dfrac{26}{3}$.   Change to an improper fraction first.

$\dfrac{26}{3} \times \dfrac{6}{1}$.   Multiply by the reciprocal of $\dfrac{1}{6}$.

$\dfrac{26 \times 6}{3} = \dfrac{26 \times 2}{1} = 52$.   (*Answer*)

Variables in the Denominator

Fraction problems get more difficult to solve when there is a variable in the denominator. To solve, find the least common denominator (LCD) of the fractions, and multiply both sides of the equation by it.

EXAMPLE:

Solve $4 - \dfrac{1}{x} = \dfrac{6}{2x}$.

The LCD of $\dfrac{1}{x}$ and $\dfrac{6}{2x}$ is $2x$.

$2x\left(4 - \dfrac{1}{x}\right) = 2x\left(\dfrac{6}{2x}\right)$.

$8x - 2 = 6$.

$8x = 8$.

$x = 1$.   (*Answer*)

Sometimes multiplying both sides of an equation by the LCD transforms the equation into an equation that is NOT equivalent to the original one. Multiplying both sides of an equation by a polynomial may introduce **extraneous roots** that do not satisfy the original equation. It is crucial to go back and check your answer in the original fractional equation.

EXAMPLE:

Solve $\dfrac{2}{(x^2 - 7x + 10)} = \dfrac{x - 1}{x - 5}$.

Factor $x^2 - 7x + 10$ into $(x - 2)(x - 5)$. Now multiply both sides of the equation by the LCD of the fractions, $(x - 2)(x - 5)$.

$\dfrac{2}{(x^2 - 7x + 10)} \times (x - 2)(x - 5) = \dfrac{x - 1}{x - 5} \times (x - 2)(x - 5)$.

$2 = (x - 1)(x - 2)$.

$2 = x^2 - 3x + 2$.

$0 = x^2 - 3x$.

$0 = x(x - 3)$.

$x = 0$ or $x = 3$.   (*Answer*)

Because you multiplied both sides of the equation by a polynomial $(x - 2)$ $(x - 5)$, check to ensure the equation does not have extraneous roots.

Substituting $x = 0$ into the original equation results in $\dfrac{2}{10} = \dfrac{-1}{-5}$ or $1/5 = 1/5$. Substituting $x = 3$ into the original equation results in $2/-2 = 2/-2$ or $-1 = -1$. Both answers check, so they are not extraneous.

Proportions are another type of problem that may have variables in the denominator. A **proportion** is an equation that sets two ratios (fractions) equal to each other. Don't worry about finding least common denominators when solving a proportion, simply **cross-multiply.**

EXAMPLE:

$\dfrac{10}{x + 4} = \dfrac{6}{x}$.

$10x = 6(x + 4)$.

$10x = 6x + 24$.

$4x = 24$.

$x = 6$.   (*Answer*)

PERCENTAGES

Converting Percentages to Decimals

Percentage problems can often be easily translated into simpler equations. Percent means "per one hundred" or "divided by one hundred." To convert a percentage to a decimal, move the decimal point two places to the left.

$$5\% = 5 \text{ out of } 100 = \frac{5}{100} = 5 \div 100 = 0.05.$$

$$\frac{3}{4}\% = \frac{3}{4} \text{ out of } 100 = \frac{\frac{3}{4}}{100} =$$

$$\frac{3}{4} \div 100 = 0.75 \div 100 = 0.0075$$

The simplest way to change a fractional percentage to a decimal is to change the fraction to a decimal first, and then move the decimal point two places to the **left.**

EXAMPLE:

Simplify $\frac{2}{5}\%$.

$$\frac{2}{5} = 0.4.$$

$0.4\% = 0.004.$ (*Answer*)

Converting Fractions to Percentages

The simplest way to change a fraction to a percentage is to change the fraction to a decimal first, and then move the decimal point two places to the **right.**

$$\frac{2}{5} = 0.4.$$

$0.4 = 40\%.$

EXAMPLE:

When written as a percentage, $7\frac{1}{4}$ is what value?

$$7\frac{1}{4} = 7.25.$$

$725\%.$ (*Answer*)

Percentage Problems

In percentage problems, the word "of" means "multiply" and the word "is" means "equals." It is often useful to set up problems in the format *a* **is** *b*% **of** *c*, and solve for the unknown variable.

EXAMPLE:

26 is 25% of what number?

$26 = 25\% \times c$ Think **a is b% of c.** $26 = a$ and $25 = b$.

$26 = \dfrac{25}{100}(c)$,   so $26 = 0.25c$.

$\dfrac{26}{0.25} = c$.

$c = 104$.   (*Answer*)

EXAMPLE:

What percentage of 12 is 4? Round answer to the nearest tenth.

$4 = b\% \times 12$.   Think **a is b% of c.** $4 = a$ and $12 = c$.

$\dfrac{4}{12} = b\%$.

$\dfrac{4}{12} = \dfrac{b}{100}$.

$\dfrac{4 \times 100}{12} = b$.

$b = \dfrac{400}{12} = 33.3\%$.   (*Answer*)

EXAMPLE:

Find 85% of 324.

$a = 85\% \times 324$.   Think **a is b% of c.** $85 = b$ and $324 = c$.

$a = 0.85 \times 324$.

$a = 275.4$.   (*Answer*)

EXPONENTS

Properties of Exponents

Given the expression 2^4, the exponent 4 tells you the number of times the base, 2, is to be used as a factor.

$2^4 = 2 \times 2 \times 2 \times 2 = 16$.

Remember that a number raised to the zero power equals one.

$a^0 = 1(a \neq 0)$. $5^0 = 1$.

Rules of Exponents

1. To multiply two powers with the same base, you **add** the exponents:

   $a^m \times a^n = a^{m+n}$. $2^2 \times 2^3 = 2^{2+3} = 2^5$.

2. To divide two powers with the same base, you **subtract** the exponents:

   $\dfrac{a^m}{a^n} = a^{m-n}$. $\dfrac{2^5}{2^3} = 2^{5-3} = 2^2$.

3. To raise a power to a power, you **multiply** the exponents:

   $(a^m)^n = a^{mn}$. $(2^2)^3 = 2^{2 \times 3} = 2^6$.

4. To raise a product to a power, you **raise each factor to the power** and **multiply:**

   $(ab)^m = a^m \times b^m$. $(2 \times 5)^3 = 2^3 \times 5^3$.

5. To raise a quotient to a power, you **raise each factor to the power** and **divide:**

   $\left(\dfrac{a}{b}\right)^m = \dfrac{a^m}{b^m}$. $\left(\dfrac{8}{4}\right)^2 = \dfrac{8^2}{4^2}$.

When simplifying expressions involving the rules of exponents, it is easiest to simplify each variable separately as shown in the next example.

EXAMPLE:

Simplify $\dfrac{30x^3y^5}{-5x^2y^3}$.   (Assume x and y do not equal 0.)

$\dfrac{30x^3y^4}{-5x^2y^3} = \dfrac{30}{-5} \times \dfrac{x^3}{x^2} \times \dfrac{y^5}{y^3}$.   Isolate each variable.

$= -6 \times x^{3-2} \times y^{5-3}$.   Use rule #2. Subtract the exponents for each base.

$= -6 \times x^1 \times y^2$.

$= -6xy^2$.   (*Answer*)

EXAMPLE:

Simplify $\dfrac{(a^3bc^3)^2}{(a^2bc)^2}$. (Assume a, b, and c do not equal 0.)

$\dfrac{(a^3bc^3)^2}{(a^2bc)^2} = \dfrac{a^{3\times2}b^2c^{3\times2}}{a^{2\times2}b^2c^2}$. Use rules #3 and #5. Multiply the exponents.

$= \dfrac{a^6}{a^4} \times \dfrac{b^2}{b^2} \times \dfrac{c^6}{c^2}$. Isolate each variable.

$= a^2 \times b^0 \times c^4$. Use rule #2. Subtract the exponents for each base.

$= a^2 \times 1 \times c^4$.

$= a^2c^4$.   (*Answer*)

Common Mistakes With Exponents

When studying for the SAT Subject Test, make sure you don't make these common mistakes:

1. $\left(-\dfrac{1}{2}\right)^{-3} \neq \dfrac{1}{8}$.

   Watch your negative exponents. The quantity $\dfrac{1}{2}$ should be put in the denominator and raised to the third power.

   $$\left(-\dfrac{1}{2}\right)^{-3} = \dfrac{1}{\left(-\dfrac{1}{2}\right)^{3}} = \dfrac{1}{\left(\dfrac{(-1)^{3}}{2^{3}}\right)} = \dfrac{8}{-1} = -8.$$

2. $3x^{3} \neq 27x^{3}$.

   Only x is raised to the third power here. $3x^{3}$ is in simplest form.

3. $2^{2} + 2^{3} \neq 2^{5}$.

   You only add the exponents when finding the **product** of two terms in the same base. $2^{2} \times 2^{3}$ would in fact equal 2^{5}. There's no rule of exponents that applies to finding the **sum** of two terms, so just simplify each term. $2^{2} + 2^{3} = 4 + 8 = 12$.

4. $4^{3} \times 4^{4} \neq 4^{12}$.

   Remember to add the exponents when the bases are the same. $4^{3} \times 4^{4} = 4^{7}$.

5. $2^{2} \times 2^{3} \neq 4^{5}$.

   It's correct to add the exponents here, but the base should remain unchanged.

6. $(a + b)^{2} \neq a^{2} + b^{2}$.

   This is a very common error. It is important to understand that raising the quantity $a + b$ to the 2nd power means that the base, $a + b$, is to be used as a factor two times. In other words, $(a + b)^{2} = (a + b)(a + b)$. You then need to multiply using the FOIL (**F**irst, **O**uter, **I**nner, **L**ast) method. $(a + b)(a + b) = a^{2} + 2ab + b^{2}$.

Rational Exponents

The previous examples focus on integral exponents. It is possible, however, to define a^{x} when x is any **rational number.** Remember that a rational number can be expressed as $\dfrac{p}{q}$ and results from dividing an integer by another (non-zero) integer.

$4^{\frac{1}{2}}$ reads as "4 to the one-half power" and equals $\sqrt{4}$.

$5^{\frac{2}{3}}$ reads as "5 to the two-thirds power" and equals $\sqrt[3]{5}^{2}$ or $\sqrt[3]{25}$. $5^{\frac{2}{3}}$ can also be represented as $\left(\sqrt[3]{5}\right)^{2}$.

$x^{\frac{a}{b}}$ equals $\sqrt[b]{x}^{a}$ or $\left(\sqrt[b]{x}\right)^{a}$ as long as $b \neq 0$. All of the rules of exponents previously discussed also apply to rational exponents.

EXAMPLE:

Simplify $81^{\frac{3}{4}}$.

$81^{\frac{3}{4}} = \left(\sqrt[4]{81}\right)^3$

$= 3^3 = 27.$ (*Answer*)

This problem can also be solved by raising 81 to the third power first.

$\sqrt[4]{81}^3 = \sqrt[4]{531,441}.$

Finding the 4th root of 531,441 is less obvious than finding the 4th root of 81 as in the solution above.

EXAMPLE:

Simplify $(8^4)^{\frac{1}{12}}$.

$(8^4)^{\frac{1}{12}} = 8^{\frac{4}{12}} = 8^{\frac{1}{3}}$

$= (2^3)^{\frac{1}{3}} = 2^1 = 2.$ (*Answer*)

Negative Exponents

Given the expression 2^{-4}, rewrite it without the negative exponent by moving 2^4 to the denominator. In other words, 2^{-4} is the reciprocal of 2^4.

$2^{-4} = \dfrac{1}{2^4} = \dfrac{1}{(2 \times 2 \times 2 \times 2)} = \dfrac{1}{16}$

Remember that expressions in simplest form typically do not contain negative exponents.

EXAMPLE:

Simplify $\dfrac{x^{-3}}{2y^3}\left(\dfrac{1}{xy}\right)^{-3}$. (Assume x and y do not equal zero)

$\dfrac{x^{-3}}{2y^3}\left(\dfrac{1}{xy}\right)^{-3} = \dfrac{x^{-3}}{2y^3}\left(\dfrac{1^{-3}}{x^{-3}y^{-3}}\right)$. Use rule #5.

$= \dfrac{1}{2x^3y^3}\left(\dfrac{x^3y^3}{1}\right)$. Simplify the negative exponents.

$= \dfrac{x^3y^3}{2x^3y^3}.$

$= \dfrac{1}{2}.$ (*Answer*)

Variables in an Exponent

Solving an equation with a variable in the exponent can be easily done if both sides can be rewritten in the same base.

EXAMPLE:

Solve $4^x = 32^{x+1}$. Recognize that 4 and 32 can be written in base 2.

$(2^2)^x = (2^5)^{x+1}$.

$2^{2x} = 2^{5(x+1)}$. Because both sides are in base 2, set the exponents equal and solve.

$2x = 5(x + 1)$.

$2x = 5x + 5$.

$-3x = 5$.

$x = -\dfrac{5}{3}$.   (*Answer*)

If both sides of the equation cannot be written in the same base, the problem is more difficult. You can take the either the **log** or **natural log** of both sides of the equation to solve for the variable in the exponent. Logarithms are discussed in detail in the Functions chapter, but here is one example.

EXAMPLE:

Solve $2^x = 5$.

First, take the natural log of both sides of the equation. A calculator is needed to do this.

$\ln 2^x = \ln 5$.

$x \ln 2 = \ln 5$.

$x = \dfrac{\ln 5}{\ln 2}$.

$x = \dfrac{1.6094}{0.6931} = 2.32$.   (*Answer*)

Note that taking the common log of both sides results in the same answer:

$x = \dfrac{\log 5}{\log 2} = 2.32$.

REAL NUMBERS

Vocabulary

Natural Numbers	{1, 2, 3, . . .}
Whole Numbers	{0, 1, 2, 3, . . .}
Integers	{. . . −2, −1, 0, 1, 2, 3, . . .}
Rational Numbers	Numbers that can be expressed as $\frac{p}{q}$ and result from dividing an integer by another (nonzero) integer. $-\frac{2}{3}, \frac{3}{4}$, 0.7, 1.333 . . . and 8 are examples of rational numbers.
Irrational Numbers	Numbers that cannot be expressed as $\frac{p}{q}$. In decimal form, they are nonterminating and nonrepeating. π and $\sqrt{2}$ are examples of irrational numbers.
Real Numbers	The set of all rational and irrational numbers.

EXAMPLE:

Which of the following is NOT an irrational number?

(A) $\sqrt{2}$ (B) π (C) $\sqrt{50}$ (D) 1.33333. . .   (E) 5.020020002. . .

1.33333 is a repeating decimal so it is rational. Irrational numbers are infinite and nonrepeating such as answer E. 5.02020202 . . . is a repeating decimal, but 5.020020002 . . . is nonrepeating because the number of zeroes continues to increase.

D) 1.333333   (*Answer*)

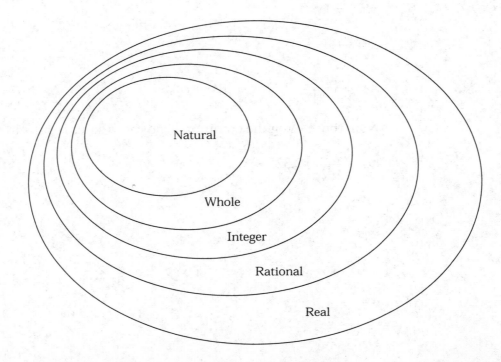

Properties of Real Numbers

It is important to understand the properties of real numbers in order to move on in algebra. Before, getting into the operations of addition and multiplication, let's review examples of the basic properties of equality. These hold true for all real numbers.

- **Reflexive Property** $x = x$. $2 = 2$.

- **Symmetric Property**   If $a = b$, then $b = a$. If $x = 1$, then $1 = x$.

- **Transitive Property**   If $a = b$, and $b = c$, then $a = c$. If $x = 1$ and $1 = y$, then $x = y$.

- **Addition Property**   If $a = b$, then $a + c = b + c$. If $x = 4$, then $x + 2 = 4 + 2$.

- **Multiplication Property**   If $a = b$, then $ac = bc$. If $x = 9$, then $3x = 3 \times 9$.

The last two properties show the fundamental principle of algebra:

What you do to one side of an equation, you MUST do to the other side.

In other words, if you add 2 to one side of an equation, you must add 2 to the other side to maintain the equality. You can perform nearly any operation on one side as long as you also perform it on the other. Most of this algebra chapter comes back to this fundamental idea. If you take the square root of one side of an equation, you must take the square root of the other side. If you cube one side of an equation, you must cube the other. You get the idea.

As you review the following properties of addition and multiplication, remember these are the properties that allow you to perform operations needed to simplify expressions and solve equations. It is important to be able to perform these operations *and* identify what property is being used. Assume a, b, and c are real numbers.

Properties of Addition

1. **Closure Property of Addition**

   The sum $a + b$ results in a unique real number.

   $3 + 11$ equals the real number 14.

2. **Commutative Property of Addition**

   $a + b = b + a$.

   $20 + 5 = 5 + 20$.

3. **Associative Property of Addition**

   $(a + b) + c = a + (b + c)$.

   $(8 + 9) + 10 = 8 + (9 + 10)$.

4. **Identity Property of Addition** (Additive Identity)

   There is a unique real number **zero** such that:

   $a + 0 = a$.

   $77 + 0 = 77$.

5. Property of Opposites (Additive Inverse)

For each real number a, there is a real unique number $-a$ such that:

$a + -a = 0$

$-a$ is the **opposite** of a. It is also called the **additive inverse** of a.

$6 + -6 = 0$.

Properties of Multiplication

1. Closure Property of Multiplication

The product $a \times b$ results in a unique real number.

3×11 equals the real number 33.

2. Commutative Property of Multiplication

$ab = ba$.

$20 \times 5 = 5 \times 20$.

3. Associative Property of Multiplication

$(a \times b) \times c = a \times (b \times c)$.

$(8 \times 9) \times 10 = 8 \times (9 \times 10)$.

4. Identity Property of Multiplication (Multiplicative Identity)

There is a unique real number **one** such that:

$a \times 1 = a$.

$77 \times 1 = 77$.

5. Property of Reciprocals (Multiplicative Inverse)

For each real number a (except 0), there is a unique real number $\dfrac{1}{a}$

such that: $a \times \dfrac{1}{a} = 1$.

$\dfrac{1}{a}$ is the **reciprocal** of a. It is also called the **multiplicative inverse**

of a.

Zero has no reciprocal because $\dfrac{1}{0}$ is undefined.

$6 \times \dfrac{1}{6} = 1$.

Distributive Property

The distributive property of multiplication over addition states that:

$a(b + c) = ab + ac$ and $(b + c)a = ba + ca$.

$3(5 + 6) = (3 \times 5) + (6 \times 5) = 15 + 30 = 45$.

EXAMPLE:

Simplify $2(6 - x + 2y)$.

$2(6 - x + 2y) = (2 \times 6) - (2 \times x) + (2 \times 2y)$. Distribute the 2.

$= 12 - 2x + 4y$.   *(Answer)*

The example shows that the distributive property also works for trinomials (expressions containing three terms). Does it apply to multiplication over subtraction? Try the next example to see that it does hold true.

EXAMPLE:

Simplify $5(4x^2 - 10)$.

$5(4x^2 - 10) = 5 \times (4x^2) - (5 \times 10)$. Distribute the 5.

$= 20x^2 - 50$.   *(Answer)*

Properties of Positive and Negative Numbers

You should be familiar with working with signed numbers by this point in your math career. Here is a review of the basic properties of positive and negative numbers.

- A positive number times a positive number equals a positive number.

  $3 \times 4 = 12$.

- A positive number times a negative number equals a negative number.

  $3 \times -4 = -12$.

- A negative number times a negative number equals a positive number.

  $-3 \times -4 = 12$.

- To subtract a number, add its opposite.

  $3 - 4 = 3 + (-4) = -1$.

  $3 - (-4) = 3 + (+4) = 7$.

- The sum of the opposites of two numbers is the opposite of their sum.

  $(-3) + (-4) = -(3 + 4) = -7$.

- $x(-1) = -x$ for all real values of x.

  $3(-1) = -3$ and $-3(-1) = -(-3) = 3$.

- $x(-y) = -(xy)$ for all real values of x and y.

  $3 \times (-4) = -(3 \times 4) = -12$.

- $x - y = -(y - x)$.

  This is a variation of the property of opposites that usually tricks students. It is often used when simplifying rational expressions and factoring, so it is important to recognize.

  $$\frac{(x - y)}{(y - x)} = -1. \qquad \frac{(x - 4)}{(4 - x)} = -1. \qquad (x - 2)(2 - x) = -(x - 2)^2.$$

ABSOLUTE VALUE

The absolute value of a number is the distance from the graph of the number on a number line to the origin. For a real number x, the absolute value of x is defined as:

$|x| = x$ if $x > 0$.

$|x| = 0$ if $x = 0$.

$|x| = -x$ if $x < 0$.

EXAMPLE:

Evaluate the expression $|x| - 2|y|$ if $x = 6$ and $y = -3$.

$|x| - 2|y| = |6| - 2|-3|$.   Substitute the given values.

$\qquad = 6 - 2 \times 3$.

$\qquad = 6 - 6 = 0$.   (*Answer*)

To solve an equation involving absolute value, think in terms of two separate equations: one where the expression inside the absolute value signs is **positive** and one where the expression inside the absolute value is **negative.**

EXAMPLE:

Solve $|x - 3| = 1$.

$x - 3 = 1$ or $-(x - 3) = 1$.   Recognize when the expression $x - 3$ is positive and negative.

$x = 4$ or $-x = -2$.

The solution set is $\{2, 4\}$.   (*Answer*)

EXAMPLE: (see the following figure)

Graph $y = |x - 1|$.

It is important to recognize immediately that y will never be negative because it equals the absolute value of an expression. Absolute value, by definition, is a positive distance. If you're unsure what happens to an absolute value graph, try plotting a few points to see what results.

When $x = 1$, $y = |1 - 1| = 0$, so the coordinate (1,0) must be part of the solution. When $x = 2$, $y = |2 - 1| = |1| = 1$, so the coordinate (2,1) must be part of the solution. When $x = 0$, $y = |0 - 1| = |-1| = 1$, so the coordinate (0,1) must be part of the solution. These three points are enough to sketch the graph, which resembles a letter "V" and has a vertex of (1,0).

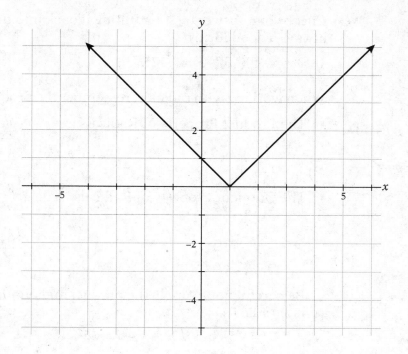

RADICAL EXPRESSIONS

Roots of Real Numbers

A radical is a symbol such as $\sqrt[n]{x}$ where n is the **index,** and x is the **radicand.** If n is not written, it is assumed to equal 2, for example $\sqrt{4}$ (read the **square root** of 4). Every positive number x has two square roots: $\sqrt{x}$ and $-\sqrt{x}$. The square roots of 16 are 4 and –4 because both 4^2 and $(-4)^2$ equal 16. The positive square root, 4 in this case, is called the **principal square root.**

EXAMPLE 1:

Solve $x^2 = 49$.
$x = 7$ or –7.
The roots are 7 and –7.

Two solutions

EXAMPLE 2:

Solve $\sqrt{x} = 6$.
Square both sides to get $x = 6^2$.
$x = 36$.

One solution

It is important to note the distinction in the examples above. When finding the roots of an equation where the variable is raised to an **even** power, remember there's a positive and negative solution. In Example 1, it is true that 49 has two real roots, but $\sqrt{49}$ has only one solution. $\sqrt{49} \neq -7$. If the variable is raised to an odd power, however, there's only **one real root.** For example, there is only one solution for x in the following example:

EXAMPLE 3:

Solve $x^3 = -125$.

Take the cube root of both sides to get $x = \sqrt[3]{-125}$.

$x = -5$.   (*Answer*)

Check your answer by substituting it back into the original equation. (This is always a good idea!)

$(-5)^3 = (-5)(-5)(-5) = -125$.

When working with radicals, remember the product and quotient properties:

- The Product Property of Radicals $\sqrt[n]{ab} = \sqrt[n]{a} \times \sqrt[n]{b}$.

$$\sqrt{4 \times 9} = \sqrt{4} \times \sqrt{9} = 2 \times 3 = 6.$$

- The Quotient Property of Radicals $\sqrt[n]{\dfrac{a}{b}} = \dfrac{\sqrt[n]{a}}{\sqrt[n]{b}}$

$$\sqrt[3]{\frac{64}{8}} = \frac{\sqrt[3]{64}}{\sqrt[3]{8}} = \frac{4}{2} = 2.$$

Be careful not to apply the product and quotient properties to finding the sum of radicals.

$$\sqrt{3^2 + 4^2} = \sqrt{5^2} \text{ but } \sqrt{3^2} + \sqrt{4^2} \neq \sqrt{5^2}.$$

Simplest Radical Form

Make sure two things are true when writing an expression, such as $\sqrt[n]{x}$, in **simplest radical form:**

1. Factor all perfect nth powers from the radicand, and

2. Rationalize the denominators so that no radicals remain in the denominator and no radicands are fractions.

Write the following examples in simplest radical form.

EXAMPLE 1:

$\sqrt{75}$

$= \sqrt{25 \times 3}$

$= \sqrt{25} \times \sqrt{3}$

$= 5\sqrt{3}$

25 is the largest perfect square factor of 75.

EXAMPLE 2:

$\sqrt[3]{54}$

$= \sqrt[3]{27 \times 2}$

$= \sqrt[3]{27} \times \sqrt[3]{2}$

$= 3\sqrt[3]{2}$

27 is the largest perfect cube factor of 54.

Rationalizing the Denominator

To rationalize a denominator containing a radical, try to create a perfect square, cube, or other nth power. Let's look at a square root with a fractional radicand first.

E X A M P L E :

Simplify $\sqrt{\dfrac{7}{3}}$.

$= \sqrt{\dfrac{7}{3} \times \dfrac{3}{3}}$. Multiplying the denominator by 3 will create a perfect square,

3^2, in the denominator. $\dfrac{3}{3}$ is another way of writing **one,** the identity

element for multiplication.

$= \sqrt{\dfrac{21}{9}}$.

$= \dfrac{\sqrt{21}}{3}$.   (*Answer*)

Solving a cube root with a fractional radicand is nearly identical. You must multiply by a perfect square this time in order to create a perfect cube in the denominator.

E X A M P L E :

Simplify $\sqrt[3]{\dfrac{15}{2}}$.

$= \sqrt[3]{\dfrac{15}{2} \times \dfrac{2^2}{2^2}}$. Multiplying the denominator by 2^2 will create a perfect cube,

2^3, in the denominator. $\dfrac{2^2}{2^2}$ is another way of writing **one,** the identity

element for multiplication.

$= \sqrt[3]{\dfrac{60}{8}}$.

$= \dfrac{\sqrt[3]{60}}{2}$.   (*Answer*)

Now let's look at rationalizing a denominator that contains a radical.

E X A M P L E :

Simplify $\dfrac{\left(\sqrt{20} - \sqrt{6}\right)}{\sqrt{3}}$.

$= \left(\dfrac{\sqrt{20} - \sqrt{6}}{\sqrt{3}} \times \dfrac{\sqrt{3}}{\sqrt{3}}\right)$. Multiplying the denominator by $\sqrt{3}$ will create a

perfect square in the denominator's radicand.

$\dfrac{\sqrt{3}}{\sqrt{3}}$ is another way of writing **one.**

$$= \frac{\left[\sqrt{3}\left(\sqrt{20} - \sqrt{6}\right)\right]}{\sqrt{9}}.$$ Distribute $\sqrt{3}$.

$$= \frac{\left(\sqrt{60} - \sqrt{18}\right)}{3}.$$ The denominator is rationalized here, but the numerator is not in simplest radical form.

$$= \frac{\left(2\sqrt{15} - 3\sqrt{2}\right)}{3}.$$ (*Answer*)

Conjugates

Conjugates are expressions in the form $\sqrt{a} + \sqrt{b}$, and $\sqrt{a} - \sqrt{b}$. Assuming a and b are integers, the product of conjugates will always equal an integer.

$$\left(\sqrt{a} + \sqrt{b}\right) \times \left(\sqrt{a} - \sqrt{b}\right) = \sqrt{a}\sqrt{a} - \sqrt{a}\sqrt{b} + \sqrt{b}\sqrt{a} - \sqrt{b}\sqrt{b} = a - b.$$

$$\left(\sqrt{19} + \sqrt{3}\right) \times \left(\sqrt{19} - \sqrt{3}\right) = \sqrt{19}\sqrt{19} - \sqrt{19}\sqrt{3} + \sqrt{3}\sqrt{19} - \sqrt{3}\sqrt{3} = 19 - 3 = 16.$$

Conjugates are useful when rationalizing a denominator containing a **binomial radical expression.**

EXAMPLE:

Simplify $\dfrac{\left(1 + \sqrt{2}\right)}{\left(1 - \sqrt{2}\right)}$.

$\dfrac{\left(1 + \sqrt{2}\right)}{\left(1 - \sqrt{2}\right)} \times \dfrac{\left(1 + \sqrt{2}\right)}{\left(1 + \sqrt{2}\right)}$. Multiply both numerator and denominator by the conjugate of the denominator $1 + \sqrt{2}$. $\dfrac{\left(1 + \sqrt{2}\right)}{\left(1 + \sqrt{2}\right)}$ is another way of writing **one.**

$$= \frac{\left(1 + 2\sqrt{2} + 2\right)}{(1 - 2)}.$$

$$= \frac{\left(3 + 2\sqrt{2}\right)}{-1}.$$ The denominator becomes an integer, -1. Now simplify.

$$= -3 - 2\sqrt{2}.$$ (*Answer*)

POLYNOMIALS

Vocabulary

A **monomial** is a single term, such as a constant, a variable, or the product of constants and variables. 7, x, and $5x^2$ are examples of monomials. **A polynomial** contains many terms. By definition, a polynomial is the sum of monomials. $x^2 - 3x + 2$ is an example of a polynomial containing the **terms** x^2, $3x$, and 2.

Polynomials can be added, subtracted, multiplied, and divided following the properties of real numbers.

Adding and Subtracting Polynomials

Polynomials can be added and subtracted by **combining like terms.** Like terms have the same variables raised to the same power. In other words, they are terms that differ only by their coefficients.

a^2b^3 and $-4a^2b^3$ are like terms that can be combined. $a^2b^3 + -4a^2b^3 = -3a^2b^3$

x^2y and $2xy$ are not like terms.

EXAMPLE:

Subtract $x^2 - 2x + 5$ from $3x - 4$.

$3x - 4 - (x^2 - 2x + 5)$.	Set up your expression. Subtract the first term from the second.
$= 3x - 4 - x^2 + 2x - 5$.	Change the subtraction to *adding the opposites.*
$= -x^2 + (3 + 2)x + (-4 + -5)$.	Combine like terms.
$= -x^2 + 5x - 9$ (*Answer*)	

Multiplying Polynomials

Multiplying polynomials involves using the distributive property. You are probably most familiar with multiplying a binomial (a polynomial with 2 terms) by another binomial. For example:

$(x + 4)(x - 6)$.

The **FOIL method** helps to remember how to multiply terms: **F**irst, **O**uter, **I**nner, **L**ast.

$(x + 4)(x - 6) = x^2 - 6x + 4x - 24$

Now, add the outer and inner products to simplify the expression.

$= x^2 - 2x - 24$.

EXAMPLE:

Multiply $(2x + 7)(2x - 7)$.

$(2x + 7)(2x - 7) = 4x^2 - 14x + 14x - 49$	FOIL
$= 4x^2 + (-14x + 14x) - 49$.	Notice that the inner and outer terms are opposites.
$= 4x^2 - 49$. (*Answer*)	

EXAMPLE:

Multiply $(5a + 1)(1 - 5a)$.

$(5a + 1)(1 - 5a) = (5a + 1)(-5a + 1)$ Rewrite $(1 - 5a)$ as the opposite of $(5a - 1)$.

$= -25a^2 + 5a - 5a + 1)$.   FOIL

$= -25a^2 + 1$.   (*Answer*)

Remembering these special products of polynomials will help when factoring.

Special Products	Examples
$(a + b)^2 = a^2 + 2ab + b^2$	$(2x + 9)^2 = 4x^2 + 36x + 81$
$(a - b)^2 = a^2 - 2ab + b^2$	$(x - 12)^2 = x^2 - 24x + 144$
$(a + b)(a - b) = a^2 - b^2$	$(x + 3y)(x - 3y) = x^2 - 9y^2$

Factoring

Now that you've reviewed multiplying polynomials, let's look at its reverse: finding factors. Factoring means expressing a polynomial as a product of other polynomials. The most basic way to factor a polynomial is to distribute out its **greatest monomial factor.** (Remember, a monomial is a single term, such as a constant, a variable, or the product of constants and variables.)

Just as 12 can be factored as $2^2 \times 3$, the polynomial $12xy^3 - 2x^2y^2$ can be factored as $2xy^2(6y - x)$. $2xy^2$ is the **greatest monomial factor,** otherwise known as the **GCF,** of the terms $12xy^3$ and $2x^2y^2$.

EXAMPLE:

Factor $xy^3 - xy^2 + x^2y$.

$xy^3 - xy^2 + x^2y = xy(y^2 - y + x)$.   The GCF of the terms is xy.

Trinomials

Some trinomials can be factored by recognizing that they are a special product. These are called **perfect square trinomials.**

$a^2 + 2ab + b^2 = (a + b)^2$.

$a^2 - 2ab + b^2 = (a - b)^2$.

EXAMPLE:

Factor $x^2 - 18x + 81$.

$x^2 - 18x + 81 = (x - 9)(x - 9)$.   Recognize that half of the second term squared equals the third term. ($\frac{1}{2} \times 18 = 9$ and $9^2 = 81$.)

$= (x - 9)^2$

When factoring, it is a good idea to check your work by multiplying the factors to get the original polynomial. Using the FOIL method, you can quickly check that $(x - 9)(x - 9)$ does, in fact, equal $x^2 - 18x + 81$.

EXAMPLE:

Factor $x^2 + x + \dfrac{1}{4}$.

$$x^2 + x + \frac{1}{4} = \left(x + \frac{1}{2}\right)\left(x + \frac{1}{2}\right).$$ Recognize that $\dfrac{1}{2}(1) = \dfrac{1}{2}$ and $\dfrac{1}{2^2} = \dfrac{1}{4}$.

$$= \left(x + \frac{1}{2}\right)^2.$$

Of course, not every trinomial is a perfect square trinomial that can be expressed as a special product. For these problems, try thinking about the FOIL method, and use trial and error.

$x^2 + 13x + 22 = (? + ?)(? + ?)$.

First $x \times x = x^2$, so begin the factorization with $(x + ?)(x + ?)$.

Last $22 = 1 \times 22$ or 2×11. Think about the factors of the last term. What two numbers will multiply to give you 22 and add to give you 13? (13 is the sum of the **O**uter and **I**nner terms.) 2 and 11 work $(x + 2)(x + 11)$.

You're not done yet. Multiply the binomials to check your work. Because the three terms in the original trinomial are positive, both binomials contain positive terms. $(x + 2)(x + 11) = x^2 + 11x + 2x + 22 = x^2 + 13x + 22$. $(x + 2)(x + 11)$ is the correct answer.

EXAMPLE:

Factor $x^2 - 2x - 35$.

$x^2 - 2x - 35 = (x + ?)(x + ?)$.   Think about the **First** terms. $x \times x = x^2$.

$35 = 1 \times 35$ or 5×7.   What two numbers will multiply to give you -35 and add to give you -2? 5 and -7 work.

$= (x + 5)(x - 7)$.   Check your work. Pay special attention to the positive and negative signs.

Difference of Perfect Squares

The product of the sum of two terms and the difference of the same terms is called the difference of perfect squares. When factoring, it is important to recognize that this is a special product.

$a^2 - b^2 = (a + b)(a - b)$.

$x^2 - 1 = x^2 - 1^2 = (x + 1)(x - 1)$.

EXAMPLE:

Factor $4x^2 - 9$.

$4x^2 - 9 = (2x + 3)(2x - 3)$.   *(Answer)*

Because both $4x^2$ and 9 are perfect squares, this binomial is a special product. Remembering this will save time when factoring.

EXAMPLE:

Factor $x^3 - 64x$.

$x^3 - 64x = x(x^2 - 64)$. Always factor out the greatest common factor first. Here the GCF is x.

$= x(x + 8)(x - 8)$.   (*Answer*)

Note that there is not a rule called "Sums of Perfect Squares." An expression such as $x^2 + 4$ cannot be further factored.

Sum and Difference Of Cubes

Factoring the sum and difference of cubes is not obvious. To save time on the SAT Subject Test, be able to recognize these equations:

1. **Sum of Cubes:** $(a^3 + b^3) = (a + b)(a^2 - ab + b^2)$.
2. **Difference of Cubes:** $(a^3 - b^3) = (a - b)(a^2 + ab + b^2)$.

EXAMPLE:

Factor $8x^3 - 125$.

Using the equation for the difference of cubes, substitute $a = 2x$ and $b = 5$.

$8x^3 - 125 = (2x - 5)(4x^2 + 10x + 25)$.   (*Answer*)

Memorizing the perfect cubes ($1^3 = 1$, $2^3 = 8$, $3^3 = 27$, $4^3 = 64$, $5^3 = 125$, $6^3 = 216$, etc.) will help when factoring the sum and difference of cubes.

QUADRATIC EQUATIONS

Factoring

Up to this point, when given a problem such as $x^2 - 8x + 9$, you would say the polynomial is unfactorable. In other words, it's prime. $x^2 - 8x + 9$ doesn't fit any of the three special products, and factoring the trinomial also doesn't work.

$x^2 - 8x + 9 = (x + ?)(x + ?)$.

What two numbers will multiply to give you 9 and add to give you -8? At first glance, 9 and 1 seem to work resulting in four possibilities:

$(x + 9)(x + 1) \ (x - 9)(x - 1) \ (x + 9)(x - 1) \ (x - 9)(x + 1)$.

None of the four, however, give you a positive 9 constant and a negative 8 coefficient for x. The **Quadratic Formula** can be used to solve a trinomial equation (in the form of a quadratic equation) whether it's factorable or not.

Before discussing the Quadratic Formula, let's take a look at quadratic equations in general. Polynomials in the form $ax^2 + bx + c$ ($a \neq 0$) are quadratic (Quadratic means "second-degree.") A quadratic equation looks like $ax^2 + bx + c = 0$. "Factorable" quadratic equations are solved by factoring and setting each factor equal to zero. The solutions are called **roots** of the quadratic, values of the variable that satisfy the equation.

EXAMPLE:

Solve $x^2 - 5x - 14 = 0$.

$x^2 - 5x - 14 = (x - 7)(x + 2) = 0$.　　Factor the trinomial.

$(x - 7) = 0$ or $(x + 2) = 0$.　　Set each factor equal to zero.

$x = 7$ or -2.

The solution set is {7, –2}.　　　(*Answer*)

Therefore, the **roots** of the quadratic equation $x^2 - 5x - 14 = 0$ are 7 and –2 because $7^2 - 5 \times 7 - 14 = 0$ and $(-2)^2 - 5 \times (-2) - 14 = 0$.

Quadratic Formula

As mentioned, the **Quadratic Formula** can be used to solve a quadratic equation, $\boldsymbol{ax^2 + bx + c = 0}$, whether it's factorable or not. The formula uses the coefficients a, b, and c to find the solutions.

$$\boxed{\begin{array}{c} \textbf{The Quadratic Formula} \\[2mm] x = \dfrac{-b \pm \sqrt{b^2 - 4ac}}{2a} \quad a \neq 0. \end{array}}$$

Remember the trinomial equation $x^2 - 8x + 9 = 0$ that we determined was "unfactorable." Let's take a look at how to solve it using the Quadratic Formula.

EXAMPLE:

Solve $x^2 - 8x + 9 = 0$.

Substitute $a = 1$, $b = -8$, and $c = 9$ into the Quadratic Formula.

$$x = \frac{\left[-b \pm \sqrt{(b^2 - 4ac)} \right]}{2a} = \frac{\left[-(-8) \pm \sqrt{((-8)^2 - 4 \times 1 \times 9)} \right]}{2 \times 1}.$$

$$x = \frac{\left[8 \pm \sqrt{(64 - 36)} \right]}{2}.$$

$$x = \frac{\left(8 \pm \sqrt{28} \right)}{2}.\quad \text{Simplify} \sqrt{28}.$$

$$x = \frac{\left(8 \pm 2\sqrt{7} \right)}{2}.\quad \text{Divide the numerator by 2.}$$

$$x = 4 \pm \sqrt{7}.\quad (\textit{Answer})$$

The Quadratic Formula can also be used to solve "factorable" quadratic equations. Earlier, we determined that the equation $x^2 - 5x - 14 = 0$ had roots of 7 and –2. Let's try to solve it a different way using the Quadratic Formula.

EXAMPLE:

Solve $x^2 - 5x - 14 = 0$ using the Quadratic Formula.

$a = 1, b = -5, c = -14.$

$$x = \frac{\left[-b \pm \sqrt{(b^2 - 4ac)}\right]}{2a} = \frac{\left[-(-5) \pm \sqrt{((-5)^2 - 4 \times 1 \times -14)}\right]}{2 \times 1}.$$

$$x = \frac{\left[5 \pm \sqrt{(25 + 56)}\right]}{2}.$$

$$x = \frac{\left(5 \pm \sqrt{81}\right)}{2}.$$

$$x = \frac{(5 \pm 9)}{2}.$$

$$x = \frac{(5 + 9)}{2} = \frac{14}{2} = 7.$$

$$x = \frac{(5 - 9)}{2} = -\frac{4}{2} = -2.$$

The solution set is {7, –2}.   (*Answer*)

Of course, the roots will be the same regardless of which method you choose to use to solve the quadratic equation.

Solving by Substitution

Sometimes equations that don't look like quadratic equations can be solved by factoring or by using the Quadratic Formula. This is true if you can rewrite the equations in quadratic form using substitution.

$x^4 - 8x^2 - 11 = 0 \quad \rightarrow$ Let $u = x^2, u^2 - 8u - 11 = 0.$

$x + 2\sqrt{x} + 5 = 0 \quad \rightarrow$ Let $u = \sqrt{x}, u^2 + 2u + 5 = 0.$

$\left(\dfrac{1}{(8x)}\right)^2 + 3\left(\dfrac{1}{(8x)}\right) - 7 = 0 \rightarrow$ Let $u = \left(\dfrac{1}{(8x)}\right), u^2 + 3u - 7 = 0.$

As in the examples above, choose a value for u so that the equation becomes quadratic in u and fits the form $au^2 + bu + c = 0.$

EXAMPLE:

Solve $x - 19\sqrt{x} + 48 = 0.$

Let $u = \sqrt{x}$, and the equation becomes $u^2 - 19u + 48 = 0.$ Is this factorable? It turns out that it is. If you're unsure, use the Quadratic Formula to find the roots.

$$u^2 - 19u + 48 = (u - 16)(u - 3) = 0.$$

$$(u - 16) = 0 \text{ or } (u - 3) = 0.$$

$$u = 16 \text{ or } u = 3.$$ You're not done yet! Substitute $\sqrt{x}$ back in for u to find x.

$$\sqrt{x} = 16 \text{ or } \sqrt{x} = 3.$$

$$x = 256 \text{ or } x = 9.$$

$\{256, 9\}.$ (*Answer*)

The Discriminant

The **discriminant** of a quadratic equation equals $b^2 - 4ac$, the radicand in the Quadratic Formula. It allows you to determine the nature of the roots of a quadratic equation without actually solving for them.

1. If $b^2 - 4ac > 0$, there are two real, unequal roots.

   When $b^2 - 4ac$ is a perfect square, there are **two real, rational roots.**

   When $b^2 - 4ac$ is not a perfect square, there are **two real, irrational roots.**

2. If $b^2 - 4ac = 0$, there is one real root. (It's called a **double root.**)

3. If $b^2 - 4ac < 0$, there are **no real roots.** (They're complex conjugate in the form $a + bi$ and $a - bi$.).

EXAMPLE:

Determine the nature of the roots of the quadratic equation $x^2 - 9x - 10 = 0$.

$$b^2 - 4ac = (-9)^2 - 4(1)(-10).$$

$$= 81 + 40 = 121. \quad \text{The discriminant is positive and a perfect square.}$$

Two real, rational roots.   (*Answer*)

Equations with Radicals

Radical equations contain radicals with variables in the radicand. To solve a radical equation, you must always isolate the radical first. Then raise both sides to the appropriate power to "undo" the radical, i.e., square a square root, cube a cube root, etc.

EXAMPLE 1:

$$\sqrt{x} = 11.$$

$$\left(\sqrt{x}\right)^2 = 11^2.$$

$$x = 121.$$

EXAMPLE 2:

$$\sqrt{x + 1} = 3.$$

$$\left(\sqrt{x + 1}\right)^2 = 3^2.$$

$$x + 1 = 9, \text{ so } x = 8.$$

EXAMPLE:

Solve $2\sqrt{x-12} - 10 = \sqrt{x-12}$.

$\sqrt{x-12} = 10$.   Combine like terms.

$\left(\sqrt{x-12}\right)^2 = 10^2$.   Isolate the radical and square both sides.

$x - 12 = 100$.

$x = 112$.   (*Answer*)

It is crucial to go back and check your answer in the original radical equation. Sometimes squaring both sides of an equation introduces **extraneous roots** that do not satisfy the original equation. When $x = 112$, $2\sqrt{112-12} - 10$ equals $\sqrt{112-12}$, so the answer checks.

When there is more than one radical in an equation, you need to square both sides multiple times. Again, remember to isolate one radical at a time.

EXAMPLE:

Solve $\sqrt{x+4} + \sqrt{x} - 6 = 0$.

$\sqrt{x+4} = 6 - \sqrt{x}$.   Isolate the radical $\sqrt{x+4}$.

$\left(\sqrt{x+4}\right)^2 = \left(6 - \sqrt{x}\right)^2$.   Square both sides.

$x + 4 = 36 - 12\sqrt{x} + x$.

$-32 = -12\sqrt{x}$.   Isolate the second radical.

$\dfrac{32}{12} = \dfrac{8}{3} = \sqrt{x}$

$\left(\dfrac{8}{3}\right)^2 = \left(\sqrt{x}\right)^2$.   Square both sides a second time.

$\dfrac{64}{9} = x$.   (*Answer*)

Remember to check your answer in the original radical equation.

◼ INEQUALITIES

The rules for solving equations also apply to inequalities. Remember that multiplying or dividing both sides of an inequality by a negative number, reverses its sign.

$-x > 8$ becomes $x < -8$.

$-\dfrac{1}{2}x < 15$ becomes $x > -30$.

Transitive Property of Inequality

The **Transitive Property of Inequality** states that for any real numbers a, b, and c:

If $a < b$ and $b < c$, then $a < c$.

It makes sense that if $3 < 4$ and $4 < 5$, then $3 < 5$.

Sometimes the transitive property is written by combining the three inequalities:

$a < b < c$ and $3 < 4 < 5$.

Addition and Multiplication Properties

The addition and multiplication properties of inequality mirror those for equalities.

Addition Property of Inequality	
If $a < b$, then $a + c < b + c$.	If $40 < 50$, then $40 + 1 < 50 + 1$.
Multiplication Property of Inequality	
If $a < b$ and c is *positive*, then $ac < bc$.	If $5 < 6$, then $5(2) < 6(2)$.
If $a < b$ and c is *negative*, then $ac > bc$.	If $5 < 6$, then $5(-2) > 6(-2)$.

EXAMPLE:

Solve $2 - x > 4 + x$.

$-2 > 2x$.

$-1 > x$.

$\{x : x < -1\}$.   (*Answer*)

This reads "the set of all x such that x is less than negative one." On a number line, the graph would begin with an open circle at -1 and extend forever in the left direction.

"And" vs. "Or"

A **conjunction** joins two sentence with "and" and is true when **both** sentences are true.

EXAMPLE:

$x > 29$ and $x < 48$.

$29 < x < 48$ is an alternate way of writing this and it's read "x is greater than 29 and less than 48."

A **disjunction** joins two sentences with "or" and is true when **at least one** of the sentences is true.

EXAMPLE:

$x > 5$ or $x < -5$.

EXAMPLE:

Solve the conjunction $0 < x - 2 \le 6$.

Rewrite the inequality using "and."

$0 < x - 2$ and $x - 2 \le 6$.

$2 < x$ and $x \le 8$.

The solution set is $\{x : 2 < x \le 8\}$.   (*Answer*)

On a number line, the graph would begin with an open circle at 2, extend to the right, and end with a closed circle at 8.

Inequalities with Absolute Value

Inequalities involving absolute value can be thought of as either a disjunction or a conjunction.

1. $|x| < n$ is equivalent to the **conjunction** $-n < x < n$.
    $|x| < 2$ is equivalent to the conjunction $-2 < x < 2$.

2. $|x| > n$ is equivalent to the **disjunction** $x < -n$ or $x > n$.
    $|x| > 2$ is equivalent to the disjunction $x < -2$ or $x > 2$.

EXAMPLE:

Solve $8 - |3x + 7| < 2$.

$-|3x + 7| < -6$.   Divide both sides by -1, reversing the sign.

$|3x + 7| > 6$. Analyze the inequality to determine if it's a conjunction or disjunction. Because the variable is on the greater than side of the inequality sign, it resembles the second example above $|x| > n$. The inequality is, therefore, a **disjunction.**

$3x + 7 > 6$ OR $3x + 7 < -6$

$3x > -1$ OR $3x < -13$

$x > -\dfrac{1}{3}$ OR $x < -\dfrac{13}{3}$

$\left\{ x : x < -\dfrac{13}{3} \text{ or } x > -\dfrac{1}{3} \right\}$.   (*Answer*)

RATIONAL EXPRESSIONS

Simplifying Rational Expressions

Rational numbers are numbers that can be expressed as $\frac{p}{q}$, a quotient of integers. Likewise, **rational expressions** are those that can be expressed as a quotient of polynomials. $\frac{(x^2 - 9)}{x}, \frac{(x^2 - 10x + 25)}{(x^2 + 100)}$, and $\frac{14xy}{xy^3}$ are examples of rational expressions. The principles of factoring are important when simplifying rational expressions. Take a moment to review some special products of polynomials.

Special Products:
$(a + b)^2 = a^2 + 2ab + b^2$
$(a - b)^2 = a^2 - 2ab + b^2$
$(a + b)(a - b) = a^2 - b^2$

EXAMPLE:

Simplify $\frac{(2x^2 - 6x)}{x^2 - 9}$.

$\frac{(2x^2 - 6x)}{x^2 - 9} = \frac{2x(x - 3)}{(x + 3)(x - 3)}$.   Factor the numerator and denominator. Recognize that the numerator has a common factor of $2x$, and the denominator is the difference of perfect squares. Now simplify by dividing the numerator and denominator by their common factor $(x - 3)$.

$\frac{2x}{x + 3}$.   *(Answer)*

Typically, rational expressions are in simplest form when they do not contain zero or negative exponents. Recall that any number raised to a zero power equals one and any number raised to a negative one power equals its reciprocal.

Multiplying and Dividing Rational Expressions

Multiplying and dividing rational expressions follow the same rules as fractions.

Multiplication Rule for Fractions $\frac{a}{b} \times \frac{c}{d} = \frac{ac}{bd}$, where $b, d \neq 0$.

Division Rule for Fractions $\frac{a}{b} \div \frac{c}{d} = \frac{a}{b} \times \frac{d}{c}$, where $b, c, d \neq 0$.

EXAMPLE:

$$\frac{4}{x^2} \div \frac{x}{4}.$$

$$\frac{4}{x^2} \div \frac{x}{4} = \frac{4}{x^2} \times \frac{4}{x}. \quad \text{Multiply by the reciprocal of } \frac{x}{4}.$$

$$= \frac{16}{x^3}. \quad (Answer)$$

EXAMPLE:

Simplify $\dfrac{(x^4 - y^4)}{(x^2 + y^2)}(x + y)^{-2}$.

Factor the first fraction. The numerator $x^4 - y^4$ is the difference of perfect squares: $x^4 - y^4 = (x^2 + y^2)(x^2 - y^2)$. The denominator $x^2 + y^2$ is the sum of perfect squares and, therefore, cannot be factored. The simplified expression is:

$$\frac{(x^2 + y^2)(x^2 - y^2)}{(x^2 + y^2)}(x + y)^{-2}.$$

Simplify the fraction by factoring out a common factor of $x^2 + y^2$:

$$\frac{(x^2 - y^2)}{1}(x + y)^{-2}.$$

Simplify the negative exponent by rewriting $(x + y)^{-2}$ as $\dfrac{1}{(x + y)^2}$. Now you have:

$$\frac{(x^2 - y^2)}{1} \times \frac{1}{(x + y)^2}.$$

The numerator of the first term is the difference of perfect squares and can be factored. In factored form, you have:

$$\frac{(x + y)(x - y)}{1} \times \frac{1}{(x + y)(x + y)}.$$

Factor out a common factor of $(x + y)$.

$$= \frac{(x - y)}{(x + y)}. \quad (Answer)$$

This example incorporates many concepts reviewed thus far: factoring the difference of perfect squares, simplifying rational expressions, finding the greatest common factor, multiplying rational expressions, and simplifying negative exponents.

Adding and Subtracting Rational Expressions

Similar to fractions, rational expressions can only be added or subtracted when they have a common denominator. The LCD is the LCM of the denominators.

EXAMPLE:

Simplify $\dfrac{1}{8x} - \dfrac{-1}{4x^2}$.

The LCM of $8x^2$ and $4x$ is $8x^2$. Express each fraction as an equivalent fraction with a denominator of $8x^2$.

$\dfrac{1}{8x} \times \dfrac{x}{x} - \dfrac{-1}{4x^2} \times \dfrac{2}{2}$.   Now simplify. Change the subtraction to adding the opposite of the 2nd term.

$\dfrac{x}{8x^2} + \dfrac{2}{8x^2}$.

$= \dfrac{(x+2)}{8x^2}$.   (*Answer*)

EXAMPLE:

Simplify $\dfrac{2}{(x-1)^2} - \dfrac{2}{(1-x^2)}$.

Recall that $1 - x^2 = -(x^2 - 1)$. The equation then becomes:

$\dfrac{2}{(x-1)^2} + \dfrac{2}{(x^2-1)}$.

The denominators can be factored as $(x-1)(x-1)$ and $(x+1)(x-1)$ resulting in an LCM of $(x+1)(x-1)^2$. Expressing each fraction with the LCM as its denominator gives you:

$\dfrac{2(x+1)}{(x+1)(x-1)^2} + \dfrac{2(x-1)}{(x^2-1)}$.

$= \dfrac{[2(x+1) + 2(x-1)]}{(x+1)(x-1)^2}$.

$= \dfrac{(2x+2+2x-2)}{(x+1)(x-1)^2}$.

$= \dfrac{4x}{(x+1)(x-1)^2}$.   (*Answer*)

Solving Equations With Rational Expressions

One way to solve equations involving rational expressions is to multiply both sides by the LCD of the rational expressions.

EXAMPLE:

Solve $\dfrac{1}{(x+2)(x-7)} + 1 = \dfrac{1}{(x-7)}$.

The LCD is $(x + 2)(x - 7)$.   Multiplying both sides by the LCD gives you:

$1 + (x + 2)(x - 7) = (x + 2)$.

$1 + x^2 - 5x - 14 = x + 2$.

$x^2 - 6x - 15 = 0$.   Because this equation is not factorable, use the Quadratic Formula to find its roots.

$$x = \frac{\left[-b \pm \sqrt{(b^2 - 4ac)}\right]}{2a} = \frac{\left(6 \pm \sqrt{96}\right)}{2} = \frac{\left(6 \pm 4\sqrt{6}\right)}{2}.$$

$x = 3 \pm 2\sqrt{6}$.   (*Answer*)

When multiplying both sides of an equation by an LCD, extraneous roots may be introduced. Always go back and check your answer in the original equation.

SYSTEMS

A **system of linear equations** is made up of two or more linear equations in the same two variables. Some examples of systems are:

EXAMPLE 1:
$2x - 4y = 10$.
$6x + y = -3$.

EXAMPLE 2:
$y = 8x - 14$.
$y = x$.

EXAMPLE 3:
$a + b = 37$.
$5a - 2b = -13$.

Systems of linear equations are also called **simultaneous equations.** The **solution** of a system is any ordered pair of the variables that satisfy all equations. For instance, in Example 2 above, the ordered pair (2, 2) is a solution of the system. When $x = 2$ and $y = 2$, both equations ($2 = 8(2) - 14$ and $2 = 2$) are satisfied. **Equivalent systems** are systems that have the same solution.

Three methods to solve systems are: (a) substitution, (b) linear combination, and (c) graphing. Here we explain the first two methods. Graphing is discussed in the Coordinate Geometry chapter.

Solving by Substitution

Just as one equation allows you to solve for one unknown variable, two equations allow you to solve for two unknowns. The substitution method involves expressing one variable in terms of the other in one equation (i.e., x in terms of y or y in terms of x) and **substituting** this value into the second equation.

EXAMPLE:

Solve the system using the substitution method:

$x + 3y = 14$.

$3x - 2y = -2$.

Choose one equation and solve for a variable. (You can choose what equation to use and for what variable to solve.) Let's solve for x in the first equation. This is the best choice because the coefficient of x is 1.

$x = -3y + 14$.

$3x - 2y = -2$.

Substitute $-3y + 14$ for x in the 2nd equation and solve for y:

$$3(-3y + 14) - 2y = -2.$$

$$-9y + 42 - 2y = -2.$$

$$-11y = -44.$$

$$y = 4.$$

Substitute 4 for y in either of the original equations in the system to solve for x:

$$x + 3(4) = 14.$$

$$x + 12 = 14.$$

$$x = 2.$$

The solution is the ordered pair (2, 4).   (*Answer*)

It is a good idea to check your answer by substituting (2, 4) back into both of the equations.

Solving by Linear Combination

Adding two linear equations results in what's called a **linear combination** of the equations. For example:

$$\begin{array}{r} x + 2y = 7 \\ + \ 3x + y \ = -8 \\ \hline 4x + 3y = -1 \end{array}$$

The linear combination method involves transforming and adding equations in order to eliminate one variable and solve for the other. The goal is to end up with one equation with one variable. Let's solve the previous example in a different way.

E X A M P L E :

Solve the system using the linear combination method.

$$x + 3y = 14.$$

$$3x - 2y = -2.$$

Let's try to eliminate x and solve for y. (You can choose to eliminate either variable here.) Start by multiplying the first equation by -3 so the coefficients of the x are opposites. Remember what you do to one side of an equation you *must* do to the other, so both sides need to be multiplied by a -3 factor.

$$-3(x + 3y = 14) \text{ becomes } -3x + -9y = -42$$

This results in the equivalent system.

$$-3x + -9y = -42.$$

$$3x - 2y = -2.$$

Add the two equations.

$$\begin{array}{r} -3x + -9y = -42 \\ + \quad 3x - 2y = -2 \\ \hline 0x - 11y = -44 \end{array}$$

It is important that one variable cancels out. If this doesn't happen, check your work for errors or try multiplying by a different number in the first step. Now that x is eliminated, you are able to solve for y.

$$-11y = -44.$$

$$y = 4.$$

Substitute 4 for y in either of the original equations in the system to solve for x:

$$3x - 2(4) = -2.$$

$$3x - 8 = -2.$$

$$3x = 6.$$

$$x = 2.$$

The solution is the ordered pair (2, 4).   (*Answer*)

This, of course, is the same answer you got by using the substitution method. Remember that you have a choice of what method to use when solving systems of linear equations.

No Solution vs. Infinite Solutions

Systems of linear equations can have three possible solution sets:

1. One solution

2. No solution

3. Infinitely many solutions

Graphing systems are discussed in the Coordinate Geometry chapter, but it is worth mentioning that one solution occurs when the two lines intersect in one point; no solution occurs when the lines are parallel; and infinitely many solutions occur when the lines are actually the same line.

When solving a system algebraically, **no solution** results from a **contradiction.** You end up with a statement that will never be true, such as $5 = 6$ or $-1 = 0$.

EXAMPLE:

Solve the system:

$$2y = x + 36.$$

$$y = \frac{1}{2}x + 4.$$

Because the 2nd equation is already solved for y in terms of x, let's substitute that value into the first equation:

$$2\left(\frac{1}{2}x + 4\right) = x + 36.$$

$$x + 8 = x + 36.$$

$$8 = 36.$$

Of course, $8 \neq 36$, so this contradiction shows the systems has no solution.

No solution.   (*Answer*)

This example can be solved an alternate way by rewriting the first equation in slope-intercept form. This results in the system:

$$y = \frac{1}{2}x + 18.$$

$$y = \frac{1}{2}x + 4.$$

Immediately you can see that these lines have the same slope, $m = \frac{1}{2}$. Therefore, they must be parallel and will, by definition, never intersect.

Infinitely many solutions, on the other hand, result from an **identity.** You end up with a statement that is always true such as $7 = 7$ or $0 = 0$.

EXAMPLE:

Solve the system:

$$y = 3x - 9.$$

$$-6x + 2y = -18.$$

Let's use the linear combination method to solve this system. Start by rewriting the first equation:

$$-3x + y = -9.$$

$$-6x + 2y = -18.$$

Multiply the first equation by -2 so the coefficients of the y are opposites:

$$6x + -2y = 18.$$

$$-6x + 2y = -18.$$

Add the equations:

$$\begin{array}{r} 6x + -2y = 18 \\ + \quad -6x + 2y = -18 \\ \hline 0x + 0y = 0. \\ 0 = 0. \end{array}$$

Zero always equals zero so this identity shows the systems has infinitely many solutions.

Infinitely many solutions.   (*Answer*)

An alternate method of solving the system is to rewrite the second equation, isolating y on the left side:

$$y = 3x - 9.$$

$$2y = 6x - 18.$$

Both of these lines have a slope of 3 and a y-intercept of 9, so they are, in fact, the same line. You may also notice that the second equation is equivalent to the first. It is simply a factor of two greater than $y = 3x - 9$.

Word Problems with Systems

Word problems with two unknowns can be solved by setting up a system and then solving it using either the substitution or linear combination method.

EXAMPLE:

Tickets for the homecoming football game cost $3 for students and $5 for the general public. Ticket sales totaled $1,396, and 316 people attended the game. How many student tickets were sold?

First define the variables. Let s = the number of student tickets and p = the number of tickets for the general public.

Because ticket sales totaled $1,396:

$3s + 5p = 1,396$.

Now use the given information on attendance to get:

$s + p = 316$.

The system looks like:

$3s + 5p = 1,396$

$s + p = 316$.

Which method, substitution or linear combination, works best here? Both produce the same solution, so it is your choice. Let's try using the linear combination method. Multiply the second equation by –3 and add to get:

$$3s + 5p = 1,396$$
$$+ \quad -3s + -3p = -948$$
$$\overline{0s + 2p = 448}$$
$$p = 224.$$

Substitute $p = 224$ into one of the original equations:

$s + 224 = 316$.

$s = 92$.

92 student tickets were sold.   (*Answer*)

As with all word problems, always make sure to answer the question asked. Although we solved for both p and s, the word problem asks for the number of student tickets.

EXAMPLE:

A mother is twice as old as her daughter. Twelve years ago she was three times as old as her daughter was then. Find the mother's present age.

Let m = the mother's age now and d = the daughter's age now. Because the mother is twice as old has her daughter, the first equation:

$m = 2d$.

Twelve years ago, the mother was $m - 12$ years old and the daughter was $d - 12$ years old. This gives you the second equation:

$m - 12 = 3(d - 12)$.

$m - 12 = 3d - 36$.

$m = 3d - 24$.

You have two equations in two unknowns, m and d. A system is needed to solve the word problem:

$m = 2d$.

$m = 3d - 24$.

Again, you can choose to solve by either the substitution or linear combination method. Let's try using substitution. Because the first equation is already solved for m in terms of d, substitute $m = 2d$ into the second equation, and solve for d.

$2d = 3d - 24$.

$24 = d$.

The word problem asks for the mother's age, so substitute $d = 24$ back into one of the original equations.

$m = 2(24)$.

$m = 48$.

The mother is 48 year old.　　　(*Answer*)

*BINOMIAL THEOREM

The **Binomial Theorem** simplifies the task of expanding a binomial expression in the form $(x + y)^n$. (Remember that a binomial is a polynomial that has two terms.) Let's look at a few values of n.

$(x + y)^0 = 1$.

$(x + y)^1 = x + y$.

$(x + y)^2 = x^2 + 2xy + y^2$.

$(x + y)^3 = x^3 + 3x^2y + 3xy^2 + y^3$.

$(x + y)^4 = x^4 + 4x^3y + 6x^2y^2 + 4xy^3 + y^4$.

$(x + y)^5 = x^5 + 5x^4y + 10x^3y^2 + 10x^2y^3 + 5xy^4 + y^5$.

Do you notice a pattern in the expansions? Each one has $n + 1$ terms. As the power of x decreases by one, the power of y increases by one, and the sum of the exponents of x and y is always n. The Binomial Theorem states that coefficient of each term in the expansion of $(x + y)^n$ is nCr, where r is the exponent of either x or y and $nCr = \dfrac{n!}{(n - r)!r!}$.

EXAMPLE:

What is the 4th term of $(a + b)^7$?

The exponent of b in the 4th term is $n - 1$ or $4 - 1 = 3$. The exponent of a must then equal $7 - 3$ or 4.

The coefficient of the 4th term is given by $_7C_4$ (or $_7C_3$ because you can choose to use either the exponent of a or b).

$$_7C_4 = \frac{7!}{(7 - 4)!4!} = \frac{7!}{3!4!} = \frac{5 \times 6 \times 7}{1 \times 2 \times 3} = 35.$$

The 4th term is $35a^4b^3$.

EXAMPLE:

What is the middle term in the expansion of $\left(4x - \frac{1}{2}y\right)^6$?

The expansion of $\left(4x - \frac{1}{2}y\right)^6$ has 7 terms, so the middle term is the 4th term.

The exponent of $\frac{1}{2}y$ is 3, so the exponent of $3x$ is also 3. The coefficient of the middle term is $_6C_3$.

$$_6C_3 = \frac{6!}{3!3!} = \frac{4 \times 5 \times 6}{1 \times 2 \times 3} = 20.$$

The middle term is:

$$20(4x)^3\left(\frac{1}{2}y\right)^3 = 20(64x^3)\left(\frac{1}{8}y^3\right) = -160x^3y^3. \qquad (Answer)$$

CHAPTER 5

SOLID GEOMETRY

This chapter provides a review of solid (i.e., three-dimensional) geometry principles. On the Level 2 test, 4–6% of the questions relate specifically to solid geometry. Note that Plane Euclidean geometry is not directly tested on the Level 2 test, although Plane Euclidean geometry principles (such as the Pythagorean Theorem, area formulas, and special right triangles) may be applied in other types of questions. By definition, solid geometry focuses on three-dimensional shapes and figures. The pie chart shows approximately how much of the Level 2 test is related to solid geometry:

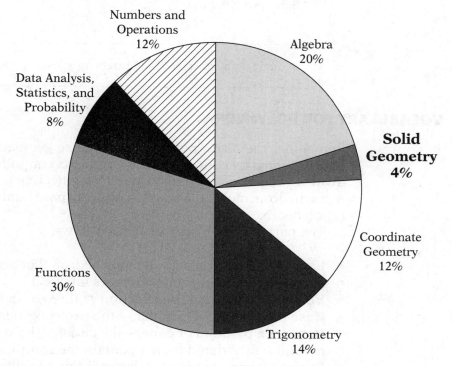

The following solid geometry topics are covered in this chapter:

1. Vocabulary for Polyhedra
2. Review of Area Formulas
3. Prisms
   a. Distance Between Opposite Vertices of a Rectangular Prism
4. Cylinders
5. Pyramids
6. Cones
7. Spheres
8. Volume Ratio of Similar Figures
9. *Coordinates in Three Dimensions

*Denotes concepts that are on the Level 2 test only.

The following reference information is provided during the Level 2 test. You do NOT need to memorize these formulas. Become familiar with the information below so that you can refer to it during the test, if necessary. These formulas are printed in the directions of the test.

Reference Information	
Right circular cone with radius r and height h:	Volume $= \dfrac{1}{3}\pi r^2 h$
Right circular cone with circumference of base c and slant height ℓ:	Lateral Area $= \dfrac{1}{2}c\ell$
Sphere with radius r:	Volume $= \dfrac{4}{3}\pi r^3$
	Surface Area $= 4\pi r^2$
Pyramid with base area B and height h:	Volume $= \dfrac{1}{3}Bh$

VOCABULARY FOR POLYHEDRA

Remember the term "polygon" from plane geometry—a many-sided closed figure created by connecting line segments endpoint to endpoint. A **polyhedron** is a many-sided solid created by connecting polygons along their sides. A polyhedron encloses a single region of space, and the plural of polyhedron is polyhedra.

The parts of a polyhedron are as follows:

- **Faces**—the flat surfaces of a polyhedron that are shaped like polygons
- **Edge**—a segment where two faces intersect
- **Vertex**—the point of intersection of three or more edges
- **Base** (of a prism or cylinder)—the two congruent, parallel faces
- **Base** (of a pyramid or cone)—the circular (for a cone) or polygonal (for a pyramid) face that does not contain the common vertex
- **Lateral faces**—the face(s) that make up the sides of the solid; for prisms, the lateral faces are always parallelograms
- **Altitude**—the segment perpendicular to the plane of both bases (for a prism or cylinder); the perpendicular segment joining the vertex to the plane of the base (for a pyramid or cone)
- **Height** (h)—the length of the altitude
- **Slant height** (ℓ)—the distance from the edge of the base to the common vertex

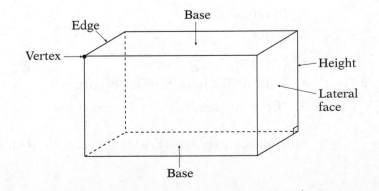

Some solids, such as prisms and pyramids, have flat faces, while others, such as cones, cylinders, and spheres, have curved faces. Solids with curved faces are not polyhedra, however, because they are not created by connecting polygons along their sides.

Let's review a few terms that are commonly used in solid geometry problems:

- **Volume** is the amount of space enclosed by a solid.
- **Surface area** is the sum of the area of all of the faces.
- **Lateral surface area** is the sum of the area of only the lateral faces (or the sides.) This is also referred to as simply the lateral area.

REVIEW OF AREA FORMULAS

Before discussing solids, here's a review of common area formulas. These may be applied when determining the volume and surface area of prisms, cylinders, cones, and pyramids.

Shape	Area Formula	Variable Definitions
Rectangle	$A = bh$	b = the length of the base h = the height, the length of the altitude
Triangle	$A = \frac{1}{2}bh$	b = the length of the base h = the height, the length of the altitude
Right Triangle	$A = \frac{1}{2}leg_1 \times leg_2$	leg_1 and leg_2 are the legs (the sides adjacent to the right angle)
Equilateral Triangle	$A = s^2\sqrt{\frac{3}{4}}$	s = the length of a side
Square	$A = s^2$	s = the length of a side
Parallelogram	$A = bh$	b = the length of the base h = the height, the length of the altitude
Rhombus	$A = bh$ or $A = \frac{1}{2}d_1d_2$	b = the length of the base h = the height, the length of the altitude d_1 and d_2 = the length of diagonals 1 and 2
Trapezoid	$A = \frac{1}{2}(b_1 + b_2)h$	b_1 and b_2 = the length of the 2 bases; i.e., the parallel sides h = the height, the length of the altitude
Regular Polygon	$A = \frac{1}{2}asn$ or $A = \frac{1}{2}ap$	a = the length of the apothem s = the length of a side n = the number of sides p = the perimeter
Circle	$A = \pi r^2$	r = the length of the radius
Sector	$A = \frac{x}{360}\pi r^2$	r = the length of the radius x = the arc measure

The shapes above should be familiar to you. A sector is a part of a circle that resembles a "slice" of the circle. Its edges are two radii and an arc.

▰▰ PRISMS

A **prism** is a polyhedron consisting of two congruent, parallel bases connected by lateral faces shaped like parallelograms. Prisms are classified by their bases: rectangular prisms have bases shaped like rectangles, triangular prisms have bases shaped like triangles, hexagonal prisms have bases shaped like hexagons, etc. A rectangular prism looks like what you would think of as a box.

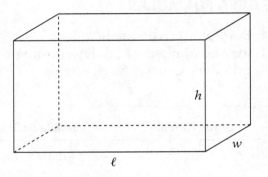

Rectangular Prism		
Surface Area	Lateral Surface Area	Volume
$S = 2\ell w + 2\ell h + 2hw$	$S = 2\ell h + 2hw$	$V = \ell wh$

In general the formula for the volume for any prism can be written as:

$$V = Bh$$

where B = the area of the base, and h = the height.

In the case of a rectangular prism, the area of the base is the product of its length and width, ℓw. Substituting ℓw for B results in $V = \ell wh$. The volume of a cube with edge s is, therefore, $V = Bh = (s^2)s = s^3$. Volume is measured in **cubic units,** such as centimeters^3, inches^3, feet^3, and meters^3.

EXAMPLE:

The volume of a square prism is equal to its lateral surface area. Find the length of the sides of the base.

Note that a square prism is not equivalent to a cube. The two bases of this prism must be squares, but the height may be any length. A square prism is equivalent to a rectangular prism whose length and width have equal measures. Draw a diagram to help solve this problem.

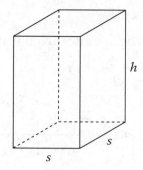

Let s equal the sides of the base and h equal the height of the prism. Use formulas for a rectangular prism and substitute s for the length and width. The volume is:

$V = \ell wh = s^2 h.$

The lateral surface area is therefore:

$S = 2\ell h + 2wh = S = 2sh + 2hs = 4hs$

Now set the volume equal to the lateral surface area and solve for s:

$s^2 h = 4sh.$ Divide both sides by h. This is ok to do because h is a length and cannot equal zero.

$s^2 = 4s.$ Divide both sides by s because s also cannot equal zero.

$s = 4.$ (*Answer*)

EXAMPLE:

The surface area of a cube is 150 cm². Find the length of its edges.

The formula for the surface area of a cube is similar to the formula for a rectangular prism, except length, width, and height are equal in a cube. If the length of an edge of the cube is s, $s = \ell = w = h$.

$S = 2\ell w + 2\ell h + 2hw$ becomes $S = 2s^2 + 2s^2 + 2s^2 = 6s^2.$

$150 = 6s^2$

$25 = s^2$

$s = 5$ cm.   (*Answer*)

Distance Between Opposite Vertices of a Rectangular Prism

Along with surface area and volume, you may be asked to determine the distance between opposite vertices of a rectangular prism. The problem can actually be solved in one of two ways: (a) by using the Pythagorean Theorem *twice* or (b) by using the distance formula.

EXAMPLE:

Find the distance from vertex P to vertex Q in the rectangular prism below.

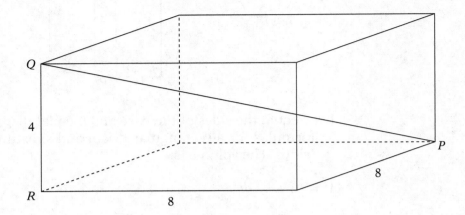

Think of $\overline{PQ}$ as the hypotenuse of a right triangle whose legs are the diagonal of the base and the edge of the prism $\overline{QR}$. First find the length of the diagonal of the base:

$RP^2 = 8^2 + 8^2.$

$RP^2 = 128.$

$RP = \sqrt{128} = 8\sqrt{2}.$

Did you recognize that $\overline{RP}$ is the hypotenuse of an isosceles right triangle? If so, you can determine the length, RP, simply by remembering the ratio of the sides of a 45°-45°-90° triangle.

Now, use the Pythagorean Theorem for a second time to determine PQ.

$PQ^2 = \left(8\sqrt{2}\right)^2 + 4^2.$

$PQ^2 = 64(2) + 16.$

$PQ^2 = 128 + 16 = 144.$

$PQ = \sqrt{144}.$

$PQ = 12.$ (*Answer*)

Another way to find the distance between opposite vertices of a rectangular prism is to use the formula:

Distance $= \sqrt{\ell^2 + w^2 + h^2}$

Try using this formula for the last example to get:

Distance $= \sqrt{8^2 + 8^2 + 4^2} = \sqrt{144} = 12.$

CYLINDERS

A **cylinder** is similar to a prism with circular bases. Right circular cylinders are the most commonly used cylinders on the Level 2 test. They consist of two congruent, parallel, circular bases joined by an **axis** that is perpendicular to each. The axis of a right circular cylinder is also its **altitude**.

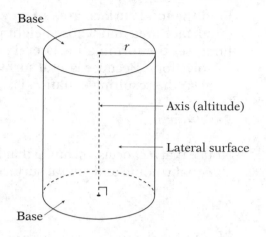

Cylinder		
Surface Area	Lateral Surface Area	Volume
$S = 2\pi r^2 + 2\pi rh$	$S = 2\pi rh$	$V = \pi r^2 h$

In general the formula for the volume for any cylinder is the same as that for any prism and can be written as:

$$V = Bh$$

where B = the area of the base and h = the height.

In the case of a right circular cylinder, the area of the base is πr^2. Substituting πr^2 for B results in $V = \pi r^2 h$.

EXAMPLE:

Find the volume of the solid created by rotating rectangle WXYZ 360° around side XY.

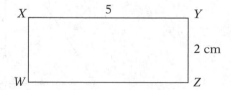

The hardest part of a problem like this is to visualize the solid formed by rotating the rectangle. Picture rectangle WXYZ rotating fully around the axis $\overline{XY}$. A right circular cylinder is created whose height is 5 cm (the length XY) and whose radius is 2 cm. (You may think of this cylinder as being "on its side" because the axis is not vertical.)

Using $r = 2$ cm and $h = 5$ cm, its volume is:

$V = \pi(2)^2(5)$.

$V = 20\pi$ cm³.   (*Answer*)

EXAMPLE:

Find the total surface area of a cylinder whose volume equals its lateral surface area and whose height is 10 inches.

First, set the formula for lateral surface area equal to that of volume to solve for r. Because lateral surface area equals $2\pi rh$, and volume equals πr^2h, the resulting equation is:

$2\pi rh = \pi r^2h$.

Notice that h cancels, meaning that height is not a factor in a cylinder having equal volume and lateral surface area. One r and π also cancel to get:

$2 = r$

Use the given information, $h = 10$, and the radius that you just found, $r = 2$, to get the cylinder's total surface area.

$S = 2\pi r^2 + 2\pi rh$

$S = 2\pi(2)^2 + 2\pi(2)(10)$

$S = 8\pi + 40\pi$

$S = 48\pi$ in².   (*Answer*)

PYRAMIDS

A **pyramid** consists of one base and triangular lateral faces that connect at a common vertex. Like prisms, pyramids are classified by their base: rectangular pyramids have a base shaped like a rectangle, triangular pyramids have a base shaped like a triangle, hexagonal pyramids have a base shaped like a hexagon, etc.

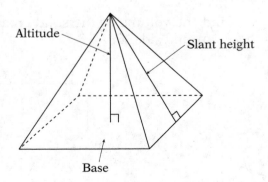

The following are formulas for a **regular pyramid.** A pyramid is regular if its base is a regular polygon (i.e., a square or equilateral triangle) and its lateral edges are congruent.

Regular Pyramid		
Surface Area	Lateral Surface Area	Volume
$S = \frac{1}{2}\ell P + B$	$S = \frac{1}{2}\ell P$	$V = \frac{1}{3}Bh$
B = area of the base	ℓ = slant height	
	P = perimeter of the base	

In general, the formula for the volume for any pyramid can be written as:

$$V = \frac{1}{3}Bh$$

where B = the area of the base, and h = the height.

In the case of a rectangular pyramid, the area of the base is the product of its length and width, ℓw. Substituting ℓw for B results in $V = \frac{1}{3}\ell wh$.

Remember that the volume formula for a pyramid, $V = \frac{1}{3}Bh$, is listed in the reference information of the Level 2 test.

EXAMPLE:

Find the volume of a pyramid whose base is an equilateral triangle with sides of length 4 cm and whose height is 9 cm.

Start by finding B, the area of the base. Recall that the area of an equilateral triangle is:

$$A = s^2\sqrt{\frac{3}{4}}.$$

$$A = 4^2\sqrt{\frac{3}{4}}.$$

$$A = 4\sqrt{3} \ cm^2.$$

Because the volume of a pyramid is given by the formula $V = \frac{1}{3}Bh$ and $h = 9$ cm, the volume is:

$$V = \frac{1}{3}Bh.$$

$$V = \frac{1}{3}\left(4\sqrt{3}\right)(9).$$

$$V = 12\sqrt{3} \ cm^3. \qquad (Answer)$$

CONES

A **cone** consists of one circular base and a lateral surface that comes to a common vertex. Right circular cones are the most commonly used cones on the Level 2 test. They consist of a circular base connected to a vertex by an **axis** perpendicular to the base. The axis of a right circular cone is also its **altitude**.

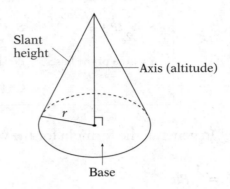

Slant height

Axis (altitude)

r

Base

Right Circular Cone		
Surface Area	Lateral Surface Area	Volume
$S = \dfrac{1}{2}c\ell + \pi r^2$	$S = \dfrac{1}{2}c\ell$	$V = \dfrac{1}{3}\pi r^2 h$
	ℓ = slant height	
	c = circumference of the base	

In general the formula for the volume for any cone is the same as that for any pyramid and can be written as:

$$V = \frac{1}{3}Bh$$

where B = the area of the base, and h = the height.

In the case of a right circular cone, the area of the base is πr^2. Substituting πr^2 for B results in $V = \dfrac{1}{3}\pi r^2 h$.

Remember that the volume formula for a right circular cone, $V = \dfrac{1}{3}\pi r^2 h$, and the lateral surface area formula, $S = \dfrac{1}{2}c\ell$, are listed in the reference information of the Level 2 test. You don't need to memorize these!

EXAMPLE:

Find the lateral area of a cone whose diameter is 12 cm and whose height is 8 cm.

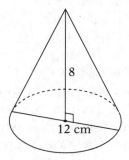

You need to solve for the circumference, c, and the slant height, ℓ, in order to use the formula for lateral surface area.

Circumference can be determined using $c = \pi d$ or $c = 2\pi r$. Because you have been given the diameter, it makes sense to use the first formula:

$C = \pi(12)$.

The radius is, therefore, half the diameter, or 6 ft. Notice that the radius and the altitude form a right triangle whose hypotenuse is the slant height. Use the Pythagorean Theorem to solve for ℓ.

$\ell^2 = 8^2 + 6^2$.

$\ell^2 = 100$.

$\ell = 10$.

Now you have enough information to solve for the lateral area.

$S = \dfrac{1}{2}c\ell$

$S = \dfrac{1}{2}(12\pi)(10)$

$S = 60\pi$ cm^2 (*Answer*)

EXAMPLE:

A right circular cylinder and a right circular cone have the same radius and volume. If the cone has a height of 18 inches, find the height of the cylinder.

To solve for the height, set the volume of each solid equal to each other:

$\pi r^2 h = \dfrac{1}{3}\pi r^2 (18)$

$h = 6$ inches   (*Answer*)

The height of the cylinder must be one-third the height of the cone, since the volume of the cone is one-third the volume of the cylinder.

EXAMPLE:

A right circular cone can have a cross section in the shape of all of the following EXCEPT:

A) a circle
B) a triangle
C) a rectangle
D) its base
E) an ellipse

A **cross section** of a solid is a figure formed when a plane intersects the solid. Try to visualize what happens when you cut a cone. A circle is obviously possible when the plane intersecting the cone is parallel to the base. The base is a possibility if the plane intersecting the cone is the same plane that contains the base. A triangle is possible is the plane cuts through the vertex of the cone and is perpendicular to the base. An ellipse results if the plane that intersects the cone is at an angle creating an oval-type figure. It is not possible to have a cross-sectional area in the shape of a rectangle. C is the correct answer.

SPHERES

A **sphere** is the set of all points in space at a given distance from a given point. Rotating a circle 360° around one of its diameters creates a sphere.

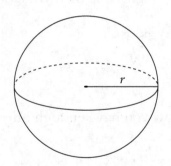

Sphere	
Surface Area	Volume
$S = 4\pi r^2$	$V = \dfrac{4}{3}\pi r^3$

Remember that the volume formula for a sphere, $V = \dfrac{4}{3}\pi r^3$, and the surface area formula, $S = 4\pi r^2$, are listed in the reference information of the Level 2 test. Again, you don't need to memorize these!

EXAMPLE:

Find the volume of a sphere whose surface area equals its volume.

First, set surface area equal to volume and solve for r.

$$4\pi r^2 = \frac{4}{3}\pi r^3.$$

$$4 = \frac{4}{3}r.$$

$$r = 3.$$

Now use the radius to solve for volume:

$$V = \frac{4}{3}\pi(3)^3.$$

$$V = 36\pi. \qquad (Answer)$$

EXAMPLE:

A ball is immersed in a cup of water and displaces 288π cubic units of water. Find the surface area of the ball.

The amount of water displaced by the ball is equivalent to its volume. Therefore, you have enough information to write an equation for the volume of the ball and solve for r.

$$\frac{4}{3}\pi r^3 = 288\pi.$$

$$r^3 = \frac{3}{4}(288).$$

$$r^3 = 216.$$

$$r = \sqrt[3]{216}.$$

$$r = 6.$$

Now substitute $r = 6$ into the surface area formula to get:

$$S = 4\pi(6)^2.$$

$$S = 144\pi \text{ units}^2 \qquad (Answer)$$

VOLUME RATIO OF SIMILAR FIGURES

Solids are said to be similar if their bases are similar, and their corresponding parts are proportional. Just as with similar polygons, **similar solids** have the same shape but different size. A square, right pyramid with a base area of 2 cm², for example, is similar to a square, right pyramid with a base area of 4 cm². The ratio of the length of corresponding parts of similar solids is called the **scale factor.**

If the scale factor of two similar solids is *m:n,* then the following ratios are true.

1. The ratio of their corresponding base perimeters or circumferences is also *m:n.*
2. The ratio of their base areas, total surface areas, and lateral surface areas is *m²:n².*
3. The ratio of their volumes is *m³:n³.*

EXAMPLE:

The lateral surface areas of two similar right cylinders are 80π in³ and 120π in³, respectively. Find the ratio of their volumes.
First determine the scale factor of the similar cylinders by comparing their lateral surface areas.
$80\pi:120\pi$ simplifies to 8:12, which simplifies to 2:3.
Therefore, the scale factor is 2:3.
Now, find the volume ratio by cubing the scale factor:

$2^3:3^3.$

8:27.   (*Answer*)

*COORDINATES IN THREE DIMENSIONS

Similar to graphing points (x, y) in a two-dimensional xy-coordinate plane, the point (x, y, z) can be graphed in a three-dimensional coordinate system having an x-axis, y-axis and z-axis. For example, the point $(2, -3, 1)$ is a solution to the equation $2x + y - z = 0$. The graph of the **ordered triple** is as shown:

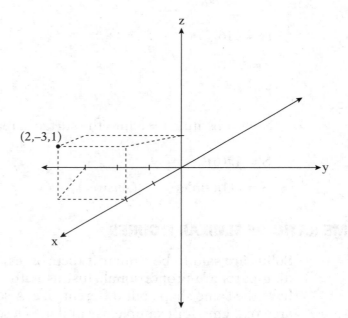

The distance between ordered triples (x_1, y_1, z_1) and (x_2, y_2, z_2) is given by the formula:

$$\textbf{Distance} = \sqrt{(x_2 - x_1)^2 + (y_2 - y_1)^2 + (z_2 - z_1)^2}.$$

EXAMPLE:

What is the distance between (0, 0, 7) and (4, 1, 0)?

The problem is asking for the length of the segment connecting the two points.

Simply apply the distance formula to get:

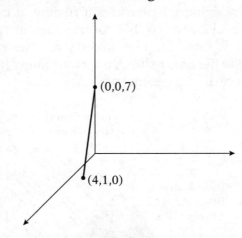

$$d = \sqrt{(4-0)^2 + (1-0)^2 + (0-7)^2}.$$

$$d = \sqrt{4^2 + 1^2 + (-7)^2}.$$

$$d = \sqrt{16 + 1 + 49}.$$

$$d = \sqrt{66} \approx 8.12. \qquad (Answer)$$

EXAMPLE:

A right circular cylinder has a height of 10 and a radius of 4. If X and Y are two points on the surface of the cylinder, what is the maximum possible length of XY?

Although this problem doesn't ask about points specifically in the form (x, y, z), it does ask you to visualize points in three-dimensions. Think of X and Y as vertices of the right triangle shown below.

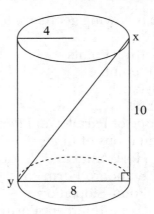

$$XY = \sqrt{8^2 + 10^2}$$

$$XY = \sqrt{64 + 100}$$

$$XY = \sqrt{164} = 2\sqrt{41} \approx 12.81 \qquad (Answer)$$

CHAPTER 6

COORDINATE GEOMETRY

This chapter provides a review of coordinate geometry principles. On the Level 2 test, 10–14% of the questions relate specifically to coordinate geometry. Coordinate geometry focuses on graphing in an *xy*-coordinate plane. The pie chart shows approximately how much of the Level 2 test is related to coordinate geometry:

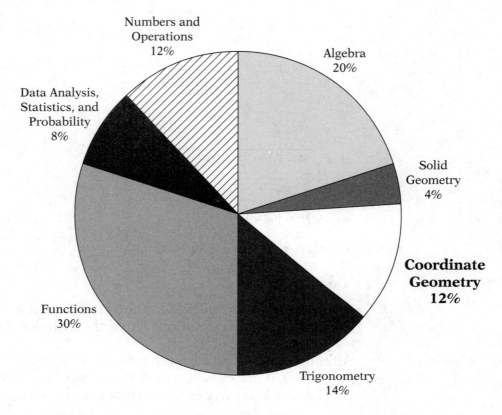

The following geometry topics are covered in this chapter:

1. Plotting Points
2. Midpoint
3. Distance
4. Slope
5. Slope of Parallel and Perpendicular Lines
6. Equations of Lines
   a. Horizontal and Vertical Lines
   b. Standard Form
   c. Point-Slope Form
   d. Slope-Intercept Form
   e. Determining x and y Intercepts
7. Circles
8. Parabolas

9. *Ellipses
10. *Hyperbolas
11. Graphing Inequalities
12. Graphing Absolute Value
13. Symmetry
14. Transformations
15. *Polar Coordinates

PLOTTING POINTS

A **plane rectangular coordinate system** is created by drawing two axes that intersect at right angles at an origin. The horizontal axis is called the **x-axis** and the vertical axis is called the **y-axis.** The axes create 4 **quadrants** in the plane, which are numbered using Roman numerals as shown:

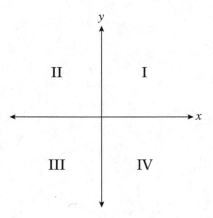

An **ordered pair** (x, y) denotes a unique point in the plane. To plot a point, simply graph the location of its x and y coordinates. The x-coordinate of a point is also referred to as the **abscissa,** while the y-coordinate is also referred to as the **ordinate.**

EXAMPLE:

Graph the following points in the same coordinate plane: A(1, 4), B(−2, −3), C(−5, 1), D(4, 0) (see graph on page 98).

_____

*Denotes concepts that are on the Level 2 test only.

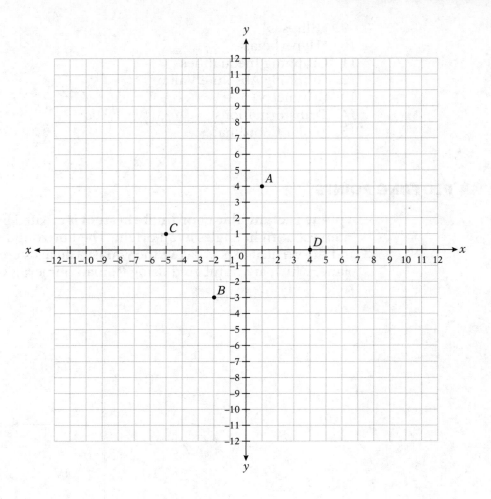

EXAMPLE:

Find three solutions of $2x + 3y = 1$.

The graph of an equation in two variables is the set of all points whose x and y coordinates satisfy the equation. To find three solutions to this equation, simply choose 3 values for x and solve for the corresponding value of y. Write y in terms of x, and create an xy-table to determine solutions of the equation.

x	$y = \dfrac{1 - 2x}{3}$	y
0	$y = \dfrac{1 - 2(0)}{3}$	$\dfrac{1}{3}$
2	$y = \dfrac{1 - 2(2)}{3}$	-1
-1	$y = \dfrac{1 - 2(-1)}{3}$	1

The graph of $2x + 3y = 1$ is a line, so there are infinitely many points that will satisfy the equation. Here three possible points are given.

$\left(1, \frac{1}{3}\right)$, $(2, -1)$, $(-1, 1)$ are three possible solutions.   (*Answer*)

MIDPOINT

The **midpoint** of a segment with endpoints (x_1, y_1) and (x_2, y_2) is the point:

$$\left(\frac{x_1 + x_2}{2}, \frac{y_1 + y_2}{2}\right)$$

Finding the midpoint of a line segment can also be thought of as finding the *average* of the x and y coordinates.

EXAMPLE:

Find the midpoint $\overline{AB}$ given the endpoints A(1, 6) and B(−3, −7).

Substitute the given coordinates into the midpoint formula to get:

$$\left(\frac{1 + -3}{2}, \frac{6 + -7}{2}\right).$$

$$\left(\frac{-2}{2}, \frac{-1}{2}\right).$$

$$\left(-1, \frac{-1}{2}\right). \quad (\textit{Answer})$$

EXAMPLE:

M is the midpoint of $\overline{AB}$. Find the coordinates of B if A has coordinates (3, 8) and M has coordinates (−4, 0).

Let the coordinates of B be (x_2, y_2), then:

$$\frac{3 + x_2}{2} = -4 \qquad \text{and} \qquad \frac{8 + y_2}{2} = 0.$$

$$3 + x_2 = -8 \qquad\qquad\qquad 8 + y_2 = 0.$$

$$x_2 = -11 \qquad\qquad\qquad\quad y_2 = -8.$$

$$B(-11, -8). \qquad (\textit{Answer})$$

DISTANCE

The **distance** between any two points (x_1, y_1) and (x_2, y_2) is:

$$d = \sqrt{(x_2 - x_1)^2 + (y_2 - y_1)^2}.$$

Some aspects of coordinate geometry, simply involve solving a plane geometry question by using an *xy*-coordinate plane. Here's an example of one.

EXAMPLE:

Find the perimeter of △ABC given its vertices are A(2, 2), B(−1, 5), and C(−5, 2).

This problem requires applying the distance formula three times to find the length of the three sides of the triangle. Solve for AB, BC, and AC as follows:

$$AB = \sqrt{(2--1)^2 + (2-5)^2} = \sqrt{(3)^2 + (-3)^2} = \sqrt{9+9} = \sqrt{18} = 3\sqrt{2}.$$

$$BC = \sqrt{(-1--5)^2 + (5-2)^2} = \sqrt{(4)^2 + (3)^2} = \sqrt{16+9} = \sqrt{25} = 5.$$

$$AC = \sqrt{(2--5)^2 + (2-2)^2} = \sqrt{(7)^2 + (0)^2} = \sqrt{49} = 7.$$

Notice that $\overline{AC}$ is a horizontal line segment, so the distance from A to C can be easily found be determining the change in the x coordinates. $|2--5| = 7$. The perimeter of the triangle is:

$$7 + 5 + 3\sqrt{2}.$$

$$12 + 3\sqrt{2}. \qquad (\textit{Answer})$$

The concept of distance can also be applied to finding the area of figures in a coordinate plane. Use the distance formula to find the length of the base and/or height of a figure, and substitute these values into the appropriate area formula. (See Chapter 5 for a review of area formulas.)

EXAMPLE:

Find the area of parallelogram ABCD given its vertices are A(3, 1), B(2, −1), C(−1, −1), and D(0, 1).

Sketch a diagram to help picture the parallelogram.

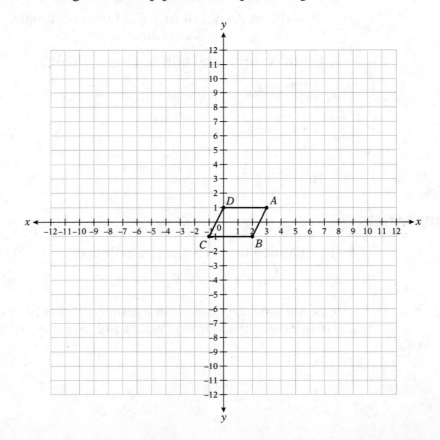

Assume $\overline{BC}$ is the base of the parallelogram, and the height is the length of the perpendicular from vertex D to side $\overline{BC}$. Notice that there is no change in the y-coordinate in the segment $\overline{BC}$, so the distance from B to C can be found simply by using absolute value.

$BC = |2 - -1| = 3$.

The height is $|1 - -1| = 2$.

The area of the parallelogram is therefore:

$A = bh = 3(2) = 6$

6 units^2.   (*Answer*)

SLOPE

Slope is the measure of the steepness of a line. The slope of a line containing the points (x_1, y_1) and (x_2, y_2) is:

$$slope = \frac{rise}{run} = \frac{change\ in\ y}{change\ in\ x} = \frac{y_2 - y_1}{x_2 - x_1}.$$

Horizontal lines have no change in y, so the slope of a horizontal line is zero.

$$m = \frac{0}{change\ in\ x} = 0.$$

Vertical lines have no change in x. Because you cannot divide by zero, vertical lines have an undefined slope.

$$m = \frac{change\ in\ y}{0} = undefined.$$

A line having **positive slope** rises from left to right, and a line having **negative slope** falls from left to right.

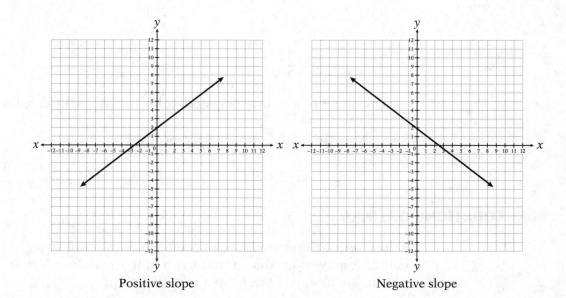

Positive slope   Negative slope

E X A M P L E :

Find the slope of the line containing the points S(6, –9) and R(–2, –5).

$$m = \frac{y_2 - y_1}{x_2 - x_1}.$$

$$m = \frac{-5 - -9}{-2 - 6}.$$

$$m = -\frac{4}{8}.$$

$$m = -\frac{1}{2}. \quad (Answer)$$

In the above example, we subtracted the coordinates of S from R. Order doesn't matter, however, as long as you choose the same order in the numerator and the denominator. We could have found the slope by subtracting the coordinates of R from S to get the same answer:

$$m = \frac{-9 - -5}{6 - -2} = -\frac{4}{8} = -\frac{1}{2}.$$

SLOPE OF PARALLEL AND PERPENDICULAR LINES

You can determine whether or not lines are parallel (never intersect) or perpendicular (intersect at a right angle) by examining their slope:

1. Parallel lines have the **same slope.** $m_1 = m_2$.

2. Perpendicular lines have slopes that are **opposite reciprocals.** $m_1 m_2 = -1$.

E X A M P L E :

Find the slope of the perpendicular bisector of $\overline{AB}$ given A(0, –2) and B(3, 3).

The slope of $\overline{AB}$ is:

$$m = \frac{y_2 - y_1}{x_2 - x_1}.$$

$$m = \frac{3 - -2}{3 - 0} = \frac{5}{3}.$$

The slope of *any* line perpendicular to $\overline{AB}$, including the perpendicular

bisector, is the opposite reciprocal of $\frac{5}{3}$.

$$m = -\frac{3}{5}. \quad (Answer)$$

EQUATIONS OF LINES

Linear equations are equations whose graphs are straight lines. Equations containing two variables x and y raised to the first power are linear. By definition, linear equations have a constant slope.

The following equations are NOT linear:

$$3x^2 + 2y^2 = 1 \qquad \frac{3}{x} + 4y = 5.$$

The following equations are linear:

$y = mx + b.$ $y - y_1 = m(x - x_1).$ $Ax + By = C.$
Slope-Intercept Form   Point-Slope Form   Standard Form

The three forms of the equation of a line are further explained in the succeeding paragraphs.

Horizontal and Vertical Lines

The most basic forms of linear equations are horizontal and vertical lines.

Horizontal lines are written in the form $y = a$, where a is any constant.

Vertical lines are written in the form $x = a$, where, again, a is any constant.

EXAMPLE:

Find the point of intersection of the lines $y = 7$ and $x = 5$.

The graph of the two lines clearly shows their intersection.

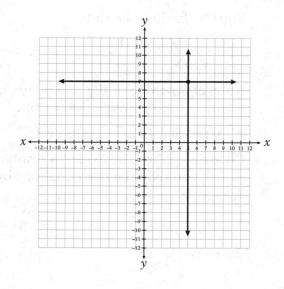

(5, 7).   (*Answer*)

Standard Form

The **standard form** of the equation of a line is:

$Ax + By = C$ (where A and B are both $\neq 0$).

The **slope** of a line in standard form is $-\dfrac{A}{B}$ (B $\neq 0$).

EXAMPLE:

Find the slope of the line $6x + 3y + 1 = 0$.

If you remember that the slope of a line in standard form is $-\dfrac{A}{B}$, this problem can be quickly solved. You may want to rewrite the equation in
standard form, although this does not affect the calculation of slope.

$6x + 3y = -1$.

$$m = -\frac{6}{3} = -2. \quad (Answer)$$

Point-Slope Form

There is exactly one line passing through a given point having a given slope.
Because this is true, a line can also be written in what is called point-slope
form. The **point-slope form** of a line containing the point (x_1, y_1) with a
slope of m is:

$$y - y_1 = m(x - x_1).$$

EXAMPLE:

Find the equation of the line in point slope form through points A(1, 10)
and B(3, 0).

Start by finding the slope:

$$m = \frac{y_2 - y_1}{x_2 - x_1} = \frac{0 - 10}{3 - 1} = \frac{-10}{2} = -5.$$

Now, choose one of the two points and substitute its x and y coordinates
into x_1 and y_1 in the point-slope form of a line. Let's choose point A:

$$y - 10 = -5(x - 1). \quad (Answer)$$

Choosing point B instead of A results in the same line. $y - 0 = -5(x - 3)$. You
can compare the two equations by rewriting each in standard form:

$y - 10 = -5(x - 1).$ $y - 0 = -5(x - 3).$

$y - 10 = -5x + 5.$ $y = -5x + 15.$

$5x + y = 15.$ $5x + y = 15.$

Slope-Intercept Form

The **slope-intercept form** of a line with a slope of m and y-intercept b is:

$$y = mx + b$$

The y-intercept is the point where the line intersects the y-axis. If the y-
intercept is 5, the line intersects the y-axis at the point $(0,5)$. If the y-intercept
is $-\dfrac{1}{2}$, the line intersects the y-axis at the point $\left(0,-\dfrac{1}{2}\right)$.

EXAMPLE:

Which of the following lines is parallel to the line $y = 5x - 1$?

(A) $y = 5x - \dfrac{1}{5}$

(B) $y = -5x - \dfrac{1}{5}$

(C) $y = -5x + \dfrac{1}{5}$

(D) $y = -\dfrac{1}{5}x - 1$

(E) $y = -\dfrac{1}{5}x + 1$

Recall that parallel lines have the same slope. Answers B, C, D, and E can quickly be eliminated because their slopes do not equal 5, the x coefficient of the given line. Answer A is the only equation in which $m = 5$, so A is the correct answer.

EXAMPLE:

Find the equation of the line with a slope of 3 containing the point (9, 7). Write your answer in slope-intercept form.

Using $m = 3$, you can write the equation of the line as:

$y = 3x + b$.

Because (9, 7) is a point on the line, let $x = 9$ and $y = 7$ and solve for b.

$7 = 3(9) + b$.

$7 = 27 + b$.

$-20 = b$.

Now you have enough information to write the slope-intercept form of the line.

$y = 3x - 20$.   (*Answer*)

Because you are given the slope of the line and a point on it, you may be inclined to immediately use the point-slope form of the line. Doing so results in the equation:

$y - 7 = 3(x - 9)$.

Now solve for y to get:

$y - 7 = 3x - 27$.

$y = 3x - 20$.

Notice that you get the same final answer.

Determining x and y Intercepts

The y-intercept of a line is the point where $x = 0$, and the x-intercept is the point where $y = 0$.

EXAMPLE:

Determine the x and y intercepts of the line $3x - 4y = 12$.

Let's first determine the y-intercept by letting $x = 0$ and solving for y.

$3(0) - 4y = 12$.

$-4y = 12$.

$y = -3$.

Now, let's determine the x-intercept by letting $y = 0$ and solving for x.

$3x - 4(0) = 12$.

$3x = 12$.

$x = 4$.

The intercepts are $(0, -3)$ and $(4, 0)$.   (*Answer*)

EXAMPLE:

Find the equation of the line with y-intercept $(0, 4)$ and x-intercept $(-3, 0)$. Write your answer in standard form.

The slope of the line is $m = \dfrac{4 - 0}{0 - (-3)} = \dfrac{4}{3}$. Because its y-intercept is $(0, 4)$, $b = 4$. In slope-intercept form, the equation of the line is:

$y = \dfrac{4}{3}x + 4$.

To determine the standard form of the equation, multiply through by 3.

$3y = 4x + 12$.

$-4x + 3y = 12$.   (*Answer*)

CIRCLES

So far, we have been focused on graphing lines in an xy-coordinate plane. The Level 2 test includes questions on curved graphs, however—mainly circles, parabolas, ellipses, and hyperbolas. Circle questions involve manipulating the standard form of the equation of a circle.

Recall that a circle is defined as the set of all points at a given distance from a given point. The set of all points at a distance of 2 units from the origin can be written as:

$x^2 + y^2 = 2^2$.

In standard form, the equation of a circle with center (h, k) and radius r is:

$(x - h)^2 + (y - k)^2 = r^2$.

The set of all points at a distance of 5 from the point (–2, 1) would, therefore, be:

$(x - 2)^2 + (y - 1)^2 = 5^2$.

EXAMPLE:

Find the x and y intercepts of the graph of $x^2 + y^2 = 9$.

First, recognize that this is the graph of a circle with center (0, 0) and radius 3. Picture the circle or sketch a graph to help visualize the intercepts.

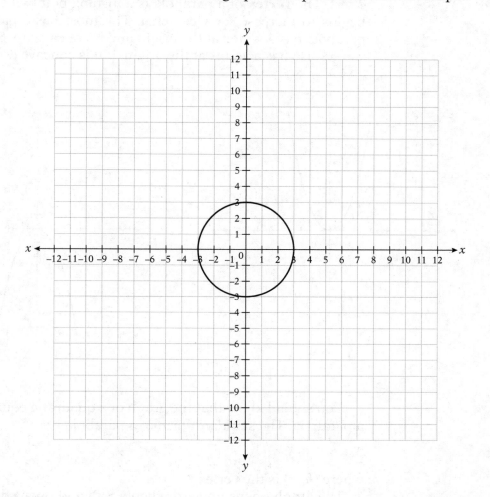

This circle is the set of all points at a distance of 3 from the origin. The intercepts can be determined by moving 3 units to the right and left of the origin, and then moving 3 units up and down from the origin.

The intercepts are (3, 0), (–3, 0), (0, 3), and (0, –3).   (*Answer*)

EXAMPLE:

Find the equation of a circle with a center in quadrant II that is tangent to both the x and y axis with a radius of 4.

Because the circle's center is in quadrant II, its x-coordinate must be negative, and its y-coordinate must be positive. The radius is 4, which tells you that the points (0, 4) and (–4, 0) are on the circle. These are the tangent points. The circle's center must, therefore, be (–4, 4).

Now you have enough information to write the standard form of the equation of the circle:

$(x - -4)^2 + (y - 4)^2 = 4^2.$

$(x + 4)^2 + (y - 4)^2 = 16.$ 　　　(*Answer*)

PARABOLAS

A **parabola** is the second type of curved graph that you may find on the Level 2 test. The **vertex** of a parabola is a turning point where a decreasing graph begins to increase, or vice versa. The most basic parabola is $y = x^2$. This parabola has a vertex at the origin and is concave up. Similarly, the graph of $y = -x^2$ also has a vertex at the origin, but is concave down.

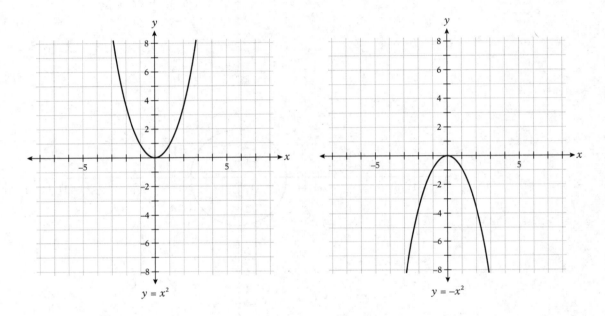

$y = x^2$　　　　　　　　　　　　$y = -x^2$

You should know that the graph of a quadratic equation $y = ax^2 + bx + c$ is a parabola. The standard form of a parabola is:

$y - k = a(x - h)^2$

where (h, k) is the vertex.

The graph opens upward when a > 0, and opens downward when a < 0. The greater $|a|$, the more narrow the graph becomes. Parabolas in this form have an axis of symmetry at $x = h$.

Parabolas can also be in the form $x - k = a(y - h)^2$. Parabolas in this form open right if $a > 0$, open left if $a < 0$, and have an axis of symmetry at $y = k$. The most basic parabolas in this form are $x = y^2$ and $x = -y^2$.

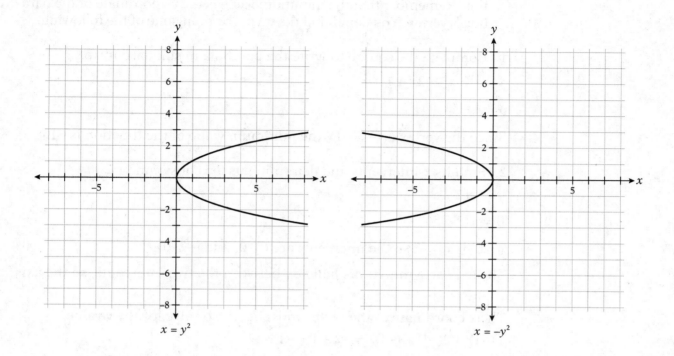

$$x = y^2 \qquad\qquad\qquad x = -y^2$$

Parabolas in the form $x - h = a(y - k)^2$ are NOT functions, though, because they do not pass the vertical line test. There is not a one-to-one correspondence been a given x-value and its corresponding y-values for these parabolas.

EXAMPLE:

Determine the vertex of the graph of $y = (x + 1)^2 + 7$.

Recognize that this is the graph of a parabola. The parabola is concave up because $a = 1$. In standard form, the equation becomes:

$$y - 7 = (x + 1)^2.$$

The vertex is $(-1, 7)$.   (*Answer*)

As mentioned, the vertex of a parabola is a turning point where a decreasing graph begins to increase, or vice versa. Because of this, the vertex represents either the maximum or minimum value of the graph. The vertex is a **maximum** if the parabola is concave down and **minimum** if the parabola is concave up. The x-coordinate of the parabola is the x-value of the maximum or minimum of the function. The **maximum value of a function** is the y coordinate of the vertex.

EXAMPLE:

Find the minimum value of the function $f(x) = 2x + x^2$.

There are many ways to go about solving for the minimum of a function like this. Remember that the minimum value is the y-coordinate of the parabola's vertex. You could find the vertex by doing one of the following:

1. Complete the square to write the parabola in standard form.

$y + 1 = x^2 + 2x + 1$

$y + 1 = (x + 1)^2$

Since the vertex is $(-1, -1)$, the minimum value of the function is -1.

2. Find its x-intercepts and determine its axis of symmetry.

$y = x(2 + x)$

$0 = x(2 + x)$

$x = 0$ or $x = -2$ so the intercepts are $(0, 0)$ and $(-2, 0)$.

The axis of symmetry is halfway between the two intercepts, so the axis is $x = -1$.

The x coordinate of the vertex must be -1, so solve for the y value.

$f(-1) = 2(-1) + (-1)^2 = -2 + 1 = -1$

3. Use the fact that the maximum or minimum value of a quadratic function occurs when $x = -\dfrac{b}{2a}$

$y = ax^2 + bx + c$

$f(x) = 2x + x^2$ meaning that $a = 1$ and $b = 2$

$-\dfrac{b}{2a} = -\dfrac{2}{2(1)} = -1$

Solve for y when $x = -1$ to get $f(x) = -1$.

4. Graph the parabola on your calculator to see where the vertex is.

The third solution above works for any parabolic function, $y = ax^2 + bx + c$. Remember that the maximum or minimum value of a function is the y value when $x = -\dfrac{b}{2a}$. The value is a maximum when a < 0 and a minimum when a > 0.

*ELLIPSES

An **ellipse** is the set of all points the sum of whose distances from two fixed points (the **foci**) is constant. The standard form of an ellipse is:

$$\frac{(x-h)^2}{a^2} + \frac{(y-k)^2}{b^2} = 1 \quad \text{for an ellipse whose major axis is horizontal}$$

$$\frac{(x-h)^2}{b^2} + \frac{(y-k)^2}{a^2} = 1 \quad \text{for an ellipse whose major axis is vertical}$$

For both equations, (h, k) is the center, $2a$ is the length of the major axis, $2b$ is the length of the minor axis, and c, the distance from each focus point to the center, is given by $c^2 = a^2 - b^2$.

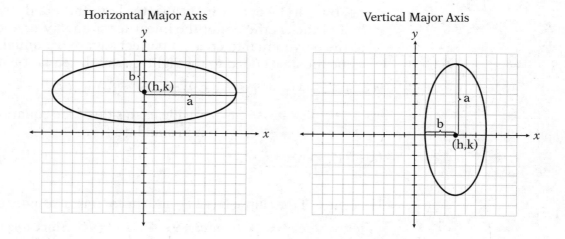

The **eccentricity,** e, of an ellipse is given by $e = \dfrac{c}{a}$ and is always less than 1 since $c < a$. As the ratio $\dfrac{c}{a}$ approaches 1, the shape of the ellipse becomes more elongated. Likewise, as the ratio $\dfrac{c}{a}$ gets smaller, the shape of the ellipse becomes nearly circular.

EXAMPLE:

What is the equation, in standard form, of the ellipse having foci at (1, 3) and (5, 3) and a major axis of length 8?

The center of the ellipse is the midpoint of the segment connecting (1, 3) and (5, 3), (3, 3). Since there is no change in y in the two focus points, the major axis of the ellipse is horizontal. A major axis of length 8 means that $2a = 8$, so $a = 4$. The distance from the center to each focus, c, is 2 units. Now, use a and c to solve for b:

$c^2 = a^2 - b^2$

$2^2 = 4^2 - b^2$

$4 = 16 - b^2$

$b = \sqrt{12} = 2\sqrt{3}$

The standard form of the equation of the ellipse is:

$$\frac{(x-3)^2}{4^2} + \frac{(y-3)^2}{\left(2\sqrt{3}\right)^2} = 1$$

$$\frac{(x-3)^2}{16} + \frac{(y-3)^2}{12} = 1. \qquad (Answer)$$

EXAMPLE:

What are the coordinates of the foci of $9x^2 + 4y^2 + 36x - 24y + 36 = 0$?

Group the x and y terms and complete the square.

$(9x^2 + 36x) + (4y^2 - 24y) = 36$

$9(x^2 + 4x) + 4(y^2 - 6y) = -36$ Now, for both the x and y expressions, take half of the coefficient of the linear term, square it, and add that value to the polynomial to create a perfect square trinomial. Of course, that value must be added to the right side of the equation, too.

$9(x^2 + 4x + 4) + 4(y^2 - 6y + 9) = -36 + 9(4) + 4(9)$

$9(x + 2)^2 + 4(y - 3)^2 = 36$ Divide each side of the equation by 36 to write it in standard form.

$$\frac{(x-2)^2}{4} + \frac{(y-3)^2}{9} = 1$$

The center of the ellipse is $(-2, 3)$ and the foci are a distance of c from the center, where $c^2 = a^2 - b^2$ or $c^2 = 9 - 4 = 5$. $c = \sqrt{5}$. Since a is the denominator of the y-term, the ellipse's major axis is vertical. Move up and down $\sqrt{5}$ units from the center to determine the foci.

The foci are $(-2, 3 \pm \sqrt{5})$.   (*Answer*)

*HYPERBOLAS

A **hyperbola** is the set of all points the difference of whose distances from two fixed points (the **foci**) is constant. The standard form of a hyperbola is:

$$\frac{(x-h)^2}{a^2} - \frac{(y-k)^2}{b^2} = 1 \text{ for a hyperbola opening right and left}$$

$$\frac{(y-k)^2}{a^2} - \frac{(x-h)^2}{b^2} = 1 \text{ for a hyperbola opening up and down}$$

For both equations, (h, k) is the center, $2a$ is the length of the transverse axis (connecting the two vertices), $2b$ is the length of the conjugate axis, and c, the distance from each focus point to the center, is given by $c^2 = a^2 + b^2$.

Horizontal Transverse Axis   Vertical Transverse Axis

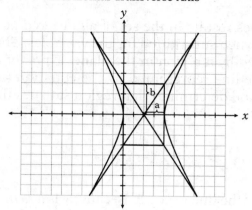
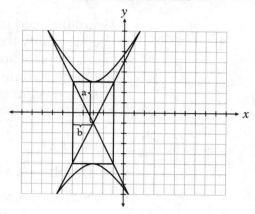

The **eccentricity,** e, of a hyperbola is given by $e = \dfrac{c}{a}$ and is always greater than 1 since $c > a$. As the ratio $\dfrac{c}{a}$ approaches 1, the branches of the hyperbola become more pointed and closer together. Likewise, as the ratio $\dfrac{c}{a}$ gets larger, the branches of the hyperbola become nearly flat.

Each hyperbola has two **asymptotes** that intersect at the center (h, k) of the hyperbola. The asymptotes are the lines containing the diagonals of a rectangle of dimensions $2a \times 2b$. The equations of the asymptotes are:

$y = k \pm \dfrac{b}{a}(x - h)$ for a hyperbola opening right and left

$y = k \pm \dfrac{a}{b}(x - h)$ for a hyperbola opening up and down

EXAMPLE:

What is the equation, in standard form, of the hyperbola having foci at (0, 5) and (8, 5) and vertices (1, 5) and (7, 5)?

The center of the hyperbola is the midpoint of the segment connecting (0, 5) and (8, 5), so the center is (4, 5). The distance from the center to the focus point (0, 5) is 4, so $c = 4$. The distance from the center to the vertex (1, 5) is 3, so $a = 3$. The hyperbola opens right and left since the transverse axis connecting (1, 5) and (7, 5) is horizontal.

$c^2 = a^2 + b^2$, so $4^2 = 3^2 + b^2$

$16 - 9 = b^2$

$\sqrt{7} = b$

It follows that the equation is:

$$\dfrac{(x-4)^2}{3^2} - \dfrac{(y-5)^2}{(\sqrt{7})^2} = 1$$

$$\dfrac{(x-4)^2}{9} - \dfrac{(y-5)^2}{7} = 1. \qquad (\textit{Answer})$$

GRAPHING INEQUALITIES

Graphing inequalities results in the set of all ordered pairs (x, y) that make the inequality true when substituted for the variables. The set is usually infinite and is illustrated by a region in the plane. Think of an inequality as an equation. Graph the line represented by the equation (assuming the given equation is linear) and determine what region satisfies the inequality. Then, shade this region.

EXAMPLE:

Graph $y < x + 5$.

Start by graphing the line $y = x + 5$. Because y is *less than* $x + 5$ and not *less than or equal to* $x + 5$, the line is dotted. Now determine whether to shade the region above or below the line. Choose a point below the line, say $(0, 2)$, and see if it satisfies the inequality.

$2 < 0 + 5$.

$2 < 5$. This is a true statement, so the region below the line $y = x + 5$ is the solution to the inequality. The graph is as follows:

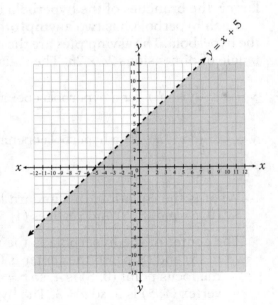

▨ GRAPHING ABSOLUTE VALUE

Absolute value graphs are v-shaped. The most basic absolute value graphs are for $y = |x|$ and $y = -|x|$.

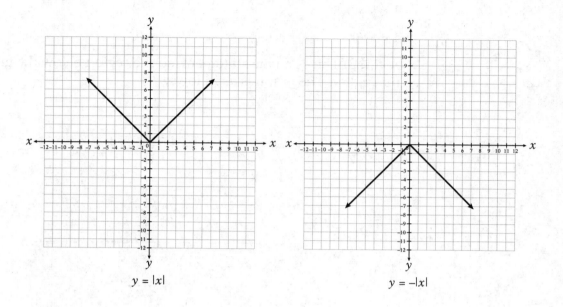

$y = |x|$ $y = -|x|$

Based on the previous example, try graphing $y = |x + 5|$. When $x = -5$, you get the turning point of the v-shaped graph. The graph is:

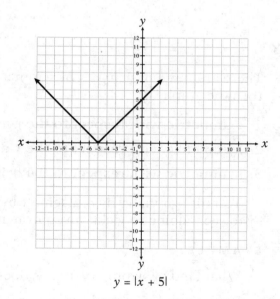

$y = |x + 5|$

Now, try graphing an absolute value inequality $y < |x + 5|$. The graph is similar to the graph of $y = |x + 5|$ with a dotted line at $y = |x + 5|$. As with any inequality, determine whether to shade above or below the line. Choose a point, say $(-8, 1)$, and see if it satisfies the inequality.

$1 < |-8 + 5|$.

$1 < |-3|$.

$1 < 3$. This is a true statement, so the region below the graph satisfies the inequality. The graph is as follows:

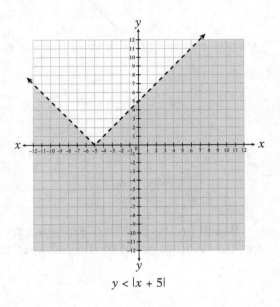

$$y < |x + 5|$$

SYMMETRY

There are three basic types of symmetry for a graph. If (x, y) is on a graph, then the graph is:

1. **symmetric with respect to the y-axis** if $(-x, y)$ is also on the graph
2. **symmetric with respect to the x-axis** if $(x, -y)$ is also on the graph
3. **symmetric with respect to the origin** if $(-x, -y)$ is also on the graph

Test for symmetry by replacing x by $-x$, y by $-y$, or both x and y by $-x$ and $-y$ to see if doing so yields an equivalent equation.

EXAMPLE:

What kind of symmetry, if any, does the graph of $y = x^2 - 16$ have?

Replacing x by $-x$ results in $y = (-x)^2 - 16$, which is equivalent to the original equation, $y = x^2 - 16$, so the graph is symmetric with respect to the y-axis.

Replacing y by $-y$ results in $-y = x^2 - 16$, which is *not* equivalent to the original equation, $y = x^2 - 16$, so the graph is not symmetric with respect to the x-axis.

Replacing x by $-x$ and y by $-y$ results in $-y = (-x)^2 - 16$, which is *not* equivalent to the original equation, $y = x^2 - 16$, so the graph is not symmetric with respect to the origin.

The graph is symmetric with respect to the y-axis.   (*Answer*)

TRANSFORMATIONS

Many graphs are simply transformations of common graphs. For example, the graph of $y = x + 3$ is simply the graph of $y = x$ shifted up 3 units.

Some common transformations of the graph of $y = f(x)$ are as follows:

- Vertical shift of c units up: $y = f(x) + c$
- Vertical shift of c units down: $y = f(x) - c$
- Horizontal shift c units left: $y = f(x + c)$
- Horizontal shift c units right: $y = f(x - c)$
- Reflected over the y-axis: $y = f(-x)$
- Reflected over the x-axis: $y = -f(x)$
- Stretched vertically by a factor of c $y = cf(x)$ for $c > 1$
- Shrunk vertically by a factor of c $y = cf(x)$ for $0 < c < 1$

Notice that the last two transformations, the vertical stretch and the vertical shrinkage, are different than the others. These cause a distortion of the shape of the graph, whereas the others simply moved the graph but left its shape unchanged.

EXAMPLE:

What is the equation of the graph of the function $y = (x + 4)^3 - 1$ shifted two units up and 5 units right?

Shifting the graph two units up results in $y = (x + 4)^3 - 1 + 2$ or $y = (x + 4)^3 + 1$.

Then, shifting the graph 5 units right results in $y = (x + 4 - 5)^3 + 1$ or $y = (x - 1)^3 + 1$.

$y = (x - 1)^3 + 1$ (*Answer*)

EXAMPLE:

The graph of $f(x) = x^2$ is translated 2 units left and reflected over the x-axis. If the resulting graph represents $h(x)$, then what is $h(4)$?

Translating the graph 2 units left results in $h(x) = (x + 2)^2$.

Then, reflecting it over the x-axis results in $h(x) = -(x + 2)^2$.

$h(4) = -(x + 2)^2 = -(4 + 2)^2 = -36.$ (*Answer*)

*POLAR COORDINATES

Points are commonly represented as (x, y) in the rectangular coordinate system, but a different system, the **polar coordinate system,** can be used as well. In the polar coordinate system, points are written in terms of their distance from a fixed point, the pole (also called the origin), and the angle between the polar axis and the ray beginning at the origin and passing through the point.

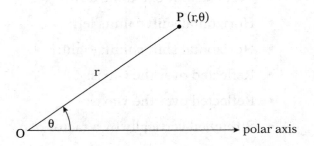

Each point is assigned polar coordinates (r, θ), where r is the **directed distance** from the origin to P, and θ is the **directed angle.** Because r is a distance, the coordinates (r, θ) and $(-r, \theta + \pi)$ actually represent the same point.

When the polar axis corresponds to the x-axis and the pole corresponds to the origin of the rectangular coordinate system, polar coordinates can be converted to rectangular coordinates (x, y) using the following relationships:

$x = r \cos \theta$

$y = r \sin \theta$

$x^2 + y^2 = r^2$

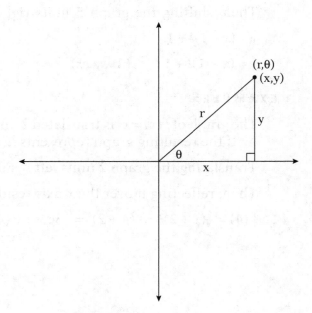

Note that in the polar coordinate system, points are not uniquely named. For example, $(3, 60°)$, $(3, -300°)$, and $(-3, 240°)$ represent the same point.

EXAMPLE:

Express the point $(3, \pi)$ in terms of rectangular coordinates.

Since $r = 3$ and $\theta = \pi$:

$x = 3 \cos \pi = -3$

$y = 3 \sin \pi = 0$

$(-3, 0)$.   (*Answer*)

EXAMPLE:

Express the point $\left(\dfrac{3}{2}, \dfrac{\sqrt{3}}{2} \right)$ in terms of polar coordinates.

Since $x^2 + y^2 = r^2$:

$$\left(\frac{3}{2}^2 + \frac{\sqrt{3}}{2}^2 \right) = r^2$$

$$\frac{9}{4} + \frac{3}{4} = r^2$$

$$r^2 = \frac{12}{4} = 3$$

$$r = \sqrt{3}$$

Now use the fact that $x = r \cos \theta$ to find θ.

$$\frac{3}{2} = \sqrt{3} \cos \theta$$

$$\cos^{-1} \left(\frac{\sqrt{3}}{2} \right) = \theta$$

$\theta = 30°$ (or $\dfrac{\pi}{6}$ in radian measure)

$(\sqrt{3}, 30°)$ (*Answer*)

CHAPTER 7

TRIGONOMETRY

This chapter provides a review of trigonometry principles. On the Level 2 test, 12–16% of the questions relate to trigonometry. Properties and graphs of trigonometric functions are not covered here but rather in the Functions chapter. The pie chart shows approximately how much of the Level 2 test is related to trigonometry:

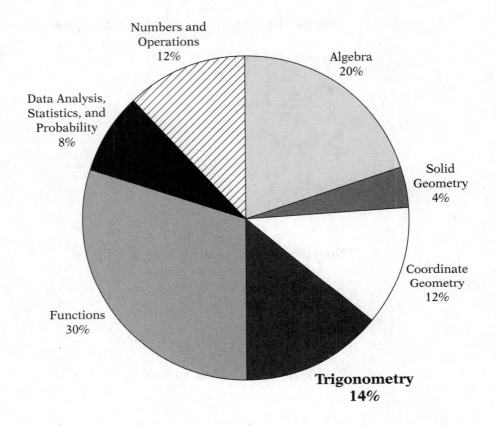

The following topics are covered in this chapter:

1. Right Triangle Trigonometry

2. Relationships Among Trigonometric Ratios
   a. Secant, Cosecant, Cotangent
   b. Cofunction Identities
   c. Inverse Functions

3. Special Right Triangles

4. Trigonometric Identities

5. *Radian Measure

6. *Law of Cosines

*Denotes concepts that are on the Level 2 test only.

7. *Law of Sines

8. *Trigonometric Equations

9. *Double Angle Formulas

RIGHT TRIANGLE TRIGONOMETRY

Trigonometry means "the measurement of triangles." One aspect of trigonometry relates to the study of the relationships between the sides and angles of right triangles, which results in the three ratios presented below. These trigonometric ratios are true when focusing on one acute angle in a right triangle. Take △*ABC*, for example:

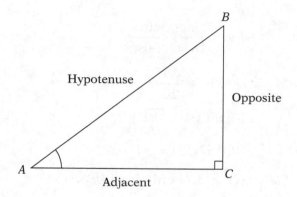

$\overline{BC}$ is the side opposite the given angle (in this case ∠*A*). $\overline{AC}$ is the side adjacent, or next to, ∠*A*. $\overline{AB}$ is the hypotenuse because it's the side opposite the 90° angle. The three trigonometric ratios for ∠*A* are:

$$\textbf{sine } \angle A = \frac{\text{opposite}}{\text{hypotenuse}} = \frac{BC}{AB}.$$

$$\textbf{cosine } \angle A = \frac{\text{adjacent}}{\text{hypotenuse}} = \frac{AC}{AB}.$$

$$\textbf{tangent } \angle A = \frac{\text{opposite}}{\text{adjacent}} = \frac{BC}{AC}.$$

The abbreviation **SOHCAHTOA** is used to remember the ratios shown above. Typically sine, cosine, and tangent are abbreviated as **sin, cos,** and **tan,** as they are on the your calculator's buttons.

EXAMPLE:

In the right triangle at the top of page 122, *m*∠*XZY* = 35°. Find the length of $\overline{XY}$. Round your answer to the nearest hundredth.

---

*Denotes concepts that are on the Level 2 test only.

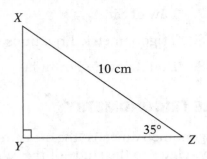

You know the length of the hypotenuse, and you're missing the length of $\overline{XY}$, the side opposite $\angle XYZ$. The sine ratio will enable you to determine $\overline{XY}$ because

$$\text{sine} = \frac{\text{opposite}}{\text{hypotenuse}}.$$

$$\sin 35° = \frac{\overline{XY}}{10}.$$

$$10\left(\sin 35° = \overline{XY}\right).$$

$$10(0.57358) = \overline{XY}.$$

$$\overline{XY} = 5.74 \text{ cm}. \qquad (\textit{Answer})$$

Make sure your calculator is set to **degree mode** to do this trigonometry problem. Angle measures on the Level 2 test may be given in radians or degrees, so know how to set your calculator to both. To check the setting of your calculator, determine $\sin 30°$. In degree mode, $\sin 30° = 0.5$. If your calculator is incorrectly set to radian mode for this problem, $\sin 30° = -0.98803$. Change your mode to degree if this is the case.

EXAMPLE:

At a distance of 45 feet from a flagpole, the angle from the ground to the top of the flagpole is 40°. Find the height of the flagpole. Round your answer to the nearest hundredth.
It may help to sketch a diagram to solve this problem.

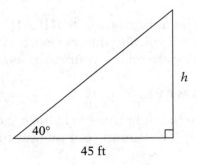

Now, determine which trigonometric ratio could be used to solve for h. You don't have enough information to use sine or cosine because you don't know the length of the hypotenuse. Tangent $= \dfrac{\text{opposite}}{\text{adjacent}}$, so:

$$\tan 40° = \frac{h}{45}.$$

$$45(\tan 40°) = h.$$

$$45(0.83910) = h.$$

$$h = 37.76 \text{ feet.} \qquad (\textit{Answer})$$

EXAMPLE:

A 15-foot ladder leans against the side of a building creating an angle of 28° with the building. How far is the base of the ladder from the side of the building?

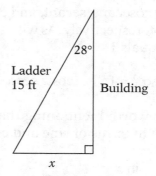

The ladder problem is commonly used in right triangle trigonometry problems. First, determine which trigonometric ratio to use. Because you know the hypotenuse and are trying to solve for the side opposite the 28° angle, it makes sense to use sine.

$$\sin 28° = \frac{x}{15}.$$

$$15(\sin 28°) = x.$$

$$x = 7.04 \text{ feet.} \qquad (\textit{Answer})$$

RELATIONSHIPS AMONG TRIGONOMETRIC RATIOS

Secant, Cosecant, Cotangent

There are three other trigonometric functions that are **reciprocal functions** of those already mentioned, sine, cosine, and tangent. Again, take a look at $\triangle ABC$:

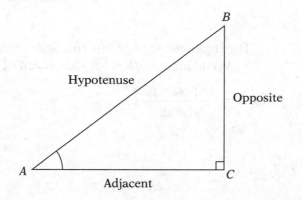

$\overline{BC}$ is the side opposite $\angle A$. $\overline{AC}$ is the side adjacent $\angle A$. $\overline{AB}$ is the hypotenuse. The three remaining trigonometric ratios for $\angle A$ are:

cosecant $\angle A = \dfrac{1}{\sin A} = \dfrac{\text{hypotenuse}}{\text{opposite}} = \dfrac{AB}{BC}$.

secant $\angle A = \dfrac{1}{\cos A} = \dfrac{\text{hypotenuse}}{\text{adjacent}} = \dfrac{AB}{AC}$.

cotangent $\angle A = \dfrac{1}{\tan A} = \dfrac{\text{adjacent}}{\text{opposite}} = \dfrac{AC}{BC}$.

The cosecant, secant, and cotangent functions are abbreviated as **csc, sec, and cot,** respectively. As with any reciprocal, a function multiplied by its reciprocal equals 1.

$$\sin x \csc x = 1 \qquad \cos x \sec x = 1 \qquad \tan x \cot x = 1$$

It is worth mentioning that the tangent and cotangent functions can be written in terms of sine and cosine as follows:

$$\tan x = \frac{\sin x}{\cos x} \qquad\qquad \cot x = \frac{\cos x}{\sin x}$$

EXAMPLE:

Given $\triangle LMN$ is a right triangle with a right angle at vertex M, find the secant of $\angle N$.

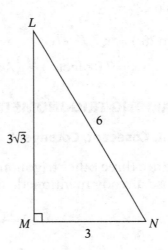

The hypotenuse of $\triangle LMN$ measures 6, and the leg adjacent to $\angle N$ measures 3. Write an equation for the secant of $\angle N$:

$$\sec N = \frac{\text{hypotenuse}}{\text{adjacent}}.$$

$$= \frac{6}{3}.$$

$$= 2. \qquad (Answer)$$

EXAMPLE:

Simplify $\cot \theta \cos \theta + \sin \theta$.

Write the cotangent function in terms of sine and cosine to get:

$$\frac{\cos \theta}{\sin \theta}(\cos \theta) + \sin \theta.$$

$$= \frac{(\cos^2 \theta + \sin^2 \theta)}{\sin \theta}.$$

$$= \frac{1}{\sin \theta}.$$

$$= \csc \theta. \qquad (Answer)$$

Cofunction Identities

Sine and cosine, tangent and cotangent, and secant and cosecant are called **cofunctions.** Notice that in $\triangle ABC$, $\angle A$ and $\angle B$ are complementary. The acute angles of any right triangle are actually complementary because the sum of all three angles in a triangle must be 180°.

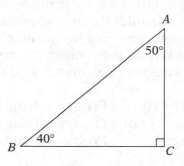

The complementary angles in $\triangle ABC$ result in the following relationships:

$\sin \angle A = \cos \angle B.$ $\sin \angle 50° = \cos \angle 40°.$

$\tan \angle A = \cot \angle B.$ or $\tan \angle 50° = \cot \angle 40°.$

$\sec \angle A = \csc \angle B.$ $\sec \angle 50° = \csc \angle 40°.$

Knowing that $\angle A + \angle B = 90°$, you can write $\angle B$ in terms of $\angle A$: $\angle B = 90 - \angle A$. Substituting this new value of $\angle B$ into the previous relationships gives you the following **cofunction identities:**

$\sin \angle A = \cos (90 - \angle A).$ $\cos \angle A = \sin (90 - \angle A).$

$\tan \angle A = \cot (90 - \angle A).$ $\cot \angle A = \tan (90 - \angle A).$

$\sec \angle A = \csc (90 - \angle A).$ $\csc \angle A = \sec (90 - \angle A).$

In general, the cofunction identities show that the sine of an angle is the cosine of its complement, and vice versa, the cosine of an angle is the sine of its complement. The same is true for secant and cosecant and tangent and cotangent.

EXAMPLE:

If csc x = sec 70°, then solve for x.

Remember that cosecant and secant are cofunctions:

csc x = sec $(90 - x)$.

Set sec $(90 - x)$ equal to sec 70° to determine x.

$90 - x = 70$.

$x = 20°$.   (*Answer*)

To check your answer, notice csc 20° = sec $(90 - 20)$°.

Inverse Functions

Trigonometry can also be used to determine the measures of angles. $\text{Sin}^{-1} x$ denotes the inverse sine of x, or the **arcsine.** $\text{Sin}^{-1} (0.707)$ means "the angle whose sine is 0.707."

To solve for the angle measure, use the $\sin^{-1}$ function on your calculator. (On most graphing calculators, this is accessed by pressing the 2nd button and then the sin button.) Try calculating $\sin^{-1} (0.707)$ using your calculator. It should equal approximately 45°.

Similarly, $\cos^{-1} x$ denotes the inverse cosine of x, or the **arccosine,** and $\tan^{-1} x$ denotes the inverse tangent of x, or the **arctangent.** Both inverse functions can be solved in the same manner as arcsine by using the $\cos^{-1}$ and $\tan^{-1}$ functions on your calculator, respectively.

Using your calculator, find the value of each of the following:

1. $\sin^{-1} (0.5)$ (You're solving for "the angle whose sine is 0.5.")
2. $\cos^{-1} (0.8)$ (You're solving for "the angle whose cosine is 0.8.")
3. $\tan^{-1} (1)$ (You're solving for "the angle whose tangent is 1.")

The answers are, in order, 30°, 36.9°, and 45°. If you didn't get these solutions, check to make sure your calculator is set in degree mode.

EXAMPLE:

Given $\triangle$ JET is a 3-4-5 right triangle with a right angle at vertex E. Determine the measures of the two acute angles. Round answers to the nearest tenth.

Let's use arcsine to solve for both angles. Remember that $\sin = \dfrac{\text{opposite}}{\text{hypotenuse}}$ and the hypotenuse of $\triangle$ JET is its longest side. The sine of one of the acute angles is, therefore, $\dfrac{3}{5}$, while the sine of the second acute angle is $\dfrac{4}{5}$. Write two expressions using arcsine:

$\sin^{-1} \left(\dfrac{3}{5} \right)$. $\sin^{-1} \left(\dfrac{4}{5} \right)$.

$= \sin^{-1} (0.6)$. $= \sin^{-1} (0.8)$.

$= 36.9°$ $= 53.1°$

The two acute angles measure 36.9° and 53.1°.   (*Answer*)

EXAMPLE:

The diagonals of a rhombus measure 24 and 10 inches. What is the measure of the larger angle of the rhombus?

Recall that the diagonals of a rhombus are perpendicular, bisect each other, and bisect the vertex angles of the rhombus. Let x and y equal the measures of the angles as shown below.

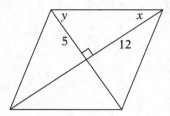

$$\tan x = \frac{5}{12}$$

$$x = \tan^{-1}\frac{5}{12} = 22.6°$$

$$\tan y = \frac{12}{5}$$

$$y = \tan^{-1}\frac{12}{5} = 67.4°$$

One angle of the rhombus measures $2(22.6) \approx 45°$, while the other angle measures $2(67.4) \approx 135°$. Since the problem asks for the greater of the two angles, $135°$ is the correct answer.

SPECIAL RIGHT TRIANGLES

Recall the two special right triangles: 45°–45°–90° and 30°–60°–90°. Here they are mentioned because the ratios of their sides occur often in right triangle trigonometry. A **45°−45°−90°** triangle is an isosceles right triangle whose sides are in the ratio $x{:}x{:}x\sqrt{2}$, while a **30°−60°−90°** triangle is a scalene right triangle whose sides are in the ratio $x{:}x\sqrt{3}{:}2x$.

For each special right triangle below, identify the sine, cosine, and tangent of the acute angles.

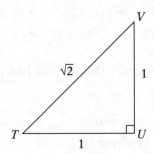

$$\sin \angle T = \frac{1}{\sqrt{2}} = \frac{1}{\sqrt{2}}\left(\frac{\sqrt{2}}{\sqrt{2}}\right) = \frac{\sqrt{2}}{2}. \qquad \sin \angle V = \frac{1}{\sqrt{2}} = \frac{1}{\sqrt{2}}\left(\frac{\sqrt{2}}{\sqrt{2}}\right) = \frac{\sqrt{2}}{2}.$$

$$\cos \angle T = \frac{1}{\sqrt{2}} = \frac{1}{\sqrt{2}}\left(\frac{\sqrt{2}}{\sqrt{2}}\right) = \frac{\sqrt{2}}{2}. \qquad \cos \angle V = \frac{1}{\sqrt{2}} = \frac{1}{\sqrt{2}}\left(\frac{\sqrt{2}}{\sqrt{2}}\right) = \frac{\sqrt{2}}{2}.$$

$$\tan \angle T = \frac{1}{1} = 1. \qquad\qquad\qquad \tan \angle V = \frac{1}{1} = 1.$$

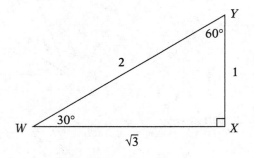

$$\sin \angle W = \frac{1}{2}. \qquad\qquad\qquad \sin \angle Y = \frac{\sqrt{3}}{2}.$$

$$\cos \angle W = \frac{\sqrt{3}}{2}. \qquad\qquad\qquad \cos \angle Y = \frac{1}{2}.$$

$$\tan \angle W = \frac{1}{\sqrt{3}} = \frac{1}{\sqrt{3}}\left(\frac{\sqrt{3}}{\sqrt{3}}\right) = \frac{\sqrt{3}}{3}. \qquad \tan \angle Y = \frac{\sqrt{3}}{1} = \sqrt{3}.$$

▓ TRIGONOMETRIC IDENTITIES

Aside from the cofunction identities and reciprocal identities (i.e., cosecant, secant, and cotangent) previously mentioned, you may encounter problems involving one key trigonometric identity on the SAT Subject Test:

$$\sin^2 x + \cos^2 x = 1.$$

An identity is an equation true for every value of the domain. Try substituting any number in for x and see what happens. Let's try $x = 25°$.

$$\sin^2(25) \quad + \cos^2(25) \quad = 1$$
$$0.422618^2 + 0.906308^2 = 1.$$

Two other Pythagorean Identities may also be encountered on the Level 2 test:

$$1 + \tan^2 x = \sec^2 x.$$
$$1 + \cot^2 x = \csc^2 x.$$

EXAMPLE:

Simplify $(4\sin x)(3\sin x) - (\cos x)(-12\cos x)$.

First, multiply the terms:

$12\sin^2 x - -12\cos^2 x$.

Notice that this resembles the identity $\sin^2 x + \cos^2 x = 1$. Now, simply factor out a 12.

$= 12(\sin^2 x + \cos^2 x)$.
$= 12(1)$.
$= 12$.   (*Answer*)

EXAMPLE:

Simplify $(1 + \sin \theta)(1 - \sin \theta)$.

Recall that $\sin^2 \theta + \cos^2 \theta = 1$, so $\cos^2 \theta = 1 - \sin^2 \theta$.

$(1 + \sin\theta)(1 - \sin\theta) =$
$1 - \sin\theta + \sin\theta - \sin^2\theta =$
$1 - \sin^2\theta =$

$\cos^2 \theta$.   (*Answer*)

EXAMPLE:

Simplify $\sec^2 20° - \tan^2 20°$.

Recall the identity $1 + \tan^2 x = \sec^2 x$. $\sec^2 20°$ can be written in terms of $\tan^2 20°$.

$\sec^2 20° - \tan^2 20° = (1 + \tan^2 20°) - \tan^2 20°$.

$= 1$.   (*Answer*)

*RADIAN MEASURE

Angles in high school mathematics are typically measured in degrees. In more advanced math courses, however, radian is a more widely used unit of measure. To convert from one to the other, use the following formula:

180° = π radians.

In other words:

$1 \text{ degree} = \dfrac{\pi}{180} \text{ radians}$ and $1 \text{ radian} = \dfrac{180}{\pi} \text{ degrees}$.

EXAMPLE:

What is the radian measure of an angle whose degree measure is 120°?

Because $1° = \dfrac{\pi}{180}$ radians, 120° equals:

$$120\left(\dfrac{\pi}{180}\right) \text{ radians.}$$

$$= \dfrac{2\pi}{3} \text{ radians} \qquad (Answer)$$

EXAMPLE:

What is the degree measure of an angle whose radian measure is $\dfrac{\pi}{3}$?

Since 1 radian $= \dfrac{180}{\pi}$ degrees, $\dfrac{\pi}{3}$ radians equals:

$$\dfrac{\pi}{3}\left(\dfrac{180}{\pi}\right) \text{ degrees}$$

$$= 60°. \qquad (Answer)$$

*LAW OF COSINES

Given △ABC:

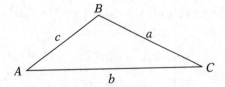

The **Law of Cosines** states:

$$c^2 = a^2 + b^2 - 2ab\cos\angle C$$

The Law of Cosines is helpful in solving for the length of the third side of a triangle given the lengths of the other two sides and the measure of their included angle. It is also used to find the measure of an angle of a triangle given the length of its three sides.

EXAMPLE:

In $\triangle ABC$, $BC = 9$, $AC = 14$, and $m\angle C = 70°$. Find AB. Round answer to one decimal place.

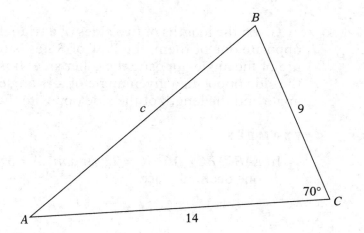

$c^2 = 9^2 + 14^2 - 2(9)(14)\cos 70°$

$c^2 = 81 + 196 - 252(0.342)$

$c^2 = 190.816$

$c = \sqrt{190.816} = 13.8$ (*Answer*)

EXAMPLE:

$\triangle ABC$ has sides measuring 3, 12, and 14 inches. What is the measure of its largest angle?

The largest angle of a triangle is opposite its longest side. Let $\angle C$ = the triangle's largest angle. The side opposite $\angle C$ is side AB, and it measures 14 inches. Using the Law of Cosines:

$14^2 = 3^2 + 12^2 - 2(3)(12)\cos C$

$14^2 = 9 + 144 - 72\cos C$

$43 = -72\cos C$

$\cos C = -\dfrac{43}{72}$

$C = \cos^{-1}-\dfrac{43}{72} \approx 126.7°$ (*Answer*)

*LAW OF SINES

Given $\triangle ABC$:

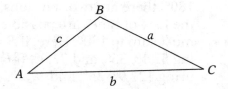

The **Law of Sines** states:

$$\sin \frac{A}{a} = \sin \frac{B}{b} = \sin \frac{C}{c}$$

Given the lengths of two sides of a triangle and the measure of the angle opposite one of them, the Law of Sines is helpful in solving for the measure of the angle opposite the other side. It is also used to find the length of the side opposite a given angle of a triangle given the measure of another angle and the length of the side opposite that angle.

EXAMPLE:

In $\triangle ABC$, $BC = 16$, $AC = 22$, and $m\angle A = 35°$. Find $m\angle B$. Round answer to one decimal place.

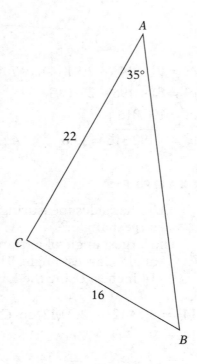

$$\frac{\sin 35°}{16} = \frac{\sin B}{22}$$

$$\frac{22(\sin 35°\ )}{16} = \sin B$$

$\sin B = 0.78867$

$B = \sin^{-1}(0.78867)$

$B = 52.1°$ or $127.9°$ (*Answer*)

Since both 52.1° and 127.9° have a sine of 0.78867 and sum to less than 180°, there are two solutions. Check to make sure your solutions using the Law of Sines are possible, noting that the three angles in a triangle must sum to 180°. Here, if $B = 52.1°$, $\triangle ABC$ would have angles measuring 52.1°, 35°, and 92.9°. If $B = 127.9°$, $\triangle ABC$ would have angles measuring 127.9°, 35°, and 17.1°.

EXAMPLE:

In $\triangle XYZ$, $XY = 3.8$ cm, $n = 39°$ and $m = 27°$. What is the length of side YZ?

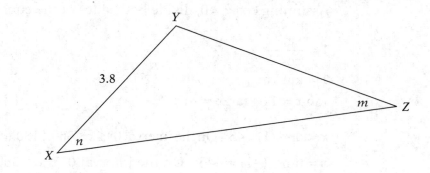

$$\frac{\sin 27°}{3.8} = \frac{\sin 39°}{YZ}$$

$$YZ = \frac{3.8(\sin 39°)}{\sin 27°}$$

$$YZ \approx 5.27 \text{ cm} \qquad (Answer)$$

*TRIGONOMETRIC EQUATIONS

Solving a trigonometric equation involves transforming the equation using the reciprocal functions, cofunctions, and/or trigonometric identities. Unlike solving other algebraic equations, trigonometric equations can have infinitely many solutions.

EXAMPLE:

Solve $2\cos \alpha = \sin \alpha$ over the interval $0° \le \alpha \le 360°$.
If $2\sin \alpha = \cos \alpha$, then:

$$2 = \frac{\sin \alpha}{\cos \alpha}$$

$$2 = \tan \alpha$$

$$\alpha = \tan^{-1} 2 = 63.4°$$

Since the problem specifies $0° \le \alpha \le 360°$, $180 + 63.4 = 243.4°$ is also a solution.

$$\alpha = 63.4° \text{ or } 243.4° \qquad (Answer)$$

EXAMPLE:

Solve $\cos^2 x = \sin^2 x$ over the interval $0° \leq x \leq 360°$.

Assuming $\cos x \neq 0$, divide both sides of the equation by $\cos^2 x$.

$$1 = \frac{\sin^2 x}{\cos^2 x}$$
$$1 = \tan^2 x$$
$$\tan x = 1 \text{ or } \tan x = -1$$

$x = \tan^{-1}(1) = 45°$. On the interval $0° \leq x \leq 360°$, $180 + 45 = 225°$ is also a solution.

$x = \tan^{-1}(-1) = -45°$. On the interval $0° \leq x \leq 360°$, $180 + -45 = 135°$ and $180 + 135 = 315°$ are solutions.

$x = 45°, 135°, 225°,$ or $315°$ (*Answer*)

As mentioned, trigonometric equations can have infinitely many solutions. Since the period of the tangent function is $180°$ (or π radians), $45°$ plus any multiple of $180°$, and $135°$ plus any multiple of $180°$ are possible solutions to the equation in the previous example.

EXAMPLE:

Solve $6\sin^2 x + \sin x - 1 = 0$ over the interval $0° \leq x \leq 360°$.

Factor the equation to get:

$$(3\sin x - 1)(2\sin x + 1) = 0$$
$$\sin x = \frac{1}{3} \text{ or } \sin x = -\frac{1}{2}$$
$$x = \sin^{-1}\left(\frac{1}{3}\right) = 19.5°$$
$$x = \sin^{-1}\left(-\frac{1}{2}\right) = -30°$$

Considering $0° \leq x \leq 360°$, the possible solutions are:

$x = 19.5°, 160.5°, 210°,$ or $330°$ (*Answer*)

*DOUBLE ANGLE FORMULAS

The **double angle formulas for sine** and **cosine** are as follows:

$$\sin 2\theta = 2\sin\theta\cos\theta \qquad \cos 2\theta = \cos^2\theta - \sin^2\theta$$

Using the trigonometric identity $\sin^2 x + \cos^2 x = 1$, the double angle formula for cosine can also be written as:

$$\cos 2\theta = 1 - 2\sin^2\theta \quad \text{or} \quad \cos 2\theta = 2\cos^2\theta - 1$$

The **double angle formula for tangent** is:

$$\tan 2\theta = \frac{2\tan\theta}{1 - \tan^2\theta}$$

EXAMPLE:

Given θ is in the first quadrant, if $\cos\theta = \dfrac{4}{5}$, what is the value of $\sin 2\theta$?

If $\cos\theta = \dfrac{4}{5}$, then $\sin\theta = \dfrac{3}{5}$. (Sketch a 3-4-5 right triangle in quadrant I if you're unsure of the value of $\sin\theta$.)

$$\sin 2\theta = 2\sin\theta\cos\theta$$
$$\sin 2\theta = 2\left(\dfrac{3}{5}\right)\left(\dfrac{4}{5}\right)$$
$$= \dfrac{24}{25} \quad (Answer)$$

EXAMPLE:

Express $2\sin 3x\cos 3x$ as a single trigonometric function.

Since the double angle formula for sine is $\sin 2\theta = 2\sin\theta\cos\theta$,

$$2\sin 3x\cos 3x = \sin 2(3x)$$
$$= \sin 6x \quad (Answer)$$

EXAMPLE:

What is the value of $2\cos^2 30° - 1$?

Since $2\cos^2\theta - 1 = \cos 2\theta$,

$$2\cos^2 30° - 1 = \cos 2(30°) = \cos 60°$$

$$\cos 60° = \dfrac{1}{2} \quad (Answer)$$

CHAPTER 8
FUNCTIONS

This chapter provides a review of functions. On the Level 2 test, 48–52% of the questions relate to Algebra and Functions combined. That translates to about 30% of the test questions relating specifically to Functions and about 20% to Algebra. The pie chart shows approximately how much of the Level 2 test is related to functions.

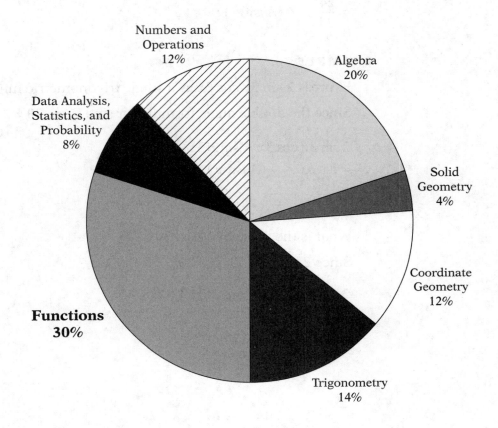

The following topics are covered in this chapter:

1. Function Notation
2. Functions vs. Relations
   a. Graphing Functions
3. Composition of Functions
   a. Identity, Zero, and Constant Functions
4. Determining the Maximum or Minimum
5. The Roots of a Quadratic Function
6. Inverse Functions
7. Rational Functions
8. Higher-Degree Polynomial Functions
9. Exponential Functions

10. *Logarithmic Functions
11. *Trigonometric Functions
12. *Inverse Trigonometric Functions
13. *Periodic Functions
14. *Piecewise Functions
15. *Recursive Functions
16. *Parametric Functions

FUNCTION NOTATION

A **function** is a set of ordered pairs of real numbers. A function is often described by a rule that creates a one-to-one correspondence between sets of input and output values. The set of all input values is called the **domain** of the function, and the set of all output values is called the **range.** Unless otherwise noted on the SAT Subject Test, the domain and range are assumed to be the set of all real numbers. Typically, a function is denoted by $f(x)$ and is read "f of x" or "the value of the function f at x." Functions can be represented by any letter, not just f, though. It is common to use f, F, g, G, h, and H to represent different functions. The following are examples of functions:

$$f(x) = x^2. \quad F(x) = 3x. \quad g(x) = (x-4)^2 + 1.$$

Take the first example, $f(x) = x^2$. When the function is evaluated for $x = 2$, the result is $f(2) = 2^2 = 4$. $f(x)$ represents the y value when a function is graphed on a xy-coordinate plane. The point $(2, 4)$ would be included in the graph of the function $f(x) = x^2$ because when $x = 2$, $f(x) = 4$.

For a set of ordered pairs to be a function:

1. For each domain value of a function, there *must* be an associated range value.

2. A domain value cannot be matched with more than one range value.

When determining the domain of a function, look for two common restrictions: dividing by zero and identifying when the radicand is negative. You want to ensure that both cases do not happen.

A **linear function** is a function in the form: $f(x) = mx + b$ where x, m, and b are real numbers.

The graph of a linear function is a straight line with slope m and y-intercept b.

A **quadratic function** is a function in the form: $f(x) = ax^2 + bx + c$ where $a \neq 0$.

The graph of a quadratic function is a parabola.

*Denotes concepts that are on the Level 2 test only.

A function is **even** if its graph is symmetric with respect to the *y*-axis, and **odd** if its graph is symmetric with respect to origin. To test for the symmetry of a function:

1. The function is even if replacing *x* with −*x* results in the original function.

   $f(-x) = f(x)$.

2. The function is odd if replacing *x* with −*x* results in the opposite of the original function.

   $f(-x) = -f(x)$.

EXAMPLE:

Which of the following mapping diagrams depicts a function?

I.
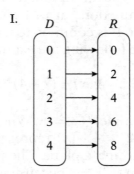

II.
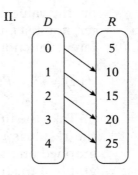

III.
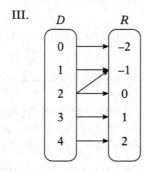

IV.
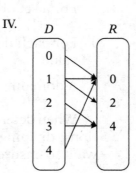

(A) I and II

(B) II and III

(C) III and IV

(D) I and IV

(E) II and IV

Remember that there must be a range associated with each domain value. II is not a function because 4 doesn't have an associated range. III cannot be a function because 2 is matched with both −1 and 0. It is ok for a range value to be mapped to more than one domain, such as shown in diagram IV. I and IV are functions. D is the correct answer.

EXAMPLE:

Find the domain of $f(x) = \sqrt{100 - x^2}$.

The domain is the set of x values for which the function is defined. In other words, it is the set of values allowed for x. We are assuming that the domain of the function is the set of real numbers. (On the SAT Subject Test, you can assume this, unless told otherwise.) The radicand, $100 - x^2$, must, therefore, be positive.

$100 - x^2 \geq 0$.

$100 \geq x^2$.

$10 \geq x$ and $10 \geq -x$.

$10 \geq x$ and $-10 \leq x$.

$-10 \leq x \leq 10$.   *(Answer)*

EXAMPLE:

Given $f(x) = 2x - 5$, find $f(x) = x - 3$.

Replace x in the original function with the expression $x - 3$.

$f(x - 3) = 2(x - 3) - 5$.

$f(x - 3) = 2x - 6 - 5$.

$f(x - 3) = 2x - 11$.   *(Answer)*

EXAMPLE:

Determine the domain of the function $g(x) = \dfrac{1}{x(x + 3)}$.

The fraction $\dfrac{1}{x(x + 3)}$ is not defined when the denominator $x(x + 3)$ equals zero. Dividing by zero is a common restriction of the domain of a function.

$x(x + 3) \neq 0$.

$x \neq 0$ or $x \neq -3$.

The domain is the set of all real numbers except 0 and -3.   *(Answer)*

EXAMPLE:

Find the domain and range of the function $f(x) = |x - 1|$ shown in the graph.

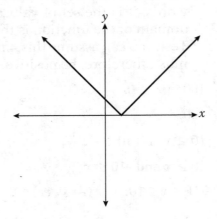

It is useful to know that "v-shaped" graphs are associated with absolute value. The domain is the set of x for which the function is defined. Are there any restrictions on x in this example? The graph shows that x is defined at zero and at all positive and negative values. The domain is the set of all real numbers. What about the range? Looking at the equation, you see that $y = |x - 1|$. Because y equals the absolute value of an expression, and absolute value, by definition, is always positive, y must be greater than or equal to zero. You can determine this from the graph because there are no points in either quadrant III or IV where y is negative.

$D = \{$all real numbers$\}$, $R = \{y: y \geq 0\}$.   (*Answer*)

FUNCTIONS VS. RELATIONS

You can test for a function algebraically or by using the vertical line test. The **vertical line test** states that any vertical line intersects the graph of a function at, at most, one point. Both tests determine if there is one and only one range (y-value) associated with a given domain (x-value).

EXAMPLE:

Is $y^2 = 5 + x$ a function?
Let's test this algebraically. Start by solving for y.

$y^2 = 5 + x.$

$y = \pm\sqrt{5 + x}.$

You can immediately see that for one value of x there are two corresponding values of y. Let $x = 4$, for example. $y = \pm\sqrt{5 + 4}$, so $y = \pm3$.

$y^2 = 5 + x$ is not a function.   (*Answer*)

EXAMPLE:

Is $x^2 + y^2 = 4$ a function?

Let's test this one using the vertical line test. You may be able recognize that the graph is a circle because $x^2 + y^2 = 4$ fits into the standard form of the equation of a circle: $(x - h)^2 + (y - k)^2 = r^2$. It center is (0,0), and its radius is 2. A vertical line intersects the circle at two points, as shown below.

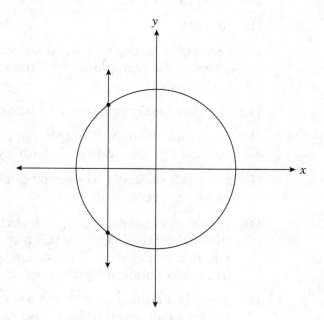

The equation does not pass the vertical line test.

$x^2 + y^2 = 4$ is not a function.   (*Answer*)

By definition, a **relation** is any set of ordered pairs. A function, therefore, is simply a type of relation consisting of ordered pairs with different x coordinates. The two parabolas below show the difference between a relation and a function.

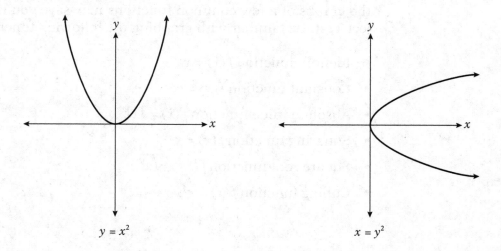

$y = x^2$ $x = y^2$

The graph of $y = x^2$ passes the vertical line test, so it is a function. The graph of $x = y^2$ does not pass the vertical line test (when $x = 4$, $y = 2$ or $y = -2$.), so it is a relation.

EXAMPLE:

Which of the following is NOT a function?

(A) $\{(x,y) : y = x\}$.

(B) $\{(x,y) : x = |y|\}$.

(C) $\{(x,y) : x^2 = y\}$.

(D) $\{(x,y) : y = \sqrt{x}\}$.

(E) $\{(x,y) : y = x^3\}$.

Each answer is written as a set notation and represents a set of ordered pairs. Answer A, for example, is read "the set of all ordered pairs (x,y) such that $y = x$."

(A) $y = x$ is a linear equation and passes the vertical line test.

(B) $x = |y|$ is a "v-shaped" graph that is concave left and does not pass the vertical line test. When $x = 5$ for example, $y = \pm 5$.

(C) $x^2 = y$ is a parabola whose vertex is the origin and is concave up, so it passes the vertical line test.

(D) $y = \sqrt{x}$ is a curve starting at the origin and moving upward in the positive x direction. Because it is a square root equation, it is not defined when x is negative. The range, y, is restricted to positive values because y equals a square root.

(E) $y = x^3$ is a cubic curve that passes through the origin. The domain is the set of all real numbers, and each x has one y associated with it.

B is not a function.   (*Answer*)

Graphing Functions

The most straightforward way to graph a function is to create an xy-table and find the coordinates of points for which the function is true. Start with the intercepts; set $y = 0$ and solve for x, then set $x = 0$ and solve for y. Knowing the graphs of a few common functions may save you time on the SAT Subject Test. Be familiar with graphing the following functions:

- Identify function $f(x) = x$.
- Constant function $f(x) = c$.
- Absolute value function $f(x) = |x|$.
- Squaring function $f(x) = x^2$.
- Square root function $f(x) = \sqrt{x}$.
- Cubing function $f(x) = x^3$.

COMPOSITION OF FUNCTIONS

Two functions can be combined to form a **composition.** $f(g(x))$ is read as "the composition of f with g." Let $f(x) = x^2$ and $g(x) = x + 1$, evaluate the following:

$f(g(x)) = f(x + 1) = (x + 1)^2$.

$g(f(x)) = g(x^2) = x^2 + 1$.

$f(f(x)) = f(x^2) = x^4$.

$f(g(2)) = f(3) = 9$.

Notice that $f(g(x))$ is not equivalent to $g(f(x))$ in this example.

EXAMPLE:

Given $g(x) = x + 3$, $h(x) = 9 - x^2$, and $g(h(x)) = 8$, find x.

$g(h(x)) = g(9 - x^2) = 9 - x^2 + 3 = 12 - x^2$.

You're given that $g(h(x)) = 8$, so set $12 - x^2$ equal to 8 and solve for x.

$12 - x^2 = 8$.

$4 = x^2$.

$x = \pm 2$.   (*Answer*)

EXAMPLE:

Given $f(x) = x^{\frac{2}{3}}$ and $g(x) = x^6$. Find $f(g(8x))$.

Start by finding $g(x)$.

$g(8x) = (8x)^6$.

Now find $f((8x)^6)$.

$f((8x)^6) = [(8x)^6]^{\frac{2}{3}} = 8^4 x^4$.

$= 4096x^4$.   (*Answer*)

Identity, Zero, and Constant Functions

The **identity function** is the function for which $y = x$. $f(x) = x$. Its graph is a diagonal line passing through the origin whose slope is 1.

The **zero function** is the function that assigns 0 to every x. $f(x) = 0$. Its graph is the horizontal line in which $y = 0$, otherwise known as the x-axis.

A **constant function** is any function that assigns a constant value c to every x. $f(x) = c$. Its graph is a horizontal line, $y = c$, whose y-intercept is the point $(0,c)$.

EXAMPLE:

Which of the following graphs represent(s) a constant function?

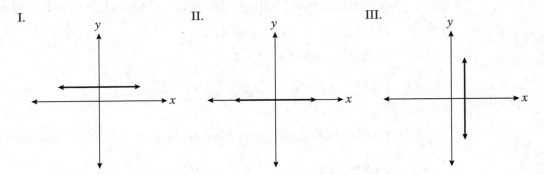

I.   II.   III.

(A) I only

(B) II only

(C) III only

(D) I and II

(E) II and III

III is not a function because it does not pass the vertical line test. I represents the constant function, $y = c$. II represents the zero function, $y = 0$, but the zero function is also a constant function.

D is the correct answer.   (*Answer*)

DETERMINING THE MAXIMUM OR MINIMUM

The graph of a function can be increasing, decreasing, or constant for intervals of its domain. A function is

- **decreasing,** if the y value decreases from left to right,

- **increasing,** if the y value increases from left to right, or

- **constant,** if the y value remains unchanged from left to right.*

Take parabola $y = x^2$, for example. The graph decreases when $y < 0$ and increases when $y > 0$. The **maximum** or **minimum** value of a function is often the point where the function changes behavior from decreasing to increasing.

> **The Maximum or Minimum of a Quadratic Function**
>
> Let $f(x) = ax^2 + bx + c$ where $a \neq 0$.
>
> If $a < 0$, the parabola is concave down and has a maximum value.
>
> If $a > 0$, the parabola is concave up and has a minimum value.
>
> The maximum or minimum is $f(x)$ when $x = -\dfrac{b}{2a}$. In other words, it's the
>
> y value of the parabola's vertex.

EXAMPLE:

Find the maximum value of the function $f(x) = -4x^2 + 3x + 1$.

Notice a is less than zero, so the function does, in fact, have a maximum value. Solve for the x coordinate of the function's vertex:

$$x = -\frac{b}{2a} = -\frac{3}{2(-4)} = \frac{3}{8}.$$

Now find the value of the function when $x = \dfrac{3}{8}$

$$f\left(\frac{3}{8}\right) = -4\left(\frac{3}{8}\right)^2 + 3\left(\frac{3}{8}\right) + 1$$

$$= -\frac{9}{16} + \frac{9}{8} + 1 = \frac{(-9 + 18 + 16)}{16} = \frac{25}{16}.$$

The maximum value is $\dfrac{25}{16}$ or 1.5625.   (*Answer*)

EXAMPLE:

A gardener has 60 feet of fencing to enclose a garden. Find the greatest possible area of the garden.

Let w = the width of the garden and l = the length of the garden.

$2w + 2l = 60$

$w + l = 30$

Write l in terms of w: $l = 30 - w$. The area of the garden is $A = lw$, so substitute $30 - w$ in for l.

$A = (30 - w)w$

Notice that this results in a quadratic equation.

$A = 30w - w^2$ where $a = -1$ and $b = 30$.

The maximum value occurs when $w = -\dfrac{b}{2a} = -\dfrac{30}{2(-1)} = 15.$

When $w = 15$, $l = 30 - 15 = 15$, so the area is 15(15) or 225 square feet.

225 square feet.   (*Answer*)

THE ROOTS OF A QUADRATIC FUNCTION

The **roots,** or solutions, of a quadratic equation are values of the variable that satisfy the equation. For example, factoring $x^2 + 2x - 15 = 0$ results in $(x + 5)$ $(x - 3) = 0$. $x = -5$ and $x = 3$ are the roots of the equation. When dealing with functions, the roots are the x values that result when $f(x) = 0$. You can also think of the roots as the x-intercepts of the graph of a function or the *zeroes* of the function.

If you're given the roots of a quadratic equation, you can use them to determine the equation itself. A quadratic equation can be thought of as:

$a[x^2 -$ (sum of the roots)$x +$ (product of the roots)$] = 0.$

EXAMPLE:

The product of the roots of a quadratic equation is -14 and their sum is -3. Find a quadratic equation whose roots have the given product and sum.

Because the sum of the two roots is -3, and the product is -14, substitute these values into the equation.

$a[x^2 -$ (sum of the roots)$x +$ (product of the roots)$] = 0.$

$a[x^2 - (-3)x + (-14)] = 0.$

Setting a equal to 1 results in one possible answer:

$x^2 + 3x - 14 = 0.$ (*Answer*)

EXAMPLE:

Find a quadratic equation with integral coefficients having roots 6 and 2.

The sum of the roots is 8 and their product is 12.

$a[x^2 -$ (sum of the roots)$x +$ (product of the roots)$] = 0.$

$a(x^2 - 8x + 12) = 0.$

Again, setting a equal to 1 results in one possible answer:

$x^2 - 8x + 12 = 0.$ (*Answer*)

EXAMPLE:

Find a quadratic equation with integral coefficients having roots $-\sqrt{2}$ and $\sqrt{2}$.

The sum of the roots is 0, and their product is -2.

$a[x^2 - 0x + (-2)] = 0.$

Setting a equal to 1 results in one possible answer:

$x^2 - 2 = 0.$ (*Answer*)

EXAMPLE:

Find a quadratic equation with integral coefficients having roots $4 + i$ and $4 - i$.

The sum of the roots is: $4 + i + 4 - i = 8$.

The product of the roots is: $(4 + i)(4 - i) = 16 - i^2 = 17$.

$a(x^2 - 8x + 17) = 0$.

Setting a equal to 1 results in one possible answer:

$x^2 - 8x + 17 = 0$.   (*Answer*)

INVERSE FUNCTIONS

The **inverse of a function** is denoted by f^{-1} and satisfies the compositions $f(f^{-1}(x)) = x$ and $f^{-1}(f(x)) = x$. All functions have an inverse, but the inverse is not necessarily a function (i.e., it doesn't have to pass the Vertical Line Test.) A function has an inverse that is also a function, however, if the original function passes the **Horizontal Line Test.** This means that if every horizontal line intersects the graph of a function in *at most* one point, then the inverse of the original function is also a function.

If (a, b) is a point on the graph of f, then (b, a) is a point on the graph of f^{-1}. In other words, the domain of f equals the range of f^{-1}, and the range of f equals the domain of f^{-1}. Because of this property, the graphs of f and f^{-1} are reflections of each other with respect to the line $y = x$. Some examples of functions and their inverse functions are as follows:

$f(x) = x + 2$. $f^{-1}(x) = x - 2$.

$g(x) = \dfrac{(x + 3)}{2}$. $g^{-1}(x) = 2x - 3$.

$h(x) = x^3 - 1$. $h^{-1}(x) = \sqrt[3]{x + 1}$.

$f(x) = x^2$.   no inverse function

$g(x) = \dfrac{1}{x}$. $g^{-1}(x) = \dfrac{1}{x}$.

$h(x) = \sqrt{x}$. $h^{-1}(x) = x^2$.

On your graphing calculator, graph $y_1 =$ one of the given functions above, $y_2 =$ its inverse function, and $y_3 = x$ to see that the function and its inverse are reflections, or "mirror images," of each other over the line $y = x$. Notice that the squaring function, $f(x) = x^2$, does not have an inverse function because it doesn't pass the Horizontal Line Test. The square root function, $h(x) = \sqrt{x}$, does, however, have an inverse function because its domain is restricted to $x \geq 0$.

To solve for the inverse of a function algebraically, interchange y and x, and solve for the new y value. This is the inverse function, if an inverse function exists. For example, take $f(x) = \dfrac{x + 4}{2}$. Replacing $f(x)$ by y results in: $y = \dfrac{x + 4}{2}$.

Now interchange x and y and solve for y:

$$x = \frac{y + 4}{2}.$$

$$2x = y + 4.$$

$$2x - 4 = y.$$

$$f^{-1} = 2x - 4.$$

Check your answer by graphing f and f^{-1} to see that they are reflections over the line $y = x$.

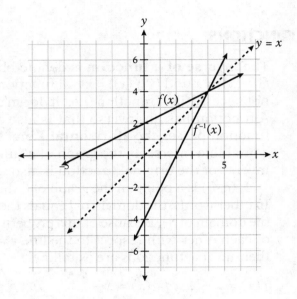

EXAMPLE:

If $f(x) = \dfrac{x + 6}{3}$, and f^{-1} is the inverse function of f, what is $f^{-1}(-1)$?

$$f(x) = \frac{x + 6}{3}.$$

$$y = \frac{x + 6}{3}.$$

$$x = \frac{y + 6}{3}.$$

$$3x = y + 6.$$

$$3x - 6 = y.$$

$$f^{-1} = 3x - 6.$$

$$f^{-1}(-1) = 3(-1) - 6 = -9. \qquad (Answer)$$

An alternate solution is to set $\dfrac{x + 6}{3} = -1$. If $(-1, n)$ is a point on the graph of the inverse function, then $(n, -1)$ must be a point on the graph of the original function. By either method, $f^{-1}(-1) = -9$.

EXAMPLE:

If $f(x) = 4x - 1$, then what is $f^{-1}(x)$?

Interchange the x and y values in the function, $f(x) = 4x - 1$ and solve for y.

$y = 4x - 1$.

$x = 4y - 1$.

$x + 1 = 4y$.

$f(x)^{-1} = \dfrac{x + 1}{4}$.   (*Answer*)

EXAMPLE:

If $g(x) = x^4$, then what is $g^{-1}(x)$?

$y = x^4$.

$x = y^4$.

$\pm\sqrt[4]{x} = y$. There is not a one-to-one correspondence between x and y values.

No inverse function.   (*Answer*)

RATIONAL FUNCTIONS

A **rational function** is defined by a rational (i.e., fractional) expression in one variable and can be written as $f(x) = \dfrac{p(x)}{q(x)}$. Unlike the linear and quadratic functions that have been discussed thus far in this chapter, rational functions are not continuous.

They contain a break in the graph at the point where the denominator equals zero. (Limits of rational functions are discussed in the Numbers and Operations chapter.) The graph of a rational function f has **vertical asymptotes** at the zeroes of the denominator $q(x)$.

EXAMPLE:

Find the domain of $f(x) = \dfrac{x^2 - 4}{x^2 - 4x}$.

The domain is the set of x values for which the function is defined, so $x^2 - 4x$ cannot equal zero.

$x^2 - 4x = 0$.

$x(x - 4) = 0$.

$x = 0$ or $x = 4$.

The domain is all real numbers except $x = 0$ and $x = 4$.   (*Answer*)

Note that the graph of $f(x) = \dfrac{x^2 - 4}{x^2 - 4x}$ has vertical asymptotes at $x = 0$ and $x = 4$. Many graphing calculators do not handle asymptotes well, so you may get a graph that appears to be continuous with "zigzags" at $x = 0$ and $x = 4$. The graph should be discontinuous at $x = 0$ and $x = 4$ because the function is undefined at these domain values. On a TI graphing calculator, try changing the Mode to Dot, instead of Connected, to view the graph better.

EXAMPLE:

Find the zeroes of $f(x) = \dfrac{x^3 - 3x}{x^2 - 9}$.

The zeroes of the function occur when $f(x) = 0$, or, in other words, at the x-intercepts of the graph.

$0 = \dfrac{x^3 - 3x}{x^2 - 9}$.

$0 = x^3 - 3x. \quad (x \neq \pm 3)$.

$0 = x(x^2 - 3)$.

$0 = x \quad$ or $\quad x^2 = 3$

$\qquad\qquad\qquad x = \pm\sqrt{3}$.

The zeroes are: $0, -\sqrt{3}, \sqrt{3}$.   (*Answer*)

EXAMPLE:

What are the equations of the asymptotes of $f(x) = \dfrac{x^3}{x^2 - 1}$?

Vertical asymptotes occur at the zeroes of the denominator.

$x^2 - 1 = 0$

$x = \pm\sqrt{1} = \pm 1$

Note there are no horizontal asymptotes, since the degree of the numerator is greater than the degree of the denominator.

$x = 1$ and $x = -1$.   (*Answer*)

HIGHER-DEGREE POLYNOMIAL FUNCTIONS

A **polynomial function** of x with degree n is given by:

$f(x) = a_n x^n + a_{n-1}x^{n-1} + \cdots + a_2 x^2 + a_1 x^1 + a_0$.

where n is a non-negative number, the coefficients of the x terms are real numbers, and $a_n \neq 0$.

A first-degree polynomial function is a **linear function:** $f(x) = ax + b\ (a \neq 0)$.

A second-degree polynomial function is a **quadratic function:** $f(x) = ax^2 + bx + c\ (a \neq 0)$.

The graphs of polynomial functions share the following properties.

1. They are continuous.

2. They have rounded curves.

3. If n (the highest exponent) is odd, and $a_n > 0$, the graph falls to the left and rises to the right.

4. If n (the highest exponent) is odd, and $a_n < 0$, the graph rises to the left and falls to the right.

5. If n (the highest exponent) is even, and $a_n > 0$, the graph rises to the left and right.

6. If n (the highest exponent) is even, and $a_n < 0$, the graph falls to the left and right.

Properties 3 through 6 describe what is known as the **Leading Coefficient Test,** which describes the right and left behavior of the graphs of functions.

EXAMPLE:

Determine the right and left behavior of the graph of $f(x) = -x^3 + 7x$.

The degree of the function is odd ($n = 3$) and its leading coefficient is -1. As $x \to -\infty$, $y \to \infty$, and as $x \to \infty$, $y \to -\infty$.

The graph rises to the left and falls to the right.   (*Answer*)

The **zeroes of a polynomial function** are the x-values when $f(x) = 0$. A function of degree n has at most n real zeroes.

EXAMPLE:

Find the real zeroes of $f(x) = x^3 - 2x^2 - 8x$.

Because $f(x)$ is a 3rd degree function, it can have, at most, 3 zeroes.

$x^3 - 2x^2 - 8x = 0$.

$x(x^2 - 2x - 8) = 0$.

$x(x - 4)(x + 2) = 0$.

$x = 0$, $x = 4$, and $x = -2$.   (*Answer*)

EXAMPLE:

Find the real zeroes of $f(x) = -x^4 + 2x^3 - x^2$.

Because $f(x)$ is a 4th degree function, it can have, at most, 4 zeroes.

$-x^4 + 2x^3 - x^2 = 0$.

$-x^2(x^2 - 2x + 1) = 0$.

$-x^2(x - 1)^2 = 0$.

$x = 0$ and $x = 1$.   (*Answer*)

Note that both $x = 0$ and $x = 1$ are **repeated zeroes.** Because n is even, the graph touches the x-axis at these points, but it does not cross the x-axis. (If n were odd, the graph would cross the x-axis at the repeated zeroes.)

Long division and synthetic division are also useful in factoring and finding the zeroes of polynomial functions.

EXAMPLE:

Divide $2x^3 - 9x^2 + 7x + 6$ by $x - 2$.

Let's divide using synthetic division:

$$
\begin{array}{r|rrrr}
2 & 2 & -9 & 7 & 6 \\
  &   & 4 & -10 & -6 \\
\hline
  & 2 & -5 & -3 & 0
\end{array}
$$

The rightmost digit, 0, is the remainder. This means that $x - 2$ divides evenly into $2x^3 - 9x^2 + 7x$.

The quotient is $2x^2 - 5x - 3$.   (*Answer*)

The **Division Algorithm** states that:

$$f(x) = d(x)q(x) + r(x),$$

where $d(x)$ is the divisor, $q(x)$ is the quotient, and $r(x)$ is the remainder. Applying this algorithm to the last example results in:

$$f(x) = (x - 2)(2x^2 - 5x - 3).$$

You can further factor $2x^2 - 5x - 3$ to get:

$$f(x) = (x - 2)(2x + 1)(x - 3).$$

Using synthetic division helps to factor polynomials that are not special products and easily factorable.

Some properties that are important in evaluating polynomial functions are:

1. **The Remainder Theorem:** If a polynomial $f(x)$ is divided by $x - r$, then the remainder, r, equals $f(r)$.

2. **The Factor Theorem:** A polynomial $f(x)$ has a factor $x - k$ if and only if $f(k) = 0$.

3. **Descartes Rule of Signs:** The number of *positive* real zeroes of a function is equal to the number of variations in sign of $f(x)$ or less than that number by an even integer. The number of *negative* real zeroes of a function is equal to the number of variations in sign of $f(-x)$ or less than that number by an even integer. (A variation in sign means that consecutive coefficients have opposite signs.)

4. **Rational Root Test:** If a polynomial function has integer coefficients, every rational zero of the function has the form $\left(\dfrac{p}{q} \right)$ (simplified to lowest terms) where $p = $ a factor of the constant term a_0, and $q = $ a factor of the leading coefficient a_n.

5. **Complex Zeroes Occur in Conjugate Pairs:** If a polynomial function has real coefficients and $a + bi$ ($b \neq 0$) is a zero of the function, then $a - bi$ is also a zero.

EXAMPLE:

Using the rational root theorem, how many possible rational roots are there for $x^4 + 2x^3 + 3x^2 + 5x + 10 = 0$?

The constant term is 10, so it can be factored as 1×10 or 2×5.

The leading coefficient is 1, so it can only be factored as 1×1.

Rational roots have the form $\left(\dfrac{p}{q} \right)$ where p is a factor of 10, and q is a factor of 1, so possible factors are: $\pm 1, \pm 2, \pm 5, \pm 10$.

There are 8 possible rational roots.　　　(*Answer*)

EXAMPLE:

Find a polynomial function of lowest degree with real coefficients if two of its roots are 2 and $3 + i$.

Because complex zeroes occur in conjugate pairs, $3 - i$ is also a zero of the function. Write the function as a product of its three factors, and then multiply to determine the function.

$f(x) = (x - 2)[x - (3 + i)][x - (3 - i)]$.

$f(x) = (x - 2)[(x - 3) + i][(3 - i) - i]$

$f(x) = (x - 2)[(x - 3)^2 - i^2]$

$f(x) = (x - 2)(x^2 - 6x + 9 - (-1))$

$f(x) = (x - 2)(x^2 - 6x + 10)$

$f(x) = x^3 - 8x^2 + 22x - 20$.　　　(*Answer*)

An alternative way to solve for the function is to recall that $x^2 - $ (sum of the roots)$x + $ (product of the roots) $= 0$. Using $3 - i + 3 + i = 6$ and $(3 - i)(3 + i) = 10$, you can quickly determine that the function is $(x - 2)(x^2 - 6x + 10) = x^3 - 8x^2 + 22x - 20$.

EXAMPLE:

How many possible positive real roots does the function $f(x) = 6x^3 - 5x^2 + 4x - 15$ have?

Use Descartes Rule of Signs to determine the number of possible positive and negative real roots.

$f(x) = 6x^3 - 5x^2 + 4x - 15$ has 3 variations in sign, so there are 3 or 1 positive roots.

$f(-x) = 6(-x)^3 - 5(-x)^2 + 4(-x) - 15 = = -6x^3 - 5x^2 - 4x - 15$ has 0 variations in sign, so there are no negative roots.

1 or 3 positive real roots are possible.　　　(*Answer*)

EXAMPLE:

Determine if $x = 2$ is a zero of the function $g(x) = x^3 - 7x + 6$.

If $x = 2$ is a zero of the function, then $x - 2$ must be a factor of the polynomial. By the factor theorem, if $g(2) = 0$, then $x - 2$ is, in fact, a factor of g.

$g(2) = (2)^3 - 7(2) + 6 = 8 - 14 + 6 = 0$.

2 is a zero of $g(x)$.   (*Answer*)

EXPONENTIAL FUNCTIONS

An exponential function f with base a is given by:

$f(x) = a^x$

where x is a real number, $a > 0$ and $a \neq 1$.
The graphs of $y = a^x$ and $y = a^{-x}$ are as follows:

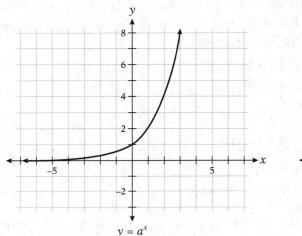
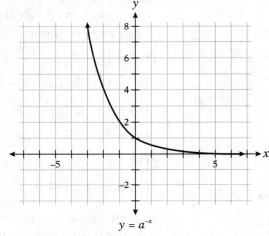

$$y = a^x \qquad\qquad\qquad\qquad y = a^{-x}$$

Notice that both have a y-intercept of 1 and a horizontal asymptote at $y = 0$. The graph of $y = a^{-x}$ is a reflection of the graph of $y = a^x$ over the y-axis.

EXAMPLE:

Use the properties of exponents to determine if the functions $f(x) = 27(3^{-x})$

and $g(x) = \left(\dfrac{1}{3}\right)^{x-3}$ are the same.

Review the properties of exponents given in the Algebra chapter if you're unsure of how to solve this problem.

$f(x) = 27(3^{-x}) = 3^3(3^{-x}) = 3^{3-x}$.

$g(x) = \left(\dfrac{1}{3}\right)^{x-3} = (3^{-1})^{x-3} = 3^{-x+3}$

$f(x)$ and $g(x)$ are the same functions.   (*Answer*)

EXAMPLE:

If $f(x) = 2^x$ and $g(x) = 3^x$, then determine when $3^x < 2^x$.

Both functions have a y-intercept of 0. Graph the functions on your graphing calculator (use the $\wedge$ button to raise 2 and 3 to the x power) to compare the curves. When $x > 0$, $3^x > 2^x$.

$3^x < 2^x$ when $x < 0$.   (*Answer*)

*LOGARITHMIC FUNCTIONS

A logarithmic function with base a is given by:

$$f(x) = \log_a x$$

where $x > 0$, $a > 0$, and $a \neq 1$.

If $y = \log_a x$ then $x = a^y$. A logarithm is an exponent. For example, $\log_2 16$ is the exponent to which 2 must be raised to get 16. Therefore, $\log_2 16 = 4$.

Try evaluating the following logarithms:

1. $\log_3 81 = 4$

2. $\log_{10} 0.1 = -1$

3. $\log_2 (-4) = $ undefined

4. $\log_4 4^{\frac{-5}{2}} = -\frac{5}{2}$

5. $\log_2 2\sqrt{2} = \frac{3}{2}$

6. $\log_9 3 = \frac{1}{2}$

7. $\log_5 1 = 0$.

The **properties of logarithms** are:

1. $\log_a 1 = 0$

2. $\log_a a = 1$

3. $\log_a a^x = x$

4. $\log_a (pq) = \log_a p + \log_a q$

5. $\log_a \left(\dfrac{p}{q} \right) = \log_a p - \log_a q$

6. $\log_a p^x = x \log_a p$

7. $a^{\log_a p} = p$

Logarithmic functions in base 10 are called **common logarithmic functions.** The log button on your calculator calculates common logs. For example, try entering log 100 into your calculator. Although the base is not written, it is assumed to be base 10. $\log_{10} 100 = 2$.

The **Change of Base Formula** states that:

$$\log_a x = \frac{\log_b x}{\log_b a},$$

where a, b, and x are positive real numbers and a and $b \neq 1$.

With the Change of Base Formula, you can use your calculator to evaluate logs in any base, not just base 10.

$$\log_2 7 = \frac{\log_{10} 7}{\log_{10} 2} = 2.807.$$

$$\log_3 35 = \frac{\log_{10} 35}{\log_{10} 3} = 3.236.$$

EXAMPLE:

Simplify $\log_5 150 - \log_5 6$.

$$\log_5 150 - \log_5 6 = \log_5 \frac{150}{6} = \log_5 25 = 2.$$

2.   (*Answer*)

EXAMPLE:

Simplify $\log_4 2 + \log_4 8$.

$$\log_4 2 - \log_4 8 = \log_4 2(8) = \log_4 16 = 2.$$

2.   (*Answer*)

EXAMPLE:

Use the properties of logarithms to express $\log_b \left(\dfrac{N^6}{M^4} \right)^{\frac{1}{3}}$ in terms of $\log_b M$ and $\log_b N$.

$$\log_b = \left(\frac{N^6}{M^4} \right)^{\frac{1}{3}} = \frac{1}{3}\left[\log_b \left(\frac{N^6}{M^4} \right) \right].$$

$$= \frac{1}{3}(\log_b N^6 - \log_b M^4).$$

$$= \frac{1}{3}(\log_b N^6 - \log_b M^4) = \frac{1}{3}(6\log_b N - 4\log_b M).$$

$$= 2\log_b N - \frac{4}{3}\log_b M. \qquad (\textit{Answer})$$

EXAMPLE:

Use the properties of logarithms to express $\log(x + 2) + 2\log x - \log(x - 4)$ as a single logarithm.

$$\log(x + 2) + 2\log x - \log(x - 4) = \log(x + 2) + \log x^2 - \log(x - 4)$$

$$= \log \frac{(x + 2)x^2}{x - 4}. \qquad (\textit{Answer})$$

E X A M P L E :

Solve $\log(x-1) - \log(x+1) = \log(x+5)$.

$\log(x-1) - \log(x+1) = \log(x+5)$.

$\log\dfrac{x-1}{x+1} = \log(x+5)$. This is true only when:

$\dfrac{x-1}{x+1} = x+5$.

$x-1 = (x+5)(x+1)$.

$x-1 = x^2 + 6x + 5$.

$0 = x^2 + 5x + 6$.

$0 = (x+3)(x+2)$.

$x = -3$ or $x = -2$.

But the logarithm function is undefined for both $x = -3$ and $x = -2$.

No solution.   (*Answer*)

The logarithmic function is the **inverse of the exponential function.** Recall that inverse functions are reflections of each other over the line $y = x$. Because of the nature of inverses, exponential equations can be solved by isolating the exponential expression and taking the logarithm of both sides. Logarithmic equations can be solved by rewriting the equation in exponential form and solving for the variable.

E X A M P L E :

Solve $6\log_3\left(\dfrac{x}{2}\right) = 11$.

$6\log_3\left(\dfrac{x}{2}\right) = 11$.

$\log_3\left(\dfrac{x}{2}\right) = \dfrac{11}{6}$.

Write the equation in exponential form to get:

$3^{\frac{11}{6}} = \dfrac{x}{2}$.

$2\left(3^{\frac{11}{6}}\right) = x$.

$x = 14.99$.   (*Answer*)

EXAMPLE:

Solve $6^{4x} = 1,000$.

Take the log of both sides to get:

$\log 6^{4x} = \log 1,000$.

$4x \log 6 = 3$.

$$x = \frac{3}{4 \log 6}$$

$x = 0.964$.   (*Answer*)

EXAMPLE:

Solve $3^{x-1} = \dfrac{1}{729}$.

Note that 729 can be written in base 3.

$3^{x-1} = \dfrac{1}{729} = \dfrac{1}{3}^6 = -3^{-6}$.

$3^{x-1} = -3^{-6}$.

When the bases are the same, simply set the exponents equal and solve for x.
    (You could also solve this equation by taking the log of both sides.)

$x - 1 = -6$.

$x = -5$.   (*Answer*)

*TRIGONOMETRIC FUNCTIONS

Trigonometric ratios, cofunctions, identities, and equations are covered in the Trigonometry chapter. Here we discuss trigonometric graphs. The graphs of all six trigonometric functions (sine, cosine, tangent, cosecant, secant, and cotangent) are periodic, meaning that the values of the functions repeat themselves at regular intervals. The sine, cosine, cosecant, and secant functions have periods of 2π, while the tangent and cotangent functions have periods of π. The graphs of sine and cosine are as follows:

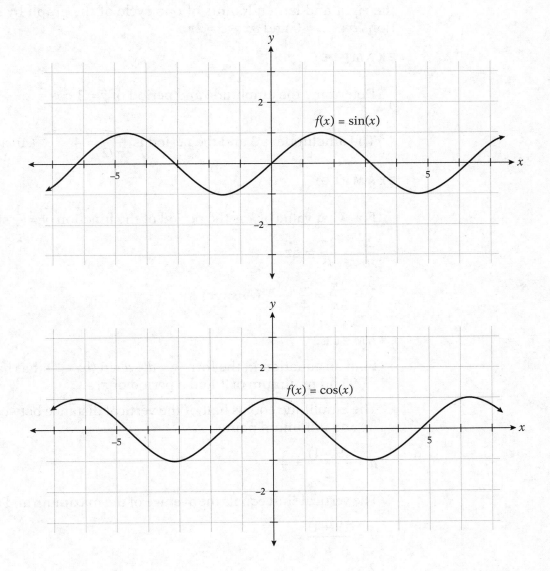

Sine is an odd function because it is symmetric with respect to the origin. Cosine is an even function because it is symmetric with respect to the y-axis. Notice that both curves are the same shape with the cosine curve equivalent to the sine curve shifted $\dfrac{\pi}{2}$ units left. Both curves also have a domain of all real numbers and a range of $-1 \le y \le 1$.

In general, the sine and cosine functions can be written as:

$$y = d + a \sin(bx - c) \quad \text{and} \quad y = d + a \cos(bx - c),$$

where d represents a vertical shift in the graph, a is the **amplitude** (the vertical stretching or shrinking), c is a horizontal shift in the graph, and b is the horizontal stretching or shrinking. $\frac{2\pi}{b}$ is the **period** of the function. The amplitude can also be thought of as half of the vertical distance between the maximum and minimum points on the graph, while the vertical shift can be thought of as the average of the maximum and minimum values. Use c to solve for the right and left endpoints of one cycle of the graph by solving the equations $bx - c = 0$ and $bx - c = 2\pi$.

EXAMPLE:

Determine the amplitude and period of $y = 3 \cos \frac{\pi}{2} x$.

The amplitude is 3 and the period is $\frac{2\pi}{\pi/2} = 4.$ (*Answer*)

EXAMPLE:

For what value of k is the period of the function $y = \frac{1}{2} \sin kx$ equal to 8π?

$$\frac{2\pi}{b} = \frac{2\pi}{k} = 8\pi.$$

$$k = \frac{2\pi}{8\pi} = \frac{1}{4}.$$ (*Answer*)

EXAMPLE:

Find an equation in the form $y = d + a \sin(bx - c)$ that has a maximum of 9 and minimum of 1 and a period of π.

The amplitude equals half of the vertical distance between the maximum and minimum points.

$$a = \frac{(9 - 1)}{2} = 4.$$

The vertical shift equals the average of the maximum and minimum values.

$$d = \frac{(9 + 1)}{2} = 5.$$

$\frac{2\pi}{b} = \pi$, so $b = 2$.

$y = 5 + 4 \sin 2x.$ (*Answer*)

(Note that $y = 5 + 4 \sin 2x$ is one possible equation where there is no horizontal shift in the graph and $a > 0$. There are, however, other possible answers.)

The tangent function is an odd function because it is symmetric with respect to the origin. It has a period of π and has asymptotes. Because $\tan x = \dfrac{\sin x}{\cos x}$, it is undefined when $\cos x = 0$. This occurs when $x = \dfrac{\pi}{2}$ or any odd multiple of $\dfrac{\pi}{2}$. As x approaches $\dfrac{\pi}{2}$, the tangent of x increases without bound. The graph of the tangent function is as follows:

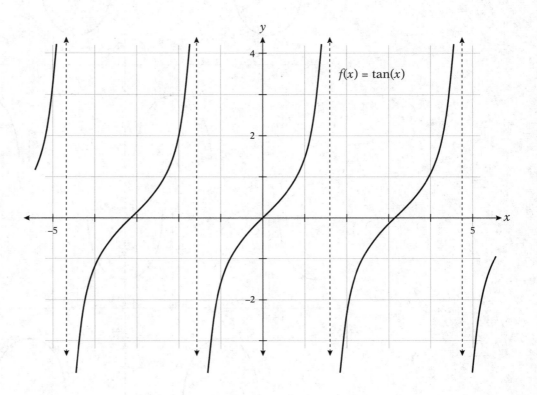

The domain of the tangent function is all real numbers except odd multiples of $\dfrac{\pi}{2}$, and its range is the set of all real numbers.

As with the graphs of sine and cosine, the tangent function can be written as:

$y = d + a \tan(bx - c)$,

where d represents a vertical shift in the graph, a is the vertical stretching or shrinking, c is a horizontal shift in the graph, and b is the horizontal stretching or shrinking. $\dfrac{\pi}{b}$ is the **period** of the function. Note that amplitude of a tangent function is undefined.

The graphs of the reciprocal functions, cosecant, secant, and cotangent, are shown below. The cosecant and cotangent functions have asymptotes at all multiples of π, while the secant function has asymptotes at all odd multiples of $\frac{\pi}{2}$.

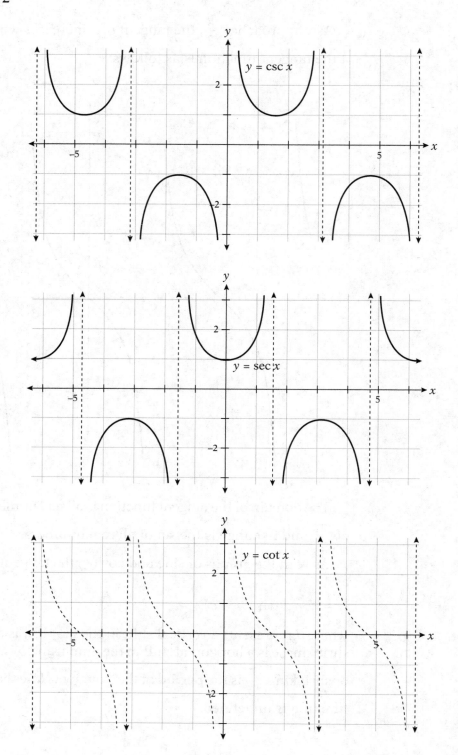

EXAMPLE:

What is the period of $y = \sec \frac{1}{2}x + 1$?

$$\frac{2\pi}{b} = \frac{2\pi}{\frac{1}{2}} = 4\pi. \qquad (Answer)$$

EXAMPLE:

For which values over the period $0 \le x < 2\pi$ is the function $y = 3\cot x$ undefined?

The cotangent is defined for all real numbers except multiples of π.

It is undefined at 0 and π.   (*Answer*)

*INVERSE TRIGONOMETRIC FUNCTIONS

The inverse trigonometric functions, arcsin ($\sin^{-1}$), arccos ($\cos^{-1}$), and arctan ($\tan^{-1}$), represent angle measures. As with any inverse function, their graphs are obtained by reflecting the original trigonometric functions over the line $y = x$. Recall that a function has an inverse if it passes the Horizontal Line Test. The trigonometric functions obviously do not pass this test, but they do have inverses on restricted domains.

The domain of $y = \sin^{-1} x$ is $-1 \le x \le 1$, and the range is $-\frac{\pi}{2} \le y \le \frac{\pi}{2}$.

The domain of $y = \cos^{-1} x$ is $-1 \le x \le 1$, and the range is $0 \le y \le \pi$.

The domain of $y = \tan^{-1} x$ is all real numbers, and the range is $-\frac{\pi}{2} \le y \le \frac{\pi}{2}$.

The graphs of these three inverse trigonometric functions are as follows (Figure 8-12):

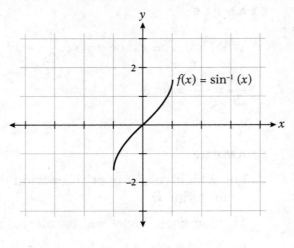

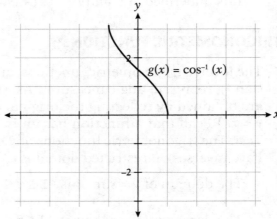

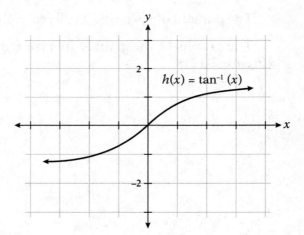

As with any inverse function, the compositions $f(f^{-1}(x)) = x$ and $f^{-1}(f(x))$ hold true. For their respective domains and ranges:

$\sin(\arcsin x) = x \quad \sin(\arcsin y) = y$

$\cos(\arccos x) = x \quad \cos(\arccos y) = y$

$\tan(\arctan x) = x \quad \tan(\arctan y) = y$

EXAMPLE:

Evaluate $\arcsin \dfrac{\sqrt{2}}{2}$.

The $\arcsin \dfrac{\sqrt{2}}{2}$ represents the angle whose sine is $\dfrac{\sqrt{2}}{2}$.

Because $\sin \dfrac{\pi}{4} = \dfrac{\sqrt{2}}{2}$, $\arcsin \dfrac{\sqrt{2}}{2} = \dfrac{\pi}{4}$. (*Answer*)

EXAMPLE:

Evaluate $\arcsin(\sin \pi)$.

$\arcsin(\sin y) = y$ is only valid for values of y in the interval $-\dfrac{\pi}{2} \le y \le \dfrac{\pi}{2}$.

π does not lie within the range of the arcsine function, but $\sin \pi = 0$.

$\arcsin(\sin \pi) = \arcsin(0) = 0$.

$\arcsin(\sin \pi) = 0$. (*Answer*)

EXAMPLE:

Evaluate $\tan(\arctan 4)$.

The domain of $\tan(\arctan x) = x$ is the set of all real numbers, so:

$\tan(\arctan 4) = 4$. (*Answer*)

EXAMPLE:

Evaluate $\sin(\arccos \dfrac{4}{5})$.

This is asking for the sine of the angle whose cosine is $\dfrac{4}{5}$. Think about a right triangle in quadrant I whose hypotenuse measures 5 and whose leg adjacent to the given angle measures 4.

The sine of the angle is $\dfrac{3}{5}$. (*Answer*)

*PERIODIC FUNCTIONS

A function is **periodic** if for every x in its domain there is some constant c such that:

$f(x + c) = f(x)$.

The smallest value of c is the period of the function. The sine and cosine functions, for example, are periodic and have a period of 2π.

EXAMPLE:

Part of the graph of a function f having period 2 is shown below. Sketch the graph of f on the interval $-4 \leq x \leq 4$.

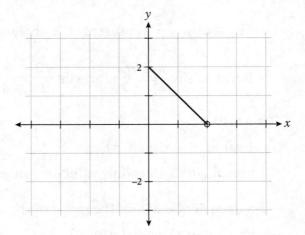

The given part of the graph represents one period. Repeat the graph to the right and left until you reach 4 and -4, respectively. The resulting graph is:

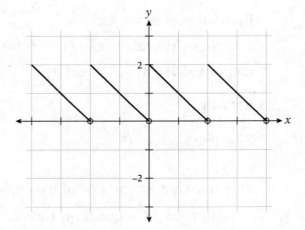

EXAMPLE:

Part of the graph of a function f having period 2 is shown below. Sketch the graph of f on the interval $-2 \leq x \leq 2$ given that the function is odd.

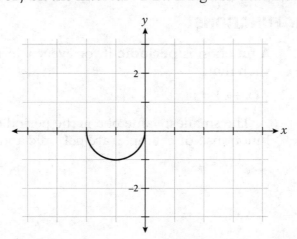

Recall that an odd function is symmetric with respect to the origin (versus an even function which is symmetric with respect to the y-axis.) Reflecting the given part of the function over the origin results in the following graph:

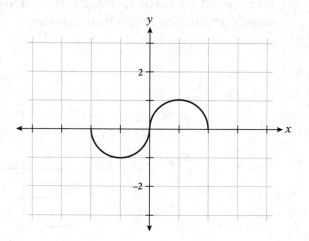

*PIECEWISE FUNCTIONS

A **piecewise function** has different rules for different intervals of its domain.

EXAMPLE:

Graph the piecewise function:

$$f(x) = \begin{cases} \dfrac{1}{2x} + 3 & \text{if } x < 0. \\ -x + 3 & \text{if } 0 \le x \le 3. \\ 3x - 9 & \text{if } x > 3. \end{cases}$$

The piecewise function has three parts and all of them are linear equations. The graph looks like the following:

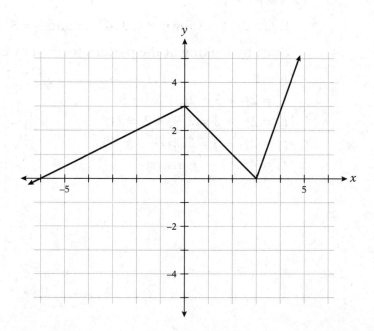

The **greatest integer function,** $f(x) = [x]$, is another example of a piecewise function. $f(x)$ equals the greatest integer less than or equal to x. $f(1.5) = [1.5] = 1$. $f(-0.5) = [-0.5] = -1$. The graph of the $f(x) = [x]$ jumps up one unit at each integer and is a horizontal segment between consecutive integers. Because of its vertical breaks, the greatest integer function is also called a step function. Its graph is as follows:

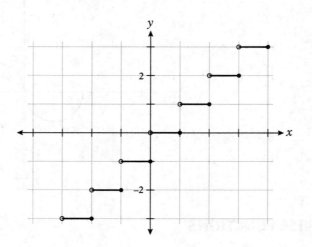

*RECURSIVE FUNCTIONS

A **recursive function** defines the terms in a sequence by relating each term to the previous ones.

The **Fibonacci Sequence** 1, 1, 2, 3, 5, 8, 13, . . . can be defined recursively as:

$a_n = a_{n-2} + a_{n-1}$ where $n \geq 2$, $a_0 = 1$ and $a_1 = 1$.

A **factorial** can also be thought of as being recursive because $n! = 1 \times 2 \times 3 \times 4 \ldots (n - 1) \times n$. In other words, $n! = (n - 1)! \times n$.

EXAMPLE:

If $f_n = 2f_{n-1} + 3$ for $n = 2, 3, 4, \ldots$ and $f_1 = 3$, then what is f_4?

Start by looking at the pattern formed by consecutive terms.

$f_1 = 3$
$f_2 = 2f_1 + 3 = 2(3) + 3 = 9$.
$f_3 = 2f_2 + 3 = 2(9) + 3 = 21$.
$f_4 = 2f_3 + 3 = 2(21) + 3 = 45$.
$f_4 = 45$.   (*Answer*)

EXAMPLE:

If $f_{n+1} = f_{n-1} + 3f_n$ for $n = 2, 3, 4, \ldots$ and $f_1 = 1$ and $f_2 = 2$, then what is f_5?

Because you are given the first two terms of the sequence, you can define the other terms using these.

$f_1 = 1$.
$f_2 = 2$.
$f_3 = f_1 + 3f_2 = 1 + 3(2) = 7$.
$f_4 = f_2 + 3f_3 = 2 + 3(7) = 23$.
$f_5 = f_3 + 3f_4 = 7 + 3(23) = 76$.
$f_5 = 76$.   (*Answer*)

*PARAMETRIC FUNCTIONS

The content in this chapter has focused on graphs involving two variables, x and y, but it is also possible to express x and y in terms of a *third* variable. This third variable is called a **parameter**. Examples of parametric equations are as follows:

$x = 12t$.
$y = -2t^2 + 12t$.

Substituting values for the parameter results in ordered pairs (x, y), which are points on the graph of the function. A curve represented by a pair of parametric equations is still plotted in an xy-coordinate plane. Plotting points as t increases gives the curve in a certain direction, which is called its orientation.

EXAMPLE:

Graph the curve determined by the parametric equations $x = t^2 - 1$ and $y = 3t$ on the interval $0 \leq t \leq 4$.

Substitute values of t to determine points on the curve.

t	0	1	2	3	4
x	−1	0	3	8	15
y	0	3	6	9	12

Now, plot the points in order to get the following graph:

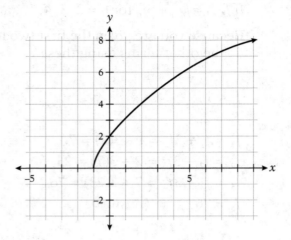

Parametric equations can also be graphed by finding an equation in terms of x and y that has the same graph. When eliminating the parameter, check the domain of the new function, since the resulting graph may contain points that are not on the graph of the original parametric equations.

EXAMPLE:

Eliminate the parameter and write the rectangular equation whose graph represents the parametric curve $x = t^2$ and $y = 4t^2 - 1$.

Substitute $x = t^2$ into the equation for y to get:

$y = 4x - 1$.

The equation is linear. The domains of the original parametric equations show that $x \geq 0$ and $y \geq -1$, however, because squaring t always results in a positive value. The domain of the rectangular equation must be $x \geq 0$.

$y = 4x - 1$ and $x \geq 0$.   (*Answer*)

CHAPTER 9

DATA ANALYSIS, STATISTICS, AND PROBABILITY

This chapter provides a review of elementary statistics. On the Level 2 test, 6–10% of the questions relate specifically to data analysis, statistics, and probability. The statistics problems on the Level 2 test focus on measures of central tendency, range, graphs and plots, regression, and basic probability. Counting problems are included in the Numbers and Operations chapter. The pie chart shows approximately how much of the Level 2 test is related to data analysis, statistics, and probability:

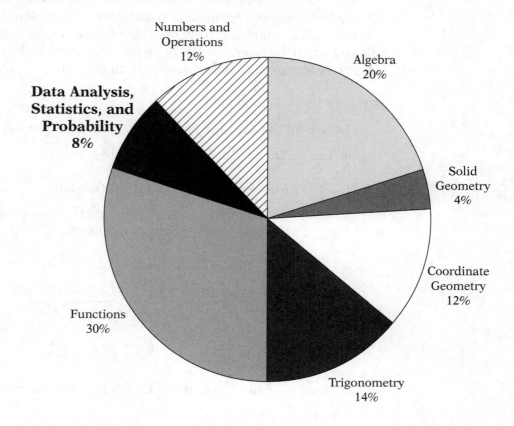

The following topics are covered in this chapter:

1. Mean, Median, Mode

2. Range

3. Interquartile Range

4. *Standard Deviation

5. Data Interpretation

---

*Denotes concepts that are on the Level 2 test only.

6. Regression
   a. Linear Regression
   b. *Quadratic Regression
   c. *Exponential Regression

7. Probability

MEAN, MEDIAN, MODE

Three different statistics are commonly used to measure central tendency. They are:

Mean—the average of the numbers
Median—the middle number (when the data is ordered)
Mode—the number that occurs the most

The mean is calculated by finding the sum of all the terms and dividing by the total number of terms. After the data are ordered, the median is simply the middle value of an odd number of terms or the average of the two middle values for an even number of terms. The mode is the most frequent value. It is possible for data to have more than one mode.

EXAMPLE:

The ages of the starting players on a high school soccer team are as follows:

14, 15, 15, 16, 16, 16, 17, 17, 17, 17, 18

Find the mean, median, and mode of the data.

1. Mean—Calculate the mean by finding the sum of all the ages and dividing that by the number of ages in question.

   The mean is

   $$\frac{14 + 15 + 15 + 16 + 16 + 16 + 17 + 17 + 17 + 17 + 18}{11}$$

   $$= \frac{178}{11} \approx 16.18.$$

2. Median—The 6th term of 11 total terms is the middle number.

   The median is 16.

3. Mode—17 occurs 4 times in the given data.

   The mode is 17.

   Mean ≈ 16.18, Median = 16, Mode = 17.   (*Answer*)

---

*Denotes concepts that are on the Level 2 test only.

EXAMPLE:

Sarah has test scores of 65, 78, 81, 82, and 90. What must she score on her 6th test to maintain an average score of 80?

Let x be Sarah's 6th test score. Because you know the average, or mean, of the data, set up an equation equal to 80 and solve for x.

$$80 = \frac{65 + 78 + 81 + 82 + 90 + x}{6}.$$

$$80 = \frac{396 + x}{6}.$$

$$480 = 396 + x.$$

$$84 = x.$$

Sarah must score 84 on her 6th test.   (*Answer*)

EXAMPLE:

Find the median and mode of the following distribution:

0, 0, 1, 4, 6, 8, 8, 9

The mode is the number that occurs the most. Because both 0 and 8 occur twice, each number is a mode.

The median is the middle number. Because there's an *even* number of terms in the given distribution, the median cannot be one of the given terms. Instead, find the median by adding the 4th and 5th terms and dividing by two. (In essence, you're finding the average of the two terms because the middle occurs between them.) The median is:

$$\frac{4 + 6}{2} = 5.$$

The mode is 0 and 8, and the median is 5.   (*Answer*)

RANGE

Range is a simple measure of data dispersion. **Range** is the difference between the largest and smallest data values. Take Sarah's test scores of 65, 78, 81, 82, and 90 from one of the previous examples. The range of her scores is 25. $90 - 65 = 25$.

EXAMPLE:

Given the daily high temperatures for the week are: 61°, 65°, 76°, 69°, 60°, 72°, and 69°, what is the range of the data?

The highest temperature is 76° and the lowest temperature is 60°, so the range is:

$$76 - 60 = 16.   (\textit{Answer})$$

EXAMPLE:

If the mean of the set of data 2, 5, 7, 9, 10, and x is 8, what is the range?
Since the mean is 8:

$$\frac{2+5+7+9+10+x}{6} = 8$$

$$33 + x = 48$$

$$x = 48 - 33 = 15$$

The range is, therefore, $15 - 2 = 13$.   (*Answer*)

INTERQUARTILE RANGE

The interquartile range is most often used in box-and-whisker plots. To determine the quartiles of a given data, find three different medians: (a) the median of the entire data set, (b) the median of the lower half of the data, the lower quartile, and (c) the median of the upper half of the data, the upper quartile. The **interquartile range** is the difference between the upper and lower quartile data values.

EXAMPLE:

Thirteen students receive the following grades on a math test:

60, 78, 90, 67, 88, 92, 81, 100, 95, 83, 83, 86, 74

What is the interquartile range of the test scores?

Start by arranging the test scores in order of lowest to highest:

60, 67, 74, 78, 81, 83, 83, 86, 88, 90, 92, 95, 100

The median of the data is 83. To find the interquartile range, find the lower quartile by determining the median of the data to the left of the median, 83. Then, find the upper quartile by determining the median of the data to the right of the median, 83.

$$\text{Lower quartile} = \frac{74 + 78}{2} = 76.$$

$$\text{Upper quartile} = \frac{90 + 92}{2} = 91.$$

The interquartile range is $91 - 76 = 15$.   (*Answer*)

*STANDARD DEVIATION

Standard deviation is another measure of data dispersion. A deviation is the difference between a data value and the mean of the data set. The **standard deviation** is given by the formula:

$$\sigma = \sqrt{\frac{\text{sum of the squares of the deviations from the mean}}{\text{number of terms in the data set}}}$$

EXAMPLE:

What is the standard deviation of the following distribution: 8, 11, 11, 13, 14, 15?

The mean of the data is:

$$8 + 11 + 11 + 13 + 14 + \frac{15}{6} = \frac{72}{6} = 12.$$

Now, determine how much each score differs from the mean. Substitute theses deviations into the standard deviation formula to get:

$$\sigma = \sqrt{\frac{(-4)^2 + (-1)^2 + (-1)^2 + 1^2 + 2^2 + 3^2}{6}} = \sqrt{5.33}.$$

$$\sigma = 2.3. \qquad (Answer)$$

EXAMPLE:

If each score in a set of scores is increased by 5, which of the following would be true statements?

I.   The mean is increased by 5.
II. The mean is unchanged.
III. The standard deviation is increased by 5.
IV. The standard deviation is unchanged.

(A) I only
(B) III only
(C) I and III only
(D) II and IV only
(E) I and IV only

Because each score is increased by 5, the mean would also increase by 5. Statement I is, therefore, true. The difference of each of the terms in the new data set from the new mean is unchanged, however. The standard deviation remains unchanged. I and IV are true statements, so Answer E is the correct choice.

DATA INTERPRETATION

Data interpretation problems involve reading data from various graphs and plots, such as histograms, pie charts, frequency distributions, bar graphs, and other types of data displays.

EXAMPLE:

The following histogram shows students' scores on a given test.

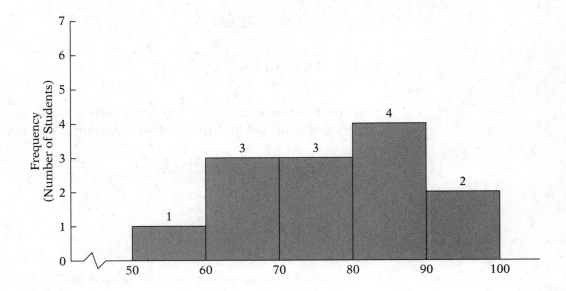

Each of the following is true EXCEPT

(A) The interval 80–89 contains the most scores.
(B) The median score is in the interval 70–79.
(C) 9 students scored 70 or above.
(D) 13 students took the test.
(E) One student got a 100%.

The most number of students scored in the interval between 80 and 89 between it is the highest bar in the histogram making answer A correct. There's not enough information to find the exact median of the data, but you can see that the middle term, the 7th term, falls in the interval between 70 and 79. Answer B is, therefore, also correct. Nine (3 + 4 + 2) students scored higher than 70, and 13 students (1 + 3 + 3 + 4 + 2) students took the test, so answers C and D are correct. That leaves E. On quickly looking at the graph, you may mistakenly think that the highest score on the test was a 100%. A histogram represents *intervals* of data, however. Two students scored in the highest interval, but you don't have enough information to conclude that a student received a 100%. E is the correct answer.

EXAMPLE:

The frequency distribution of the average daily temperatures in June is shown below. Determine the mean temperature. Round your answer to the nearest integer.

Temperature	Frequency
59	2
60	5
61	6
62	6
63	5
64	3
65	2
66	1

The mean is the sum of all the temperatures divided by the total number of days in question. Adding up the frequencies results in:

$2 + 5 + 6 + 6 + 5 + 3 + 2 + 1 = 30$ days.

June actually has 30 days, so this number makes sense. Now find the sum of the 30 given temperatures and divide by 30.

$$\frac{59(2) + 60(5) + 61(6) + 62(6) + 63(5) + 64(3) + 65(2) + 66(1)}{30}$$

$$= \frac{1,859}{30}$$

$$\approx 61.97$$

62 degrees.   (*Answer*)

REGRESSION

Three different regressions are included on the Level 2 test: Linear, Quadratic, and Exponential. In regression problems, you are asked to determine the model that best fits a set of data. Linear models are in the form: $y = ax + b$. Quadratic models are in the form: $y = ax^2 + bx + c$. Lastly, exponential models are in the form: $y = ab^x$.

All three can be determined by using the LinReg, QuadReg, and ExpReg functions under STAT—CALC on your TI graphing calculator.

Linear Regression

The line of best fit, or the **linear regression line,** is the line, $y = ax + b$, that best represents the relationship between the data sets in a scatter plot.

EXAMPLE:

> The students at Crawford High School volunteer each week as part of the school's community service program. If the scatter plot below represents the number of hours volunteered each week, which of the following equations best represents the line of best fit?

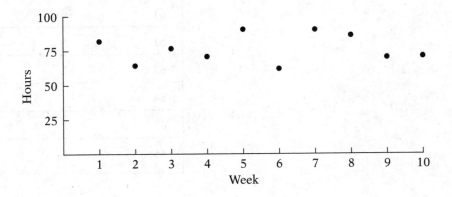

> (A) $y = 5x + 25$
> (B) $y = -5x + 25$
> (C) $y = 25x$
> (D) $y = 5x + 75$
> (E) $y = 75$

> The line that best represent the data is a horizontal line whose y-intercept is approximately 75. Answer E is the correct choice.
> Now, let's try an example using the LinReg feature of your TI graphing calculator.

EXAMPLE:

> The table below shows the number of running shoes sold by a certain manufacturer from 2001 to 2005. Find the line of best fit for the data.

Year	Number of Shoes Sold (millions)
2001	4.0
2002	4.8
2003	5.7
2004	5.9
2005	6.5

First, enter the data into List 1 and List 2 of your calculator. Let 2000 correspond to $x = 0$. Press STAT, ENTER and enter the x values in L1 and the y values in L2.

Then, find the equation of the line of best fit by pressing STAT, CALC, 4 LinReg, and ENTER. Your screen should show the following:

LinReg

$y = ax + b$

$a = .61$

$b = 3.55$

The line of best fit is $y = 0.61x + 3.55$.   (*Answer*)

Although it was not asked in this problem, you can graph the line and the scatter plot to check your equation. Press Y=, VARS, 5 Statistics, >, >, and 1 RegEQ to enter the regression equation. Then, press 2nd STAT PLOT, 1, ENTER to turn on Plot 1 and select L1 as Xlist and L2 as Ylist. Press GRAPH to display both the scatter plot and the line of best fit. (Press ZOOM 9 to automatically adjust the window to the data entered.)

*Quadratic Regression

The **quadratic regression model,** is the parabola, $y = ax^2 + bx + c$, that best represents the relationship between the data sets in a scatter plot. Let's use the QuadReg feature of your TI graphing calculator to find the quadratic equation that best represents the given data.

EXAMPLE:

The table below shows the participation in soccer in the United States from 1975 to 2000. Find the quadratic model for the data.

Year	Participants in Soccer (millions)
1975	12.1
1980	10.2
1985	9.4
1990	12.6
1995	15.0
2000	19.3

First, enter the data into List 1 and List 2 of your calculator. Let 1900 correspond to $x = 0$. Press STAT, ENTER and enter the x values in L1 and the y values in L2.

Then, find the equation of the parabola of best fit by pressing STAT, CALC, 5 QuadReg, and ENTER. Your screen should show the following: (Here it is rounded to 2 decimal places.)

QuadReg

$y = ax^2 + bx + c$

$a = .03$

$b = -5.17$

$c = 223.55$

The quadratic model for the data is $y = 0.03x^2 - 5.17x + 223.55$.   (*Answer*)

Again, although it was not asked in this problem, you can graph the parabola and the scatter plot to check your equation. Press Y=, VARS, 5 Statistics, >, >, and 1 RegEQ to enter the regression equation. Then, press 2nd STAT PLOT, 1, ENTER to turn on Plot 1 and select L1 as Xlist and L2 as Ylist. Press GRAPH to display both the scatter plot and the parabola of best fit. (Press ZOOM 9 to automatically adjust the window to the data entered.)

*Exponential Regression

The **exponential regression model,** is the exponential curve, $y = ab^x$, that best represents the relationship between the data sets in a scatter plot. Let's use the ExpReg feature of your TI graphing calculator to find the exponential equation that best represents the given data.

EXAMPLE:

Find the exponential function that best fits the data in the table below.

x	0	1	2	3	4	5
y	3	3.3	3.7	4.5	5.2	6.4

First, enter the data into List 1 and List 2 of your calculator. Press STAT, ENTER and enter the x values in L1 and the y values in L2.
Then, find the equation of the exponential curve of best fit by pressing STAT, CALC, 0 ExpReg, and ENTER. Your screen should show the following: (Here it is rounded to 2 decimal places.)

ExpReg

$y = a*b^x$

$a = 2.87$

$b = 1.17$

The exponential model for the data is $y = 2.87(1.17)^x$.   (*Answer*)

You can graph the exponential curve and the scatter plot to check your equation. Press Y =, VARS, 5 Statistics, >, >, and 1 RegEQ to enter the regression equation. Then, press 2nd STAT PLOT, 1, ENTER to turn on Plot 1 and select L1 as Xlist and L2 as Ylist. Press GRAPH to display both the scatter plot and the best-fitting exponential function. (Press ZOOM 9 to automatically adjust the window to the data entered.)

PROBABILITY

An **experiment** is an occurrence in which you do not necessarily get the same results when it is repeated under similar conditions. The **sample space** is the set of all possible outcomes of an experiment. When you toss a coin, the possible outcomes are heads, H, or tails, T. The sample space of a coin toss is written as $\{H, T\}$. The sample space for rolling a die, for example, is $\{1, 2, 3, 4, 5, 6\}$. An **event** is a set of outcomes and is a subset of the sample space.

If all outcomes are equally likely, the **probability** that an event, E, occurs is:

$$P(E) = \frac{\text{the number of possible outcomes of } E}{\text{the total number of possible outcomes}}.$$

EXAMPLE:

Two dice are rolled. Find the probability that the sum of the two numbers is less than 4.

When the two dice are rolled there are:

$6 \times 6 = 36$ total possible outcomes.

The sum of the two dice must, however, be less than 4. If the first die is a 1, the second could be 1 or 2. If the first die is 2, the second die could be a 1. If the first die is a 3, 4, 5, or, 6, there are no possibilities that the second roll will result in a sum of less than 4. The possible outcomes are therefore:

$\{(1, 1), (1, 2), (2, 1)\}$

The probability is $\dfrac{\text{the number of possible outcomes}}{\text{the total number of possible outcomes}} = \dfrac{3}{36} = \dfrac{1}{12}.$

$\dfrac{1}{12}.$ (*Answer*)

EXAMPLE:

The are 12 pieces of colored chalk in a package—3 white, 3 yellow, 3 orange, and 3 green. If two pieces are selected at random, find the probability that both will be yellow.

The probability of choosing the first yellow piece of chalk is:

$$P(Y_1) = \frac{3}{12} = \frac{1}{4}$$

Once one piece is chosen, there are only 11 pieces left in the package. The probability of choosing the second piece of yellow chalk is:

$$P(Y_2) = \frac{2}{11}$$

The answer is therefore: $\frac{1}{4}\left(\frac{2}{11}\right) = \frac{2}{44} = \frac{1}{22}$

$\frac{1}{22}$.   *(Answer)*

Notice that in the previous problem the first piece of chalk is *not replaced* before the second is drawn. This decreases the total number of outcomes to 11 when the second piece of chalk is selected.

EXAMPLE:

The probability of passing this week's math test is 70%, and the probability of passing this week's English test is 80%. What is the probability of failing both tests?

To get the probability that an event will NOT occur, subtract the probability that the event *will* occur from 1.

The probability of not passing this week's math test is: 1 – 70% = 30%.

The probability of not passing this week's English test is: 1 – 80% = 20%.

Notice that these are **independent events,** meaning that passing the math test is not dependent on how you do on the English test and vice versa. Multiply the probability of not passing both tests to get:

30%(20%) = 6%

6%.   *(Answer)*

EXAMPLE:

The probability that Juan does his math homework tonight is $\frac{2}{5}$, that Nicole does her homework is $\frac{9}{10}$, and that Amy does her homework is $\frac{7}{9}$. What is the probability that at least one of them does their homework tonight?

These are independent events, since any one person doing their homework does not affect the other students doing theirs. Since the problem asks for the probability that at least one student does their homework, you need to consider one student, 2 students, and all 3 students doing their homework. The easiest way to solve the problem is to determine the probability that *none* of them do their homework.

The probability that Juan does NOT do his homework is $1 - \frac{2}{5} = \frac{3}{5}$.

The probability that Nicole does NOT do her homework is $1 - \frac{9}{10} = \frac{1}{10}$.

The probability that Amy does NOT do her homework is $1 - \frac{7}{9} = \frac{2}{9}$.

The probability that none of them do their homework is therefore:

$$\frac{3}{5} \times \frac{1}{10} \times \frac{2}{9} = \frac{1}{75}.$$

The probability that at least one student does their homework is:

$$1 - \frac{1}{75} = \frac{74}{75}. \qquad (Answer)$$

CHAPTER 10
NUMBERS AND OPERATIONS

This chapter provides a review of number sense and operations. On the Level 2 test, 10–14% of the questions relate to Numbers and Operations (formerly called Miscellaneous topics). These questions cover items outside the realm of the algebra, geometry, trigonometry, and statistics found on the rest of the test.

The College Board claims that students are not expected to have studied every topic on the SAT Math Level 2 test. You should expect some test questions, especially those under the Numbers and Operations category, to seem unfamiliar to you.

The pie chart shows approximately how much of the Level 2 test is related to Numbers and Operations:

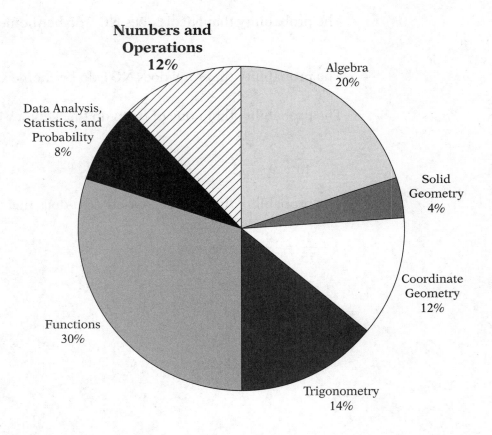

The following topics are covered in this chapter:

1. Invented Operations
2. "In Terms of" Problems
3. Ratio and Proportion
4. Complex Numbers
5. Counting Problems

6. Number Theory
7. Logic
8. Matrices
9. Sequences
   a. Arithmetic Sequences
   b. Geometric Sequences
10. *Series
11. *Vectors
12. *Limits

▉ INVENTED OPERATIONS

"Invented operations" appear often in standardized tests. This type of question introduces a new symbol that represents a made up mathematical operation. Think back to learning what the symbols $+, -, \times, \div, \sqrt{}$ represent. When presented with a plus sign, $+$, you learned to add the number on the left of the symbol to the number on the right. Don't panic when the symbol presented in one of these problems looks unfamiliar. It should, because the symbol is made up for the problem.

EXAMPLE:

The operation ◉ is defined for all real numbers x and y by the equation:

x ◉ $y = 4x + \dfrac{y^2}{2}$. If n ◉ $4 = 12$, find the value of n.

Remember that ◉ should NOT look familiar to you. Don't panic because you don't know what the symbol means! The question defines the symbol for you:

x ◉ $y = 4x + \dfrac{y^2}{2}$.

When $x = n$, and $y = 4$, the result is 12. Substitute n and 4 into the equation for x and y, and solve for n.

n ◉ $4 = 4n + \dfrac{4^2}{2} = 12$.

$4n + 8 = 12$.

$4n = 4$

$n = 1$.   (*Answer*)

EXAMPLE:

The operation ▼ is defined for all real numbers a and b by the equation:

a ▼ $b = |a|^b$. If -6 ▼ $n = 216$, find the value of n.

Just like the previous example, the question defines the symbol ▼ for you:

a ▼ $b = |a|^b$.

---

*Denotes concepts that are on the Level 2 test only.

When $a = -6$ and $b = n$, the result is 216. Substitute -6 and n into the equation for a and b, and solve for n.

$$-6 \blacktriangledown n = \left| -6 \right|^n = 216.$$

$$6^n = 216.$$

6 raised up to some power, n, equals 216. You know that $6^1 = 6$ and $6^2 = 36$. You may or may not know off the top of your head what 6^3 equals. $6 \times 6 \times 6 = 36 \times 6 = 216$. (On a graphing calculator, type $6 \wedge 3$.)

$$n = 3. \qquad (Answer)$$

"IN TERMS OF" PROBLEMS

Sometimes on the Level 2 test, you may be faced with one equation with more than one unknown variable. You don't have enough information to solve for an unknown, but you can solve for one variable *in terms of* the other variables.

EXAMPLE:

Given $2x - 3y = x - 6y + 9$, solve for y in terms of x.

Your goal is to isolate y on one side of the equation. This will give you the solution for y *in terms of* x.

$$2x - 3y = x - 6y + 9$$

$$2x + 3y = x + 9.$$

$$3y = -x + 9.$$

$$y = \frac{-x + 9}{3}. \qquad (Answer)$$

EXAMPLE:

Given $a + b = \dfrac{x}{d} + \dfrac{x}{c}$, find the value of x in terms of a, b, c, and d.

Again, your goal is to isolate x on one side of the equation. Start by multiplying both sides by the LCD, cd.

$$a + b = \frac{x}{d} + \frac{x}{c}.$$

$$cd(a + b) = cx + dx.$$

$$cd(a + b) = x(c + d).$$

$$\frac{cd(a + b)}{(c + d)} = x. \qquad (Answer)$$

RATIO AND PROPORTION

A **proportion** is an equation that sets two ratios (fractions) equal to each other. Don't worry about finding least common denominators when solving a proportion, simply **cross multiply.**

EXAMPLE:

$$\frac{12}{x+4} = \frac{8}{x}.$$

$$12x = 8(x+4).$$

$$12x = 8x + 32.$$

$$4x = 32.$$

$$x = 8. \qquad (Answer)$$

EXAMPLE:

If 0.3 cm³ of a substance weighs 5 grams, how many grams will 0.8 cm³ of the same substance weigh?

Let x = the weight of 0.8 cm³ of the substance. Then, set up a proportion to solve for x.

$$\frac{0.3}{5} = \frac{0.8}{x}.$$

$$0.3x = 5(0.8).$$

$$x = \frac{4}{0.3} \approx 13.33 \text{ grams.} \qquad (Answer)$$

COMPLEX NUMBERS

A **complex number** is a number in the form $a + bi$ where both a and b are real numbers. The complex number system encompasses all of the real and imaginary numbers. a is the real part of a complex number, and bi is the imaginary part. Recall that $i = \sqrt{-1}$.

Two complex numbers are equal when their real parts and imaginary parts are equal. For example, if $7 - i = a + bi$, then $a = 7$ and $b = -1$.

Add complex numbers by adding their real parts and then adding their imaginary parts:

$$(a + bi) + (c + di) = (a + c) + (b + d)i.$$

$$(5 + 6i) + (-4 - 2i) = (5 + -4) + (6 + -2)i = 1 + 4i.$$

Multiply complex numbers by using the FOIL method as you would when multiplying any two binomials. Because $i = \sqrt{-1}$, $i^2 = (\sqrt{-1})(\sqrt{-1}) = -1$. Once you use FOIL, remember to simplify the i^2 term.

$$(a + bi)(c + di) = (ac - bd) + (ad + bc)i.$$

$$(5 + 6i)(-4 - 2i) = -20 - 10i - 24i - 12i^2 = -20 - 34i - 12(-1) = -8 - 34i.$$

Similar to rationalizing the denominator of a radical expression by multiplying by the conjugate, the quotient of complex numbers is simplified by multiplying the numerator and denominator by the **complex conjugate** of the denominator. The complex numbers $a + bi$ and $a - bi$ are complex conjugates.

$$(a + bi)(a - bi) = a^2 - abi + bai - b^2i^2 = a^2 + b^2.$$

$$(5 + 6i)(5 - 6i) = 25 - 30i + 30i - 36i^2 = 25 + 36 = 61.$$

EXAMPLE:

Simplify the quotient $\dfrac{8-i}{5+i}$.

Multiply the numerator and denominator by the conjugate of $5 + i$, $5 - i$.

$$\dfrac{8-i}{5+i} \times \dfrac{5-i}{5-i} = \dfrac{40 - 8i - 5i + i^2}{25 - i^2}$$

$$= \dfrac{40 - 13i + (-1)}{25 - (-1)}$$

$$\dfrac{40 - 13i - 1}{25 + 1} = \dfrac{39 - 13i}{26}.$$ Now express the answer in the form $a + bi$.

$$\dfrac{39}{26} - \dfrac{13}{26}i = \dfrac{3}{2} - \dfrac{1}{2}i.$$

EXAMPLE:

Simplify $\left(\sqrt{3} + \sqrt{-6}\right)\left(\sqrt{3} - \sqrt{-6}\right)$.

Express the radicals in pure imaginary form first. $\sqrt{-6} = i\sqrt{6}$. Then, multiply

$$\left(\sqrt{3} + \sqrt{-6}\right)\left(\sqrt{3} - \sqrt{-6}\right) = \left(\sqrt{3} + i\sqrt{6}\right)\left(\sqrt{3} - i\sqrt{6}\right)$$

$$= \sqrt{3}\left(\sqrt{3}\right) - i\sqrt{18} + i\sqrt{18} - i^2(6).$$

$$= 3 - (-1)(6) = 3 + 6 = 9. \qquad \textit{(Answer)}$$

Notice in the previous example that $\sqrt{-6} \times \sqrt{-6} \neq \sqrt{36}$. When both radicands are negative, you must express them as imaginary numbers and then simplify.

In the example above, $\sqrt{-6} \times \sqrt{-6}$ became $i\sqrt{6} \times i\sqrt{6} = i^2\sqrt{36} = -6$.

Raising i to consecutive powers creates the following pattern:

$i^1 = i \qquad i^5 = i$

$i^2 = -1 \qquad i^6 = -1$

$i^3 = -i \qquad i^7 = -i$

$i^4 = 1 \qquad i^8 = 1$

To determine the value of i^n, divide n by 4. A remainder of zero corresponds to $i^4 = 1$. A remainder of 1 corresponds to $i^1 = i$. A remainder of 2 corresponds to $i^2 = -1$, and a remainder of 3 corresponds to $i^3 = -i$. For example, $i^{21} = i$, since $21 \div 4$ has a remainder of 1.

EXAMPLE:

Which of the following is equivalent to 1?

(A) i^{29}

(B) i^{30}

(C) i^{31}

(D) i^{32}

(E) i^{33}

i^n is equivalent to 1 when n is a factor of 4. Since 32 is divisible by 4, D is the correct answer choice. (Simplifying the other answers results in $i^{29} = i^1 = i$, $i^{30} = i^2 = -1$, $i^{31} = i^3 = -i$, and $i^{33} = i^1 = i$.)

You may be asked to find the **absolute value of a complex number** on the Level 2 test. Since the absolute value of any number is its distance from the origin, the absolute value of any complex number can be found by using the Pythagorean Theorem.

$$|a + bi| = \sqrt{a^2 + b^2}$$

EXAMPLE:

If $z = 3 - 4i$, then what does $|z|$ equal?

$$|z| = |3 - 4i| = \sqrt{(3^2 + (-4)^2)}$$

$$\sqrt{(9 + 16)} = \sqrt{25} = 5. \qquad (Answer)$$

COUNTING PROBLEMS

The **Fundamental Counting Principle** states that if one action can be done in a ways, and for each of these a second action can be done in b ways, the number of ways the two actions can be done in order is $a \times b$.

For example, if an automobile manufacturer produces 4 different models of cars and each one is available in 5 different colors, there are:

$4 \times 5 = 20$.

20 different combinations of car model and color which can be created.

Mutually exclusive events are events that cannot occur at the same time. For example, when you roll a die, you either roll a 1, 2, 3, 4, 5, or 6. 1, 2, 3, 4, 5, and 6 are mutually exclusive events. When you flip a coin, you get either heads or tails. Heads and tails are also mutually exclusive. If the possibilities being counted are mutually exclusive, then the total number of possibilities is the **sum** of the number of possibilities in each group.

EXAMPLE:

How many positive integers between 0 and 100 can be created using the digits 1, 2, 3, 4, and 5?

Consider all the possible 1-digit and 2-digit integers that can be created using 1, 2, 3, 4, or 5. These are *mutually exclusive* events.

| 1-digit integers: | 5 possibilities for the ones digit |
| 2-digit integers | (5 possibilities for the tens digit)(5 possibilities for the ones digit) |

Because the possibilities being counted are mutually exclusive, find the sum of the number of possibilities in each group.

$5 + 5(5) = 30$.

30 integers can be created. (*Answer*)

EXAMPLE:

John's high school offers 6 math courses, 4 English courses, and 3 science courses to students in his grade level. How many schedules are possible if John chooses a course in each subject?

Use the Fundamental Counting Principle to get:

$6 \times 4 \times 3 = 72$ schedules.

72 schedules.   (*Answer*)

EXAMPLE:

In how many different ways can a 15-question true or false quiz be answered? Assume every question must be answered.

There are 15 "events" and each one has two possible outcomes. Using the Fundamental Counting Principle, you get:

$2 \times 2 \times 2 \times 2 \times 2 \times 2 \times 2 \times 2 \times 2 \times 2 \times 2 \times 2 \times 2 \times 2 \times 2 = 2^{15} = 32{,}768$.

32,768 possible combinations of answers.   (*Answer*)

Now, try the previous example assuming that you can leave questions blank. The number of true/false questions doesn't change, but now you have 3 possible outcomes for each question—true, false, or blank. The answer becomes 3^{15} or 14,348,907 possible combinations.

EXAMPLE:

Rosemarie wears a uniform to work. As part of her uniform, she can wear one of 3 pairs of pants, one of 4 shirts, and one of two hats. How many pant-shirt-hat combinations are possible?

Again, use the Fundamental Counting Principle to get:

$3 \times 4 \times 2 = 24$

24 possible pant-shirt-hat combinations.   (*Answer*)

EXAMPLE:

A certain state makes license plates consisting of 6 symbols (letters and numbers), and it is a requirement that the letters always come before the numbers. How many license plates of 6 symbols (letters and numbers) can be made using at least one letter in each?

There are 6 mutually exclusive events possible—license plates with 1, 2, 3, 4, 5, or 6 letters. Recognize that there are 26 possibilities for choosing a letter and 10 possibilities for choosing a number (the digits 0 through 9) and it's ok to use a number or letter more than once.

1 Letter and 5 Numbers:	$26 \times 10 \times 10 \times 10 \times 10 \times 10 = 2{,}600{,}000$.
2 Letters and 4 Numbers:	$26 \times 26 \times 10 \times 10 \times 10 \times 10 = 6{,}760{,}000$.
3 Letters and 3 Numbers:	$26 \times 26 \times 26 \times 10 \times 10 \times 10 = 17{,}576{,}000$.
4 Letters and 2 Numbers:	$26 \times 26 \times 26 \times 26 \times 10 \times 10 = 45{,}697{,}600$.
5 Letters and 1 Number:	$26 \times 26 \times 26 \times 26 \times 26 \times 10 = 118{,}813{,}760$.
6 Letters:	$26 \times 26 \times 26 \times 26 \times 26 \times 26 = 308{,}915{,}776$.

The total number of possible license plates is the sum of the 6 mutually exclusive events:

$2,600,000 + 6,760,000 + 17576,000 + 45,697,600 + 118,813,760 + 308,915,776$

$= 500,363,136.$

500,363,136 possible license plates.   *(Answer)*

EXAMPLE:

How many different seating arrangements can be made for 5 students in a row of 5 desks?

This problem is different from the previous ones because order matters. Choose the student to sit in the first desk. There are 5 possibilities for choosing that student. Once one student is seated, he or she cannot be chosen again, so there are only 4 possible students that can be chosen to sit in the 2nd desk. Using that logic, there are 3 possible students to choose for the 3rd desk, 2 for the 4th, and 1 for the 5th. The problem can be solved using multiplication:

$5 \times 4 \times 3 \times 2 \times 1 = 120$

Notice that $5 \times 4 \times 3 \times 2 \times 1 = 5!$. You can use a **factorial** to solve problems in which order matters. A **permutation** is an ordered arrangement of elements. The number of permutations of n objects is $n!$. Hence, there are 5! possible permutations in this problem.

120 seating arrangements.   *(Answer)*

NUMBER THEORY

Number theory questions have to do with such concepts as: properties of positive and negative numbers, properties of prime numbers, properties of integers, and properties of odd and even numbers. The following examples show possible number theory questions found on the Level 2 test.

EXAMPLE:

If a and b are both positive, a is odd, and b is even, which of the following must be odd?

(A) $b + 2a$

(B) ab

(C) $\dfrac{b}{a}$

(D) a^b

(E) b^a

Think of the terms in the expressions as being odd or even. The table below illustrates whether the answers are odd or even and gives a numeric example for each.

Answer	In Words	Example	Even or Odd?
$b + 2a$	even + 2(odd)	$4 + 2(3) = 10$	Even
ab	odd × even	$3(2) = 6$	Even
$\dfrac{b}{a}$	even ÷ odd	$\dfrac{12}{3} = 4$ $\dfrac{20}{3} \approx 6.67$	Even (if it is an integer)
a^b	odd raised to an even power	$3^2 = 9$	Odd
b^a	even raised to an odd power	$2^3 = 8$	Even

The correct answer is D.

EXAMPLE:

If a is positive and b is negative, which of the following must be negative?

(A) $a + b$

(B) $a + |b|$

(C) $a - |b|$

(D) $|ab|$

(E) $|a|b$

Answers B and D are always positive because of the absolute value. Answers A and C could result in a positive or a negative value, so you cannot say that the expressions *must* result in a negative value. In answer E, $|a|$ is positive and b is negative. The product of a positive number and a negative number is always negative.

The correct answer is E.

▄▄ LOGIC

The logic questions on the Level 2 test have to do with conditional statements, converses, inverses, and contrapositives. **A conditional statement** is an if-then statement that may or may not be true. Some examples of conditional statements are as follows:

If two lines are perpendicular, then they intersect at a 90° angle.

If given two points, then there is one and only one line determined by them.

If today is Saturday, then it is the weekend.

If today is the weekend, then it is Saturday.

Notice that the first three conditional statements are true, but the forth one is not. If today is the weekend, then it could also be Sunday. The **negation** of an if-then statement is formed by inserting the word *not* into the statement. Negating the statement "All right angles measure 90°," for example, results in: "All right angles do not measure 90°."

Three other if-then statements are created by switching and/or negating the if and then parts of a given conditional statement.

Name	General Form	Example	True or False?
Conditional	If p, then q.	If $\angle Y$ measures 100°, then it is obtuse.	True
Converse	If q, then p.	If $\angle Y$ is obtuse, then it measures 100°.	False
Inverse	If not p, then not q.	If $\angle Y$ does not measure 100°, then it is not obtuse.	False
Contrapositive	If not q, then not p.	If $\angle Y$ is not obtuse, then it does not measure 100°.	True

Let's take a look at what happens when the given conditional statement is false.

Name	General Form	Example	True or False?
Conditional	If p, then q.	If two angles are supplementary, then they are right angles.	False
Converse	If q, then p.	If two angles are right angles, then they are supplementary.	True
Inverse	If not p, then not q.	If two angles are not supplementary, then they are not right angles.	True
Contrapositive	If not q, then not p.	If two angles are not right angles, then they are not supplementary.	False

Notice that when the given conditional statement is true, the contrapositive is also true. When the given conditional statement is false, the contrapositive is also false. This means that the contrapositive is *logically equivalent* to the conditional statement, and, because of this, logic questions on the Level 2 test often ask about the contrapositive.

EXAMPLE:

The statement "if John lives in Boston, then he lives in Massachusetts" is logically equivalent to which of the following?

I.   If John lives in Massachusetts, then he lives in Boston.

II. If John does not live in Boston, then he does not live in Massachusetts.

III. If John does not live in Massachusetts, then he does not live in Boston.

   (A) I only

   (B) II only

   (C) III only

   (D) I and II only

   (E) I, II, and III

The given statement is a conditional in the form "if p, then q" and it is a true statement. If you recall the properties of converse, inverse, and contrapositive statements, you can immediately determine that the contrapositive will also be true. The contrapositive is in the form "if not q, then not p" and coincides with answer III above.

If you don't recall the properties of converse, inverse, and contrapositive statements, take a look at each statement individually. I and II are false statements so they cannot be logically equivalent to the given statement. The only possible answer is III.

The correct answer is C.

MATRICES

A **matrix** is a rectangular array of numbers written in brackets. Each number in a matrix is called an **element.** The dimensions of a matrix equal the number of rows by the number of columns, where the number of rows is always given first.

Two matrices are equal if the have the same dimensions and all corresponding elements are equal.

EXAMPLE:

What is the value of x, y, and z?

$$\begin{bmatrix} x - z & 2x + z \\ 4 - y & 0 \end{bmatrix} = \begin{bmatrix} -2 & 8 \\ -5y & 0 \end{bmatrix}$$

Set corresponding elements equal to each other to solve for the three variables. Let's start with y.

$4 - y = -5y$

$4 = -4y$

$y = -1$

There are two elements written in terms of x and z. Set up a system to solve for x using the linear combination method to eliminate z.

$$\begin{aligned} x - z &= -2 \\ + 2x + z &= 8 \\ \hline 3x &= 6 \\ x &= 2 \end{aligned}$$

Since $x - z = -2$, $2 - z = -2$, so $z = 4$.

$x = 2$, $y = -1$, and $z = 4$.   (*Answer*)

To add matrices of the same dimension, simply find the sum of corresponding elements. Addition of matrices of different dimension is undefined.

A scalar is a real number in matrix terms. The **scalar product** of a real number n and the matrix X is the matrix nX. Each element of nX is n times its corresponding element in the given matrix X.

EXAMPLE:

Solve for the matrix X.

$$X + 3\begin{bmatrix} 1 & 0 \\ -2 & 4 \end{bmatrix} = \begin{bmatrix} \frac{1}{2} & 3 \\ -1 & 0 \end{bmatrix}$$

First, find the scalar product:

$$X + \begin{bmatrix} 3 & 0 \\ -6 & 12 \end{bmatrix} = \begin{bmatrix} \frac{1}{2} & 3 \\ -1 & 0 \end{bmatrix}$$

Add the inverse of the second matrix to both sides.

$$X = \begin{bmatrix} \frac{1}{2} & 3 \\ -1 & 0 \end{bmatrix} + \begin{bmatrix} -3 & 0 \\ 6 & -12 \end{bmatrix}$$

$$X = \begin{bmatrix} -\frac{5}{2} & 3 \\ 5 & -12 \end{bmatrix}.$$ (*Answer*)

The **product of two matrices** $X_{a \times b}$ and $Y_{b \times c}$ is an $a \times c$ matrix. Notice that the two matrices X and Y share a dimension of b. Two matrices can only be multiplied if the number of columns of the first matrix equals the number of rows of the second matrix. Multiplying a 2×2 matrix by a 2×1 matrix results in a 2×1 matrix with the following elements:

$$\begin{bmatrix} a & b \\ c & d \end{bmatrix} \begin{bmatrix} x \\ y \end{bmatrix} = \begin{bmatrix} ax + by \\ cx + dy \end{bmatrix}$$

Matrix multiplication is not commutative.

The **identity matrix** is a matrix whose diagonal from the upper left corner to the lower right has elements of 1 and all other elements are 0.

EXAMPLE:

A small shop has three full-time employees. The table below shows the number of hours worked by each employee during a given weekend. If James earns $8 an hour, Joe earns $7.50, and Celia earns $7, find a matrix expression that results in the total amount of money spent on salaries for each of the two days.

	Saturday	Sunday
James	8	4
Joe	6	6
Celia	4	2

You want to sum the three salaries for each day, so set up a matrix of the three hourly salaries.

$$[8 \quad 7.50 \quad 7]$$

Since this is a 1×3 matrix and the hours given in the table form a 3×2 matrix, their product will be a 1×2 matrix.

$$[8 \quad 7.50 \quad 7]\begin{bmatrix} 8 & 4 \\ 6 & 6 \\ 4 & 2 \end{bmatrix} \quad (Answer)$$

Although it was not asked in the problem, the product of the two matrices is:

$$[8(8) + 7.5(6) + 7(4) \quad 8(4) + 7.5(6) + 7(2)] = [137 \quad 91]$$

This means that $137 was spent on salaries on Saturday and $91 was spent on salaries on Sunday.

$$: X = \begin{bmatrix} a & b \\ c & d \end{bmatrix}$$

The **determinant** is a real number associated with each matrix. The determinant of a 2×2 matrix X is defined as:

$$\det X = \begin{vmatrix} a & b \\ c & d \end{vmatrix} = ad - bc$$

EXAMPLE:

Solve for x given

$$\begin{vmatrix} 4 & 7 \\ -2 & x \end{vmatrix} = 0$$

$$4x - (-14) = 0$$

$$4x = -14$$

$$x = -\frac{14}{4} = -\frac{7}{2}. \quad (Answer)$$

SEQUENCES

A **sequence** is a set of numbers listed in a certain order. You can also think of a sequence as a function whose domain is the set of consecutive positive integers. a_n is a term in the sequence, and n is the number of the term. **Finite sequences** have a limited number of terms, while **infinite sequences** continue indefinitely. Some examples of infinite sequences are as follows:

$1, 2, 3, 4, 5, \ldots n, \ldots$

$2, 4, 6, 8, 10, \ldots 2n \ldots$

$3, 9, 27, 81, 243, \ldots 3^n, \ldots$

$1, 4, 9, 16, 25, \ldots n^2 \ldots$

$1, 4, 7, 10, 13, \ldots 3n - 2, \ldots$

In general, infinite sequences are in the form: $a_1, a_2, a_3, a_4, a_5, \ldots a_n, \ldots$.

Arithmetic Sequences

If the difference between consecutive terms in a sequence is a constant, the sequence is an **arithmetic sequence.** The constant difference between terms is called the **common difference** and is represented by d. In a given arithmetic sequence $a_1, a_2, a_3, a_4, a_5, \ldots$, the difference between any two consecutive terms must equal d: $a_2 - a_1 = d$, $a_3 - a_2 = d$, $a_4 - a_3 = d$, etc.

The **nth term of an arithmetic sequence** can be found using the equation $a_n = dn + c$, where d is the common difference, n is the number of the term, and c is a constant. Alternately, the equation $a_n = a_1 + (n - 1)d$ (where a_1 is the first term of the sequence) also represents the nth term of an arithmetic sequence.

EXAMPLE:

Find the nth term of the arithmetic sequence $6, 10, 14, 18, 22, \ldots$.

Because the sequence is arithmetic, there is a common difference between consecutive terms. $d = 10 - 6 = 4$. The nth term must be in the form:

$a_n = dn + c$.

$a_n = 4n + c$.

Because $a_1 = 6$, you can write an expression for the first term and solve for c.

$6 = 4(1) + c$.

$2 = c$.

The formula for the nth term is $a_n = 4n + 2$.   (*Answer*)

Notice the last example can also be solved using the equation $a_n = a_1 + (n - 1)d$. Substituting $a_1 = 6$ and $d = 4$, results in:

$a_n = 6 + (n - 1)4$.

$a_n = 6 + 4n - 4 = 4n + 2$.

EXAMPLE:

How many numbers between 50 and 500 are divisible by 11?

Determine an arithmetic sequence to represent the numbers between 50 and 500 divisible by 11. The common difference between terms is 11. The first term of the sequence is 55 and the last is 495 ($45 \times 11 = 495$).

$a_n = a_1 + (n-1)d$.

$a_n = 55 + (n-1)11$.

$495 = 55 + (n-1)11$.

$440 = (n-1)11$.

$40 = n - 1$.

$n = 41$ terms.   (*Answer*)

Geometric Sequences

If the ratio between consecutive terms in a sequence is a constant, the sequence is a **geometric sequence.** The constant ratio between terms is called the **common ratio** and is represented by r. In a given geometric sequence $a_1, a_2, a_3, a_4, a_5, \ldots$, the ratio between any two consecutive terms must equal r: $\dfrac{a_2}{a_1} = r,\ \dfrac{a_3}{a_2} = r,\ \dfrac{a_4}{a_3} = r$, etc. and r cannot equal zero.

The ***n*th term of a geometric sequence** can be found using the equation $a_n = a_1 r^{n-1}$, where r is the common ratio, n is the number of the term, and a_1 is the first term of the sequence. Using this formula, every geometric sequence can be written as follows:

$a_1, a_2, a_3, a_4, a_5, \ldots a_n, \ldots$ *or*

$a_1, a_1 r^1, a_1 r^2, a_1 r^3, a_1 r^4, \ldots a_1 r^{n-1}, \ldots$

EXAMPLE:

Find the *n*th term of the geometric sequence: $3, \dfrac{3}{2}, \dfrac{3}{4}, \dfrac{3}{8}, \dfrac{3}{16}, \ldots$

This is a geometric sequence because there is a common ratio.

$r = \dfrac{3/2}{3} = \dfrac{3}{6} = \dfrac{1}{2}$.

Substitute the values $r = \dfrac{1}{2}$ and $a_1 = 3$ into the formula for the *n*th terms to get:

$a_n = a_1 r^{n-1}$.

$a_n = 3\left(\dfrac{1}{2}\right)^{n-1}$.   (*Answer*)

EXAMPLE:

The second term of a geometric sequence is $\dfrac{1}{2}$ and the 5th term is $\dfrac{1}{128}$.

Find the common ratio.

Start by writing the two given terms in $a_n = a_1 r^{n-1}$ form.

$$a_2 = a_1 r^1 = \frac{1}{2} \quad \text{and} \quad a_5 = a_1 r^4 = \frac{1}{128}.$$

You can then write a_5 in terms of a_2.

$$a_2 \times r \times r \times r = a_5.$$

$$\frac{1}{2} \times r \times r \times r = \frac{1}{128}.$$

$$\frac{1}{2} r^3 = \frac{1}{128}.$$

$$r^3 = \frac{2}{128} = \frac{1}{64}.$$

$$r = \sqrt[3]{\frac{1}{64}} = \frac{1}{4}.$$

$$\frac{1}{4}. \quad (Answer)$$

*SERIES

A series is the sum of the terms of a sequence.

The **sum of a finite arithmetic sequence** is: $S_n = \dfrac{n}{2}(a_1 + a_n)$.

The **sum of a finite geometric sequence** is: $S_n = a_1 \left(\dfrac{1 - r^n}{1 - r} \right)$ where $r \neq 1$.

The **sum of an infinite geometric sequence** is: $S = \dfrac{a_1}{1 - r}$ where $-1 < r < 1$.

EXAMPLE:

Find the sum of the terms in the sequence 2, 4, 6, 8, 10, 12, 14, 16, 18, 20, 22, 24, 26, 28, 30.

Of course, you could simply add these 15 terms to get an answer. A better way is to recognize that this is, in fact, an arithmetic sequence. $n = 15$, $a_1 = 2$, and $a_n = 30$. Substitute these values into the formula for the sum of a finite arithmetic sequence to get:

$$S_n = 2 + 4 + 6 + 8 + 10 + 12 + 14 + 16 + 18 + 20 + 22 + 24 + 26 + 28 + 30$$

$$S_n = \frac{n}{2}(a_1 + a_n)$$

$$S_n = \frac{15}{2}(2 + 30)$$

$$S_n = \frac{15}{2}(32)$$

$$S_n = 15(16) = 240$$

240. (Answer)

EXAMPLE:

Find the sum of the integers from 1 to 200.

The integers from 1 to 200 form an arithmetic sequence having 200 terms. $n = 200$, $a_1 = 1$, and $a_n = 200$. Substitute these values into the formula for the sum of a finite arithmetic sequence to get:

$$S_n = 1 + 2 + 3 + 4 + 5 + \cdots + 100$$

$$S_n = \frac{n}{2}(a_1 + a_n)$$

$$S_n = \frac{200}{2}(1 + 200)$$

$$S_n = 100(201) = 20{,}100$$

20,100.   (*Answer*)

EXAMPLE:

Find the sum of the geometric sequence: $1, \dfrac{7}{10}, \dfrac{49}{100}, \ldots$

Divide the second term by the first term to determine the common ratio, $r = \dfrac{7}{10}$.

Since this is an infinite geometric sequence, find its sum by using the formula:

$$S = \frac{a_1}{1 - r}$$

$$S = \frac{1}{1 - \dfrac{7}{10}}$$

$$S = \frac{1}{\dfrac{3}{10}}$$

$$S = \frac{10}{3}.$$ (*Answer*)

EXAMPLE:

Evaluate $\displaystyle\sum_{k=1}^{10} 5(-2)^k$.

The sigma notation reads "the sum of $5(-2)^k$ for values of k from 1 to 10." Essentially, you are finding the sum of the first 10 terms of a geometric series with a common ratio of -2. The series is: $-10 + 20 - 40 + 80 - \cdots + 5120$.

$$S_n = a_1\left(\frac{1 - r^n}{1 - r}\right)$$

$$S_{10} = \frac{-10\left[1 - (-2)^{10}\right]}{1 - (-2)}$$

$$= \frac{-10(1 - 1024)}{3}$$

$$= 3{,}410. \qquad (Answer)$$

*VECTORS

A vector quantity is a quantity that has both size and direction. A **vector** is represented by an arrow whose length is proportional to the size of the vector quantity and whose direction is the direction of the vector quantity. For example, a vector can represent the path of a boat or plane. Equivalent vectors have the same size and direction.

If vector v is given by (v_1, v_2) and vector u is given by (u_1, u_2), then their **resultant** is:

$(v_1 + u_1, v_2 + u_2)$. The **norm** is the length of a vector. The norm of vector v is represented by $\|v\|$ where $\|v\| = \sqrt{(v_1^2 = v_2^2)}$. A vector whose norm equals one is the unit vector.

Two vectors v and u are perpendicular if their dot product equals zero. Their dot product is given by: $v \cdot u = v_1 u_1 + v_2 u_2 = 0$. It results in a real number, not another vector.

EXAMPLE:

Let $v = (4, 5)$ and $u = (-1, 2)$. What is the resultant of v and u?

The resultant is the sum of $v + u$.

$(v_1 + u_1, v_2 + u_2)$

$(4 - 1, 5 + 2)$

$(3, 7). \qquad (Answer)$

EXAMPLE:

If $v = (8, 2)$, then what is the norm of v?

$$\|v\| = \sqrt{(v_1{}^2 + v_2{}^2)} = \sqrt{(8^2 + 2^2)} = \sqrt{68}$$

$2\sqrt{17}$.   (*Answer*)

EXAMPLE:

If $u = (5, -2)$, find a vector perpendicular to u.

Let $v = (x, y)$. For vectors to be perpendicular, their dot product must equal zero.

$$v \cdot u = v_1 u_1 + v_2 u_2 = 0$$

$$5x - 2y = 0$$

One possible solution is $v = (2, 5)$, since $5(2) - 2(5) = 0$.

$v = (2, 5)$.   (*Answer*)

*LIMITS

The **limit** of a function is the value that the function approaches as x approaches a given value. Limits occur in rational functions when the domain approaches an undefined value.

EXAMPLE:

If $f(x) = \dfrac{x^2 - 9}{x - 3}$, what value does the function approach as x approaches 3?

Of course, the function is undefined when $x = 3$ because the denominator cannot equal zero. There are many ways to go about solving this problem, so here are three methods:

(1) Factor the numerator and denominator. Then, simplify the expression and evaluate it when $x = 3$.

$$\frac{x^2 - 9}{x - 3} = \frac{(x - 3)(x + 3)}{x - 3} = x + 3$$

Substituting $x = 3$ results in $3 + 3 = 6$.

(2) Substitute numbers close to 3 for x and evaluate the function.

Let $x = 2.99$. $\dfrac{2.99^2 - 9}{2.99 - 3} = 5.99$

(3) Graph the function on your calculator and see how the graph behaves around $x = 3$.

In any case, the function approaches 6 as x approaches 3.   (*Answer*)

EXAMPLE:

$$\lim_{x \to 5} \frac{x^3 - 6x^2 + 5x}{x^2 - 25} =$$

Factor the numerator and denominator to get:

$$\frac{x^3 - 6x^2 + 5x}{x^2 - 25} = \frac{x(x^2 - 6x + 5)}{(x - 5)(x + 5)}$$

$$= \frac{x(x - 5)(x - 1)}{(x - 5)(x + 5)}$$

$$= \frac{x(x - 1)}{(x + 5)}$$

Now, substitute $x = 5$ to find the limit as x approaches 5.

$$= \frac{5(5 - 1)}{(5 + 5)} = \frac{20}{10} = 2$$

The limit as x approaches 5 is 2.   (*Answer*)

EXAMPLE:

If $f(x) = \frac{3x+3}{4x-8}$, what value does the function approach as x approaches infinity?

Imagine that x is getting infinitely larger. You could substitute $x = 1{,}000$ or $x = 10{,}000$ into the function and evaluate it.

$$f(1{,}000) = \frac{3(1000) + 3}{4(1000) - 8} = 0.75225$$

Or you could factor the numerator and denominator:

$$f(x) = \frac{3x + 3}{4x - 8} = \frac{3(x + 1)}{4(x - 2)}$$

The value of $\frac{(x + 1)}{(x - 2)}$ approaches 1 as x gets infinitely larger.

The function, therefore, approaches $\frac{3}{4}$.   (*Answer*)

PART III
EIGHT PRACTICE TESTS

PRACTICE TEST 1

The following pages contain eight full-length SAT Math Level 2 Practice Tests. Treat each practice test as the actual test and complete it in one 60-minute sitting. Use the following answer sheet to fill in your multiple-choice answers. Once you have completed each practice test:

1. Check your answers using the Answer Key.
2. Review the Answers and Solutions.
3. Fill in the "Diagnose Your Strengths and Weaknesses" sheet, and determine areas that require further preparation.

PRACTICE TEST 1
MATH LEVEL 2

ANSWER SHEET

Tear out this answer sheet and use it to complete the practice test. Determine the BEST answer for each question. Then, fill in the appropriate oval using a No. 2 pencil.

1. (A) (B) (C) (D) (E)	21. (A) (B) (C) (D) (E)	41. (A) (B) (C) (D) (E)
2. (A) (B) (C) (D) (E)	22. (A) (B) (C) (D) (E)	42. (A) (B) (C) (D) (E)
3. (A) (B) (C) (D) (E)	23. (A) (B) (C) (D) (E)	43. (A) (B) (C) (D) (E)
4. (A) (B) (C) (D) (E)	24. (A) (B) (C) (D) (E)	44. (A) (B) (C) (D) (E)
5. (A) (B) (C) (D) (E)	25. (A) (B) (C) (D) (E)	45. (A) (B) (C) (D) (E)
6. (A) (B) (C) (D) (E)	26. (A) (B) (C) (D) (E)	46. (A) (B) (C) (D) (E)
7. (A) (B) (C) (D) (E)	27. (A) (B) (C) (D) (E)	47. (A) (B) (C) (D) (E)
8. (A) (B) (C) (D) (E)	28. (A) (B) (C) (D) (E)	48. (A) (B) (C) (D) (E)
9. (A) (B) (C) (D) (E)	29. (A) (B) (C) (D) (E)	49. (A) (B) (C) (D) (E)
10. (A) (B) (C) (D) (E)	30. (A) (B) (C) (D) (E)	50. (A) (B) (C) (D) (E)
11. (A) (B) (C) (D) (E)	31. (A) (B) (C) (D) (E)	
12. (A) (B) (C) (D) (E)	32. (A) (B) (C) (D) (E)	
13. (A) (B) (C) (D) (E)	33. (A) (B) (C) (D) (E)	
14. (A) (B) (C) (D) (E)	34. (A) (B) (C) (D) (E)	
15. (A) (B) (C) (D) (E)	35. (A) (B) (C) (D) (E)	
16. (A) (B) (C) (D) (E)	36. (A) (B) (C) (D) (E)	
17. (A) (B) (C) (D) (E)	37. (A) (B) (C) (D) (E)	
18. (A) (B) (C) (D) (E)	38. (A) (B) (C) (D) (E)	
19. (A) (B) (C) (D) (E)	39. (A) (B) (C) (D) (E)	
20. (A) (B) (C) (D) (E)	40. (A) (B) (C) (D) (E)	

PRACTICE TEST 1

Time: 60 minutes

Directions: Select the BEST answer for each of the 50 multiple-choice questions. If the exact solution is not one of the five choices, select the answer that is the best approximation. Then, fill in the appropriate oval on the answer sheet.

Notes:

1. A calculator will be needed to answer some of the questions on the test. Scientific, programmable, and graphing calculators are permitted. It is up to you to determine when and when not to use your calculator.
2. Angles on the Level 2 test are measured in degrees and radians. You need to decide whether your calculator should be set to degree mode or radian mode for a particular question.
3. Figures are drawn as accurately as possible and are intended to help solve some of the test problems. If a figure is not drawn to scale, this will be stated in the problem. All figures lie in a plane unless the problem indicates otherwise.
4. Unless otherwise stated, the domain of a function f is assumed to be the set of real numbers x for which the value of the function, $f(x)$, is a real number.
5. Reference information that may be useful in answering some of the test questions can be found below.

Reference Information	
Right circular cone with radius r and height h:	Volume $= \dfrac{1}{3}\pi r^2 h$
Right circular cone with circumference of base c and slant height ℓ:	Lateral Area $= \dfrac{1}{2}c\ell$
Sphere with radius r:	Volume $= \dfrac{4}{3}\pi r^3$
	Surface Area $= 4\pi r^2$
Pyramid with base area B and height h:	Volume $= \dfrac{1}{3}Bh$

PRACTICE TEST 1 QUESTIONS

1. If $\sqrt[3]{8x^3 - 5} = 3$, then $x =$

   (A) 4
   (B) 1.59
   (C) 2.35
   (D) 0.40
   (E) 0.06

2. $\dfrac{10!}{3!7!} =$

   (A) 1
   (B) 60
   (C) 120
   (D) 240
   (E) 720

3. Which of the following lines is perpendicular to the line $y = \dfrac{3}{2}x + 7$?

   (A) $y = \dfrac{3}{2}x - 7$

   (B) $y = -\dfrac{3}{2}x + 7$

   (C) $y = \dfrac{2}{3}x + 7$

   (D) $y = -\dfrac{2}{3}x + 7$

   (E) $y = \dfrac{3}{2}x + \dfrac{1}{7}$

4. If $f(x, y) = \dfrac{1}{4}x - y$, then which of the following is equal to $f(8, 3)$?

   (A) $f(12, 2)$
   (B) $f(16, 6)$
   (C) $f(4, 0)$
   (D) $f(2, 1)$
   (E) $f(-12, -2)$

5. If $f(x) = x^2 + 1$, then $f(f(4)) =$

   (A) 17
   (B) 256
   (C) 34
   (D) 290
   (E) 144

GO ON TO THE NEXT PAGE

6. Assuming $a \neq 0$, $\dfrac{5 - \dfrac{1}{a}}{a^{-1}} =$

(A) $5a - 1$

(B) $\dfrac{5a - 1}{a^2}$

(C) 4

(D) $\dfrac{1 - 5a}{a^2}$

(E) $1 - 5a$

7. If $\sec \theta = 2$, then $\cos \theta \sec \theta =$

(A) 2

(B) 4

(C) $\dfrac{1}{4}$

(D) 1

(E) 0

8. If $16x^4 - 9 = 4$, then x could equal which of the following?

(A) 1.34

(B) -0.95

(C) 0.87

(D) 0.90

(E) 1.05

9. If a hexahedral die is rolled 2 times, what is the probability of *not* rolling a 6 both times?

(A) $\dfrac{1}{6}$

(B) $\dfrac{5}{6}$

(C) $\dfrac{1}{36}$

(D) $\dfrac{25}{36}$

(E) $\dfrac{2}{3}$

10. What is the range of $f(x) = \sqrt{4 - x^2}$?

(A) $y \geq 0$

(B) $y \geq 2$

(C) $-2 \leq y \leq 2$

(D) $0 \leq y \leq 2$

(E) $y \leq 2$

GO ON TO THE NEXT PAGE

11. The probability that John wins a game is $\frac{4}{5}$, and, independently, the probability that Meghan wins is $\frac{9}{11}$. What is the probability that Meghan wins and John loses the game?

   (A) $\frac{18}{55}$

   (B) $\frac{45}{44}$

   (C) $\frac{36}{55}$

   (D) $\frac{16}{25}$

   (E) $\frac{9}{55}$

12. In Figure 1, what is the value of θ?

   (A) 49.8°
   (B) 57.8°
   (C) 40.2°
   (D) 32.2°
   (E) 32.9°

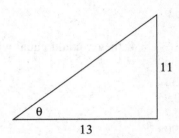

Figure 1

13. $\log_2 16\sqrt{2} =$

   (A) $\frac{7}{2}$

   (B) 5

   (C) 4

   (D) 2

   (E) $\frac{9}{2}$

14. Which of the following is a polynomial with roots 0, 4, and *i*?

   (A) $x^3 - 4x^2 + x - 4$
   (B) $x^3 - (4 + i)x^2 + 4ix$
   (C) $x^4 - 4x^3 + x^2 - 4x$
   (D) $x^2 - 4x$
   (E) $x^4 - 4x^3 - x^2 + 4x$

GO ON TO THE NEXT PAGE

15. In Figure 2, $x =$

(A) $r \sin \theta$
(B) $r \cos \theta$
(C) $r - y$
(D) r^2
(E) $y \tan \theta$

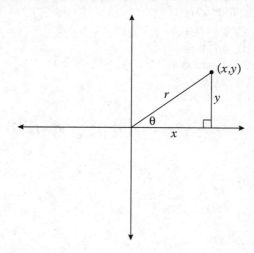

Figure 2

16. If θ is an acute angle and $\sin \theta = \dfrac{3}{4}$, then $\cos 2\theta =$

(A) $-\dfrac{1}{8}$

(B) $-\dfrac{7}{25}$

(C) 1

(D) -2

(E) $-\dfrac{1}{2}$

17. For all x such that $x > 0$, $f(x) = \log_3 x$. What does $f^{-1}(x)$ equal?

(A) x^3
(B) 3^x
(C) $\sqrt[3]{x}$
(D) $\log_x 3$
(E) $3^{\frac{1}{x}}$

18. What are the asymptote(s) of $f(x) = \dfrac{6x^2}{4 - x^2}$?

(A) $x = 2$ and $x = -2$
(B) $y = -6$
(C) $x = 2$
(D) $x = 2$, $x = -2$, and $y = -6$
(E) $y = -5$

19. If $3^{5-x} = 81^{x+1}$, what does x equal?

(A) $\dfrac{1}{3}$

(B) 3

(C) $\dfrac{4}{5}$

(D) $\dfrac{1}{2}$

(E) $\dfrac{1}{5}$

GO ON TO THE NEXT PAGE

20. The graph of $16x^2 + 8y^2 - 32x + 8y = 0$ is which of the following?

    (A) a hyperbola
    (B) an ellipse
    (C) a parabola
    (D) a circle
    (E) a semicircle

21. If $f(x) = 2x + 5$ and $g(x) = \dfrac{1}{6 + x}$, then $fg(12) =$

    (A) 29
    (B) $\dfrac{1}{18}$
    (C) $\dfrac{29}{18}$
    (D) 47
    (E) 11

22. Seven integers are arranged from least to greatest. If the median is 9 and the only mode is 7, what is the least possible range for the 7 numbers?

    (A) 4
    (B) 5
    (C) 6
    (D) 8
    (E) 12

23. The graph of $x^2 - xy = 4$ has which of the following symmetries?

    (A) Symmetric with respect to the x-axis
    (B) Symmetric with respect to the y-axis
    (C) Symmetric with respect to the origin
    (D) Symmetric with respect to both axes
    (E) None

24. Which of the following is *not* equivalent to i^{21}?

    (A) i^{17}
    (B) i^9
    (C) i^{105}
    (D) i^{45}
    (E) i^{31}

25. Cost is a function of the number of units produced as given by: $C(n) = 0.01n^2 - 90n + 25,000$. How many units, n, produce a minimum cost C?

    (A) 500
    (B) 4,500
    (C) 9,000
    (D) 18,000
    (E) $-177,500$

26. $\sqrt[5]{\sqrt[4]{\sqrt[3]{\sqrt{n}}}}$ =

    (A) $n^{\frac{1}{17}}$

    (B) $n^{\frac{1}{19}}$

    (C) $n^{\frac{1}{60}}$

    (D) $n^{\frac{1}{120}}$

    (E) $n^{\frac{77}{60}}$

27. Which of the following is the equation of a line with x-intercept $(6, 0)$ and y-intercept $(0, -15)$?

    (A) $y = \dfrac{5}{2}x - 15$

    (B) $y = -\dfrac{5}{3}x - 15$

    (C) $y = -\dfrac{5}{2}x - 6$

    (D) $y = -\dfrac{2}{5}x + 15$

    (E) $y = \dfrac{5}{2}x - 6$

28. Which of the following describes the right and left behavior of the graph of $f(x) = -3x^7 + 2x^5 - 3x + 6$?

    (A) Rises right and left
    (B) Falls right and left
    (C) Falls left, rises right
    (D) Rises left, falls right
    (E) Cannot be determined

29. If $x + 2$ is a factor of $x^4 + x^3 + 3x^2 + kx - 10$, then $k =$

    (A) -5
    (B) -13
    (C) 15
    (D) 13
    (E) 5

30. By the Rational Root Test, how many possible rational roots does $f(x) = 6x^3 - 5x^2 + 4x - 15$ have?

    (A) 6
    (B) 12
    (C) 16
    (D) 24
    (E) 32

31. In Figure 3, two segments are tangent to a circle of radius 3. Points S and T are the points of tangency. What is the length of ST?

    (A) 6
    (B) 1.9
    (C) 5.8
    (D) 1.6
    (E) 2.9

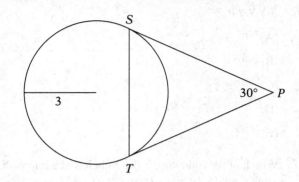

Figure 3

32. $2,500 is invested at a rate of 4.5% compounded monthly. The value of the investment in t years can be modeled by the equation $A = 2500\left(1 + \dfrac{0.045}{12}\right)^{12t}$. How long will it take for the investment to double?

    (A) 10.2 years
    (B) 15.4 years
    (C) 18.8 years
    (D) 25 years
    (E) 185.2 years

33. If the 2nd term of an arithmetic sequence is 7, and the 6th term is 23, then what is the 90th term of the sequence?

    (A) 270
    (B) 356
    (C) 359
    (D) 360
    (E) 363

34. The product of 45,454,545,454,545 and 1,234 contains how many digits?

    (A) 14
    (B) 15
    (C) 16
    (D) 17
    (E) 18

GO ON TO THE NEXT PAGE

35. Which of the following equations has the graph shown in Figure 4?

    (A) $y = \sin\dfrac{1}{2}x$

    (B) $y = 2\sin x$

    (C) $y = \sin 2x$

    (D) $y = \dfrac{1}{2}\sin x$

    (E) $y = \dfrac{1}{2}\sin 2x$

USE THIS SPACE AS SCRATCH PAPER

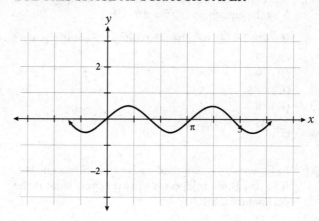

Figure 4

36. In $\triangle ABC$ in Figure 5, $AB = 3.4$ cm, $x = 43°$, and $y = 29°$. What is the length of side BC?

    (A) 4.8
    (B) 2.4
    (C) 4.3
    (D) 2.8
    (E) 5.7

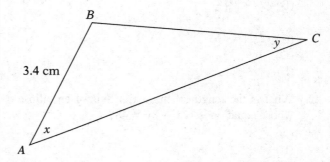

Figure 5

37. Pam has a term average of 84% in history. If this makes up 75% of her overall grade and the final exam makes up the remaining 25%, what will her overall grade be if she receives a 92% on the final exam?

    (A) 90%
    (B) 88%
    (C) 87.5%
    (D) 86%
    (E) 85%

38. What is the length of the segment connecting A(−4, 2, 1) to B(7, 5, −3)?

    (A) 5.8
    (B) 12.1
    (C) 11.6
    (D) 132
    (E) 146

39. A line has parametric equations $x = 8 - t$ and $y = 10 + 2t$ where t is the parameter. What is the slope of the line?

    (A) −1
    (B) −2
    (C) 26
    (D) 2
    (E) $\dfrac{1}{2}$

GO ON TO THE NEXT PAGE

40. The operation Φ is defined for all real numbers a and b by the equation: $a \Phi b = a^{-b} - 3b$

    If $n \Phi -2 = 70$, which of the following could equal n?

    (A) 7
    (B) 9
    (C) −8
    (D) 8.7
    (E) $\dfrac{1}{8}$

41. In Figure 6, the length of each edge of the cube is s. If A and B are midpoints of two edges, what is the perimeter of ABCD?

    (A) $4s\sqrt{5}$

    (B) $2s + s\sqrt{\dfrac{5}{2}}$

    (C) $2s + s\sqrt{5}$
    (D) $3s$
    (E) $4s$

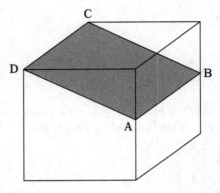

Figure 6

42. What is the length of the major axis of an ellipse whose equation is $12x^2 + 8y^2 = 48$?

    (A) 2.45
    (B) 4
    (C) 4.90
    (D) 6
    (E) 12

43. What is the y-intercept of the line tangent to the circle $x^2 + y^2 = 1$ at the point $\left(\dfrac{3}{5}, \dfrac{4}{5}\right)$?

    (A) 0.80
    (B) 1
    (C) 1.20
    (D) 1.25
    (E) 1.60

44. $\lim\limits_{x \to 3} \dfrac{(3x^2 - 7x - 6)}{(x^2 - 9)} =$

    (A) 0
    (B) 1.6
    (C) 1.8
    (D) 2.4
    (E) No limit exists

45. If a function is an odd function, then $f(-x) = -f(x)$ for all values of x in the domain. Which of the following is an odd function?

    (A) $f(x) = \sin x$
    (B) $f(x) = \cos x$
    (C) $f(x) = x^2 - 10$
    (D) $f(x) = 4^x$
    (E) $f(x) = \log_2 x$

GO ON TO THE NEXT PAGE

46. If $12 \sin^2 x + \sin x - 1 = 0$ over the interval $180° \le x \le 360°$, then $x =$

(A) 14.5°
(B) −19.5°
(C) 194.5° or 344.5°
(D) 199.5°
(E) 199.5° or 340.5°

47. If $i^2 = -1$, then which of the following equals $(15 - 8i)^{\frac{1}{2}}$?

(A) $2 - 2i$
(B) $4 - i$
(C) $2 + 2i$
(D) $4 + i$
(E) $2 + 3i$

48. $\dfrac{\tan \theta + \cot \theta}{\tan \theta} =$

(A) 1
(B) $\csc^2 \theta$
(C) $\sin^2 \theta$
(D) $\cot \theta$
(E) $\sec^2 \theta$

49. What is the sum of the infinite series

$$1 - \frac{1}{5} + \frac{1}{25} - \frac{1}{125} + \cdots?$$

(A) $\dfrac{5}{6}$

(B) $\dfrac{1}{5}$

(C) $\dfrac{6}{5}$

(D) $-\dfrac{5}{6}$

(E) $-\dfrac{6}{5}$

50. What is the middle term in the expansion of

$$\left(3x - \frac{1}{3}y\right)^8 ?$$

(A) $0.86x^4y^4$
(B) $-70x^4y^4$
(C) $5,670x^4y^4$
(D) $70x^4y^4$
(E) $81x^4y^4$

S T O P

IF YOU FINISH BEFORE TIME IS CALLED, YOU MAY CHECK YOUR WORK ON THIS TEST ONLY.
DO NOT TURN TO ANY OTHER TEST IN THIS BOOK.

ANSWER KEY

1. B	11. E	21. C	31. C	41. C
2. C	12. C	22. A	32. B	42. C
3. D	13. E	23. C	33. C	43. D
4. E	14. C	24. E	34. D	44. C
5. D	15. B	25. B	35. E	45. A
6. A	16. A	26. D	36. A	46. E
7. D	17. B	27. A	37. D	47. B
8. B	18. D	28. D	38. B	48. B
9. D	19. E	29. E	39. B	49. A
10. D	20. B	30. D	40. C	50. D

ANSWERS AND SOLUTIONS

1. **B** First, cube both sides of the equation.

$$\sqrt[3]{(8x^3 - 5)} = 3.$$

$$8x^3 - 5 = 3^3 = 27.$$

$$8x^3 = 32.$$

$$x^3 = 4.$$

$$x = 4^{\frac{1}{3}} \approx 1.59.$$

2. **C** Recall that factorial is represented by the "!" symbol. $10! = 10 \times 9 \times 8 \times 7 \times 6 \times 5 \times 4 \times 3 \times 2 \times 1$.

In this problem, 10! can be written in terms of 7! $10! = 10 \times 9 \times 8 \times 7!$ Now, simplify the fraction by dividing through by a factor of 7!.

$$\frac{10!}{3!7!} = \frac{10 \times 9 \times 8}{3 \times 2 \times 1}$$

$$= 120.$$

3. **D** Perpendicular lines have slopes that are opposite reciprocals of each other. The given line is written in slope-intercept form $y = mx + b$ where $m =$ slope. Its slope is $\frac{3}{2}$. The opposite reciprocal of $\frac{3}{2}$ is $-\frac{2}{3}$. Answer D is the only line with this slope.

4. **E**

$$f(8, 3) = \frac{1}{4}(8) - (3) = 2 - 3 = -1.$$

Answer E is the only choice that also results in –1.

$$f(-12, -2) = \frac{1}{4}(-12) - (-2) = -3 + 2 = -1.$$

5. **D**

$$f(4) = 4^2 + 1 = 17.$$

$$f(f(4)) = f(17) = 17^2 + 1 = 290.$$

6. **A**

$$\frac{5 - \dfrac{1}{a}}{a^{-1}} = \frac{5 - \dfrac{1}{a}}{\dfrac{1}{a}}.$$

Multiply the numerator and denominator by the LCD, a, to get:

$$\frac{5 - \dfrac{1}{a}}{\dfrac{1}{a}} \times \frac{a}{a} = \frac{5a - 1}{1} = 5a - 1$$

7. **D** Secant is the reciprocal function of the cosine function. If $\sec \theta = 2$, then $\cos \theta = \dfrac{1}{2}$.

$$\cos \theta \sec \theta = \frac{1}{2}(2) = 1.$$

8. **B**

$$16x^4 - 9 = 4.$$

$$16x^4 = 13.$$

$$x^4 = \frac{13}{16}.$$

$$x = \pm\left(\frac{13}{16}\right)^{\frac{1}{4}} = \pm 0.95.$$

9. **D** The probability of rolling a 6 is $\dfrac{1}{6}$, so the probability of NOT rolling a 6 is $1 - \dfrac{1}{6}$ or $\dfrac{5}{6}$. The probability of not rolling a 6 on both rolls is:

$$\frac{5}{6}\left(\frac{5}{6}\right) = \frac{25}{36}.$$

10. **D** Graph $f(x) = \sqrt{4 - x^2}$ on your graphing calculator to see that it is the graph of a semicircle centered at the origin with a radius of 2 units. Because $f(x)$ equals the square root of an expression, it must be a positive value, and $y \geq 0$ is part of the range. There is an upper limit on y, however. The maximum y-value occurs when $x = 0$.

$$f(0) = \sqrt{4 - 0^2} = 2.$$

The range is between 0 and 2, inclusive.

11. **E** Because the two events are independent, the probability that Meghan wins and John loses is the product of the two probabilities. The probability that John loses is: $1 - \dfrac{4}{5} = \dfrac{1}{5}$.

$$P = \frac{9}{11}\left(\frac{1}{5}\right) = \frac{9}{55}.$$

12. **C** You know the length of the side opposite and the side adjacent to θ, so use arctangent to solve for the angle measure.

$$\text{Tan}^{-1}\left(\frac{11}{13}\right) = 40.2°.$$

13. **E** Remember that a logarithm is an exponent. You're trying to determine to what exponent to raise the base, 2, to equal $16\sqrt{2}$.

$$\log_2 16\sqrt{2} = \log_2 2^4 (2)^{\frac{1}{2}}.$$

By the properties of exponents
$$2^4(2)^{\frac{1}{2}} = 2^{4 + \frac{1}{2}} = 2^{\frac{9}{2}}.$$

$$\log_2 2^{\frac{9}{2}} = \frac{9}{2}.$$

14. **C** Complex roots occur in conjugate pairs. If i is a root of the polynomial, then $-i$ is also a root. Use the four roots to determine the factors of the polynomial. Then multiply to get the polynomial.

$$x(x - 4)(x - i)(x + i) =$$

$$x(x - 4)(x^2 + 1) =$$

$$x(x^3 - 4x^2 + x - 4) =$$

$$x^4 - 4x^3 + x^2 - 4x.$$

15. **B** Recall that in the polar coordinate system $x = r \cos \theta$. Alternatively, use right triangle trigonometry to determine cosine θ.

$$\cos \theta = \frac{x}{r}.$$

Now solve for x: $x = r \cos \theta$.

16. **A** In a right triangle, if $\sin \theta = \dfrac{3}{4}$, the leg opposite θ measures 3 and the hypotenuse measures 4. Use the Pythagorean Theorem to solve for the side adjacent to θ.

$$a^2 + 3^2 = 4^2.$$

$$a^2 = 16 - 9 = 7.$$

$$a = \sqrt{7}.$$

$$\cos \theta = \sqrt{\frac{7}{4}}.$$

Recall that the double angle formula for cosine is:

$$\cos 2\theta = \cos^2 \theta - \sin^2 \theta.$$

$$\cos 2\theta = \left(\sqrt{\frac{7}{4}}\right)^2 - \left(\frac{3}{4}\right)^2 = \frac{7}{17} - \frac{9}{16} = -\frac{2}{16} = -\frac{1}{8}.$$

17. **B** The inverse of the logarithmic function is the exponential function. The inverse of $f(x) = \log_3 x$ is, therefore, $f^{-1}(x) = 3^x$.

You can also determine this by graphing $f(x) = \log_3 x$ and $f^{-1}(x) = 3^x$ on your calculator and observing that their graphs are reflections of each other over the line $y = x$.

18. **D** In a rational function, asymptotes occur when the denominator approaches 0 because division by 0 is undefined.

$$4 - x^2 = 0.$$

$$4 = x^2.$$

$$x = \pm 2.$$

Vertical asymptotes, therefore, occur at $x = 2$ and $x = -2$. Because the degree of the numerator equals the degree of the denominator, a horizontal asymptote occurs at the quotient of the coefficients of the x^2 terms.

$$\frac{6}{-1} = -6.$$

The line $y = -6$ is a horizontal asymptote. (To verify the three asymptotes, graph the function on your graphing calculator.)

19. **E** Because $81 = 3^4$, both sides of the equation can be written in base 3.

$$3^{5-x} = 81^{x+1}.$$

$$3^{5-x} = 3^{4(x+1)}.$$

Now, set the exponents equal to each other and solve for x.

$$5 - x = 4x + 4.$$

$$1 = 5x.$$

$$x = \frac{1}{5}.$$

20. **B** Because both the x and y terms are raised to the 2nd power, the graph cannot be a parabola. Note that the x^2 and y^2 terms have different coefficients, and both are positive. The graph would, therefore, be an ellipse.

$$16x^2 + 8y^2 - 32x + 8y - 1 = 0.$$

$$\frac{(x-1)^2}{\frac{9}{8}} + \frac{\left[y + \left(\frac{1}{2}\right)\right]^2}{\frac{9}{4}} = 1.$$

21. **C** $fg(12)$ is the product of $f(12)$ and $g(12)$.

$$f(12) = 2(12) + 5 = 29.$$

$$g(12) = \frac{1}{6+12} = \frac{1}{18}.$$

$$fg(12) = 29\left(\frac{1}{18}\right) = \frac{29}{18}.$$

22. **A** Because the median is 9, the 4th term when arranged from least to greatest is 9. The mode is 7, so either 2 or 3 of the integers less than 9 equal 7. Note that 7 is the only mode. Because the problem asks for the *least* possible range, assume that three of the integers equal 7.

There are two possible scenarios for determining the numbers greater than the median:

7, 7, 7, 9, 10, 10, 11,

7, 7, 7, 9, 10, 11, 11.

Note that if 7 occurs three times, then one of the integers greater than 9 can occur twice. In either case, however, the range equals 11–7, or 4.

23. **C** To check for x-axis symmetry, replace x by $-x$.

$(-x)^2 - (-x)y = 4$ is not equivalent to the original equation.

To check for y-axis symmetry, replace y by $-y$.

$x^2 - x(-y) = 4$ is not equivalent to the original equation.

To check for origin symmetry, replace x by $-x$ and y by $-y$.

$(-x)^2 - (-x)(-y) = 4$ is equivalent to the original equation, so the graph is symmetric with respect to only the origin.

24. **E** Raising the imaginary number i to an exponent follows the pattern:

$$i^1 = i.$$

$$i^2 = -1.$$

$$i^3 = -i.$$

$$i^4 = 1.$$

$21 \div 4 = 5$ remainder 1, so i^{21} is equivalent to $i^1 = i$. Raising i to any power that results in a remainder of 1 when the exponent is divided by 4 will also equal i^1 or i. $31 \div 4 = 7$ remainder 3, so i^{31} is equivalent to $i^3 = -i$, not i.

25. **B** The minimum value of a quadratic equation

$ax^2 + bx + c$ occurs when $x = -\dfrac{b}{2a}$. When graphed the

minimum occurs at the vertex of a parabola that is concave up.

$$C(n) = 0.01x^2 - 90x + 25{,}000.$$

$$n = -\frac{b}{2a} = -\frac{(-90)}{2(0.01)} = 4{,}500 \text{ units.}$$

26. **D**

$$\sqrt[5]{\left(\sqrt[4]{\left(\sqrt[3]{\left(\sqrt{n}\right)}\right)}\right)} = \left(\left(\left(n^{\frac{1}{2}}\right)^{\frac{1}{3}}\right)^{\frac{1}{4}}\right)^{\frac{1}{5}}.$$

When raising a power to a power, multiply the exponents.

$$\frac{1}{2} \times \frac{1}{3} \times \frac{1}{4} \times \frac{1}{5} = \frac{1}{120}.$$

$$\sqrt[5]{\left(\sqrt[4]{\left(\sqrt[3]{\left(\sqrt{n}\right)}\right)}\right)} = n^{\frac{1}{120}}.$$

27. **A** The slope of the line with x-intercept $(6, 0)$ and y-intercept $(0, -15)$ is:

$$m = \frac{y_2 - y_1}{x_2 - x_1} = \frac{-15 - 0}{0 - 6} = \frac{15}{6} = \frac{5}{2}.$$

The y-intercept is given as -15. In slope-intercept form $y = mx + b$ the equation is therefore:

$$y = \frac{5}{2}x + (-15).$$

$$y = \frac{5}{2}x - 15.$$

28. **D** The degree of the polynomial is odd and the leading coefficient is negative. $(a_n = -3)$ By the Leading Coefficient Test, the graph rises left and falls right.

29. **E** If $x + 2$ is a factor of $x^4 + x^3 + 3x^2 + kx - 10$, then $f(-2) = 0$.

$$f(-2) = (-2)^4 + (-2)^3 + 3(-2)^2 + k(-2) - 10 = 0.$$

$$16 - 8 + 12 + k(-2) - 10 = 0.$$

$$-2k + 10 = 0.$$

$$-2k = -10.$$

$$k = 5.$$

Alternatively, divide $x^4 + x^3 + 3x^2 + kx - 10$ by $x + 2$ using either synthetic or long division. The remainder, $-2k + 10$, must equal zero for $x + 2$ to be a factor of the polynomial.

$$-2k + 10 = 0.$$

$$k = 5.$$

30. **D** The Rational Root Test states that if a polynomial function has integer coefficients, every rational zero of the function has the form $\dfrac{p}{q}$ (simplified to lowest terms) where $p =$ a factor of the constant term a_0 and $q =$ a factor of the leading coefficient a_n. Here $a_0 = -15$ and $a_n = 6$.

The factors of -15 are 1, 15, 3, and 5, and the factors of 6 are 1, 6, 2, and 3.

$$\frac{p}{q} = \pm 1, \ \pm \frac{1}{2}, \ \pm \frac{1}{3}, \ \pm \frac{1}{6}, \ \pm 3, \ \pm \frac{3}{2}, \ \pm 5,$$

$$\pm \frac{5}{2}, \ \pm \frac{5}{3}, \ \pm \frac{5}{6}, \ \pm 15, \ \pm \frac{15}{2}.$$

Remember not to duplicate terms and write each in simplest form. There are 24 possible roots.

31. **C** Draw the radius to the point of tangency T. The radius is perpendicular to the tangent segment. Then, draw the segment connecting P to the center of the circle. $\angle P$ is bisected and the new segment is also perpendicular to ST. The central angle measures 75° and the new figure is as follows:

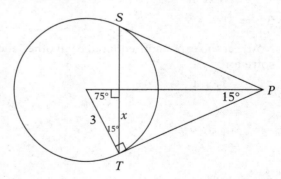

Let $x =$ half the length of ST as shown. Use the radius, 3, as the hypotenuse of the small right triangle in the interior of the circle to solve for x.

$$\cos 15° = \frac{x}{3}.$$

$$x = 3 \cos 15° \approx 2.898.$$

$$ST = 2(2.898) \approx 5.796 \approx 5.8.$$

32. **B** If the investment doubles, $A = \$5,000$.

$$5,000 = 2,500\left(1 + \frac{0.045}{12}\right)^{12t}.$$

$$2 = \left(1 + \frac{0.045}{12}\right)^{12t}.$$

$$2 = 1.00375^{12t}.$$

Now, take either the log or natural log of both sides of the equation to solve for the variable, t, in the exponent.

$$\log 2 = \log (1.00375)^{12t}.$$

$$\log 2 = 12t \log 1.00375.$$

$$\log 2 = 0.0195t.$$

$$t \approx 15.4 \text{ years.}$$

33. **C** The nth term of an arithmetic sequence is given by the equation: $a_n = a_1 + (n-1)d$, where $d =$ the common difference between consecutive terms and $a_1 =$ the first term of the sequence.

The difference between 23 and 7 represents $4d$ because the sequence increases by $6 - 2 = 4$ terms.

$$4d = 23 - 7.$$

$$4d = 16d$$

$$d = 4$$

Knowing that $a_2 = 7$, you can solve for a_1:

$$a_2 = a_1 + (2-1)4 = 7.$$

$$a_1 + 4 = 7.$$

$$a_1 = 3.$$

The 90th term is, therefore:

$$a_{90} = 3 + (90-1)4 = 359.$$

34. **D** Multiplying 45,454,545,454,545 by the units digit of 1,234, 4, results in a 14-digit product. Multiplying 45,454,545,454,545 by the tens digit of 1,234, 3, results in a 15-digit product because it is necessary to use a zero placeholder for the units digit. Similarly, multiplying by the hundreds digit requires 2 placeholders, and multiplying by the thousands digit requires 3 placeholders. The product will contain:

$$14 + 3 = 17 \text{ digits.}$$

On your calculator, the product may be displayed as $5.609 \ldots \text{E}16$, which represents $5.609 \ldots \times 10^{16}$. In decimal form, this results in a 5 followed by 16 digits.

35. **E** The figure is the graph of the sine function with amplitude $\frac{1}{2}$ and period π. The equation is, therefore,

$$y = \frac{1}{2} \sin 2x.$$

36. **A** Use the Law of Sines to determine the length of BC.

$$\frac{\sin A}{a} = \frac{\sin B}{b} = \frac{\sin C}{c}.$$

$$\frac{\sin 29°}{3.4} = \frac{\sin 43°}{BC}.$$

$$BC = \frac{3.4(\sin 43°)}{\sin 29°}.$$

$$BC \approx 4.8 \text{ cm.}$$

37. **D**

$$0.75(84) + 0.25(92) = 86.$$

Her overall grade will be 86%.

38. **B** The distance between ordered triples (x_1, y_1, z_1) and (x_2, y_2, z_2) is given by the formula:

$$\text{Distance} = \sqrt{(x_2 - x_1)^2 + (y_2 - y_1)^2 + (z_2 - z_1)^2}.$$

$$\text{Distance} = \sqrt{(7 - -4)^2 + (5 - 2)^2 + (-3 - 1)^2}.$$

$$= \sqrt{11^2 + 3^2 + (-4)^2}.$$

$$= \sqrt{146} \approx 12.1.$$

39. **B**

To find the slope of the line, write the parametric equations as a single equation in terms of x and y. Because $x = 8 - t$, $t = 8 - x$. Substitute this value of t into the equation for y:

$$y = 10 + 2(8 - x).$$

$$y = 10 + 16 - 2x.$$

$$y = -2x + 26.$$

The equation of the line is in slope-intercept form, so the slope of the line is the coefficient of the x term, -2.

40. **C** Because $a \, \Phi \, b = a \, \Phi \, b = a^{-b} - 3b$,

$$n \, \Phi - 2 = n^{-(-2)} - 3(-2).$$

$$n^2 + 6 = 70.$$

$$n^2 = 64.$$

$$n = \pm 8.$$

Answer C, -8, is one possible solution for n.

41. **C** AD is the hypotenuse of a right triangle with legs measuring s and $\frac{s}{2}$. Use the Pythagorean Theorem to solve for AD.

$$AD^2 = s^2 + \left(\frac{s}{2}\right)^2.$$

$$AD^2 = s^2 + \frac{s^2}{4}.$$

$$AD^2 = \frac{5^2}{4}.$$

$$AD = \frac{s\sqrt{5}}{2}$$

AD = BC, so the perimeter of ABCD is:

$$s + \frac{s\sqrt{5}}{2} + s + \frac{s\sqrt{5}}{2} = 2s + s\sqrt{5}.$$

42. **C** The standard form of the equation of an ellipse is:

$\frac{(x-h)^2}{a^2} + \frac{(y-k)^2}{b^2} = 1$ for an ellipse whose major axis is horizontal, and $\frac{(x-h)^2}{b^2} + \frac{(y-k)^2}{a^2} = 1$ for an ellipse whose major axis is vertical. In both cases, $2a$ = the length of the major axis.

First, divide both sides of the equation by 48 to write it in standard form.

$$12x^2 + 8y^2 = 48.$$

$$\frac{x^2}{4} + \frac{y^2}{6} = 1.$$

This ellipse has a vertical major axis because a must be greater than b. $a = \sqrt{6}$. The length of the major axis is $2\sqrt{6} \approx 4.90$.

43. **D** The line tangent to the circle $x^2 + y^2 = 1$ at $\left(\frac{3}{5}, \frac{4}{5}\right)$ is perpendicular to the radius drawn from the point of tangency.

Note that the equation $x^2 + y^2 = 1$ represents a circle centered at the origin with a radius of one unit.

The line containing the radius from point $\left(\frac{3}{5}, \frac{4}{5}\right)$ has a slope of $m = \dfrac{\frac{3}{5}}{\frac{4}{5}} = \frac{4}{3}$. Any line perpendicular to the radius will have a slope equivalent to the opposite reciprocal of $\frac{4}{3}$, which is $-\frac{3}{4}$.

Now, find the equation of the line containing the point $\left(\frac{3}{5}, \frac{4}{5}\right)$ with a slope of $-\frac{3}{4}$. In point-slope form, the equation is:

$$y - \frac{4}{5} = -\frac{3}{4}\left(x - \frac{3}{5}\right).$$

$$y = -\frac{3}{4}x + \frac{9}{20} + \frac{4}{5}.$$

$$y = -\frac{3}{4}x + \frac{25}{20} = -\frac{3}{4}x + \frac{5}{4}.$$

The y-intercept is $\frac{5}{4}$ or 1.25.

44. **C**

$$\frac{3x^2 - 7x - 6}{x^2 - 9} = \frac{3x + 2, \, x - 3}{x - 3, \, x + 3}$$

$$= \frac{3x + 2}{x + 3}.$$

The values of the function are equal to $\dfrac{3x + 2}{x + 3}$ for all x except $x = \pm 3$. As x approaches 3, the value of the function approaches:

$$\frac{3(3) + 2}{3 + 3} = \frac{11}{6} \approx 1.8.$$

45. **A** A function is odd if replacing x with $-x$ results in the opposite of the original function. Its graph is symmetric with respect to the origin. Instead of algebraically determining which of the given functions satisfy the equation $f(-x) = -f(x)$, graph them on your graphing calculator. You can see that the sine function is symmetric to the origin.

$f(x) = \cos x$ is symmetric with respect to the y-axis. $f(x) = x^2 - 10$ is also symmetric with respect to the y-axis. $f(x) = 4^x$ and $f(x) = \log_2 x$ are inverse functions and reflections of each other over the line $y = x$. They are not symmetric with respect to the origin.

Answer A, $f(x) = \sin x$, is the correct answer choice.

46. **E** Factor the equation to get:

$$(4\sin x - 1)(3\sin x + 1) = 0.$$

$$\sin x = \frac{1}{4} \text{ or } \sin x = -\frac{1}{3}.$$

$$x = \sin^{-1}\left(\frac{1}{4}\right) = 14.478°.$$

$$x = \sin^{-1}\left(-\frac{1}{3}\right) = 19.471°.$$

Considering $0° \le x \le 360°$, the possible solutions are:

$$x = 14.48°, \ 165.52°, \ 199.47°, \text{ or } 340.53°.$$

The problem specifies the interval $180° \le x \le 360°$, however. 199.5° or 340.5° are the correct answers.

47. **B** The problem is asking for the square root of $15 - 8i$. Square the answer choices to determine which one results in $15 - 8i$. Remember that $i^2 = -1$.

$$(4 - i)(4 - i) = 16 - 8i + i^2.$$

$$= 16 - 8i - 1 = 15 - 8i.$$

48. **B**

$$\frac{\tan \theta \cot \theta}{\tan \theta} =$$

$$\frac{\dfrac{\sin \theta}{\cos \theta} + \dfrac{\cos \theta}{\sin \theta}}{\left(\dfrac{\sin \theta}{\cos \theta}\right)}.$$

Multiply the numerator and denominator by the LCD, $\cos \theta \sin \theta$:

$$\frac{\dfrac{\sin \theta}{\cos \theta} + \dfrac{\cos \theta}{\sin \theta}}{\dfrac{\sin \theta}{\cos \theta}} \times \frac{\cos \theta \sin \theta}{\cos \theta \sin \theta}$$

$$= \frac{\sin^2 \theta + \cos^2 \theta}{\sin^2 \theta}$$

$$= \frac{1}{\sin^2 \theta}$$

$$= \csc^2 \theta.$$

49. **A** The first term in the series, a_1, is 1. Divide the second term by the first term to determine the common ratio, $r = -\dfrac{1}{5}$. Because this is an infinite geometric sequence, find its sum by using the formula:

$$S = \frac{a_1}{1 - r}.$$

$$S = \frac{1}{1 - \dfrac{-1}{5}}.$$

$$S = \frac{1}{\dfrac{6}{5}} = \frac{5}{6}.$$

50. **D** The middle term of $\left(3x - \dfrac{1}{3}y\right)^8$ has the coefficient $_8C_4$.

$$\frac{8!}{4!4!} = \frac{5 \times 6 \times 7 \times 8}{1 \times 2 \times 3 \times 4} = 70.$$

$$70(3x)^4\left(-\frac{1}{3}y\right)^4 =$$

$$70(3^4)(x^4)\left(-\frac{1}{3}^4\right)(y^4) =$$

$$70x^4y^4.$$

■■■ DIAGNOSE YOUR STRENGTHS AND WEAKNESSES

Check the number of each question answered correctly and "X" the number of each question answered incorrectly.

Algebra	1	2	6	8	13	19	26	32	47	50	Total Number Correct
10 questions											

Solid Geometry	38	41	Total Number Correct
2 questions			

Coordinate Geometry	3	15	20	27	42	43	Total Number Correct
6 questions							

Trigonometry	7	12	16	31	36	46	48	Total Number Correct
7 questions								

Functions	4	5	10	14	17	18	21	23	25	28	29	30	35	39	45	Total Number Correct
15 questions																

Data Analysis, Statistics, and Probability	9	11	22	37	Total Number Correct
4 questions					

Numbers and Operations	24	33	34	40	44	49	Total Number Correct
6 questions							

Number of correct answers – $\frac{1}{4}$ (Number of incorrect answers) = Your raw score

_____ – $\frac{1}{4}$ (_____) = _____

Compare your raw score with the approximate SAT Subject Test score below:

	Raw Score	SAT Subject Test Approximate Score
Excellent	43–50	770–800
Very Good	33–43	670–770
Good	27–33	620–670
Above Average	21–27	570–620
Average	11–21	500–570
Below Average	< 11	< 500

PRACTICE TEST 2

Treat this practice test as the actual test and complete it in one 60-minute sitting. Use the following answer sheet to fill in your multiple-choice answers. Once you have completed the practice test:

1. Check your answers using the Answer Key.
2. Review the Answers and Solutions.
3. Fill in the "Diagnose Your Strengths and Weaknesses" sheet and determine areas that require further preparation.

PRACTICE TEST 2
MATH LEVEL 2

ANSWER SHEET

Tear out this answer sheet and use it to complete the practice test. Determine the BEST answer for each question. Then, fill in the appropriate oval using a No. 2 pencil.

1. Ⓐ Ⓑ Ⓒ Ⓓ Ⓔ	21. Ⓐ Ⓑ Ⓒ Ⓓ Ⓔ	41. Ⓐ Ⓑ Ⓒ Ⓓ Ⓔ
2. Ⓐ Ⓑ Ⓒ Ⓓ Ⓔ	22. Ⓐ Ⓑ Ⓒ Ⓓ Ⓔ	42. Ⓐ Ⓑ Ⓒ Ⓓ Ⓔ
3. Ⓐ Ⓑ Ⓒ Ⓓ Ⓔ	23. Ⓐ Ⓑ Ⓒ Ⓓ Ⓔ	43. Ⓐ Ⓑ Ⓒ Ⓓ Ⓔ
4. Ⓐ Ⓑ Ⓒ Ⓓ Ⓔ	24. Ⓐ Ⓑ Ⓒ Ⓓ Ⓔ	44. Ⓐ Ⓑ Ⓒ Ⓓ Ⓔ
5. Ⓐ Ⓑ Ⓒ Ⓓ Ⓔ	25. Ⓐ Ⓑ Ⓒ Ⓓ Ⓔ	45. Ⓐ Ⓑ Ⓒ Ⓓ Ⓔ
6. Ⓐ Ⓑ Ⓒ Ⓓ Ⓔ	26. Ⓐ Ⓑ Ⓒ Ⓓ Ⓔ	46. Ⓐ Ⓑ Ⓒ Ⓓ Ⓔ
7. Ⓐ Ⓑ Ⓒ Ⓓ Ⓔ	27. Ⓐ Ⓑ Ⓒ Ⓓ Ⓔ	47. Ⓐ Ⓑ Ⓒ Ⓓ Ⓔ
8. Ⓐ Ⓑ Ⓒ Ⓓ Ⓔ	28. Ⓐ Ⓑ Ⓒ Ⓓ Ⓔ	48. Ⓐ Ⓑ Ⓒ Ⓓ Ⓔ
9. Ⓐ Ⓑ Ⓒ Ⓓ Ⓔ	29. Ⓐ Ⓑ Ⓒ Ⓓ Ⓔ	49. Ⓐ Ⓑ Ⓒ Ⓓ Ⓔ
10. Ⓐ Ⓑ Ⓒ Ⓓ Ⓔ	30. Ⓐ Ⓑ Ⓒ Ⓓ Ⓔ	50. Ⓐ Ⓑ Ⓒ Ⓓ Ⓔ
11. Ⓐ Ⓑ Ⓒ Ⓓ Ⓔ	31. Ⓐ Ⓑ Ⓒ Ⓓ Ⓔ	
12. Ⓐ Ⓑ Ⓒ Ⓓ Ⓔ	32. Ⓐ Ⓑ Ⓒ Ⓓ Ⓔ	
13. Ⓐ Ⓑ Ⓒ Ⓓ Ⓔ	33. Ⓐ Ⓑ Ⓒ Ⓓ Ⓔ	
14. Ⓐ Ⓑ Ⓒ Ⓓ Ⓔ	34. Ⓐ Ⓑ Ⓒ Ⓓ Ⓔ	
15. Ⓐ Ⓑ Ⓒ Ⓓ Ⓔ	35. Ⓐ Ⓑ Ⓒ Ⓓ Ⓔ	
16. Ⓐ Ⓑ Ⓒ Ⓓ Ⓔ	36. Ⓐ Ⓑ Ⓒ Ⓓ Ⓔ	
17. Ⓐ Ⓑ Ⓒ Ⓓ Ⓔ	37. Ⓐ Ⓑ Ⓒ Ⓓ Ⓔ	
18. Ⓐ Ⓑ Ⓒ Ⓓ Ⓔ	38. Ⓐ Ⓑ Ⓒ Ⓓ Ⓔ	
19. Ⓐ Ⓑ Ⓒ Ⓓ Ⓔ	39. Ⓐ Ⓑ Ⓒ Ⓓ Ⓔ	
20. Ⓐ Ⓑ Ⓒ Ⓓ Ⓔ	40. Ⓐ Ⓑ Ⓒ Ⓓ Ⓔ	

PRACTICE TEST 2

Time: 60 minutes

> **Directions:** Select the BEST answer for each of the 50 multiple-choice questions. If the exact solution is not one of the five choices, select the answer that is the best approximation. Then, fill in the appropriate oval on the answer sheet.

Notes:

1. A calculator will be needed to answer some of the questions on the test. Scientific, programmable, and graphing calculators are permitted. It is up to you to determine when and when not to use your calculator.
2. Angles on the Level 2 test are measured in degrees and radians. You need to decide whether your calculator should be set to degree mode or radian mode for a particular question.
3. Figures are drawn as accurately as possible and are intended to help solve some of the test problems. If a figure is not drawn to scale, this will be stated in the problem. All figures lie in a plane unless the problem indicates otherwise.
4. Unless otherwise stated, the domain of a function f is assumed to be the set of real numbers x for which the value of the function, $f(x)$, is a real number.
5. Reference information that may be useful in answering some of the test questions can be found below.

Reference Information	
Right circular cone with radius r and height h:	Volume $= \dfrac{1}{3}\pi r^2 h$
Right circular cone with circumference of base c and slant height ℓ:	Lateral Area $= \dfrac{1}{2}c\ell$
Sphere with radius r:	Volume $= \dfrac{4}{3}\pi r^3$ Surface Area $= 4\pi r^2$
Pyramid with base area B and height h:	Volume $= \dfrac{1}{3}Bh$

PRACTICE TEST 2 QUESTIONS

1. If $x^5 = 8^4$, $x =$

   (A) 0.13
   (B) 5.28
   (C) 13.45
   (D) 819.20
   (E) 6,208.37

2. If $f(x) = e^{2x}$ and $g(x) = x^{-2}$, then $f(g(4)) =$

   (A) 0.07
   (B) 2,981
   (C) 1.13
   (D) 1.27
   (E) 7.89

3. If $\dfrac{m}{3m - n} = \dfrac{1}{5}$, then $\dfrac{n}{m} =$

   (A) -2
   (B) $-\dfrac{1}{2}$
   (C) $\dfrac{1}{2}$
   (D) 2
   (E) $\dfrac{3}{5}$

4. For all $x \neq 0$, $\dfrac{1}{x} + \dfrac{2}{x^2} + \dfrac{3}{x^3} =$

   (A) $\dfrac{6}{x^3}$
   (B) $\dfrac{6}{x^6}$
   (C) $\dfrac{(x^2 + x + 1)}{x^3}$
   (D) $\dfrac{(x^2 + 2x + 3)}{x^3}$
   (E) $\dfrac{(x^2 + 5)}{x^3}$

5. What is the reciprocal of $6 + i$?

   (A) $\dfrac{1}{6}$
   (B) $\dfrac{6 - i}{35}$
   (C) $\dfrac{6 + i}{36}$
   (D) $\dfrac{6 - i}{37}$
   (E) $\dfrac{6 - i}{36}$

GO ON TO THE NEXT PAGE

6. In factored form, $x^3 - 2x^2 + 2x - 4 =$

   (A) $(x-2)(x+2)^2$
   (B) $(x-2)(x+2)(x+1)$
   (C) $(x-2)^2(x+2)$
   (D) $(x-2)^3$
   (E) $(x-2)(x^2+2)$

USE THIS SPACE AS SCRATCH PAPER

7. $\sqrt[3]{20x^2y^7} \cdot \sqrt[3]{50x^4y^2} =$

   (A) $20^{\frac{1}{3}}(50^{\frac{1}{3}})x^6y^9$

   (B) $70^{\frac{1}{3}}x^2y^3$

   (C) $10x^{\frac{8}{3}}y^{\frac{14}{3}}$
   (D) $10x^2y^3$

   (E) $1{,}000x^{\frac{8}{3}}y^{\frac{14}{3}}$

8. If $\dfrac{x+2}{x-5} \geq 0$, then which of the following describes x?

   (A) $x \geq -2$
   (B) $-2 \leq x < 5$
   (C) $x \leq -2$ or $x > 5$
   (D) $x > 5$
   (E) $x \leq -2$ or $x \geq 5$

9. Which of the following expressions represents the statement "N varies jointly with the square of x and with y"?

   (A) $N = kx^2y$

   (B) $N = \dfrac{k}{y\sqrt{x}}$

   (C) $N = ky\sqrt{x}$
   (D) $N = kx^2y^2$

   (E) $N = \dfrac{k}{x^2y}$

10. What is the vertex of the parabola given by $f(x) = x^2 - 6x + 5$?

    (A) $(-3, 4)$
    (B) $(3, -4)$
    (C) $(3, 4)$
    (D) $(3, -3)$
    (E) $(4, -4)$

GO ON TO THE NEXT PAGE

11. In Figure 1, $\cot \theta = 1.33$. $\sin \theta =$

    (A) 0.01
    (B) 0.63
    (C) 0.60
    (D) 0.75
    (E) 0.80

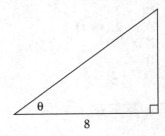

Figure 1

12. What are the zeroes of $f(x) = 8x^3 - 2x^2 - 3x$?

    (A) $\left\{-\dfrac{1}{2}, \dfrac{3}{4}\right\}$

    (B) $\left\{-\dfrac{3}{4}, \dfrac{1}{2}\right\}$

    (C) $\left\{-\dfrac{1}{2}, \dfrac{1}{2}, \dfrac{3}{4}\right\}$

    (D) $\left\{-\dfrac{3}{4}, 0, \dfrac{1}{2}\right\}$

    (E) $\left\{-\dfrac{1}{2}, 0, \dfrac{3}{4}\right\}$

13. The probability that it will snow tomorrow is $\dfrac{2}{3}$ and, independently, the probability that it will also snow the day after tomorrow is $\dfrac{1}{5}$. What is the probability that it will snow tomorrow but *not* the day after tomorrow?

    (A) $\dfrac{2}{15}$

    (B) $\dfrac{2}{5}$

    (C) $\dfrac{3}{4}$

    (D) $\dfrac{8}{15}$

    (E) $\dfrac{22}{15}$

14. An operation is defined on any three real numbers by $a \,\square\, b \,\square\, c = a(c - b)$. If $2 \,\square\, 1 \,\square\, x = 10$, then $x =$

    (A) −6
    (B) −4
    (C) 5
    (D) 6
    (E) 4

GO ON TO THE NEXT PAGE

15. If $(x - 1)^{\frac{2}{3}} = 25$, then $x =$

   (A) 8.5
   (B) 15,625
   (C) 124
   (D) 125
   (E) 126

16. If $\cos 2\theta = \dfrac{3}{4}$, then $\dfrac{1}{\cos^2\theta - \sin^2\theta} =$

   (A) -1
   (B) $\dfrac{3}{4}$
   (C) $\dfrac{4}{3}$
   (D) 4
   (E) 1

17. What does the angle $-\dfrac{5\pi}{12}$ equal in degree measure?

   (A) $-75°$
   (B) $-15°$
   (C) $-150°$
   (D) $37.5°$
   (E) $-52.5°$

18. If $f(x) = \dfrac{4x^2 - 9}{2x + 3}$, what value does the function approach as x approaches $-\dfrac{3}{2}$?

   (A) 0.02
   (B) 0
   (C) -4.33
   (D) -6
   (E) -9

19. If i is a zero of the polynomial $p(x)$, then which of the following must be a factor of $p(x)$?
   (A) $-i$
   (B) x^2
   (C) $x^2 + 1$
   (D) $x^2 - 1$
   (E) $x^2 - 2ix + 1$

GO ON TO THE NEXT PAGE

20. For all $x \neq 2$, $f(x) = (x-2)(2-x)^{-1}$. Which of the following must be a true statement?

    I.　　$f(1) = f(-1)$
    II.　$f(4) = f(0)$
    III.　$f\left(\dfrac{1}{2}\right) = f(-2)$

    (A)　I only
    (B)　III only
    (C)　I and II only
    (D)　II and III only
    (E)　I, II, and III

21. If $f(x) = 5x - 1$ and $g(f(-3)) = 18$, then $g(x)$ could be which of the following?

    (A)　$x + 2$
    (B)　$-x + 2$
    (C)　$-2x - 12$
    (D)　$\dfrac{x}{4} + 14$
    (E)　$x + 4$

22. Which of the following is a y-intercept of the hyperbola $\dfrac{y^2}{9} - \dfrac{x^2}{16} = 1$?

    (A)　$(0, -3)$
    (B)　$(0, 4)$
    (C)　$(3, 0)$
    (D)　$(0, 81)$
    (E)　$(0, 9)$

23. What is the length of segment DE in Figure 2?

    (A)　3.46
    (B)　4.47
    (C)　6
    (D)　6.16
    (E)　11

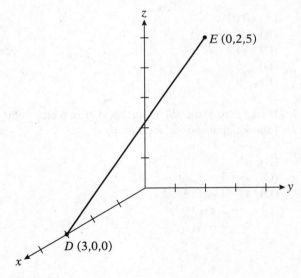

Figure 2

24. A car is purchased for $24,500. If it decreases in value at a rate of 7% per year, how much will it be worth in 5 years?

    (A) $15,851
    (B) $15,925
    (C) $17,044
    (D) $22,785
    (E) $32,787

25. $f(x) = 4^x$ for all real values of x. If $p > 1$ and $q > 1$, then $f^{-1}(p)f^{-1}(q) =$

    (A) 4^{p+q}
    (B) $\log_4 p \log_4 q$
    (C) $\log_4 pq$
    (D) $\log_4 p + \log_4 q$
    (E) $\log_p 4 \log_q 4$

26. If $\log_b 6 = 36$, then $b =$

    (A) 0.17
    (B) 0.50
    (C) 1.05
    (D) 1.50
    (E) 2

27. $\tan (\arccos 0.75) =$

    (A) 0.66
    (B) 0.75
    (C) 0.80
    (D) 0.88
    (E) 41.4

28. Five-sixths of the students in class are passing with a grade of C– or better. Three-fourths of the students in the same class are passing with a grade of B– or better. What fraction of the class is not passing with a grade of B– or better but is passing with a grade of C– or better?

    (A) $\dfrac{5}{8}$

    (B) $\dfrac{1}{12}$

    (C) $\dfrac{1}{6}$

    (D) $\dfrac{1}{4}$

    (E) $\dfrac{1}{15}$

USE THIS SPACE AS SCRATCH PAPER

GO ON TO THE NEXT PAGE

29. What is the radius of the circle $x^2 + y^2 - 14x + 4y + 44 = 0$?

    (A) 2.2
    (B) 3
    (C) 6.6
    (D) 9
    (E) 44

30. Which of the following equations has the graph shown in Figure 3?

    (A) $y = \cos 2x$
    (B) $y = 2\cos x$
    (C) $y = 2\cos 2x$
    (D) $y = 2\cos \dfrac{x}{2}$
    (E) $y = \cos \dfrac{x}{2}$

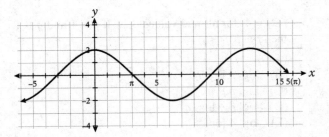

Figure 3

31. What is the range of the piecewise function
$$f(x) = \begin{cases} x^2 & x > 3 \\ -\dfrac{2}{3}x + 11 & x \le 3 \end{cases} ?$$

    (A) All real numbers
    (B) $y \ge 0$
    (C) $-3 \le y \le 3$
    (D) $y \le 3$
    (E) $y \ge 9$

32. If vector $v = (-3, 7)$ and vector $u = (2, -1)$, then vector $u - v =$

    (A) $(-5, 8)$
    (B) $(-1, 6)$
    (C) $(-8, 5)$
    (D) $(-6, -7)$
    (E) $(5, -8)$

33. A cube has edges of length 3. If P and Q are points on its surface, what is the maximum straight-line distance from P to Q?

    (A) $3\sqrt{2}$
    (B) $3\sqrt{3}$
    (C) 6
    (D) $3\sqrt{5}$
    (E) 9

34. If a is any positive integer, then which of the following is *not* a true statement?

    (A) $2a + 1$ is always an odd integer.
    (B) $\sqrt{a}$ is always a real number.
    (C) $\sqrt{-a}$ is always an imaginary number.
    (D) a^3 is always an odd integer.
    (E) The product of a and $\dfrac{1}{a}$ always equals 1.

GO ON TO THE NEXT PAGE

35. If $\dfrac{n}{x^2 - 36} = \dfrac{1}{x - 6} + \dfrac{1}{x + 6}$, then $n =$

   (A) x
   (B) $2x$
   (C) $2(x + 6)$
   (D) $2(x - 6)$
   (E) 2

36. If $f(x) = x^3$ and $h(x)$ is obtained by shifting $f(x)$ down 4 units and right 2 units, then $h(x) =$

   (A) $(x - 2)^3 + 4$
   (B) $(x + 2)^3 - 4$
   (C) $(x - 2)^3 - 4$
   (D) $(x - 4)^3 - 2$
   (E) $4 - (x - 2)^3$

37. If the lines $y_1 = (n + 2)x + 10$ and $y_2 = (n - 4)x + 2$ are perpendicular, then n could equal which of the following?

   (A) 3.45
   (B) 3.83
   (C) 1
   (D) 0.5
   (E) −6

38. The graph of $y = -x^4 + 12x - 18$

   (A) intersects the x-axis at exactly one point.
   (B) intersects the x-axis at exactly two points.
   (C) intersects the x-axis at exactly three points.
   (D) intersects the x-axis at exactly four points.
   (E) does not intersect the x-axis.

39. Which of the following is equivalent to the equation $x^2 + 5x + y^2 - 1 = 0$ in polar form?

   (A) $r^2 + 5r \cos \theta - 1 = 0$
   (B) $r = 5r \cos \theta + 1$
   (C) $r^2 = 5r \cos \theta$
   (D) $r^2 + 5r \sin \theta - 1 = 0$
   (E) $r^2 = -5r \sin \theta$

40. If A is a 2×3 matrix, and B is a 3×4 matrix, then the product of A times $3B$ is a matrix of which of the following dimensions?

   (A) 6×4
   (B) 2×3
   (C) 2×4
   (D) 3×3
   (E) 2×12

41. $(\sec \theta + \tan \theta)(\sec \theta - \tan \theta) =$

   (A) $\sec^2 \theta$
   (B) 1
   (C) $\tan^2 \theta - \sec^2 \theta$
   (D) −1
   (E) $2\sec^2 \theta - 1$

GO ON TO THE NEXT PAGE

42. The linear regression model $C = 13.2m + 20.5$ relates the calories burned using a new exercise machine (C) to the number of minutes a person uses the machine (m). Which of the following statements about this model must be true?

   I.   When a person spends 22 minutes using the machine, the predicted number of calories burned is approximately 311.

   II. There is relatively no correlation between C and m.

   III. A person burns approximately 13.2 calories each minute he or she uses the machine.

(A) I only
(B) III only
(C) I and II only
(D) I and III only
(E) I, II, and III

43. If (x, y) is a point on the graph of $f(x)$, then which of the following is a point on the graph of $f^{-1}(x)$?

(A) $(-x, -y)$
(B) $(-x, y)$
(C) (y, x)
(D) $(x, -y)$
(E) $(-y, -x)$

44. The graph of $y = -2x + 7$ can be expressed as a set of parametric equations. If $x = 1 - t$, and $y = f(t)$, then what does $f(t)$ equal?

(A) $2t - 7$
(B) $-2t + 5$
(C) $2t + 9$
(D) $-\frac{1}{2}t - 7$
(E) $2t + 5$

45. If $x_0 = 5$ and $x_{n+1} = x_n\sqrt{x_n + 4}$, then $x_4 =$

(A) 23.4
(B) 65.4
(C) 544.6
(D) 12,709.8
(E) 12,756.4

46. If $f(x) = 6^x$, then $f\left(\log_7 \frac{1}{343}\right) =$

(A) -3
(B) -18
(C) $\frac{1}{216}$
(D) $\frac{1}{1,296}$
(E) 216

GO ON TO THE NEXT PAGE

47. How long is the base of an isosceles triangle if the other two sides measure 20 cm and each base angle measures 28°?

(A) 12.7
(B) 28.3
(C) 30.6
(D) 35.3
(E) 88.6

48. A committee of 4 people is to be selected from a group of 8 women and 4 men. Assuming the selection is made randomly, what is the probability that the committee consists of 2 women and 2 men?

(A) $\dfrac{56}{165}$

(B) $\dfrac{6}{495}$

(C) $\dfrac{28}{495}$

(D) $\dfrac{28}{165}$

(E) $\dfrac{34}{495}$

49. In terms of θ, what is the area of the triangle in Figure 4?

(A) $2 \sin^2 \theta$
(B) $4 \sin \theta \cos \theta$
(C) $\dfrac{1}{2} \tan \theta$
(D) $2 \sin \theta \cos \theta$
(E) $\dfrac{1}{2} \theta$

50. If f is a function whose graph is the line segment shown in Figure 5, then $f^{-1}(6.2) =$

(A) 0.44
(B) 0.76
(C) 0.89
(D) 1.11
(E) 1.77

USE THIS SPACE AS SCRATCH PAPER

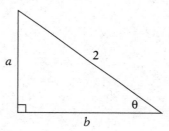

Figure 4

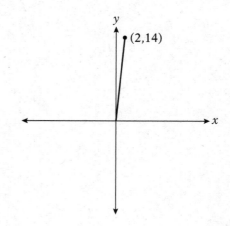

Figure 5

S T O P

IF YOU FINISH BEFORE TIME IS CALLED, YOU MAY CHECK YOUR WORK ON THIS TEST ONLY.
DO NOT TURN TO ANY OTHER TEST IN THIS BOOK.

■ ANSWER KEY

1. B	11. C	21. B	31. E	41. B
2. C	12. E	22. A	32. E	42. D
3. A	13. D	23. D	33. B	43. C
4. D	14. D	24. C	34. D	44. E
5. D	15. E	25. B	35. B	45. E
6. E	16. C	26. C	36. C	46. C
7. D	17. A	27. D	37. B	47. D
8. C	18. D	28. B	38. E	48. A
9. A	19. C	29. B	39. A	49. D
10. B	20. E	30. D	40. C	50. C

■ ANSWERS AND SOLUTIONS

1. **B** Take the fifth root of both sides of the equation to solve for x:

$$x^5 = 8^4.$$

$$(x^5)^{\frac{1}{5}} = (8^4)^{\frac{1}{5}}.$$

$$x = 8^{\frac{4}{5}} = 5.27803 \approx 5.28.$$

2. **C** You will need to use the e^x function on your calculator for this problem.

$$g(4) = 4^{-2} = \frac{1}{16} = 0.0625.$$

$$f(g(4)) = f(0.0625) = e^{2(0.0625)}.$$

$$= 1.133148 \approx 1.13.$$

3. **A** Transform the equation and isolate $\dfrac{n}{m}$:

$$\frac{m}{(3m - n)} = \frac{1}{5}.$$

$$3m - n = 5m.$$

$$-2m = n.$$

$$-2 = \frac{n}{m}.$$

4. **D** The LCD of the three fractions is x^3.

$$\frac{1}{x} + \frac{2}{x^2} + \frac{3}{x^3} =$$

$$\frac{x^2}{x^3} + \frac{2x}{x^3} + \frac{3}{x^3} =$$

$$\frac{(x^2 + 2x + 3)}{x^3}.$$

5. **D** The complex conjugate of $6 + i$ is $6 - i$. To simplify the fraction, multiply the numerator and the denominator by the complex conjugate. Recall that $i^2 = -1$.

$$\frac{1}{6 + i} = \frac{1}{6 + i} \times \frac{6 - i}{6 - i}$$

$$= \frac{6 - i}{(6 + i)(6 - i)} = \frac{6 - i}{36 - i^2}$$

$$= \frac{6 - i}{36 - (-1)} = \frac{6 - i}{37}.$$

6. **E** Factor by grouping terms:

$$x^3 - 2x^2 + 2x - 4 = (x^3 - 2x^2) + (2x - 4).$$

Now, distribute common factors:

$$(x^3 - 2x^2) + (2x - 4) = x^2(x - 2) + 2(x - 2)$$
$$= (x - 2)(x^2 + 2).$$

7. **D** First, determine the product of the radicands. Then, take the cube root of each term.

$$\sqrt[3]{20x^2y^7} \cdot \sqrt[3]{50x^4y^2} =$$
$$\sqrt[3]{[(20)(50)(x^2x^4)(y^7y^2)]} =$$
$$\sqrt[3]{1000x^6y^9} =$$
$$1000^{\frac{1}{3}} x^{\frac{6}{3}} y^{\frac{9}{3}} =$$
$$10x^2y^3.$$

8. **C** This problem involves a rational expression. Find the critical points where the numerator and denominator equal zero. Then, determine which intervals satisfy the inequality.

$$\frac{x + 2}{x - 5} \geq 0$$

Critical points: $x = -2$ and $x = 5$.

Note that $x \neq 5$, however, because the denominator cannot equal zero.

Test when $x = 0$. $\frac{2}{-5} \geq 0$ is not a true statement, so the interval between -2 and 5 is not part of the solution. The solution is the interval $x \leq -2$ or $x > 5$.

9. **A** "N varies jointly with the square of x and with y" is equivalent to "N is jointly proportional to the square of x and with y." If N was *inversely* proportional to the square of x and with y, the x and y terms would be in the denominator.

The square of x translates to x^2, not $\sqrt{x}$, so $N = kx^2y$ is the correct answer.

10. **B** Complete the square to write the equation of the parabola in standard form.

$$f(x) = x^2 - 6x + 5.$$
$$y = x^2 - 6x + 5.$$
$$y - 5 = x^2 - 6x.$$
$$y - 5 + 9 = x^2 - 6x + 9.$$
$$y + 4 = (x - 3)^2.$$

The vertex is $(3, -4)$. You can also verify this answer by graphing the function on your graphing calculator.

11. **C** Because $\cot \theta = 1.33$, $\tan \theta = \frac{1}{1.33} = 0.75$.

$$\tan^{-1}(0.75) \approx 36.87°.$$
$$\sin 36.87° \approx 0.6.$$

Alternatively, recognize that for $\cot \theta$ to equal 1.33, the triangle has sides measuring 6–8–10. $\cot \theta = \frac{8}{6} = 1.33$.

$\sin \theta = \frac{6}{10} = 0.6$.

12. **E** Set the polynomial equal to zero and factor.

$$8x^3 - 2x^2 - 3x = 0.$$
$$x(8x^2 - 2x - 3) = 0.$$
$$x(2x + 1)(4x - 3) = 0.$$
$$x = 0 \ \ or \ -\frac{1}{2} \ \ or \ x = \frac{3}{4}.$$

13. **D** Because the events are independent, find the product of their probabilities.

The probability that it will NOT snow the day after tomorrow is:

$$1 - \frac{1}{5} = \frac{4}{5}.$$

The probability that it will snow tomorrow but *not* the day after tomorrow is:

$$\frac{2}{3} \times \frac{4}{5} = \frac{8}{15}.$$

14. **D**

$$a \,\square\, b \,\square\, c = a(c - b).$$

$$2 \,\square\, 1 \,\square\, x = 2(x - 1) = 10.$$

$$x - 1 = 5.$$

$$x = 6.$$

15. **E** Raise each side of the equation to the $\frac{3}{2}$ power to solve for x:

$$(x - 1)^{\frac{3}{2}} = 25.$$

$$\left[(x - 1)^{\frac{2}{3}}\right]^{\frac{3}{2}} = 25^{\frac{3}{2}}.$$

$$x - 1 = 25^{\frac{3}{2}} = (5^2)^{\frac{3}{2}} = 5^3.$$

$$x = 125 + 1 = 126.$$

16. **C** The double angle formula for cosine is:

$$\cos 2\theta = \cos^2 \theta - \sin^2 \theta.$$

Because $\cos 2\theta = \frac{3}{4}$, $\cos^2 \theta - \sin^2 \theta$ also equals $\frac{3}{4}$

$$\frac{1}{\cos^2 \theta - \sin^2 \theta} = \frac{1}{\frac{3}{4}} = \frac{4}{3}.$$

17. **A** Recall that π radians = 180°. To convert the given angle to degrees, multiply it by $\frac{180}{\pi}$.

$$\frac{5\pi}{12} \times \frac{180}{\pi} = -\frac{5(180)}{12} = -75°$$

18. **D** Factor the numerator and denominator. Then, simplify the expression and evaluate it when $x = -\frac{3}{2}$.

$$f(x) = \frac{4x^2 - 9}{2x + 3} = \frac{(2x - 3)(2x + 3)}{2x + 3} = 2x - 3.$$

When $x = -\frac{3}{2}$, $2\left(-\frac{3}{2}\right) - 3 = -3 - 3 = -6.$

19. **C** Recall that complex zeroes occur in conjugate pairs. If i is a zero of the polynomial $p(x)$, then $-i$ is also a zero. One factor of the polynomial is $(x - i)$ $(x + i)$.

$$(x - i)(x + i) = x^2 + ix - ix - i^2$$

$$= x^2 - i^2 = x^2 - (-1) = x^2 + 1.$$

20. **E** Recognize that $2 - x = -(x - 2)$.

$$f(x) = (x - 2)(2 - x)^{-1} = -\frac{x - 2}{x - 2} - 1.$$

The function $f(x) = (x - 2)(2 - x)^{-1}$ equals -1 for all values of x except $x = 2$.

$$f(1) = f(-1) = f(4) = f(0) = f\left(\frac{1}{2}\right)$$

$$= f(-2) = -1.$$

Statements I, II, and III are true.

21. **B**

$$f(-3) = 5(-3) - 1 = -16.$$

For $g(f(-3))$ to equal 18, $g(-16)$ must equal 18. There are many possible functions that would have an output of 18 when -16 is the input. Of the possible answers, Answer B is the only one that works.

$$g(-16) = -(-16) + 2 = 16 + 2 = 18.$$

22. **A** One way to determine the y-intercept is to set x equal to zero and solve for y.

$$\frac{y^2}{9} - \frac{x^2}{16} = 1.$$

$$\frac{y^2}{9} - \frac{0}{16} = 1.$$

$$\frac{y^2}{9} = 1.$$

$$y^2 = 9.$$

$$y = \pm 3.$$

The point $(0, -3)$ is one possible answer.

23. **D**

$$\text{Distance} = \sqrt{(x_2 - x_1)^2 + (y_2 - y_1)^2 + (z_2 - z_1)^2}$$

$$= \sqrt{(3 - 0)^2 + (0 - 2)^2 + (0 - 5)^2}$$

$$= \sqrt{3^2 + (-2)^2 + (-5)^2}$$

$$= \sqrt{9 + 4 + 25}$$

$$= \sqrt{38} \approx 6.16.$$

24. **C** Note that the car is decreasing in value. The value of the car can be calculated using the equation:

$$A = 24{,}500(1 - 0.07)^5.$$

$$A = 24{,}500(0.93)^5.$$

$$A \approx \$17{,}044.$$

25. **B** The inverse of the exponential function $f(x) = 4^x$ is the logarithmic function $f^{-1}(x) = \log_4 x$.

$$f^{-1}(p)f^{-1}(q) = \log_4 p \log_4 q.$$

26. **C** If $\log_b 6 = 36$, then $b^{36} = 6$. Take the 36th root of each side of the equation.

$$(b^{36})^{\frac{1}{36}} = 6^{\frac{1}{36}}.$$

$$b = 6^{\frac{1}{36}} = 1.05.$$

27. **D** First, find the angle whose cosine is 0.75.

$$\cos^{-1}(0.75) = 41.4096°.$$

Then, determine the tangent of the angle.

$$\tan 41.4096° \approx 0.88.$$

28. **B** Find the difference between the two fractions.

$$\frac{5}{6} - \frac{3}{4} = \frac{10 - 9}{12} = \frac{1}{12}.$$

$\frac{1}{12}$ of the class is passing with a grade of C– or better but not a grade of B– or better.

29. **B** Complete the square to get the standard form of the equation of the circle.

$$x^2 + y^2 - 14x + 14y + 44 = 0.$$

$$(x^2 - 14x) + (y^2 + 4y) = -44.$$

$$(x^2 - 14x + 49) + (y^2 + 4y + 4) = -44 + 49 + 4.$$

$$(x^2 - 7)^2 + (y + 2)^2 = 9.$$

Its radius is: $\sqrt{9} = 3$ units.

30. **D** The figure is the graph of the cosine function with amplitude 2 and period 4π. Therefore, the equation is,

$$y = 2 \cos \frac{2\pi}{4\pi} x = 2 \cos \frac{x}{2}.$$

31. **E** The graph is linear when $x \le 3$. Because the function only looks at the ray formed when $x \le 3$, the ray starts at $(3, 9)$ and extends upward in the negative direction of x. When $x > 3$, the graph is a parabola whose lowest point is $(3, 9)$. All y values greater than or equal to 9 satisfy the range.

32. **E** Vector $v = (-3, 7)$ and vector $u = (2, -1)$.

$$u - v = (2 - (-3), -1 - 7).$$

$$u - v = (5, -8).$$

33. **B** The maximum straight line distance is the distance between opposite vertices of the cube. Recall that distance between opposite vertices of any rectangular prism is:

$$\text{Distance} = \sqrt{l^2 + w^2 + h^2}$$

$$= \sqrt{3^2 + 3^2 + 3^2}$$

$$= \sqrt{27} = 3\sqrt{3}.$$

34. **D** The statement "a^3 is always an odd integer" is not always true. One counterexample is $2^3 = 8$.

35. **B** Multiply both sides of the equation by the LCD, $(x + 6)(x - 6)$, to get:

$$n = (x + 6) + (x - 6).$$

$$n = 2x.$$

36. **C** Shifting $f(x)$ down 4 units results in:

$$h(x) = f(x) - 4.$$

$$h(x) = x^3 - 4.$$

Then, shifting the function right 2 units results in:

$$h(x) = (x - 2)^3 - 4.$$

37. **B** The slopes of perpendicular lines are opposite reciprocals. If $y_1 = (n + 2)x + 10$ and $y_2 = (n - 4)x + 2$ are perpendicular, then:

$$(n + 2)(n - 4) = -1.$$

$$n^2 - 2n - 8 = -1.$$

$$n^2 - 2n - 7 = 0.$$

Use the Quadratic Formula to determine that $n = 3.828$ and $n = -1.828$ are solutions for n. 3.8 is the correct answer choice.

38. **E** Graph the equation $y = -x^4 + 12x - 18$ on your calculator to observe that it never intersects the x-axis. Answer E is the best answer choice.

39. **A** In the polar coordinate system, $x^2 + y^2 = r^2$ and $x = r \cos \theta$. Substituting these values into the given equation results in:

$$x^2 + 5x + y^2 - 1 = 0.$$

$$r^2 - 5r \cos \theta - 1 = 0.$$

40. **C** The product of a 2×3 matrix and a 3×4 matrix is a 2×4 matrix. Recall that the number of columns in the first matrix must be equal to the number of rows in the second matrix for matrix multiplication to be defined.

41. **B**

$$(\sec \theta + \tan \theta)(\sec \theta - \tan \theta) = \sec^2 \theta - \tan^2 \theta.$$

Recall that one of the Pythagorean Identities is $1 + \tan^2 \theta = \sec^2 \theta$. Substituting $1 + \tan^2 \theta$ for $\sec^2 \theta$ results in:

$$1 + \tan^2 \theta - \tan^2 \theta = 1.$$

42. **D** Based on the model $C = 13.2m + 20.5$, there is a positive correlation between the calories burned and the number of minutes a person uses a machine. (If datapoints were graphed, they would cluster about a line with a slope of approximately 13.2.) Statements I and III are true based on the linear model, but II is not true. Answer D is the correct answer choice.

43. **C** The inverse function $f^{-1}(x)$ is the reflection of $f(x)$ over the line $y = x$. If (x, y) is a point on the graph of $f(x)$, then (y, x) is point on the graph of the inverse.

44. **E** Substitute $x = 1 - t$ into the equation for y to solve for y in terms of t.

$$y = f(t) = -2(1 - t) + 7.$$

$$y = -2 + 2t + 7.$$

$$y = 2t + 5.$$

45. **E** The function $x_{n+1} = x_n \sqrt{(x_n + 4)}$ is recursive. Because you are given the first term of the sequence, you can define the other terms using it.

$$x_0 = 5.$$

$$x_1 = 5\sqrt{9} = 15.$$

$$x_2 = 15\sqrt{19} = 65.38.$$

$$x_3 = 65.83\sqrt{69.38} = 544.62.$$

$$x_4 = 544.62\sqrt{548.62} \approx 12{,}756.4.$$

46. **C** First, evaluate $\log_7 \dfrac{1}{343}$:

$$\log_7 \dfrac{1}{343} = -3 \text{ since } 7^{-3} = \dfrac{1}{343}.$$

If $f(x) = 6^x$, then $f(-3) = 6^{-3} = \dfrac{1}{216}$.

47. **D** If each base angle measures $28°$, the vertex angle of the isosceles triangle measures $180 - 2(28) = 124°$. Let $x =$ the length of the base. By the Law of Sines:

$$\dfrac{\sin 28°}{20} = \dfrac{\sin 124°}{x}.$$

$$x \sin 28° = 20 \sin 124°.$$

$$x = 35.3 \ cm.$$

48. **A** First, determine the number of possible ways to choose 4 people from a group of 12.

$$_{12}C_4 = \dfrac{12!}{4!8!} = 495$$

Then, determine how many possible ways to choose 2 women from 8 and 2 men from 4.

$$_8C_2 = \dfrac{8!}{2!6!} = 28.$$

$$_4C_2 = \dfrac{4!}{2!2!} = 6.$$

The probability that the committee consists of 2 women and 2 men is, therefore,

$$\dfrac{28(6)}{495} = \dfrac{168}{495} = \dfrac{56}{165}.$$

49. **D** There are many ways to go about writing an expression for the area of the triangle. You know the formula for the area of any triangle is $A = \frac{1}{2}$ (base $\times$ height). In the given figure, $A = \frac{1}{2} ab$.

Now, use trigonometric ratios to write a and b in terms of θ.

$$\sin\,\theta = \frac{a}{2} \qquad a = 2\sin\,\theta.$$

$$\cos\,\theta = \frac{b}{2} \qquad b = 2\cos\,\theta.$$

Substituting these values of a and b into the area equation results in:

$$A = \frac{1}{2}(2\sin\,\theta)(2\cos\,\theta).$$

$$A = 2\sin\,\theta\,\cos\,\theta.$$

50. **C** Recall that if (x, y) is a point on the graph of f, then (y, x) is a point on the graph of f^{-1}. $f^{-1}(6.2)$ corresponds to the point $(x, 6.2)$ on the graph of f.

Reflect f over the line $y = x$ to get the graph of f^{-1}. The new line segment passes through the origin and has a slope of $\frac{2}{14} = \frac{1}{7}$.

$$f^{-1}(6.2) = \frac{1}{7}(6.2) = 0.89.$$

▬▬▬ DIAGNOSE YOUR STRENGTHS AND WEAKNESSES

Check the number of each question answered correctly and "X" the number of each question answered incorrectly.

Algebra	1	3	4	6	7	8	9	15	24	35	Total Number Correct
10 questions											

Solid Geometry	23	33	Total Number Correct
2 questions			

Coordinate Geometry	22	29	36	37	38	39	Total Number Correct
6 questions							

Trigonometry	11	16	17	27	41	47	49	Total Number Correct
7 questions								

Functions	2	10	12	19	20	21	25	26	30	31	43	44	45	46	50	Total Number Correct
15 questions																

Data Analysis, Statistics, and Probability	13	28	42	48	Total Number Correct
4 questions					

Numbers and Operations	5	14	18	32	34	40	Total Number Correct
6 questions							

Number of correct answers $-\dfrac{1}{4}$ **(Number of incorrect answers) = Your raw score**

_____ $-\dfrac{1}{4}$ (_____) = _____

Compare your raw score with the approximate SAT Subject Test score below:

	Raw Score	SAT Subject Test Approximate Score
Excellent	43–50	770–800
Very Good	33–43	670–770
Good	27–33	620–670
Above Average	21–27	570–620
Average	11–21	500–570
Below Average	< 11	<500

PRACTICE TEST 3

Treat this practice test as the actual test and complete it in one 60-minute sitting. Use the following answer sheet to fill in your multiple-choice answers. Once you have completed the practice test:

1. Check your answers using the Answer Key.
2. Review the Answers and Solutions.
3. Fill in the "Diagnose Your Strengths and Weaknesses" sheet and determine areas that require further preparation.

PRACTICE TEST 3

MATH LEVEL 2

ANSWER SHEET

Tear out this answer sheet and use it to complete the practice test. Determine the BEST answer for each question. Then, fill in the appropriate oval using a No. 2 pencil.

1. Ⓐ Ⓑ Ⓒ Ⓓ Ⓔ	21. Ⓐ Ⓑ Ⓒ Ⓓ Ⓔ	41. Ⓐ Ⓑ Ⓒ Ⓓ Ⓔ
2. Ⓐ Ⓑ Ⓒ Ⓓ Ⓔ	22. Ⓐ Ⓑ Ⓒ Ⓓ Ⓔ	42. Ⓐ Ⓑ Ⓒ Ⓓ Ⓔ
3. Ⓐ Ⓑ Ⓒ Ⓓ Ⓔ	23. Ⓐ Ⓑ Ⓒ Ⓓ Ⓔ	43. Ⓐ Ⓑ Ⓒ Ⓓ Ⓔ
4. Ⓐ Ⓑ Ⓒ Ⓓ Ⓔ	24. Ⓐ Ⓑ Ⓒ Ⓓ Ⓔ	44. Ⓐ Ⓑ Ⓒ Ⓓ Ⓔ
5. Ⓐ Ⓑ Ⓒ Ⓓ Ⓔ	25. Ⓐ Ⓑ Ⓒ Ⓓ Ⓔ	45. Ⓐ Ⓑ Ⓒ Ⓓ Ⓔ
6. Ⓐ Ⓑ Ⓒ Ⓓ Ⓔ	26. Ⓐ Ⓑ Ⓒ Ⓓ Ⓔ	46. Ⓐ Ⓑ Ⓒ Ⓓ Ⓔ
7. Ⓐ Ⓑ Ⓒ Ⓓ Ⓔ	27. Ⓐ Ⓑ Ⓒ Ⓓ Ⓔ	47. Ⓐ Ⓑ Ⓒ Ⓓ Ⓔ
8. Ⓐ Ⓑ Ⓒ Ⓓ Ⓔ	28. Ⓐ Ⓑ Ⓒ Ⓓ Ⓔ	48. Ⓐ Ⓑ Ⓒ Ⓓ Ⓔ
9. Ⓐ Ⓑ Ⓒ Ⓓ Ⓔ	29. Ⓐ Ⓑ Ⓒ Ⓓ Ⓔ	49. Ⓐ Ⓑ Ⓒ Ⓓ Ⓔ
10. Ⓐ Ⓑ Ⓒ Ⓓ Ⓔ	30. Ⓐ Ⓑ Ⓒ Ⓓ Ⓔ	50. Ⓐ Ⓑ Ⓒ Ⓓ Ⓔ
11. Ⓐ Ⓑ Ⓒ Ⓓ Ⓔ	31. Ⓐ Ⓑ Ⓒ Ⓓ Ⓔ	
12. Ⓐ Ⓑ Ⓒ Ⓓ Ⓔ	32. Ⓐ Ⓑ Ⓒ Ⓓ Ⓔ	
13. Ⓐ Ⓑ Ⓒ Ⓓ Ⓔ	33. Ⓐ Ⓑ Ⓒ Ⓓ Ⓔ	
14. Ⓐ Ⓑ Ⓒ Ⓓ Ⓔ	34. Ⓐ Ⓑ Ⓒ Ⓓ Ⓔ	
15. Ⓐ Ⓑ Ⓒ Ⓓ Ⓔ	35. Ⓐ Ⓑ Ⓒ Ⓓ Ⓔ	
16. Ⓐ Ⓑ Ⓒ Ⓓ Ⓔ	36. Ⓐ Ⓑ Ⓒ Ⓓ Ⓔ	
17. Ⓐ Ⓑ Ⓒ Ⓓ Ⓔ	37. Ⓐ Ⓑ Ⓒ Ⓓ Ⓔ	
18. Ⓐ Ⓑ Ⓒ Ⓓ Ⓔ	38. Ⓐ Ⓑ Ⓒ Ⓓ Ⓔ	
19. Ⓐ Ⓑ Ⓒ Ⓓ Ⓔ	39. Ⓐ Ⓑ Ⓒ Ⓓ Ⓔ	
20. Ⓐ Ⓑ Ⓒ Ⓓ Ⓔ	40. Ⓐ Ⓑ Ⓒ Ⓓ Ⓔ	

PRACTICE TEST 3

Time: 60 minutes

Directions: Select the BEST answer for each of the 50 multiple-choice questions. If the exact solution is not one of the five choices, select the answer that is the best approximation. Then, fill in the appropriate oval on the answer sheet.

Notes:

1. A calculator will be needed to answer some of the questions on the test. Scientific, programmable, and graphing calculators are permitted. It is up to you to determine when and when not to use your calculator.

2. Angles on the Level 2 test are measured in degrees and radians. You need to decide whether your calculator should be set to degree mode or radian mode for a particular question.

3. Figures are drawn as accurately as possible and are intended to help solve some of the test problems. If a figure is not drawn to scale, this will be stated in the problem. All figures lie in a plane unless the problem indicates otherwise.

4. Unless otherwise stated, the domain of a function f is assumed to be the set of real numbers x for which the value of the function, $f(x)$, is a real number.

5. Reference information that may be useful in answering some of the test questions can be found below.

Reference Information	
Right circular cone with radius r and height h:	Volume $= \dfrac{1}{3}\pi r^2 h$
Right circular cone with circumference of base c and slant height ℓ:	Lateral Area $= \dfrac{1}{2}c\ell$
Sphere with radius r:	Volume $= \dfrac{4}{3}\pi r^3$
	Surface Area $= 4\pi r^2$
Pyramid with base area B and height h:	Volume $= \dfrac{1}{3}Bh$

▨ PRACTICE TEST 3 QUESTIONS

USE THIS SPACE AS SCRATCH PAPER

1. If $\dfrac{1-x}{x} = \dfrac{4-4x}{x}$, then $\dfrac{1-x}{x} =$

   (A) -1
   (B) 0
   (C) $\dfrac{1}{4}$
   (D) 1
   (E) 4

2. A number k is increased by 10. If the fifth root of that result equals -2, $k =$

   (A) -42
   (B) -22
   (C) -11.1
   (D) 22
   (E) 32

3. $\dfrac{[(n+1)!]^3}{(n!)^3} =$

   (A) n
   (B) $n+1$
   (C) n^3
   (D) $(n+1)^3$
   (E) $\left(\dfrac{n+1}{n}\right)^3$

4. What is the distance between the points in space $J(11, 4, -1)$ and $T(-2, 0, 3)$?

   (A) 10.63
   (B) 12.37
   (C) 13.00
   (D) 14.18
   (E) 14.49

5. If $\sin x = 0.45$, then $\cos\left(\dfrac{x}{2}\right) =$

   (A) 0.45
   (B) 0.52
   (C) 0.71
   (D) 0.89
   (E) 0.97

6. What is the domain of $f(x) = \sqrt{9-x^2}$?

   (A) $x \le 3$
   (B) $x \ge -3$
   (C) $-3 \le x \le 3$
   (D) $x \ge -3$ or $x \ge 3$
   (E) All real numbers

GO ON TO THE NEXT PAGE

7. If $7a^4 = 28 a^2$, then which of the following are the possible values of a?

(A) 2
(B) −2 or 2
(C) 4
(D) −2 or 0 or 2
(E) 0

8. If $f(x) = 2x + \sqrt[3]{x}$, then $f(f(8)) =$

(A) 18
(B) 36
(C) 38.6
(D) 40.2
(E) 42

9. How many 4-person committees can be formed from a group of 9?

(A) 24
(B) 126
(C) 1,512
(D) 3,024
(E) 362,880

10. What is the magnitude of vector v with initial point $(3, -5)$ and terminal point $(-2, 7)$?

(A) 4
(B) 5
(C) 12
(D) 13
(E) 25

11. If $2\sqrt{x} - \sqrt{2x + 1} - 1 = 0$, then what is the value of x?

(A) −2
(B) 1
(C) 2
(D) 4
(E) 0

12. If the graph of the equation $y = mx + 4$ has points in the 4th quadrant, then which of the following must be true for m?

(A) $m = 0$
(B) $m < 0$
(C) $0 < m < 1$
(D) $m > 0$
(E) $m = -4$

GO ON TO THE NEXT PAGE

13. The operation † is defined for all real numbers a and b, $b \neq 0$, as $a \dagger b = \dfrac{\left(\dfrac{a}{2}\right)}{b}$. If $10 \dagger n = n \dagger \dfrac{1}{10}$, then which of the following could be a solution for n?

(A) $\dfrac{1}{2}$

(B) 1

(C) $5\sqrt{2}$

(D) -10

(E) 10

14. What is the middle term of the expansion of $(x + 2)^6$?

(A) $15x^4$

(B) $20x^3$

(C) $60x^4$

(D) $160x^3$

(E) $240x^3$

15. Which of the following is a zero of $f(x) = 6x^3 - 5x^2 + 4x - 15$?

(A) -1.50

(B) 0.33

(C) 1.00

(D) 1.25

(E) 1.50

16. A triangle has sides measuring 4, 4, and 6 inches. What is the measure of its largest angle?

(A) $82.8°$

(B) $97.2°$

(C) $41.4°$

(D) $120.0°$

(E) $178.2°$

17. Which of the following is the equation of the circle whose diameter is the line segment connecting points $(1, -4)$ and $(3, 6)$?

(A) $(x - 2)^2 + (y - 1)^2 = 26$

(B) $(x - 1)^2 + (y + 4)^2 = 104$

(C) $(x + 2)^2 + (y + 1)^2 = 26$

(D) $(x + 2)^2 + (y + 1)^2 = 25$

(E) $(x - 2)^2 + (y - 1)^2 = 5.1$

GO ON TO THE NEXT PAGE

18. A cell phone provider charges $0.40 for the first minute of a call and $0.20 for each additional minute or each additional portion of a minute. The cost of a call, C, is given by the model $C = 0.40 + 0.20 \lceil t \rceil$ where t is the number of minutes over the first minute and $\lceil t \rceil$ is the least integer greater than or equal to t. What is the cost of a 12.25-minute call?

(A) $2.60
(B) $2.65
(C) $2.80
(D) $2.85
(E) $3.00

19. Some number c is added to the three numbers 1, 13, and 61 to create the first three terms of a geometric sequence. What is the value of c?

(A) 1
(B) $\dfrac{1}{2}$
(C) 2
(D) 3
(E) 5

20. A right circular cylinder has a height of 12 and a radius of 3. If X and Y are two points on the surface of the cylinder, what is the maximum possible length of XY?

(A) $3\sqrt{17}$
(B) 6
(C) $6\sqrt{5}$
(D) $5\sqrt{6}$
(E) $9\sqrt{5}$

21. A teacher gives a test to two algebra classes. The first class has 18 students, and the second has 24 students. If the average for the first class is 84%, and x is the overall average grade for all of the students, then which of the following statements is true?

(A) $84 \leq x \leq 93.1$
(B) $42 \leq x \leq 92$
(C) $36 \leq x \leq 93.1$
(D) $36 \leq x \leq 92$
(E) $42 \leq x \leq 84$

GO ON TO THE NEXT PAGE

22. What is the remainder when the polynomial $x^4 - 5x^2 - 10x - 12$ is divided by $x + 2$?

   (A) 4
   (B) −36
   (C) −20
   (D) 2
   (E) −4

23. What is the maximum value of $f(x) = 3 - (x + 1)^2$?

   (A) −3
   (B) −1
   (C) 1
   (D) 3
   (E) 9

24. If $\sin \theta = \dfrac{1}{2}\cos \theta$, then what is the smallest positive value of θ?

   (A) 26.57°
   (B) 30°
   (C) 53.14°
   (D) 60°
   (E) 63.43°

25. What is the sum of the integers from 1 to 300?

   (A) 9,000
   (B) 44,850
   (C) 45,150
   (D) 90,000
   (E) 90,300

26. The hyperbola given by the equation $9x^2 - y^2 - 36x - 6y + 18 = 0$ is centered at

   (A) $(2, -3)$
   (B) $(3, -3)$
   (C) $(-3, 2)$
   (D) $(2, 6)$
   (E) $(-2, 3)$

27. Which of the following lines are asymptotes of the graph of $f(x) = \dfrac{3(x^2 - 9)}{x^2 - 4}$?

   I. $x = \pm 2$
   II. $x = 3$
   III. $y = 3$

      (A) I only
      (B) II only
      (C) I and II only
      (D) I and III only
      (E) I, II, and III

28. In a geometry exercise, there is a 0.15 probability a protractor is in error of 1° or more. If 5 protractors are used, what is the probability that all of them are in error of 1° or more?

    (A) 0.000076
    (B) 0.60
    (C) 0.15
    (D) 0.75
    (E) 7.6

29. For all θ, $(\sin θ + \sin (-θ))(\cos θ + \cos (-θ)) =$

    (A) $2 \sin θ$
    (B) 0
    (C) 1
    (D) $2 \cos θ$
    (E) $4 \sin θ \cos θ$

30. If $12 \sin^2 θ + 5 \sin θ - 2 = 0$, then what is the smallest positive value of θ?

    (A) 8.6°
    (B) 14.5°
    (C) 20.9°
    (D) 41.8°
    (E) 83.6°

31. What value does $f(x) = \dfrac{5x - 11}{2x + 11}$ approach as x gets infinitely large?

    (A) $-\dfrac{5}{2}$

    (B) $\dfrac{2}{5}$

    (C) 1

    (D) $\dfrac{5}{2}$

    (E) 11

32. If $7.8^a = 3.4^b$, then $\dfrac{b}{a} =$

    (A) 0.361
    (B) 0.596
    (C) 1.408
    (D) 1.679
    (E) 2.294

33. A point has rectangular coordinates (6, 8). If the polar coordinates are (10, θ), then θ =

    (A) 21.8°
    (B) 36.9°
    (C) 53.1°
    (D) 60°
    (E) 76°

USE THIS SPACE AS SCRATCH PAPER

GO ON TO THE NEXT PAGE

34. The graph of $f(x) = x^3$ is translated 6 units up, 2 units right, and reflected over the x-axis. If the resulting graph represents $g(x)$, then $g(-1) =$

    (A) −21
    (B) 5
    (C) 14
    (D) 21
    (E) 33

USE THIS SPACE AS SCRATCH PAPER

35. $(6 \sin x)(3 \sin x) - (9 \cos x)(-2 \cos x) =$

    (A) 1
    (B) −18
    (C) 18
    (D) −1
    (E) $18 \sin^2 x - 18 \cos^2 x$

36. If a coin is tossed three times, what is the probability that exactly two heads will appear?

    (A) $\dfrac{3}{8}$

    (B) $\dfrac{3}{7}$

    (C) $\dfrac{1}{2}$

    (D) $\dfrac{1}{4}$

    (E) $\dfrac{5}{8}$

37. If $f(x) = \sqrt[3]{2x^3 - 5}$, then $f^{-1}(2.5) =$

    (A) 1.74
    (B) 2.18
    (C) 2.37
    (D) 2.97
    (E) 5.12

38. Which of the following is an even function?

    (A) $f(x) = x^3 + 2$
    (B) $f(x) = (x - 1)^2 + 1$
    (C) $f(x) = -x^2 + 1$
    (D) $f(x) = \sin x$
    (E) $f(x) = (x + 2)^4$

39. All of the following functions have a period of 2 except which one?

    (A) $y = \sin \pi x + 2$
    (B) $y = 2 \cos \pi x$
    (C) $y = 4 \sin \pi x$
    (D) $y = \dfrac{1}{2} \cos 2\pi x + 1$
    (E) $y = 2 \csc \pi x$

GO ON TO THE NEXT PAGE

40. The daytime high temperatures for the first 9 days in January in Boston were 19, 21 16, 22, 28, 34, 30, 28, 36 degrees Fahrenheit. What is the standard deviation of the temperatures?

(A) 4.90
(B) 6.48
(C) 10
(D) 19.44
(E) 42

41. The graph in Figure 1 could be a portion of the graph of which of the following functions?

I. $f(x) = x^4 + ax^3 + bx^2 + cx + d.$
II. $F(x) = -x^4 + ax^3 + bx^2 + cx + d.$
III. $g(x) = x^6 + ax^5 + bx^4 + cx^3 + dx^2 + ex + f.$

(A) I only
(B) III only
(C) I and II only
(D) I and III only
(E) I, II, and III

42. If $f(x) = \ln\ e^{\frac{x}{2}}$, then what is the smallest possible integer x such that $f(x) > 100$?

(A) 51
(B) 99
(C) 101
(D) 199
(E) 201

43. If $\log_3 (x - 9) = \log_9 (x - 3)$, then $x =$

(A) 30
(B) 7
(C) 9
(D) 7 or 12
(E) 12

44. If $\lceil n \rceil$ represents the greatest integer less than or equal to n, then which of the following is the solution to $-11 + 4\lceil n \rceil = 5$?

(A) $n = 4$
(B) $4 < n < 5$
(C) $-2 \leq n < -1$
(D) $4 \leq n < 5$
(E) $4 < n \leq 5$

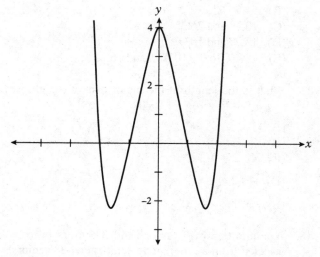

Figure 1

GO ON TO THE NEXT PAGE

45. If a rectangular prism has faces with areas of 8, 10 and 20 units², then what is its volume?

    (A) 20
    (B) 40
    (C) 80
    (D) 400
    (E) 1,600

46. If $\tan 4x = 2 \cot 4x$ and $0 \le x \le 180°$, then $x =$

    (A) 13.7°
    (B) 54.7°
    (C) 13.7° and 76.3°
    (D) 13.7° and 103.7°
    (E) 13.7°, 76.3°, 103.7°, and 166.3°

47. What is the length of the major axis of the ellipse $x^2 + 4y^2 - 2x + 16y + 13 = 0$?

    (A) 1
    (B) 2
    (C) 4
    (D) $4\sqrt{2}$
    (E) $2\sqrt{17}$

48. A committee of 3 juniors and 3 seniors is to be selected from a group of 15 juniors and 28 seniors. How many different committees are possible?

    (A) 420
    (B) 455
    (C) 3,276
    (D) 1,490,580
    (E) 1.32×10^{12}

49. $f(x) = \cos(\arctan x)$ and $g(x) = \tan(\arccos x)$. If $0 \le x \le \dfrac{\pi}{2}$, then $g\left(f\left(\dfrac{\pi}{8}\right)\right) =$

    (A) 0.374
    (B) 0.393
    (C) 0.931
    (D) 1.167
    (E) 2.342

50. Given the graph of $f(x)$ in Figure 2, $f(f(5)) =$

    (A) 0
    (B) 1
    (C) 2
    (D) 3
    (E) 4

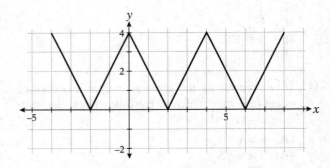

Figure 2

S T O P

IF YOU FINISH BEFORE TIME IS CALLED, YOU MAY CHECK YOUR WORK ON THIS TEST ONLY.
DO NOT TURN TO ANY OTHER TEST IN THIS BOOK.

ANSWER KEY

1. B	11. D	21. C	31. D	41. D
2. A	12. B	22. A	32. D	42. E
3. D	13. B	23. D	33. C	43. D
4. D	14. D	24. A	34. D	44. D
5. E	15. E	25. C	35. C	45. B
6. C	16. B	26. A	36. A	46. E
7. D	17. A	27. D	37. B	47. C
8. C	18. C	28. A	38. C	48. D
9. B	19. D	29. B	39. D	49. B
10. D	20. C	30. B	40. B	50. A

ANSWERS AND SOLUTIONS

1. **B**

$$\frac{1-x}{x} = \frac{4-4x}{x}.$$

$$\frac{1-x}{x} = 4\left(\frac{1-x}{x}\right).$$

$$\frac{1-x}{x} = 0.$$

2. **A**

$$(k+10)^{\frac{1}{5}} = -2.$$

Raise each side of the equation to the fifth power to solve for k.

$$\left[(k+10)^{\frac{1}{5}}\right]^5 = (-2)^5.$$

$$k+10 = -32.$$

$$k = -42.$$

3. **D**

$$\frac{[(n+1)!]^3}{(n!)^3} =$$

$$\left[\frac{(n+1)!}{(n!)}\right]^3 =$$

$$\left[\frac{n!(n+1)}{(n!)}\right]^3 =$$

$$(n+1)^3.$$

4. **D** The distance between ordered triples (x_1, y_1, z_1) and (x_2, y_2, z_2) is given by the formula:

$$\text{Distance} = \sqrt{(x_2-x_1)^2 + (y_2-y_1) + (z_2-z_1)^2}.$$

$$= \sqrt{(11--2)^2 + (4-0)^2 + (-1-3)^2}$$

$$= \sqrt{13^2 + 4^2 + (-4)^2}$$

$$= \sqrt{13^2 + 4^2 + (-4)^2}$$

$$= \sqrt{201} \approx 14.18.$$

5. **E**

If $\sin x = 0.45$, the angle whose sine is 0.45 is:

$$\sin^{-1}(0.45) = 26.74°$$

$$\cos\left(\frac{26.74}{2}\right)° = 0.97$$

6. **C** The radicand must be greater than or equal to zero.

$$9 - x^2 \geq 0.$$

$$9 \geq x^2.$$

$$-3 \leq x \leq 3.$$

7. **D**

$$7a^4 = 28a^2.$$

$$7a^4 - 28a^2 = 0.$$

$$7a^2 - (a^2 - 4) = 0.$$

$$7a^2 - (a-2)(a+2) = 0.$$

$$a = 0, 2, \text{ or } -2.$$

8. **C**

First, determine $f(8)$.

$$f(8) = 2(8) + \sqrt[3]{8} = 16 + 2 = 18.$$

Now, determine $f(18)$.

$$f(8) = 2(18) + \sqrt[3]{18} = 36 + 2.621 \approx 38.6$$

9. **B**

$$\frac{9!}{4!(9-4)!} = \frac{9!}{4!5!}$$

$$= \frac{6 \times 7 \times 8 \times 9}{1 \times 2 \times 3 \times 4}$$

$$= 126.$$

10. **D** The components of v are given by $(3 - (-2), -5 - 7)$, or $(5, -12)$. The magnitude is the length of v.

$$\|v\| = \sqrt{[5^2 + -12^2]}$$

$$\|v\| = \sqrt{169}$$

$$\|v\| = 13$$

11. **D** Isolate the radical expressions and square both sides of the equation.

$$2\sqrt{x} - \sqrt{2x+1} - 1 = 0.$$

$$2\sqrt{x} - 1 = \sqrt{2x+1}.$$

$$\left(2\sqrt{x} - 1\right)^2 = \left(\sqrt{2x+1}\right)^2.$$

$$4x - 4\sqrt{x} + 1 = 2x + 1.$$

$$2x = 4\sqrt{x}.$$

$$x = 2\sqrt{x}.$$

Now square both sides a second time.

$$x^2 = \left(2\sqrt{x}\right)^2.$$

$$x^2 = 4x.$$

$$x^2 - 4x = 0.$$

$$x(x - 4) = 4.$$

$$x = 0 \text{ or } x = 4.$$

Because the radicand of a square root must be greater than zero, 4 is the only solution.

12. **B** Because the y-intercept of the line $y = mx + 4$ is positive, then the slope of the line must be negative in order for part of the line to fall in the 4th quadrant. $m < 0$ is the correct answer choice.

13. **B**

If $a \dagger b = \dfrac{\frac{a}{2}}{b}$, then :

$$10 \dagger n = \frac{\left(\frac{10}{2}\right)}{n} = \frac{5}{n}.$$

$$n \dagger \frac{1}{10} = \frac{\left(\frac{n}{2}\right)}{\left(\frac{1}{10}\right)} = \frac{5n}{1} = \frac{5n}{1} = 5n.$$

Now, set the two expressions equal to each other and solve for n.

$$\frac{5}{n} = 5n.$$

$$5 = 5n^2.$$

$$n^2 = 1.$$

$$n = \pm 1.$$

Answer B is the only possible answer choice.

14. **D** The middle term in the binomial expansion of $(x + 2)^6$ is given by:

$$_6C_3x^32^3 =$$

$$\frac{6!}{3!3!}(x^3)(8) =$$

$$20(x^3)(8) = 160x^3.$$

15. **E** Try substituting the given values into the function for x to determine which results in $f(x) = 0$.

$$f(1.5) = 6(1.5)^3 - 5(1.5)^2 + 4(1.5) - 15 = 0.$$

An alternative solution is to divide the polynomial by the factor $\left(x - \frac{3}{2}\right)$. Doing so results in a zero remainder. You could also graph the function to determine that $\frac{3}{2}$ is an x-intercept.

16. **B** The largest angle of a triangle is opposite its longest side. Let θ = the largest angle of the triangle. θ is opposite the side measuring 6 inches. Using the Law of Cosines:

$$6^2 = 4^2 + 4^2 - 2(4)(4)\cos\theta.$$

$$36 = 16 + 16 - 32\cos\theta.$$

$$4 = -32\cos\theta.$$

$$\cos\theta = -\frac{4}{32}.$$

$$\theta = \cos^{-1} - \frac{4}{32} \approx 97.2°$$

17. **A** The midpoint of the line segment connecting $(1, -4)$ and $(3, 6)$ is the center of the circle.

Midpoint: $\left(\frac{1+3}{2}, \frac{-4+6}{2}\right)$ or $(2, 1)$

The radius of the circle is half the length of the line segment connecting the two points.

$$\frac{1}{2}\sqrt{[(3-1)^2 + (6+4)^2]} \approx \frac{1}{2}(10.2) \approx 5.099.$$

Therefore, the standard form of the equation of the circle is $(x - 2)^2 + (y - 1)^2 = 26$.

18. **C** The model uses the greatest integer function. Evaluate the model for $t = 11.25$. Remember that the cost of the first minute is $0.40. 12 is the least integer greater than or equal to 11.25.

$$C = 0.40 + 0.20\lceil t \rceil.$$

$$C = 0.40 + 0.20\lceil 11.25 \rceil.$$

$$C = 0.40 + 0.20(12) = \$2.80.$$

19. **D** For the three terms to be part of a geometric sequence there must be a common ratio between consecutive terms. Add c to each of the three terms to get the progression $1 + c$, $13 + c$, $61 + c$. Now, set the common ratios equal to each other and solve for c.

$$\frac{13 + c}{1 + c} = \frac{61 + c}{13 + c}.$$

$$(13 + c)(13 + c) = (1 + c)(61 + c)$$

$$169 + 26c + c^2 = 61 + 62c + c^2.$$

$$108 = 36c.$$

$$c = 3.$$

20. **C** Think of X and Y as vertices of a right triangle with one leg measuring 6 units (the diameter of the cylinder's base) and one leg measuring 12 units (the height).

$$XY = \sqrt{6^2 + 12^2}$$

$$XY = \sqrt{36 + 144}$$

$$XY = \sqrt{180} = 6\sqrt{5}$$

21. **C** The average grade for the first class is 84%, so the sum of the grades is 18(84) or 1,512. There are 42 total students in both classes and the least possible sum for the second class is 0.

$$\frac{1,512 + 0}{42} = 36$$

The greatest possible sum for the second class is 100(24) or 2,400.

$$\frac{1,512 + 2,400}{42} = 93.1.$$

The correct answer choice is, therefore, $36 \leq x \leq 93.1$.

22. **A** Use either synthetic or long division to divide $x^4 - 5x^2 - 10x - 12$ by $x + 2$. Remember to include a zero placeholder for the x^3 term.

$$-2 \; | \; 1 \quad 0 \quad -5 \quad -10 \quad -12$$
$$\underline{\quad -2 \quad 4 \quad 2 \quad 16}$$
$$1 \; -2 \; -1 \quad -8 \quad 4$$

The remainder is 4.

23. **D** The maximum value of $f(x) = 3 - (x + 1)^2$ is the y-coordinate of its vertex.

$$f(x) = 3 - (x + 1)^2.$$
$$y - 3 = -(x + 1)^2.$$

The vertex is $(-1, 3)$, so the maximum value is 3.

24. **A**

$$\sin\theta = \frac{1}{2}\cos\theta.$$
$$\tan\theta = \frac{1}{2}.$$
$$\tan^{-1}\left(\frac{1}{2}\right) \approx 26.57°$$

25. **C** The integers from 1 to 300 form an arithmetic sequence having 300 terms. $n = 300$, $a_1 = 1$, and $a_n = 300$. Substitute these values into the formula for the sum of a finite arithmetic sequence to get:

$$S_n = 1 + 2 + 3 + 4 + 5 + \cdots + 300.$$
$$S_n = \frac{n}{2}(a_1 + a_n).$$
$$S_n = \frac{300}{2}(1 + 300).$$
$$S_n = 150(301) = 45,150.$$

26. **A** Complete the square to write the equation of the hyperbola in standard form.

$$9x^2 - y^2 - 36x - 6y + 18 = 0.$$
$$(9x^2 - 36x) - (y^2 + 6y) = -18.$$
$$9(x^2 - 4x + 4) - (y^2 + 6y + 9) = -18 + 36 - 9.$$
$$9(x - 2)^2 - (y + 3)^2 = 9.$$
$$(x - 2)^2 - \frac{(y + 3)^2}{9} = 1.$$

The center of the hyperbola is $(2, -3)$.

27. **D** The function $f(x) = \frac{3(x^2 - 9)}{x^2 - 4}$ has vertical asymptotes at the zeroes of the denominator.

$$x^2 - 4 = 0.$$
$$x = \pm 2.$$

Because the degree of the numerator equals the degree of the denominator, a horizontal asymptote exists at $y = \frac{3}{1} = 3$.

Statements I and III are, therefore, true.

28. **A** The probability that all 5 protractors are in error of 1° or more is:

$$0.15(0.15)(0.15)(0.15)(0.15) \approx 7.6 \times 10^{-5}.$$

29. **B**

$$(\sin\theta + \sin(-\theta))(\cos\theta + \cos(-\theta)) =$$
$$(\sin\theta + -\sin\theta)(\cos\theta + \cos\theta) =$$
$$(0)(2\cos\theta) = 0.$$

30. **B**

Factor the equation and solve for θ.
$$12\sin^2\theta + 5\sin\theta - 2 = 0.$$
$$(3\sin\theta + 2)(4\sin\theta - 1) = 0.$$
$$\sin = -\frac{2}{3} \text{ or } \sin\theta = \frac{1}{4}.$$
$$\theta \approx -41.8° \text{ or } 14.5°$$

14.5° is the smallest positive value of θ.

31. **D** Graph the function to see that it has a horizontal asymptote at $y = \frac{5}{2}$.

Alternately, you can evaluate the function at a large value of x. For example, let $x = 10,000$:

$$f(10,000) = \frac{5(10,000) - 11}{2(10,000) + 11} = 2.49807.$$

The function approaches $\frac{5}{2}$ as x gets infinitely large.

32. **D** Take the logarithm of both sides of the equation to solve for $\frac{b}{a}$.

$$7.8^a = 3.4^b.$$

$$a \log 7.8 = b \log 3.4.$$

$$\frac{b}{a} = \frac{\log 7.8}{\log 3.4}.$$

$$\frac{b}{a} \approx 1.679.$$

33. **C** Because the rectangular coordinates (x, y) are $(6, 8)$:

$$\tan \theta = \frac{y}{x} = \frac{8}{6}.$$

$$\tan^{-1} \frac{8}{6} 53.1°$$

34. **D** Translating the graph of $f(x) = x^3$ 6 units up and 2 units right results in:

$$f(x) = (x - 2)^3 + 6.$$

Then, reflecting it over the x-axis results in:

$$g(x) = -(x - 2)^3 - 6.$$

Now, evaluate the function for $x = -1$.

$$g(-1) = -(-1 - 2)^3 - 6 = 27 - 6 = 21.$$

35. **C**

$$(6 \sin x)(3 \sin x) - (9 \cos x)(-2 \cos x) =$$

$$18 \sin^2 x + 18 \cos^2 x =$$

$$18(\sin^2 x + \cos^2 x) =$$

$$18(1) = 18.$$

36. **A** There are 8 possible outcomes when a coin is tossed three times:

TTT	TTH
HHH	HHT
THH	HTT
THT	HTH

Three out of the 8 have exactly two heads, so the probability is $\frac{3}{8}$.

37. **B** Exchange the x and y values and solve for the inverse of f.

$$f(x) = \sqrt[3]{2x^3 - 5}.$$

$$y = \sqrt[3]{2x^3 - 5}.$$

$$x = \sqrt[3]{2y^3 - 5}.$$

$$\frac{x^3 + 5}{2} = y^3.$$

$$y = \sqrt[3]{\left(\frac{x^3 + 5}{2} \right)} = f^{-1}(x).$$

$$f^{-1}(2.5) = \sqrt[3]{\left(\frac{2.5^3 + 5}{2} \right)} \approx 2.18$$

38. **C** Recall that a function is even if it is symmetric with respect to the y-axis and $f(-x) = f(x)$.

Graph the functions on your calculator to determine which one has y-axis symmetry. $f(x) = -x^2 + 1$ is the correct answer choice.

39. **D** All of the functions have a period of $\frac{2\pi}{\pi}$ or 2 with the exception of $y = \frac{1}{2} \cos 2\pi x + 1$. It has a period of $\frac{2\pi}{2\pi} = 1$. Answer D is the correct answer choice.

40. **B** First, determine the mean of the 9 temperatures.

$$\text{Mean} = \frac{\text{sum}}{9}$$

$$= \frac{16 + 19 + 21 + 22 + 28 + 28 + 30 + 34 + 36}{9}$$

$$= \frac{234}{9} = 26.$$

Now use the deviation of each temperature from the mean to determine the variance.

$$\text{variance} = \frac{\begin{array}{c} -10^2 + -7^2 + -5^2 + -4^2 \\ + 2^2 + 2^2 + 4^2 + 8^2 + 10^2 \end{array}}{9}$$

$$= \frac{378}{9} = 42$$

The standard deviation is the square root of the variance.

$$\sigma = \sqrt{42} \approx 6.48$$

41. **D** The graph has 4 zeroes, so it could be the graph of either the 4th degree polynomial in statement I or the 6th degree polynomial in statement III. Because the leading coefficient in statement II is negative, the graph of $F(x)$ would fall to the left and right.

42. **E** Since $f(x) = \ln e^{\frac{x}{2}}$ must be greater than 100:

$$\frac{x}{2} > 100.$$

$$x > 200.$$

The smallest possible integer greater than 200 is 201.

43. **D** Use the change of base formula to rewrite the right side of the equation.

$$\log_3(x - 9) = \log_9(x - 3).$$

$$\log_3(x - 9) = \frac{\log_3(x - 3)}{\log_3 9}.$$

$$\log_3(x - 9) = \frac{\log_3(x - 3)}{2}.$$

Now, solve for x.

$$2\log_3(x - 9) = \log_9(x - 3).$$

$$(x - 9)^2 = x - 3.$$

$$x^2 - 18x + 81 = x - 3.$$

$$x^2 - 19x + 84 = 0.$$

$$(x - 7)(x - 12) = 0.$$

$$x = 7 \text{ or } 12.$$

7 is an extraneous solution, however, because the log of a negative number is undefined. $x = 12$ is the only solution.

44. **D**

$$-11 + 4[n] = 5.$$

$$4[n] = 16.$$

$$[n] = 4.$$

4 is the greatest integer less than or equal to n, so n must be on the interval $4 \leq n < 5$.

45. **B** Let w = the width, l = the length, and h = the height of the prism. Using the three given areas:

$$wh = 8.$$

$$wl = 10.$$

$$lh = 20.$$

Use substitution to solve for the variables. Because $wh = 8$, $w = \dfrac{8}{h}$.

$$wl = \left(\frac{8}{h}\right)l = 10.$$

$$l = \frac{10h}{8} = \frac{5h}{4}.$$

Substitute this value of l into the third equation to get:

$$lh = \frac{5h}{4}(h) = 20.$$

$$5h^2 = 80.$$

$$h^2 = 16.$$

$$h = 4.$$

If $h = 4$, then $w(4) = 8$, and $w = 2$. $2l = 10$, so $l = 5$.

The volume is, therefore, $5 \times 2 \times 4 = 40$ units^3.

46. **E**

$$\tan 4x = 2 \cot 4x.$$

$$\tan 4x = \frac{2}{\tan 4x}.$$

$$(\tan 4x)^2 = 2.$$

$$\tan 4x = \sqrt{2}.$$

$$\tan^{-1}\sqrt{2} \approx 54.7°.$$

$$x = \frac{54.7}{4} \approx 13.7°.$$

On the interval $0 \leq x \leq 180$, $x = 13.7°$, $76.3°$, $103.7°$, and $166.3°$.

47. **C** Complete the square to write the equation of the ellipse in standard form.

$$x^2 + 4y^2 - 2x + 16y + 13 = 0.$$

$$(x^3 - 2x) + 4(y^2 + 4y) = -13$$

$$(x^2 - 2x + 1) + 4(y^2 + 4y + 4) = -13 + 1 + 16.$$

$$(x - 1)^2 + 4(y + 2)^2 = 4.$$

$$\frac{(x - 1)^2}{4} + (y + 2)^2 = 1.$$

$a = \sqrt{4} = 2$. The length of the major axis is $2a$, or 4 units.

48. **D** The number of possible committees is given by $_{15}C_3 \times {}_{28}C_3$.

$$\frac{15!}{12!3!} \times \frac{28!}{25!3!} = 455 \times 3,276 = 1,490,580.$$

49. **B**

$$f\left(\frac{\pi}{8}\right) = \cos\left(\arctan\frac{\pi}{8}\right) \approx 0.9308.$$

$$g(0.9308) = \tan(\arccos 0.9308) \approx 0.393.$$

50. **A** Don't waste time trying to determine what function fits the graph. Simply use the graph to determine the y value when $x = 5$.

$$f(5) = 2.$$
$$f(f(5)) = f(2) = 0.$$

▮▮▮ DIAGNOSE YOUR STRENGTHS AND WEAKNESSES

Check the number of each question answered correctly and "X" the number of each question answered incorrectly.

Algebra	1	2	3	7	11	14	32	43	44	Total Number Correct
9 questions										

Solid Geometry	4	20	45	Total Number Correct
3 questions				

Coordinate Geometry	12	17	26	33	34	47	Total Number Correct
6 questions							

Trigonometry	5	16	24	29	30	35	46	Total Number Correct
7 questions								

Functions	6	8	15	18	22	23	27	37	38	39	41	42	49	50	Total Number Correct
14 questions															

Data Analysis, Statistics, and Probability	21	28	36	40	Total Number Correct
4 questions					

Numbers and Operations	9	10	13	19	25	31	48	Total Number Correct
7 questions								

Number of correct answers $- \frac{1}{4}$ **(Number of incorrect answers) = Your raw score**

_____ $- \frac{1}{4}$ (_____) = _____

Compare your raw score with the approximate SAT Subject Test score below:

	Raw Score	SAT Subject Test Approximate Score
Excellent	43–50	770–800
Very Good	33–43	670–770
Good	27–33	620–670
Above Average	21–27	570–620
Average	11–21	500–570
Below Average	< 11	< 500

PRACTICE TEST 4

Treat this practice test as the actual test and complete it in one 60-minute sitting. Use the following answer sheet to fill in your multiple-choice answers. Once you have completed the practice test:

1. Check your answers using the Answer Key.
2. Review the Answers and Solutions.
3. Fill in the "Diagnose Your Strengths and Weaknesses" sheet and determine areas that require further preparation.

PRACTICE TEST 4
MATH LEVEL 2

ANSWER SHEET

Tear out this answer sheet and use it to complete the practice test. Determine the BEST answer for each question. Then, fill in the appropriate oval using a No. 2 pencil.

1. (A) (B) (C) (D) (E)	21. (A) (B) (C) (D) (E)	41. (A) (B) (C) (D) (E)
2. (A) (B) (C) (D) (E)	22. (A) (B) (C) (D) (E)	42. (A) (B) (C) (D) (E)
3. (A) (B) (C) (D) (E)	23. (A) (B) (C) (D) (E)	43. (A) (B) (C) (D) (E)
4. (A) (B) (C) (D) (E)	24. (A) (B) (C) (D) (E)	44. (A) (B) (C) (D) (E)
5. (A) (B) (C) (D) (E)	25. (A) (B) (C) (D) (E)	45. (A) (B) (C) (D) (E)
6. (A) (B) (C) (D) (E)	26. (A) (B) (C) (D) (E)	46. (A) (B) (C) (D) (E)
7. (A) (B) (C) (D) (E)	27. (A) (B) (C) (D) (E)	47. (A) (B) (C) (D) (E)
8. (A) (B) (C) (D) (E)	28. (A) (B) (C) (D) (E)	48. (A) (B) (C) (D) (E)
9. (A) (B) (C) (D) (E)	29. (A) (B) (C) (D) (E)	49. (A) (B) (C) (D) (E)
10. (A) (B) (C) (D) (E)	30. (A) (B) (C) (D) (E)	50. (A) (B) (C) (D) (E)
11. (A) (B) (C) (D) (E)	31. (A) (B) (C) (D) (E)	
12. (A) (B) (C) (D) (E)	32. (A) (B) (C) (D) (E)	
13. (A) (B) (C) (D) (E)	33. (A) (B) (C) (D) (E)	
14. (A) (B) (C) (D) (E)	34. (A) (B) (C) (D) (E)	
15. (A) (B) (C) (D) (E)	35. (A) (B) (C) (D) (E)	
16. (A) (B) (C) (D) (E)	36. (A) (B) (C) (D) (E)	
17. (A) (B) (C) (D) (E)	37. (A) (B) (C) (D) (E)	
18. (A) (B) (C) (D) (E)	38. (A) (B) (C) (D) (E)	
19. (A) (B) (C) (D) (E)	39. (A) (B) (C) (D) (E)	
20. (A) (B) (C) (D) (E)	40. (A) (B) (C) (D) (E)	

PRACTICE TEST 4

Time: 60 minutes

Directions: Select the BEST answer for each of the 50 multiple-choice questions. If the exact solution is not one of the five choices, select the answer that is the best approximation. Then, fill in the appropriate oval on the answer sheet.

Notes:

1. A calculator will be needed to answer some of the questions on the test. Scientific, programmable, and graphing calculators are permitted. It is up to you to determine when and when not to use your calculator.
2. Angles on the Level 2 test are measured in degrees and radians. You need to decide whether your calculator should be set to degree mode or radian mode for a particular question.
3. Figures are drawn as accurately as possible and are intended to help solve some of the test problems. If a figure is not drawn to scale, this will be stated in the problem. All figures lie in a plane unless the problem indicates otherwise.
4. Unless otherwise stated, the domain of a function f is assumed to be the set of real numbers x for which the value of the function, $f(x)$, is a real number.
5. Reference information that may be useful in answering some of the test questions can be found below.

Reference Information	
Right circular cone with radius r and height h:	Volume $= \dfrac{1}{3}\pi r^2 h$
Right circular cone with circumference of base c and slant height ℓ:	Lateral Area $= \dfrac{1}{2}c\ell$
Sphere with radius r:	Volume $= \dfrac{4}{3}\pi r^3$
	Surface Area $= 4\pi r^2$
Pyramid with base area B and height h:	Volume $= \dfrac{1}{3}Bh$

▰▰ PRACTICE TEST 4 QUESTIONS

1. If $x^5 = 6^8$, then $x =$

   (A) 2.17
   (B) 3.06
   (C) 9.6
   (D) 17.58
   (E) 1,296

2. If $f(x) = x^2 + 3x$, then $f(3x) =$

   (A) $3(x^2 + 3x)$
   (B) $9(x + 1)$
   (C) $9x^2 + 9x$
   (D) $3x^2 + 9x$
   (E) $9x^2 + 6x$

3. If (x, y) is a point on the graph of a function, then which of the following must be a point on the graph of the inverse of the function?

   (A) (y, x)
   (B) $(-x, -y)$
   (C) $(-y, -x)$
   (D) $(x, -y)$
   (E) $(-x, y)$

4. What real values of a and b satisfy the equation $a + b + 9i = 6 + (2a - b)i$?

   (A) $a = 5, b = -1$
   (B) $a = 5, b = 1$
   (C) $a = 6, b = 0$
   (D) $a = 4, b = 2$
   (E) $a = 1, b = 5$

5. Standing 20 feet away from a flagpole, the angle of elevation of the top of the pole is 42°. Assuming the flagpole is perpendicular to the ground, what is its height?

   (A) 18 ft
   (B) 22 ft
   (C) 13 ft
   (D) 15 ft
   (E) 16 ft

6. If $\sin \theta = \dfrac{8}{17}$ and $\dfrac{\pi}{2} < \theta < \pi$, then $\tan \theta =$

   (A) $-\dfrac{15}{17}$

   (B) $-\dfrac{8}{15}$

   (C) $-\dfrac{8}{17}$

   (D) $\dfrac{8}{15}$

   (E) $\dfrac{8}{17}$

7. Which of the following is an equation of the line with an x-intercept of 4 and a y-intercept of -3?

   (A) $\dfrac{3}{4}x - y = -3$

   (B) $\dfrac{3}{4}x + y = -3$

   (C) $\dfrac{4}{3}x - y = 3$

   (D) $\dfrac{4}{3}x + y = -3$

   (E) $\dfrac{3}{4}x - y = 3$

8. The graph of which of the following functions is symmetric with respect to the origin?

   (A) $f(x) = e^x$
   (B) $g(x) = (x - 3)^2$
   (C) $h(x) = (x + 1)^3$
   (D) $G(x) = 2 \sin x$
   (E) $F(x) = x^3 - 1$

9. If $-4 + \sqrt{2 - x} = x$, then $x =$

   (A) -7 or -2
   (B) 7 or 2
   (C) -7 only
   (D) -2 only
   (E) -2 or 7

10. If $\log_3 x + 2 \log_3 x = 4$, then $x =$

    (A) 4.33
    (B) 2.28
    (C) 2
    (D) 1.33
    (E) 81

GO ON TO THE NEXT PAGE

11. If $f(x) = x^2 + 3$ for $-1 \leq x \leq 3$, then what is the range of f?

   (A) $y \geq 0$
   (B) $y \geq 3$
   (C) $-1 \leq y \leq 3$
   (D) $4 \leq y \leq 12$
   (E) $3 \leq y \leq 12$

USE THIS SPACE AS SCRATCH PAPER

12. What is the length of the edge of a cube having the same total surface area as a rectangular prism measuring 3 cm by 4 cm by 8 cm?

   (A) 22.7 cm
   (B) 4.8 cm
   (C) 136 cm
   (D) 5.8 cm
   (E) 11.7 cm

13. What is the maximum value of $f(x) = 4 - (x + 1)^2$?

   (A) -1
   (B) 4
   (C) 1
   (D) -4
   (E) -5

14. A teacher has a test bank of 12 questions. If she wishes to create a test using 8 of the questions, how many different combinations of 8 questions are possible?

   (A) 96
   (B) 495
   (C) 2,950
   (D) 11,800
   (E) 1.996×10^7

15. The number of tails showing when a pair of coins was tossed ten times was {0, 1, 2, 2, 1, 1, 0, 2, 0, 1}. What is the mean of the data?

   (A) 0
   (B) 0.5
   (C) 1
   (D) 1.5
   (E) 2

16. If a point has polar coordinates $(2, \pi)$, then what are its rectangular coordinates?

   (A) $(0, -2)$
   (B) $(2, 0)$
   (C) $(-2, -2)$
   (D) $(-2, 0)$
   (E) $(0, 2)$

GO ON TO THE NEXT PAGE

17. Figure 1 shows one cycle of the graph of $y = 3 \sin x + 1$ for $0 \le x < 2\pi$. What are the coordinates of the point where the minimum value of the function occurs on this interval?

    (A) $(\pi, -3)$

    (B) $\left(\dfrac{3\pi}{2}, -3\right)$

    (C) $(\pi, -2)$

    (D) $\left(\dfrac{5\pi}{4}, -2\right)$

    (E) $\left(\dfrac{3\pi}{2}, -2\right)$

USE THIS SPACE AS SCRATCH PAPER

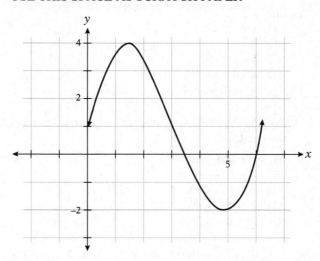

Figure 1

18. Valerie's average score on the first three math tests of the term is 89%. If she earns an 81% on the fourth test, what will her new average be?

    (A) 87%
    (B) 85%
    (C) 86.8%
    (D) 88%
    (E) 85.5%

19. If a circle has a radius of 6 cm, then what is the length of the arc intercepted by a central angle of 210°?

    (A) $\dfrac{7\pi}{6}$

    (B) $\dfrac{7\pi}{2}$

    (C) 7π

    (D) $\dfrac{15\pi}{2}$

    (E) 8π

20. What is the domain of $f(x) = \dfrac{1}{\sqrt{16 - x^2}}$?

    (A) $x \ne \pm 4$
    (B) $x < 4$
    (C) $x > -4$
    (D) $-4 < x < 4$
    (E) $x < -4$ or $x > 4$

21. If $f(x) = 2x^3 - 1$, then $f^{-1}(f(5)) =$

    (A) -1
    (B) 5
    (C) $\sqrt[3]{3}$
    (D) 1
    (E) 249

GO ON TO THE NEXT PAGE

22. If $x = 4 \cos \theta$ and $y = 4 \sin \theta$, then $\sqrt{x^2 + y^2} =$

   (A) 1
   (B) 4
   (C) 16
   (D) $4 \sin \theta \cos \theta$
   (E) $4(\cos \theta + \sin \theta)$

23. Which of the following quadratic equations has roots $8 + i$ and $8 - i$?

   (A) $x^2 - 16x + 65 = 0$
   (B) $x^2 + 16x - 65 = 0$
   (C) $x^2 - 16x + 63 = 0$
   (D) $x^2 + 16x - 63 = 0$
   (E) $x^2 + 16x + 65 = 0$

24. If A is a point on the unit circle in Figure 2, then what are the coordinates of A?

   (A) $(\sin 30°, \cos 30°)$

   (B) $\left(\sqrt{\dfrac{2}{2}}, \sqrt{\dfrac{2}{2}} \right)$

   (C) $\left(\dfrac{1}{2}, \sqrt{\dfrac{3}{2}} \right)$

   (D) $\left(\dfrac{1}{2}, \dfrac{1}{2} \right)$

   (E) $\left(\sqrt{\dfrac{3}{2}}, \dfrac{1}{2} \right)$

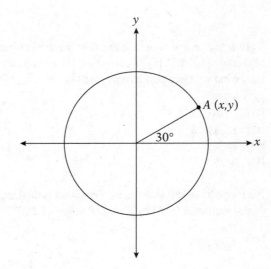

Figure 2

25. What are the real zeroes of $f(x) = -x^4 - 6x^3 - 9x^2$?

   (A) $\{3\}$
   (B) $\{-3, 3\}$
   (C) $\{0, -3\}$
   (D) $\{0, -3, 3\}$
   (E) $\{0\}$

26. In $\triangle ABC$ in Figure 3, $\dfrac{(\cos A \ \cot B)}{\csc A} =$

   (A) $\dfrac{a^2 b}{c^3}$

   (B) $\dfrac{b^2}{c^2}$

   (C) 1

   (D) $\dfrac{a^2}{c^2}$

   (E) $\dfrac{a^3}{bc^2}$

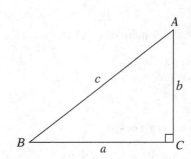

Figure 3

GO ON TO THE NEXT PAGE

27. Which single transformation can replace rotating a polygon 30° clockwise, followed by 110° counter-clockwise, followed by 15° clockwise all about the same center of rotation?

    (A) 155° clockwise
    (B) 95° counterclockwise
    (C) 275° clockwise
    (D) 65° counterclockwise
    (E) 80 counterclockwise

28. The solution set of $5x + 2y > 0$ lies in which quadrants?

    (A) I only
    (B) I and II
    (C) I, II, and IV
    (D) II, III, and IV
    (E) I, II, III, and IV

29. If $\tan \theta = \dfrac{5}{12}$, then $\cos \theta =$

    (A) $\dfrac{12}{13}$

    (B) $\pm\dfrac{12}{13}$

    (C) $\dfrac{5}{13}$

    (D) $\pm\dfrac{5}{13}$

    (E) $\dfrac{12}{11}$

30. The cube in Figure 4 has edges of length 4 cm. If point B is the midpoint of the edge, what is the perimeter of $\triangle ABC$?

    (A) 8.94
    (B) 11.31
    (C) 12.94
    (D) 14.60
    (E) 15.87

31. If $\dfrac{n!}{3} = (n-1)!$ then $n =$

    (A) 1
    (B) 2
    (C) 3
    (D) 4
    (E) 5

USE THIS SPACE AS SCRATCH PAPER

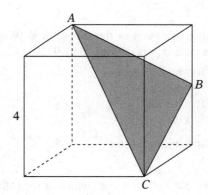

Figure 4

GO ON TO THE NEXT PAGE

32. The sides of a triangle are 5, 6, and 7 cm. What is the measure of the angle opposite the 5 cm side?

    (A) 44.4°
    (B) 53.8°
    (C) 57.1°
    (D) 78.5°
    (E) 90.0°

33. Given the statement "If $\angle ABC$ is a right angle, then it measures 90°," an indirect proof of the statement could begin with which of the following assumptions?

    (A) $\angle ABC$ does not measure 90°.
    (B) $\angle ABC$ measures 90°.
    (C) $\angle ABC$ is a right angle.
    (D) $\angle ABC$ is an obtuse angle.
    (E) $\angle ABC$ measures 30°.

34. If $8^{k+2} = 9^k$, then $k =$

    (A) −37.3
    (B) −0.9
    (C) 0.1
    (D) 1.9
    (E) 35.3

35. If $\sqrt{a} = 4.718$, then $\sqrt{13a} =$

    (A) 8
    (B) 17
    (C) 36
    (D) 61
    (E) 80

36. A varies inversely as the square of B. What is the effect on B if A is multiplied by 9?

    (A) It is multiplied by 3.
    (B) It is multiplied by 9.
    (C) It is divided by 3.
    (D) It is divided by 9.
    (E) It is multiplied by $\dfrac{1}{81}$.

37. If $x(x + 5)(x - 2) > 0$, then which of the following is the solution set?

    (A) $-5 < x < 2$
    (B) $x < -5$ or $0 < x < 2$
    (C) $x > 2$
    (D) $-5 < x < 0$ or $x > 2$
    (E) $x < -5$ or $x > 2$

GO ON TO THE NEXT PAGE

38. If $\log_4 (x^2 - 5) = 3$, then which of the following could equal x?

    (A) 7.7
    (B) 8.3
    (C) 4.6
    (D) 8
    (E) 69

39. If $5,000 is invested at a rate of 5.8% compounded daily, how much will the investment be worth in 3 years?

    (A) 5,117
    (B) 5,597
    (C) 5,921
    (D) 5,943
    (E) 5,950

40. $\triangle MNO$ in Figure 5 is an equilateral triangle. What is the slope of segment MN?

    (A) $-\sqrt{\dfrac{3}{3}}$

    (B) -1

    (C) $-\sqrt{3}$

    (D) -2

    (E) $\sqrt{\dfrac{3}{3}}$

41. A new computer does a calculations in b hours, and an old computer does c calculations in d minutes. If the two computers work together, how many calculations do they perform in m minutes?

    (A) $m\left(\dfrac{ac}{60bd}\right)$

    (B) $60m\left(\dfrac{a}{b} + \dfrac{c}{d}\right)$

    (C) $m\left(\dfrac{60a}{b} + \dfrac{c}{d}\right)$

    (D) $m\left(\dfrac{a}{b} + \dfrac{c}{d}\right)$

    (E) $m\left(\dfrac{a}{60b} + \dfrac{c}{d}\right)$

42. If the 15th term of an arithmetic sequence is 120, and the 30th term is 270, then what is the first term of the sequence?

    (A) -30
    (B) -20
    (C) 10
    (D) 20
    (E) 30

USE THIS SPACE AS SCRATCH PAPER

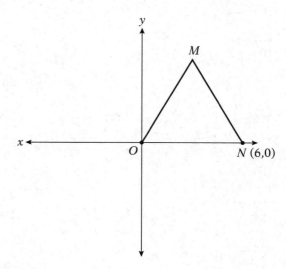

Figure 5

GO ON TO THE NEXT PAGE

43. If −1 is a zero of the function $f(x) = 2x^3 + 3x^2 - 20x - 21$, then what are the other zeroes?

(A) 1 and 3

(B) −3 and 3

(C) $-\dfrac{7}{2}$ and 3

(D) −3 and 1

(E) $-\dfrac{7}{2}$ and 1 and 3

44. If $f(x) = \dfrac{x^2 + 7x + 6}{x^2 - 2x - 3}$, what value does the function approach as x approaches −1?

(A) $-\dfrac{7}{2}$

(B) $-\dfrac{5}{4}$

(C) −1

(D) −2

(E) $-\dfrac{1}{2}$

45. Which of the following is NOT a factor of $x^5 + x^3 + 2x^2 - 12x + 8$?

(A) $x - 1$

(B) $x + 2$

(C) $x - 2i$

(D) $x^2 + 4$

(E) $x - 2$

46. $\displaystyle\sum_{k=0}^{8} (-1)^k 3k =$

(A) −108

(B) −12

(C) 84

(D) 12

(E) 108

47. A line has parametric equations $x = 6t - 2$, and $y = -8 + 4t$. Given t is the parameter, what is the slope of the line?

(A) $\dfrac{3}{28}$

(B) $\dfrac{2}{3}$

(C) $\dfrac{3}{2}$

(D) $\dfrac{28}{3}$

(E) $\dfrac{4}{3}$

GO ON TO THE NEXT PAGE

48. $|7 + i| =$

    (A) $5\sqrt{2}$

    (B) $2\sqrt{2}$

    (C) $2\sqrt{5}$

    (D) 3

    (E) $\sqrt{6}$

49. In how many ways can 10 people be divided into two groups if one group has 6 people and the other has 4?

    (A) 60
    (B) 120
    (C) 210
    (D) 720
    (E) 5,040

50. In how many ways can the letters of the word TEACH be arranged using all of the letters?

    (A) 15
    (B) 30
    (C) 60
    (D) 120
    (E) 720

USE THIS SPACE AS SCRATCH PAPER

S T O P

IF YOU FINISH BEFORE TIME IS CALLED, YOU MAY CHECK YOUR WORK ON THIS TEST ONLY.
DO NOT TURN TO ANY OTHER TEST IN THIS BOOK.

ANSWER KEY

1. D	11. E	21. B	31. C	41. E
2. C	12. B	22. B	32. A	42. B
3. A	13. B	23. A	33. A	43. C
4. B	14. B	24. E	34. E	44. B
5. A	15. C	25. C	35. B	45. E
6. B	16. D	26. D	36. C	46. D
7. E	17. E	27. D	37. D	47. B
8. D	18. A	28. C	38. B	48. A
9. D	19. C	29. B	39. E	49. C
10. A	20. D	30. E	40. C	50. D

ANSWERS AND SOLUTIONS

1. **D** Take the fifth root of both sides of the equation to solve for x.

$$x^5 = 6^8.$$

$$x^5 = 1,679,616.$$

$$x = (1,679,616)^{\frac{1}{5}}.$$

$$x \approx 17.58.$$

2. **C** Given $f(x) = x^2 + 3x$,

$$f(3x) = x^2 + 3x,$$

$$f(3x) = (3x)^2 + 3(3x),$$

$$f(3x) = 9x^2 + 9x.$$

3. **A** The graph of the inverse of a function is the graph of the function reflected over the line $y = x$. If (x, y) is a point on f, then (y, x), the reflection of the point over the line $y = x$, is on the graph of f^{-1}.

4. **B** Because $a + b + 9i = 6 + (2a - b)i$, $a + b = 6$ and $2a - b = 9$. Set up a system and use the linear combination method to solve for a and b.

$$a + b = 6$$
$$+ \quad 2a - b = 9$$
$$\overline{3a + 0b = 15.}$$
$$a = 5.$$

$$5 + b = 6, so \ b = 1.$$

5. **A** Let $h =$ the height of the flagpole.

$$\tan 42° = \frac{h}{20}.$$

$$h = 20(\tan 42°) \approx 18 \text{ feet.}$$

6. **B** Think of sine either in terms of the opposite leg and hypotenuse of a right triangle or in terms of the point (x, y) and r of a unit circle. Because $\dfrac{\pi}{2} < \theta < \pi$, θ lies in quadrant II, and the tangent $\left(\dfrac{\sin\theta}{\cos\theta}\right)$ must be negative.

$$\sin\theta = \frac{8}{17} = \frac{y}{r}$$

Because $r = \sqrt{x^2 + y^2}$:

$$17 = \sqrt{x^2 + 8^2}.$$

$$x = 15.$$

$$\tan\theta = -\frac{y}{x} = -\frac{8}{15}.$$

7. **E** The line passes through the points $(4, 0)$ and $(0, -3)$. The slope of the line is $m = \dfrac{-3 - 0}{0 - 4} = \dfrac{3}{4}$. Because the y-intercept is given, you can easily write the equation in slope-intercept form.

$$y = mx + b.$$

$$y = \frac{3}{4}x - 3.$$

$$\frac{3}{4}x - y = 3.$$

8. **D** The sine function is an odd function, which means it is symmetric with respect to the origin. Graph $G(x) = 2\sin x$ on your calculator to determine that it does, in fact, have origin symmetry.

9. **D** Isolate the radical expression and square both sides of the equation to solve for x.

$$-4 + \sqrt{2 - x} = x.$$

$$\sqrt{2 - x} = x + 4.$$

$$2 - x = x^2 + 8x + 16.$$

$$0 = x^2 + 9x + 14.$$

$$0 = (x + 2)(x + 7).$$

$$x = -7 \text{ or } -2.$$

Squaring both sides of the equation may introduce extraneous roots, however, so check the two solutions in the original equation.

When $x = -2$, $-4 + \sqrt{[2 - (-2)]} = -2$. $-4 + 2 = -2$.

When $x = -7$, $-4 + \sqrt{[2 - (-7)]} = -7$. $-4 + 3 \neq -7$.

$x = -7$ is not a solution of the original equation, so $x = -2$ is the only answer.

10. **A**

$$\log_3 x + 2\log_3 x = 4.$$

$$3\log_3 x = 4.$$

$$\log_3 x = \frac{4}{3}.$$

$$3^{\frac{4}{3}} = x.$$

$$x = 4.33.$$

11. **E** The graph of $f(x) = x^2 + 3$ is a parabola with vertex $(0, 3)$ and concave up. Because the domain is specified, the curve has a beginning and an ending point.

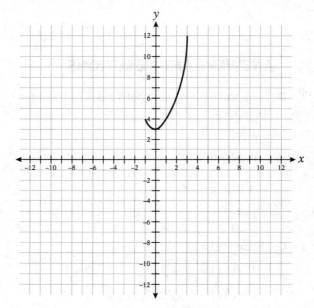

When $x = -1$, $y = 4$, and when $x = 3$, $y = 12$. The range is the set of all possible y values, so don't forget to include the vertex whose y value is less than 4. The range is $3 \leq y \leq 12$.

12. **B** The surface area of the prism is:

$$SA = 2(3)(4) + 2(3)(8) + 2(4)(8) = 136 \text{ cm}^2.$$

The surface area of the cube is given by the formula $SA = 6e^2$, where $e = $ the length of an edge of the cube.

$$136 = 6e^2.$$

$$22.67 = e^2.$$

$$e = 4.8 \text{ cm}.$$

13. **B** The maximum value of the function is the y-coordinate of the parabola's vertex. For the function $f(x) = 4 - (x + 1)^2$, the vertex is $(-1, 4)$. (You can check this by graphing the parabola on your graphing calculator.) The maximum value is, therefore, 4.

An alternate way of solving for the maximum is to find the y-value when $x = -\dfrac{b}{2a}$. In this case, $x = -\dfrac{(-2)}{2(-1)} = -1$, so $y = 4 - (-1 + 1)^2 = 4$.

14. **B**

$$_{12}C_8 = \frac{12!}{8!(12-8)!}.$$

$$= \frac{9 \times 10 \times 11 \times 12}{1 \times 2 \times 3 \times 4}.$$

$$= 495.$$

15. **C** The mean is the sum of the data divided by the number of terms.

$$\frac{(0 + 1 + 2 + 2 + 1 + 1 + 0 + 2 + 0 + 1)}{10} =$$

$$\frac{10}{10} = 1.$$

16. **D** Because the polar coordinates are $(2, \pi)$, $(r, \theta) = (2, \pi)$.

$$x = r \cos \theta = 2 \cos \pi = 2(-1) = -2.$$

$$y = r \sin \theta = 2 \sin \pi = 2(0) = 0.$$

The rectangular coordinates are $(-2, 0)$.

17. **E** The graph of $y = 3 \sin x + 1$ is the graph of $y = \sin x$ shifted up 1 unit with an amplitude of 3. The minimum value occurs at the point where $x = \dfrac{3\pi}{2}$. The y-coordinate at that point is -2.

18. **A** Let s = the sum of the scores of Valerie's first three tests.

$$\frac{s}{3} = 89.$$

$$s = 267.$$

Valerie's new average is $\dfrac{267 + 81}{4} = 87\%$.

19. **C** Use the formula $s = r\theta$, where s = the arc length and r = the radius of the circle. Convert 210° to radian measure first.

$$210\left(\frac{\pi}{180}\right) = \left(\frac{7\pi}{6}\right) \text{ radians.}$$

Now, solve for the arc length:

$$s = 6\left(\frac{7\pi}{6}\right) = 7\pi \text{ cm.}$$

20. **D** The denominator cannot equal zero and the radicand must be positive.

$$16 - x^2 > 0.$$

$$-x^2 > -16.$$

$$x^2 > 16.$$

$$-4 < x < 4.$$

21. **B** This problem can be done quickly and with little work if you recall that the composition of a function and its inverse function, $f^{-1}(f(x))$ and $f(f^{-1}(x))$, equal x.

$$f^{-1}(f(5)) = 5.$$

22. **B**

$$\sqrt{(x^2 + y^2)} = \sqrt{(4 \cos \theta)^2 + (4 \sin \theta)^2}$$

$$= \sqrt{16(\cos^2 \theta + \sin^2 \theta)}$$

Recognize that you can use one of the Pythagorean Identities, $\cos^2 \theta + \sin^2 \theta = 1$, to simplify the expression.

$$\sqrt{16(\cos^2 \theta + \sin^2 \theta)} = \sqrt{16(1)} = 4.$$

23. **A** The sum of the roots is: $8 + i + 8 - i = 16$.

The product of the roots is: $(8 + i)(8 - i) = 64 - i^2 = 65$.

The quadratic equation is, therefore, given by the equation:

$a[x^2 - (\text{sum of the roots})x + (\text{product of the roots})] = 0$.

$$a(x^2 - 16x + 65) = 0.$$

Setting a equal to 1 results in one possible answer:

$$x^2 - 16x + 65 = 0.$$

24. **E** Because the circle is a unit circle, the coordinates of A are $(\cos 30°, \sin 30°)$. This can be simplified to $\left(\sqrt{\dfrac{3}{2}}, \dfrac{1}{2}\right)$.

If you don't know what the cosine and sine of 30° equal, let (x, y) be the coordinates of A, and draw a right triangle with legs of length x and y. The triangle is a 30°-60°-90° triangle, so use the ratios of the sides of this special right triangle to determine that the coordinates of point A are $\left(\sqrt{\dfrac{3}{2}}, \dfrac{1}{2}\right)$.

25. **C**

$$-x^4 - 6x^3 - 9x^2 = 0.$$

$$-x^2(x^2 + 6x + 9) = 0.$$

$$-x^2(x + 3)^2 = 0.$$

$$x = 0 \text{ and } x = -3.$$

26. **D** Using right triangle trigonometry to determine values for the three trigonometric functions.

$$\cos A = \frac{\text{adjacent}}{\text{hypotenuse}} = \frac{b}{c}.$$

$$\cot B = \frac{\text{adjacent}}{\text{opposite}} = \frac{a}{b}.$$

$$\csc A = \frac{1}{\sin A} = \frac{\text{hypotenuse}}{\text{opposite}} = \frac{c}{a}.$$

$$\frac{\cos A \cot B}{\csc A} = \frac{\dfrac{b}{c}\left(\dfrac{a}{b}\right)}{\dfrac{c}{a}}.$$

$$= \frac{\dfrac{a}{c}}{\dfrac{c}{a}} = \frac{a^2}{c^2}.$$

27. **D** Rotating a polygon 30° clockwise, followed by 110° counterclockwise, followed by 15° clockwise all about the same center of rotation is equivalent to rotating it $30 + (-110) + (15) = -65°$. 65° counterclockwise is the correct answer.

28. **C** Solve the inequality for y to get $y > -\dfrac{5}{2}x$. Then, graph the linear equation $y = -\dfrac{5}{2}x$. The solution to the inequality is the shaded area above the line, and that region falls in quadrants I, II, and IV.

29. **B**

$$\tan \theta = \frac{5}{12} = \frac{y}{x}.$$

$$\cos \theta = \frac{x}{r} \text{ where } r = \sqrt{(x^2 + y^2)}.$$

First solve for r to get:

$$r = \sqrt{(x^2 + y^2)} = \sqrt{(12^2 + 5^2)} = 13.$$

Therefore, $\cos \theta = \pm\dfrac{12}{13}$.

30. **E** Because B is the midpoint of the edge of the cube, use the Pythagorean Theorem to determine the measure of AB and BC.

$$AB = BC = \sqrt{4^2 + 2^2} = \sqrt{20} = 2\sqrt{5}.$$

The remaining side, AC, is the hypotenuse of a right triangle with legs of lengths 4 and $4\sqrt{2}$.

$$AC = \sqrt{4^2 + (4\sqrt{2})^2} = \sqrt{48} = 4\sqrt{3}$$

The perimeter of

$$\triangle ABC = 2\sqrt{5} + 2\sqrt{5} + 4\sqrt{3} = 15.87 \text{ cm}.$$

31. **C**

$$\frac{n!}{3} = (n - 1)!$$

$$\frac{n!}{(n - 1)!} = 3.$$

$$n = 3.$$

32. **A** The Law of Cosines states: $c^2 = a^2 + b^2 - 2ab \cos \angle C$.

$5^2 = 6^2 + 7^2 - 2(6)(7) \cos \angle C$, where C is the angle opposite the 5-cm side.

$$25 = 85 - 84 \cos \angle C.$$

$$-60 = -84 \cos \angle C.$$

$$\cos^{-1}\left(\frac{60}{84}\right) = 44.4° .$$

33. **A** "$\angle ABC$ does not measure 90°" is the negation of the conclusion of the given statement. It is the correct assumption to use to begin an indirect proof.

34. **E** Take the log of both sides of the equation to solve for k.

$$\log(8^{k+2}) = \log(9^k).$$

$$(k + 2)\log 8 = k\log 9.$$

$$k + 2 = k\left(\frac{\log 9}{\log 8}\right).$$

$$k + 2 = 1.0557k.$$

$$k = 35.3.$$

35. **B**

$$\sqrt{13a} = \sqrt{13}(\sqrt{a}) = (\sqrt{13})(4.718)$$

$$= 17.$$

36. **C** A and B are inversely proportional. When A is multiplied by 9, B is divided by $\sqrt{9}$. Answer C is the correct answer choice.

37. **D** The critical points of the inequality $x(x + 5)$ $(x - 2) > 0$ are $x = 0, -5,$ and 2. Evaluate the 4 intervals created by these points by determining if the inequality is satisfied on each interval. $-5 < x < 0$ or $x > 2$ is the correct answer choice.

38. **B** If $\log_4 (x^2 - 5) = 3$, then $4^3 = x^2 - 5$.

$$64 = x^2 - 5.$$

$$69 = x^2.$$

$$x = 8.3.$$

39. **E** $A = P\left(1 + \dfrac{r}{n}\right)^{nt}$, where n is the number of times the investment is compounded per year.

$$A = 5{,}000\left(1 + \frac{0.058}{365}\right)^{365(3)}.$$

$$A = 5{,}000(1.0001589)^{1095}.$$

$$A \approx 5{,}950.$$

40. **C** Because $\triangle MNO$ is equilateral, you can break it into two 30°–60°–90° right triangles. The x-coordinate of point M is the midpoint of ON, which is 3. The y-coordinate of point M can be determined by using the ratios of the sides of a 30°–60°–90° triangle. The side opposite the 30° angle is 3, so the side opposite the 60° angle is $3\sqrt{3}$. Point M, therefore, has coordinates $(3, 3\sqrt{3})$.

The slope of MN is $-3\sqrt{\dfrac{3}{3}} = -\sqrt{3}$.

41. **E** The new computer does a calculations in b hours, so it does $\dfrac{a}{60b}$ calculations in one minute. Add the individual rates together and multiply their sum by m minutes.

$$m\left(\frac{a}{60b} + \frac{c}{d}\right).$$

42. **B** Because the 15th term of an arithmetic sequence is 120 and the 30th term is 270, the common ratio between consecutive terms is $\dfrac{270 - 120}{30 - 15} = \dfrac{150}{15} = 10$.

$$a_n = a_1 + (n - 1)d.$$

$$120 = a_1 + (15 - 1)10.$$

$$-20 = a_1.$$

43. **C** If $x = -1$ is a zero of the function, then $x + 1$ is a factor of the polynomial. Use either long division or synthetic division to determine that $(2x^3 + 3x^2 - 20x - 21) \div (x + 1) = 2x^2 + x - 21$.

$$2x^2 + x - 21 = 0.$$

$$(2x + 7)(x - 3) = 0.$$

$$x = -\frac{7}{2} \text{ or } x = 3.$$

44. **B** Factor the numerator and denominator. Then, simplify the expression and evaluate it when $x = -1$.

$$f(x) = \frac{x^2 + 7x + 6}{x^2 - 2x - 3} = \frac{(x + 6)(x + 1)}{(x - 3)(x + 1)}$$

$$= \frac{(x + 6)}{(x - 3)}.$$

When $x = -1$, $\dfrac{(x + 6)}{(x - 3)} = -\dfrac{5}{4}$.

45. E One way to solve this problem is to verify that if $x - a$ is a factor of the polynomial, then a is a zero.

$$f(1) = (1)^5 + (1)^3 + 2(1)^2 - 12(1) + 8 = 0.$$

$$f(-2) = (-2)^5 + (-2)^3 + 2(-2)^2 - 12(-2) + 8 = 0.$$

$$f(2i) = (2i)^5 + (2i)^3 + 2(2i)^2 - 12(2i) + 8 = 0.$$

$$f(-2i) = (-2i)^5 + (-2i)^3 + 2(-2i)^2 - 12(-2i) + 8 = 0.$$

$$f(2) = (2)^5 + (2)^3 + 2(2)^2 - 12(2) + 8 = 32.$$

Note, to determine if $x^2 + 4$ is a factor of the polynomial, check that $x - 2i$ is a factor because $(x - 2i)(x - 2i) = x^2 + 4$. $f(2)$ results in a remainder of 32, so $x - 2$ is not a factor of the polynomial.

46. D Substitute $k = 0, 1, 2, \ldots 8$ into the summation to get:

$$0 - 3 + 6 - 9 + 12 - 15 + 18 - 21 + 24 = 12.$$

47. B Because $x = 6t - 2$, $t = \dfrac{x + 2}{6}$. Substitute this value into the second equation to get:

$$y = 8 + 4\left(\frac{x + 2}{6}\right).$$

$$3y = 24 + 2x + 4.$$

$$y = \frac{2}{3}x + \frac{28}{3}.$$

The slope of the resulting line is $\dfrac{2}{3}$.

48. A Recall that the absolute value of a complex number is given by: $|a + bi| = \sqrt{(a^2 + b^2)}$.

$$|7 + i| = \sqrt{(7^2 + 1^2)} = \sqrt{50} = 5\sqrt{2}.$$

49. C Choosing 6 people out of the 12 results in the following:

$$_{10}C_6 = \frac{10!}{6!(10 - 6)!} = \frac{10!}{6!4!}$$

$$= \frac{7 \times 8 \times 9 \times 10}{1 \times 2 \times 3 \times 4}$$

$$= 210.$$

Note that once the 6 members are chosen, the remaining 4 people are automatically placed in the second group.

50. D Find the number of permutations of five letters taken five at a time.

$$5! = 5 \times 4 \times 3 \times 2 \times 1 = 120.$$

■ DIAGNOSE YOUR STRENGTHS AND WEAKNESSES

Check the number of each question answered correctly and "X" the number of each question answered incorrectly.

Algebra	1	9	31	34	35	36	37	39	41	Total Number Correct
9 questions										

Solid Geometry	12	30	Total Number Correct
2 questions			

Coordinate Geometry	7	16	24	27	28	40	Total Number Correct
6 questions							

Trigonometry	5	6	19	22	26	29	32	Total Number Correct
7 questions								

Functions	2	3	8	10	11	13	17	20	21	23	25	38	43	45	47	Total Number Correct
15 questions																

Data Analysis, Statistics, and Probability	15	18	Total Number Correct
2 questions			

Numbers and Operations	4	14	33	42	44	46	48	49	50	Total Number Correct
9 questions										

Number of correct answers $-\dfrac{1}{4}$ **(Number of incorrect answers) = Your raw score**

_____ $-\dfrac{1}{4}$ (_____) = _____

Compare your raw score with the approximate SAT Subject Test score below:

	Raw Score	SAT Subject Test Approximate Score
Excellent	43–50	770–800
Very Good	33–43	670–770
Good	27–33	620–670
Above Average	21–27	570–620
Average	11–21	500–570
Below Average	< 11	< 500

PRACTICE TEST 5

Treat this practice test as the actual test and complete it in one 60-minute sitting. Use the following answer sheet to fill in your multiple-choice answers. Once you have completed the practice test:

1. Check your answers using the Answer Key.
2. Review the Answers and Solutions.
3. Fill in the "Diagnose Your Strengths and Weaknesses" sheet, and determine areas that require further preparation.

PRACTICE TEST 5
MATH LEVEL 2

ANSWER SHEET

Tear out this answer sheet and use it to complete the practice test. Determine the BEST answer for each question. Then, fill in the appropriate oval using a No. 2 pencil.

1. Ⓐ Ⓑ Ⓒ Ⓓ Ⓔ	21. Ⓐ Ⓑ Ⓒ Ⓓ Ⓔ	41. Ⓐ Ⓑ Ⓒ Ⓓ Ⓔ
2. Ⓐ Ⓑ Ⓒ Ⓓ Ⓔ	22. Ⓐ Ⓑ Ⓒ Ⓓ Ⓔ	42. Ⓐ Ⓑ Ⓒ Ⓓ Ⓔ
3. Ⓐ Ⓑ Ⓒ Ⓓ Ⓔ	23. Ⓐ Ⓑ Ⓒ Ⓓ Ⓔ	43. Ⓐ Ⓑ Ⓒ Ⓓ Ⓔ
4. Ⓐ Ⓑ Ⓒ Ⓓ Ⓔ	24. Ⓐ Ⓑ Ⓒ Ⓓ Ⓔ	44. Ⓐ Ⓑ Ⓒ Ⓓ Ⓔ
5. Ⓐ Ⓑ Ⓒ Ⓓ Ⓔ	25. Ⓐ Ⓑ Ⓒ Ⓓ Ⓔ	45. Ⓐ Ⓑ Ⓒ Ⓓ Ⓔ
6. Ⓐ Ⓑ Ⓒ Ⓓ Ⓔ	26. Ⓐ Ⓑ Ⓒ Ⓓ Ⓔ	46. Ⓐ Ⓑ Ⓒ Ⓓ Ⓔ
7. Ⓐ Ⓑ Ⓒ Ⓓ Ⓔ	27. Ⓐ Ⓑ Ⓒ Ⓓ Ⓔ	47. Ⓐ Ⓑ Ⓒ Ⓓ Ⓔ
8. Ⓐ Ⓑ Ⓒ Ⓓ Ⓔ	28. Ⓐ Ⓑ Ⓒ Ⓓ Ⓔ	48. Ⓐ Ⓑ Ⓒ Ⓓ Ⓔ
9. Ⓐ Ⓑ Ⓒ Ⓓ Ⓔ	29. Ⓐ Ⓑ Ⓒ Ⓓ Ⓔ	49. Ⓐ Ⓑ Ⓒ Ⓓ Ⓔ
10. Ⓐ Ⓑ Ⓒ Ⓓ Ⓔ	30. Ⓐ Ⓑ Ⓒ Ⓓ Ⓔ	50. Ⓐ Ⓑ Ⓒ Ⓓ Ⓔ
11. Ⓐ Ⓑ Ⓒ Ⓓ Ⓔ	31. Ⓐ Ⓑ Ⓒ Ⓓ Ⓔ	
12. Ⓐ Ⓑ Ⓒ Ⓓ Ⓔ	32. Ⓐ Ⓑ Ⓒ Ⓓ Ⓔ	
13. Ⓐ Ⓑ Ⓒ Ⓓ Ⓔ	33. Ⓐ Ⓑ Ⓒ Ⓓ Ⓔ	
14. Ⓐ Ⓑ Ⓒ Ⓓ Ⓔ	34. Ⓐ Ⓑ Ⓒ Ⓓ Ⓔ	
15. Ⓐ Ⓑ Ⓒ Ⓓ Ⓔ	35. Ⓐ Ⓑ Ⓒ Ⓓ Ⓔ	
16. Ⓐ Ⓑ Ⓒ Ⓓ Ⓔ	36. Ⓐ Ⓑ Ⓒ Ⓓ Ⓔ	
17. Ⓐ Ⓑ Ⓒ Ⓓ Ⓔ	37. Ⓐ Ⓑ Ⓒ Ⓓ Ⓔ	
18. Ⓐ Ⓑ Ⓒ Ⓓ Ⓔ	38. Ⓐ Ⓑ Ⓒ Ⓓ Ⓔ	
19. Ⓐ Ⓑ Ⓒ Ⓓ Ⓔ	39. Ⓐ Ⓑ Ⓒ Ⓓ Ⓔ	
20. Ⓐ Ⓑ Ⓒ Ⓓ Ⓔ	40. Ⓐ Ⓑ Ⓒ Ⓓ Ⓔ	

PRACTICE TEST 5

Time: 60 minutes

Directions: Select the BEST answer for each of the 50 multiple-choice questions. If the exact solution is not one of the five choices, select the answer that is the best approximation. Then, fill in the appropriate oval on the answer sheet.

Notes:

1. A calculator will be needed to answer some of the questions on the test. Scientific, programmable, and graphing calculators are permitted. It is up to you to determine when and when not to use your calculator.
2. Angles on the Level 2 test are measured in degrees and radians. You need to decide whether your calculator should be set to degree mode or radian mode for a particular question.
3. Figures are drawn as accurately as possible and are intended to help solve some of the test problems. If a figure is not drawn to scale, this will be stated in the problem. All figures lie in a plane unless the problem indicates otherwise.
4. Unless otherwise stated, the domain of a function f is assumed to be the set of real numbers x for which the value of the function, $f(x)$, is a real number.
5. Reference information that may be useful in answering some of the test questions can be found below.

Reference Information	
Right circular cone with radius r and height h:	Volume $= \dfrac{1}{3}\pi r^2 h$
Right circular cone with circumference of base c and slant height ℓ:	Lateral Area $= \dfrac{1}{2}c\ell$
Sphere with radius r:	Volume $= \dfrac{4}{3}\pi r^3$
	Surface Area $= 4\pi r^2$
Pyramid with base area B and height h:	Volume $= \dfrac{1}{3}Bh$

▨ PRACTICE TEST 5 QUESTIONS

1. If $\sqrt[3]{8x^3 - 1} = 2$, then $x =$

    (A) -1.5
    (B) 1.04
    (C) 1.50
    (D) 2.08
    (E) 4.5

2. $\dfrac{12!}{4!9!} =$

    (A) 24
    (B) 33
    (C) 55
    (D) 330
    (E) $1,320$

3. Which of the following lines is parallel to the line $y = \dfrac{3}{4}x + 5$?

    (A) $y = \dfrac{3}{4}x - 5$

    (B) $y = -\dfrac{3}{4}x + 5$

    (C) $y = \dfrac{4}{3}x + 5$

    (D) $y = -\dfrac{4}{3}x + 5$

    (E) $y = -\dfrac{4}{3}x - 5$

4. If $f(x, y) = \dfrac{1}{2}x + y$, then which of the following is equal to $f(14, 3)$?

    (A) $f(12, 2)$
    (B) $f(16, -2)$
    (C) $f(-20, 0)$
    (D) $f(8, 6)$
    (E) $f(-2, 12)$

5. If $f(x) = x^3 + 1$, then $f(f(2)) =$

    (A) 7
    (B) 9
    (C) 126
    (D) 729
    (E) 730

GO ON TO THE NEXT PAGE

6. What is the value of k if

$$\frac{1}{(x-2)(x+4)} = \frac{h}{(x-2)} + \frac{k}{(x+4)}?$$

(A) 2

(B) −4

(C) $-\frac{1}{6}$

(D) $\frac{1}{6}$

(E) −2

7. If $\csc \theta = 3$, then $\sin \theta \csc \theta =$

(A) 3

(B) 6

(C) $\frac{1}{3}$

(D) 1

(E) −1

8. If $9x^4 - 4 = 7$, then x could equal which of the following?

(A) −1.05

(B) 0.31

(C) 0.95

(D) 1.11

(E) 1.22

9. The boys' basketball team scored an average of 54 points per game in their first 5 games of the season. The girls' basketball team scored an average of 59 points per game in their first 6 games. What was the average of points scored in all 11 games?

(A) 56.5

(B) 56.7

(C) 56.0

(D) 57.1

(E) 62.4

10. What is the range of $f(x) = \sqrt{16 - x^2}$?

(A) $y \geq 0$

(B) $y \geq 4$

(C) $-4 \leq y \leq 4$

(D) $0 \leq y \leq 4$

(E) $y \leq 4$

USE THIS SPACE AS SCRATCH PAPER

GO ON TO THE NEXT PAGE

11. The probability that Mike hits a target is $\frac{4}{7}$, and, independently, the probability that Michelle hits it is $\frac{5}{8}$. What is the probability that Mike hits the target and Michelle does not?

(A) $\frac{3}{14}$

(B) $\frac{3}{8}$

(C) $\frac{4}{14}$

(D) $\frac{3}{7}$

(E) $\frac{55}{56}$

12. In Figure 1, what is the value of θ?
    (A) 1°
    (B) 23.6°
    (C) 42.5°
    (D) 47.5°
    (E) 66.4°

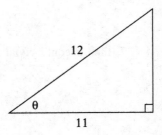

Figure 1

13. $\log_3 27\sqrt{3} =$

(A) $\frac{7}{2}$

(B) $9\sqrt{3}$
(C) 9
(D) 3

(E) $\frac{3}{2}$

14. Which of the following is a polynomial with roots 0 and $5 + i$?

(A) $x^2 - 5x$
(B) $x^2 - 10x + 26$
(C) $x^3 - 10x^2 + 24x$
(D) $x^3 - 10x^2 + 26x$
(E) $x^3 - 10x^2 + 25x$

GO ON TO THE NEXT PAGE

15. In Figure 2, the polar coordinates of the point shown are (4, 40°). What is the value of r?

    (A) $4 \cos \theta$
    (B) $4 \sin \theta$
    (C) 3.3
    (D) 4
    (E) 5.2

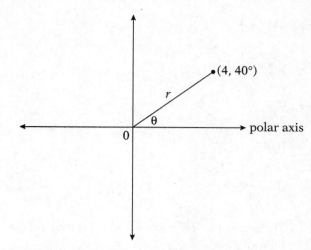

Figure 2

16. If $\theta > 0$ and $\cos \theta = \dfrac{2}{3}$, then $\sin 2\theta =$

    (A) 0.50
    (B) 0.75
    (C) 0.99
    (D) 2.23
    (E) 2.98

17. For all x such that $x > 0$, $f(x) = \log_8 x$. What does $f^{-1}(x)$ equal?

    (A) x^8
    (B) 8^x
    (C) $\sqrt[8]{x}$
    (D) $\log_x 8$
    (E) $8^{\frac{1}{x}}$

18. Which of the following is an asymptote of $f(x) = \tan 2x$?

    (A) $x = \dfrac{\pi}{2}$
    (B) $x = \pi$
    (C) $x = \dfrac{\pi}{3}$
    (D) $x = \dfrac{\pi}{6}$
    (E) $x = \dfrac{\pi}{4}$

GO ON TO THE NEXT PAGE

19. If $8^{2-x} = 512^{x+1}$, what does x equal?

   (A) $-\dfrac{1}{4}$

   (B) $-\dfrac{1}{2}$

   (C) $\dfrac{1}{4}$

   (D) $\dfrac{1}{2}$

   (E) $\dfrac{5}{4}$

20. The graph of $x^2 - y^2 - 3x + 4y - 5 = 0$ is which of the following?

   (A) a circle
   (B) an ellipse
   (C) a parabola
   (D) a hyperbola
   (E) a semicircle

21. If $f(x) = x + 3$ and $g(x) = \dfrac{1}{4 - x}$, then $f/g(-1) =$

   (A) $\dfrac{2}{5}$

   (B) $\dfrac{9}{5}$

   (C) $\dfrac{5}{2}$

   (D) 6
   (E) 10

22. Given the set of data 1, 2, 2, 3, 3, 3, 4, 4, 4, 4 which of the following is a true statement?

   (A) mean < median < mode
   (B) mean ≤ median ≤ mode
   (C) mean ≤ mode ≤ median
   (D) median < mode < mean
   (E) median < mean < mode

23. The graph of $y = -2 \cos \pi x$ has which of the following symmetries?

   (A) Symmetric with respect to the y-axis
   (B) Symmetric with respect to the x-axis
   (C) Symmetric with respect to the origin
   (D) Symmetric with respect to both axes
   (E) None

GO ON TO THE NEXT PAGE

24. If 7, $\dfrac{23}{2}$, and 16 are the first three terms of an arith-

    metic sequence, then what is the sum of the first 15 terms of the sequence?

    (A) 77
    (B) 472.5
    (C) 577.5
    (D) 945
    (E) 1,155

25. A laptop purchased new for $2,800 depreciates at a rate of 22% per year. How much is it worth after 30 months?

    (A) 636
    (B) 1,505
    (C) 1,621
    (D) 1,874
    (E) 2,034

26. Which of the following is the solution of $|2x - 4| < 1$?

    (A) $\dfrac{3}{2} < x < \dfrac{5}{2}$

    (B) $x < \dfrac{5}{2}$

    (C) $x < \dfrac{3}{2}$ or $x > \dfrac{5}{2}$

    (D) $x > 0$

    (E) $x \le \dfrac{3}{2}$ or $x \ge \dfrac{5}{2}$

27. Which of the following is the equation of a line with x-intercept $(-3, 0)$ and y-intercept $(0, -5)$?

    (A) $5x + 3y = 15$
    (B) $3x + 5y = -15$
    (C) $5x - 3y = -15$
    (D) $5x + 3y = -15$
    (E) $-5x + 3y = 15$

GO ON TO THE NEXT PAGE

28. The graph in Figure 3 represents a portion of the graph of which of the following functions?

    (A) $f(x) = 2 \cos (x + \pi)$
    (B) $f(x) = \sin 2x$
    (C) $f(x) = -2 \sin x$

    (D) $f(x) = \cos\left(x + \dfrac{\pi}{2} \right)$

    (E) $f(x) = 2 \sin x$

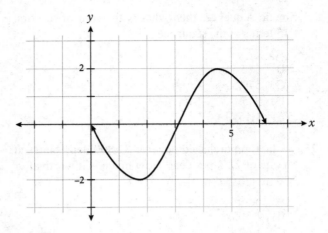

Figure 3

29. If $x + 3$ is a factor of $x^5 + 2x^4 - kx^3 + 3x^2$, then $k =$

    (A) −3
    (B) −2
    (C) −1
    (D) 2
    (E) 3

30. By the Rational Root Test, how many possible rational roots does $f(x) = 4x^3 - x^2 + 10x - 6$ have?

    (A) 3
    (B) 8
    (C) 14
    (D) 16
    (E) 24

31. What are the solutions to the system: $xy + 6 = 0$ and $x - y = 5$?

    (A) $\{(-3, 2), (-2, 3)\}$
    (B) $\{(-2, -3), (-3, -2)\}$
    (C) $\{(1, -6), (-6, 1)\}$
    (D) $\{(6, 1), (-1, -6)\}$
    (E) $\{(2, -3), (3, -2)\}$

32. $1,000 is invested at a rate of $r\%$ compounded quarterly. The value of the investment in t years can be modeled by the equation $A = 1,000\left(1 + \dfrac{\left(\dfrac{r}{100} \right)}{4} \right)^{4t}$.

    If the investment doubles in 12 years, what is the value of r?

    (A) 4.7
    (B) 5.8
    (C) 6.1
    (D) 10.2
    (E) 11.6

GO ON TO THE NEXT PAGE

33. Given the three vectors $\vec{u}, \vec{v},$ and $\vec{w}$ in Figure 4, which of the following expressions denotes the vector operation shown?

    (A) $\vec{u} + \vec{v} = \vec{w}$
    (B) $\vec{u} + \vec{w} = \vec{v}$
    (C) $\vec{v} - \vec{u} = \vec{w}$
    (D) $\vec{v} + \vec{w} = \vec{u}$
    (E) $\vec{v} - \vec{w} = \vec{u}$

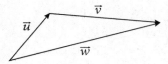

Figure 4

34. The product of 212,121,212,121 and 33,333 contains how many digits?

    (A) 14
    (B) 15
    (C) 16
    (D) 17
    (E) 18

35. What is the maximum value of the function $f(x) = \dfrac{1}{x}$ over the interval $\dfrac{1}{2} \le x \le \dfrac{3}{2}$?

    (A) $\dfrac{1}{2}$

    (B) $\dfrac{3}{2}$

    (C) 2

    (D) $\dfrac{2}{3}$

    (E) infinity

36. In $\triangle ABC$ in Figure 5, $BC = 6.3$ cm, $x = 49°$, and $y = 22°$. What is the length of side AB?

    (A) 2.4
    (B) 2.9
    (C) 3.1
    (D) 4.8
    (E) 12.7

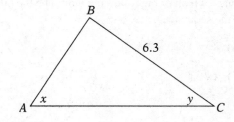

Figure 5

37. The rectangle in Figure 6 is rotated about side WZ. What is the volume of the resulting solid?

    (A) 432
    (B) 108π
    (C) 432π
    (D) 72π
    (E) 330

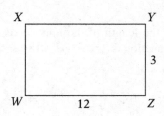

Figure 6

GO ON TO THE NEXT PAGE

38. What is the length of the segment connecting $A(0, -1, 7)$ to $B(5, 4, -2)$?

    (A) 7.7
    (B) 8.7
    (C) 10.7
    (D) 11.4
    (E) 131

USE THIS SPACE AS SCRATCH PAPER

39. Kate needs to complete 5 more courses: calculus, English, French, computer science, and history, in order to graduate from high school. She plans to schedule the courses during the first 5 periods of the school day, and all 5 courses are offered during each of the 5 periods. How many different schedules are possible?

    (A) 25
    (B) 24
    (C) 240
    (D) 120
    (E) 60

40. If the operation $\blacklozenge$ is defined for all real numbers a and b as $a \blacklozenge b = b^{2a}$. If $n \blacklozenge 5 = 125$, then $n =$

    (A) 1
    (B) 2
    (C) 3
    (D) $\dfrac{3}{2}$
    (E) $\dfrac{1}{2}$

41. If the pattern of the terms $3\sqrt{3}, 27, 81\sqrt{3}, \ldots$ continues, which of the following would be the 6th term of the sequence?

    (A) $(3\sqrt{3})^6$
    (B) $(\sqrt{3})^6$
    (C) 3^6
    (D) $(3\sqrt{3})^5$
    (E) 3^7

42. What is the length of the minor axis of an ellipse whose equation is $25x^2 + 9y^2 - 18y - 216 = 0$?

    (A) 3
    (B) 5
    (C) 6
    (D) 9
    (E) 10

GO ON TO THE NEXT PAGE

43. Which of the following is the equation of a circle with center $(-1, 7)$ and a radius of length 3?

    (A) $(x+1)^2 - (y+7)^2 = 9$
    (B) $(x+1)^2 + (y-7)^2 = 3$
    (C) $(x-1)^2 + (y+7)^2 = 3$
    (D) $(x+1)^2 + (y-7)^2 = 9$
    (E) $(x-1)^2 + (y+7)^2 = 9$

44. $\lim\limits_{x\to 1} \dfrac{8x^2 - 11x + 3}{x^2 - 1} =$

    (A) 1.7
    (B) 2.2
    (C) 2.5
    (D) 3
    (E) No limit exists.

45. If a function is an even function, then $f(-x) = f(x)$ for all values of x in the domain. Which of the following is an even function?

    (A) $f(x) = \tan x$
    (B) $f(x) = |x+1|$
    (C) $f(x) = x^3 - 1$
    (D) $f(x) = 2^x$
    (E) $f(x) = x^4 - 2x^2 + 7$

46. If $x = \arctan(-4)$ and $x + y = 320°$, then $\cos y =$

    (A) -0.44
    (B) 0.24
    (C) 0.73
    (D) 0.81
    (E) 1

47. If $i^2 = -1$, then which of the following equals $(5 - 12i)^{\frac{1}{2}}$?

    (A) $2 - 2i$
    (B) $3 - 2i$
    (C) $2 + 2i$
    (D) $3 + 2i$
    (E) $2 + 3i$

48. $\tan^4 \theta + 2\tan \theta + 1 =$

    (A) $\sec^2 \theta$
    (B) $2\sec^2 \theta$
    (C) $\sec^4 \theta$
    (D) $\cos^4 \theta$
    (E) 1

GO ON TO THE NEXT PAGE

49. The right circular cylinder in Figure 7 has a diameter of 6 cm and a height of 8 cm. A cylindrical hole is created through the center as shown, with a radius of 1 cm. What is the total surface area of the solid?

(A) 34π
(B) 66π
(C) 80π
(D) 82π
(E) 84π

USE THIS SPACE AS SCRATCH PAPER

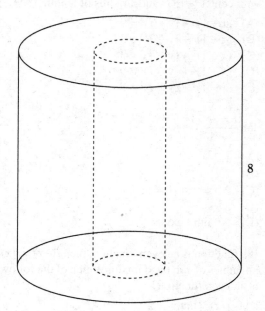

8

Figure 7

50. How many real solutions does the system $x^2 + y^2 = 25$ and $xy = 10$ have?

(A) 0
(B) 1
(C) 2
(D) 3
(E) 4

S T O P

IF YOU FINISH BEFORE TIME IS CALLED, YOU MAY CHECK YOUR WORK ON THIS TEST ONLY.
DO NOT TURN TO ANY OTHER TEST IN THIS BOOK.

■ ANSWER KEY

1. B	11. A	21. E	31. E	41. A
2. C	12. B	22. B	32. B	42. C
3. A	13. A	23. A	33. A	43. D
4. D	14. D	24. C	34. C	44. C
5. E	15. D	25. B	35. C	45. E
6. C	16. C	26. A	36. C	46. D
7. D	17. B	27. D	37. B	47. B
8. A	18. E	28. C	38. D	48. C
9. B	19. A	29. D	39. D	49. C
10. D	20. D	30. D	40. D	50. E

■ ANSWERS AND SOLUTIONS

1. **B** First, cube both sides of the equation.

$$\sqrt[3]{8x^3 - 1} = 2.$$
$$8x^3 - 1 = 2^3 = 8.$$
$$8x^3 = 9.$$
$$x^3 = \frac{9}{8}.$$
$$x = \left(\frac{9}{8}\right)^{\frac{1}{3}} \approx 1.04.$$

2. **C** Recall that factorial is represented by the "!" symbol.

$$12! = 12 \times 11 \times 10 \times 9 \times 8 \times 7 \times 6 \times 5 \times 4 \times 3 \times 2 \times 1$$
$$\frac{12!}{4!9!} = \frac{10 \times 11 \times 12}{1 \times 2 \times 3 \times 4}$$
$$= 55.$$

3. **A** Parallel lines have the same slopes. The given line is written in slope-intercept form $y = mx + b$ where m = slope. Its slope is $\frac{3}{4}$. Answer A is the only line with this slope.

4. **D**

$$f(14, 3) = \frac{1}{2}(14) + 3 = 7 + 3 = 10.$$

Answer D is the only choice that also results in 10.

$$f(8, 6) = \frac{1}{2}(8) + 6 = 4 + 6 = 10$$

5. **E**

$$f(2) = 2^3 + 1 = 9.$$
$$f(f(2)) = f(9) = 9^3 + 1 = 730.$$

6. **C** Start by multiplying both sides by the LCD:

$$\frac{1}{(x - 2)(x + 4)} = \frac{h}{(x - 2)} + \frac{k}{(x + 4)}$$
$$1 = h(x + 4) + k(x - 2).$$

Solving for k may not be immediately obvious. One way to solve for k is to substitute –4 for x, so the h term cancels out.

$$1 = h(-4 + 4) + k(-4 - 2).$$
$$1 = k(-6).$$
$$k = -\frac{1}{6}.$$

7. **D** Cosecant is the reciprocal function of the sine function. If $\csc \theta = 3$, then $\sin \theta = \dfrac{1}{3}$.

$$\sin \theta \csc \theta = \frac{1}{3}(3) = 1.$$

8. **A**

$$9x^4 - 4 = 7.$$

$$9x^4 = 11.$$

$$x^4 = \frac{11}{9}.$$

$$x = \pm\left(\frac{11}{9}\right)^{\frac{1}{4}} = \pm 1.05.$$

9. **B** The boys' team scored a total of 5(54) or 270 points in their first 5 games. The girls' team scored a total of 6(59) or 354 points in their first 6 games. The average for all 11 games is:

$$\frac{270 + 354}{11} = 56.7 \text{ points.}$$

10. **D** Because $f(x)$ equals the square root of an expression, it must be a positive value and $y \geq 0$ is part of the range. There is an upper limit on y, however. The maximum y-value occurs when $x = 0$.

$$f(0) = \sqrt{16 - 0^2} = 4.$$

The range is between 0 and 4, inclusive.

11. **A** Because the two events are independent, the probability that Michelle does not hit the target and Mike does hit the target is the product of the two probabilities. The probability of Michelle missing the target is: $1 - \dfrac{5}{8} = \dfrac{3}{8}$.

$$P = \frac{4}{7}\left(\frac{3}{8}\right) = \frac{3}{14}.$$

12. **B** You know the length of the side adjacent to θ and the hypotenuse of the triangle, so use arccosine to solve for the angle measure.

$$\cos^{-1}\left(\frac{11}{12}\right) = 23.6°.$$

13. **A** A logarithm is an exponent. Determine to what exponent to raise the base, 3, to equal $27\sqrt{3}$.

$$\log_3 27\sqrt{3} = \log_3 3^3 (3)^{\frac{1}{2}}.$$

By the properties of exponents $3^3 (3)^{\frac{1}{2}} = 3^{3+\frac{1}{2}} = 3^{\frac{7}{2}}$.

$$\log_3 3^{\frac{7}{2}} = \frac{7}{2}.$$

14. **D** Complex roots occur in conjugate pairs. If $5 + i$ is a root of the polynomial, then $5 - i$ is also a root. Use the three roots to determine the factors of the polynomial. Then multiply to determine the polynomial.

$$x[x - (5 + i)][x - (5 - i)] =$$

$$x[(x - 5) - i][(5 - i) + i)] =$$

$$x[(x - 5)^2 - i^2)] =$$

$$x(x^2 - 10x + 25 + 1) =$$

$$x(x^2 - 10x + 26) =$$

$$x^3 - 10x^2 + 26x.$$

15. **D** Recall that in the polar coordinate system the coordinates of a point are in the form (r, θ) where r is the directed distance from the pole and θ is the directed angle. Because the point shown has polar coordinates (4, 40°), you don't need to do any work to determine that $r = 4$.

16. **C** One way to solve this is to think of a right triangle. If $\cos \theta = \dfrac{2}{3}$, $\sin \theta =$

$$a^2 + 2^2 = 3^2.$$

$$a^2 = 9 - 4 = 5.$$

$$a = \sqrt{5}.$$

$$\sin \theta = \frac{\sqrt{5}}{3}.$$

Recall that the double angle formula for sine is:

$$\sin 2\theta = 2 \sin \theta \cos \theta.$$

$$\sin 2\theta = 2\left(\frac{\sqrt{5}}{3}\right)\left(\frac{2}{3}\right) = \frac{4\sqrt{5}}{9} \approx 0.99.$$

17. **B** The inverse of the logarithmic function is the exponential function. The inverse of $f(x) = \log_8 x$ is, therefore, $f^{-1}(x) = 8^x$.

18. **E** The graph of $y = \tan x$ has asymptotes when $\cos x = 0$. That means that asymptotes occur when x equals all odd multiples of $\frac{\pi}{2}$.

The graph of $f(x) = \tan 2x$ is similar to the graph of $y = \tan x$ with a period of $\frac{\pi}{2}$. Instead of an asymptote occurring at $x = \frac{\pi}{2}$, one will occur at $x = \frac{\left(\frac{\pi}{2}\right)}{2}, x = \frac{\pi}{4}$.

(Graph the function on your calculator to confirm there is an asymptote at $x = \frac{\pi}{4}$.)

19. **A** Because $8^3 = 512$, both sides of the equation can be written in base 8.

$$8^{2-x} = 512^{x+1}.$$

$$8^{2-x} = 8^{3(x+1)}.$$

Now, set the exponents equal to each other and solve for x.

$$2 - x = 3x + 3.$$

$$-1 = 4x.$$

$$x = -\frac{1}{4}.$$

20. **D** Because the x^2 and y^2 terms have different signs, the graph is a hyperbola.

21. **E** $f/g(-1)$ is the quotient of $f(-1)$ and $g(-1)$.

$$f(-1) = -1 + 3 = 2$$

$$g(-1) = \frac{1}{(4-(-1))} = \frac{1}{5}$$

$$f/g(-1) = 2\bigg/\left(\frac{1}{5}\right) = 10.$$

22. **B** Because there are 10 terms in the data set, the median is the average of the 5th and 6th terms. The median is, therefore, 3. The mode is 4, and the mean is the sum of the data divided by 10 : $\frac{30}{10} = 3$.

$$3 \leq 3 \leq 4.$$

mean $\leq$ median $\leq$ mode

23. **A** The cosine function is an even function, so it is symmetric with respect to the y-axis. To verify the symmetry, graph the equation using your graphing calculator.

24. **C** First, find the common difference between consecutive terms in the sequence. $\frac{23}{2} - 7 = \frac{9}{2}$.

The 15th term of the sequence is therefore:

$$a_n = a_1 + (n-1)d.$$

$$a_{15} = 7 + (15-1)\left(\frac{9}{2}\right).$$

$$a_{15} = 7 + (14)\left(\frac{9}{2}\right) = 70.$$

Use the equation for the sum of a finite arithmetic sequence, $S_n = \frac{n}{2}(a_1 + a_n)$, to determine the sum of the first 15 terms.

$$S_{15} = \frac{15}{2}(7 + 70).$$

$$S_{15} = \frac{15}{2}(77) = 577.5.$$

25. **B**

$$A = 2{,}800(1 - 0.22)^{2.5}.$$

$$A = 2{,}800(0.78)^{2.5}.$$

$$A = 1{,}505.$$

26. **A**

$$|2x - 4| < 1.$$

$$-1 < 2x - 4 < 1.$$

$$3 < 2x < 5.$$

$$\frac{3}{2} < x < \frac{5}{2}.$$

27. **D** The slope of the line with x-intercept $(-3, 0)$ and y-intercept $(0, -5)$ is:

$$m = \frac{-5 - 0}{0 - (-3)} = -\frac{5}{3}.$$

The y-intercept is given as -5. In slope-intercept form, $y = mx + b$, the equation is therefore:

$$y = -\frac{5}{3}x - 5.$$

$$5x + 3y = -15.$$

28. **C** The graph shows the sine curve, $y = \sin x$, reflected over the x-axis with an amplitude of 2. The function corresponding with the graph is, therefore, $f(x) = -2 \sin x$.

29. **D** If $x + 3$ is a factor of $x^5 + 2x^4 - kx^3 + 3x^2$, then $f(-3) = 0$.

$$f(-3) = (-3)^5 + 2(-3)^4 - k(-3)^3 + 3(-3)^2 = 0.$$

$$-54 - k(-27) = 0.$$

$$27k = 54.$$

$$k = 2.$$

30. **D** The Rational Root Test states that if a polynomial function has integer coefficients, every rational zero of the function has the form $\frac{p}{q}$ (simplified to lowest terms) where p = a factor of the constant term a_0 and q = a factor of the leading coefficient a_n. Here $a_0 = -6$ and $a_n = 4$.

The factors of 6 are 1, 6, 2, and 3, while the factors of 4 are 1, 4, and 2.

$$\frac{p}{q} = \pm 1, \pm \frac{1}{2}, \pm \frac{1}{4}, \pm 2, \pm 3, \pm \frac{3}{2}, \pm \frac{3}{4}, \pm 6.$$

Remember not to duplicate terms and write each in simplest form. There are 16 possible roots.

31. **E** Because $x - y = 5$, solve for x, and substitute this value into the first equation.

$$x = 5 + y.$$

$$xy + 6 = 0.$$

$$(5 + y)y + 6 = 0.$$

$$5y + y^2 + 6 = 0.$$

$$y^2 + 5y + 6 = 0.$$

$$(y + 2)(y + 3) = 0.$$

$$y = -2 \text{ or } y = -3.$$

Because $x = 5 + y$, $x = 3$ when $y = -2$ and $x = 2$ when $y = 2$.

32. **B** If the investment doubles, $A = \$2,000$.

$$2,000 = 1,000\left(1 + \frac{r}{400}\right)^{4(12)}$$

$$2 = \left(1 + \frac{r}{400}\right)^{48}$$

Now, take either the log or natural log of both sides of the equation to solve for r.

$$\ln 2 = 48 \ln\left(1 + \frac{r}{400}\right).$$

$$0.0144405 = \ln\left(1 + \frac{r}{400}\right).$$

$$e^{0.0144405} = 1.014545 = 1 + \frac{r}{400}.$$

$$0.014545 = \frac{r}{400}.$$

$$r = 5.8.$$

33. **A** Vectors are added head to tail. Here, when $\vec{u}$ and $\vec{v}$ are added the resulting vector, $\vec{w}$, extends from the tail of $\vec{u}$ to the head of $\vec{v}$. $\vec{u} + \vec{v} = \vec{w}$ is the operation depicted in the figure.

34. **C** Multiplying 212,121,212,121 by the ones digit of 33,333 results in a 12-digit product. Multiplying 212,121,212,121 by the tens digit of 33,333 results in a 13-digit product because it is necessary to use a zero placeholder for the ones digit. Similarly, multiplying by the hundreds digit requires 2 placeholders, multiplying by the thousands digit requires 3 placeholders, and multiplying by the ten-thousands digit requires 4 placeholders. The product will contain:

$$12 + 4 = 16 \text{ digits}$$

35. **C** The graph of the function $f(x) = \frac{1}{x}$ has asymptotes of the y and x axes. As x approaches zero, the value of the function approaches infinity. Because the domain is restricted to the interval $\frac{1}{2} \leq x \leq \frac{3}{2}$, the maximum value of the function occurs when $x = \frac{1}{2}$.

$$f(x) = \frac{1}{\frac{1}{2}} = 2.$$

36. **C** Use the Law of Sines to determine the length of AB.

$$\frac{\sin A}{a} = \frac{\sin B}{b} = \frac{\sin C}{c}.$$

$$\frac{\sin 22°}{AB} = \frac{\sin 49°}{6.3}.$$

$$AB = \frac{6.3(\sin 22°)}{\sin 49°}.$$

$$AB \approx 3.1 \text{ cm.}$$

37. **B** Rotating the rectangle creates a cylinder of radius 3 and height 12. The volume of the cylinder is:

$$V = \pi r^2 h = \pi(3)^2(12) = 108\pi.$$

38. **D** The distance between ordered triples (x_1, y_1, z_1) and (x_2, y_2, z_2) is given by the formula:

$$\text{Distance} = \sqrt{(x_2 - x_1)^2 + (y_2 - y_1)^2 + (z_2 - z_1)^2}.$$

$$\text{Distance} = \sqrt{(5 - 0)^2 + (4 - (-1))^2 + (-2 - 7)^2}.$$

$$= \sqrt{5^2 + 5^2 + (-9)^2}.$$

$$= \sqrt{131} \approx 11.4.$$

39. **D** Kate chooses one course out of the five for her first period class. She chooses one course out of the remaining four for her second period class. Then, she chooses one out of the remaining three for her third period class and one out of the remaining two for her fourth period class.

$$5 \times 4 \times 3 \times 2 \times 1 = 120.$$

40. **D** Because $n \blacklozenge 5 = 125$, $5^{2n} = 125$.

$$5^3 = 125, \text{ so } 2n \text{ must equal } 3.$$

$$2n = 3.$$

$$n = \frac{3}{2}.$$

41. **A** The given sequence is a geometric sequence whose nth term is $(3\sqrt{3})^n$.

$$(3\sqrt{3})^1 = 3\sqrt{3}.$$

$$(3\sqrt{3})^2 = 9(3) = 27.$$

$$(3\sqrt{3})^3 = 3^3(\sqrt{3})^3 = 27(3\sqrt{3}) = 81\sqrt{3}.$$

The 6th term is, therefore, $(3\sqrt{3})^6$.

42. **C** The standard form of the equation of an ellipse is:

$\frac{(x - h)^2}{a^2} + \frac{(y - k)^2}{b^2} = 1$ for an ellipse whose major axis

is horizontal, and $\frac{(x - h)^2}{b^2} + \frac{(y - k)^2}{a^2} = 1$ for an ellipse

whose major axis is vertical. In both cases, $2b =$ the length of the minor axis.

First, complete the square and write the equation in standard form.

$$25x^2 + 9y^2 - 18y - 216 = 0.$$

$$25x^2 + 9(y^2 - 2y) = 216.$$

$$25x^2 + 9(y^2 - 2y + 1) = 216 + 9.$$

$$\frac{x^2}{9} + \frac{(y - 1)^2}{25} = 1.$$

This ellipse has a horizontal major axis because a must be greater than b. $b = \sqrt{9} = 3$. The length of the minor axis is $2(3) = 6$.

43. **D** The general equation of a circle is:

$(x - h)^2 + (y - k)^2 = r^2$ where (h, k) is the center, and r is the length of the radius. The equation of a circle with center $(-1, 7)$ and a radius of length 3 is:

$$(x - -1)^2 + (y - 7)^2 = 3^2.$$

$$(x + 1)^2 + (y - 7)^2 = 9.$$

44. **C**

$$\frac{8x^2 - 11x + 3}{x^2 - 1} = \frac{(8x - 3)(x - 1)}{(x - 1)(x + 1)}$$

$$= \frac{8x - 3}{x + 1}$$

As x approaches 1, the value of the function approaches:

$$\frac{8(1) - 3}{1 + 1} = \frac{5}{2} = 2.5.$$

45. **E** A function is even if replacing x with $-x$ results in the original function. Its graph is symmetric with respect to the y-axis. You can either test for symmetry by algebraically determining which of the given functions satisfy the equation $f(-x) = f(x)$, or by graphing them on your graphing calculator.

$$f(x) = x^4 - 2x^2 + 7.$$

$$f(-x) = (-x)^4 - 2(-x)^2 + 7$$

$$= x^4 - 2x^2 + 7 = f(x).$$

46. **D** Because $x = \arctan(-4)$, $x = -75.964°$.

$$x + y = 320°.$$

$$-75.964° + y = 320°.$$

$$y = 395.96°.$$

$$\cos y = \cos 395.96° \approx 0.81.$$

47. **B** The problem is asking for the square root of $5 - 12i$. Square the answer choices to determine which one results in $5 - 12i$. Remember that $i^2 = -1$.

$$(3 - 2i)(3 - 2i) = 9 - 12i + 4i^2$$

$$= 9 - 12i - 4 = 5 - 12i.$$

48. **C** Factor the expression and use the trigonometric identity $1 + \tan^2 x = \sec^2 x$ to simplify.

$$\tan^4 \theta + 2\tan\theta + 1 = (\tan^2 \theta + 1)(\tan^2 \theta + 1)$$

$$= (\sec^2 \theta)(\sec^2 \theta) = \sec^4 \theta.$$

49. **C** The total surface area consists of the area of the 2 bases of the large cylinder plus the lateral surface area of the large cylinder plus the lateral surface area of the inner cylinder *minus* the area of the 2 bases of the inner cylinder. Let $R = 3$, the radius of the large cylinder, and $r = 1$, the radius of the inner cylinder. The total surface area is:

$$SA = 2\pi(R)^2 + 2\pi Rh + 2\pi rh - 2\pi r^2.$$

$$SA = 2\pi(3)^2 + 2\pi(3)(8) + 2\pi(1)(8) - 2\pi(1)^2.$$

$$SA = 18\pi + 48\pi + 16\pi - 2\pi.$$

$$SA = 80\pi \text{ cm}^2.$$

50. **E** Graph the two equations, $x^2 + y^2 = 25$ and $xy = 10$, to determine how many points of intersection there are. The graph of $x^2 + y^2 = 25$ is a circle centered at the origin with a radius of 5. On your calculator, graph:

$$y_1 = \sqrt{(25 - x^2)}.$$

$$y_2 = -\sqrt{(25 - x^2)}.$$

$$y_3 = \frac{10}{x}.$$

The graphs intersect at four points.

▦ DIAGNOSE YOUR STRENGTHS AND WEAKNESSES

Check the number of each question answered correctly and "X" the number of each question answered incorrectly.

Algebra	1	6	8	13	19	25	26	31	32	50	Total Number Correct
10 questions											

Solid Geometry	37	49	Total Number Correct
2 questions			

Coordinate Geometry	3	15	20	27	38	42	43	Total Number Correct
7 questions								

Trigonometry	7	12	16	36	46	48	Total Number Correct
6 questions							

Functions	4	5	10	14	17	18	21	23	28	29	30	35	45	Total Number Correct
13 questions														

Data Analysis, Statistics, and Probability	9	11	22	39	Total Number Correct
4 questions					

Numbers and Operations	2	24	33	34	40	41	44	47	Total Number Correct
8 questions									

Number of correct answers $-\frac{1}{4}$ (Number of incorrect answers) = Your raw score

$$\underline{\hspace{6cm}} -\frac{1}{4} (\underline{\hspace{6cm}}) = \underline{\hspace{3cm}}$$

Compare your raw score with the approximate SAT Subject Test score below:

	Raw Score	SAT Subject Test Approximate Score
Excellent	43–50	770–800
Very Good	33–43	670–770
Good	27–33	620–670
Above Average	21–27	570–620
Average	11–21	500–570
Below Average	< 11	< 500

PRACTICE TEST 6

Treat this practice test as the actual test and complete it in one 60-minute sitting. Use the following answer sheet to fill in your multiple-choice answers. Once you have completed the practice test:

1. Check your answers using the Answer Key.
2. Review the Answers and Solutions.
3. Fill in the "Diagnose Your Strengths and Weaknesses" sheet and determine areas that require further preparation.

PRACTICE TEST 6
MATH LEVEL 2

███ **ANSWER SHEET**

Tear out this answer sheet and use it to complete the practice test. Determine the BEST answer for each question. Then, fill in the appropriate oval using a No. 2 pencil.

1. (A) (B) (C) (D) (E)	21. (A) (B) (C) (D) (E)	41. (A) (B) (C) (D) (E)
2. (A) (B) (C) (D) (E)	22. (A) (B) (C) (D) (E)	42. (A) (B) (C) (D) (E)
3. (A) (B) (C) (D) (E)	23. (A) (B) (C) (D) (E)	43. (A) (B) (C) (D) (E)
4. (A) (B) (C) (D) (E)	24. (A) (B) (C) (D) (E)	44. (A) (B) (C) (D) (E)
5. (A) (B) (C) (D) (E)	25. (A) (B) (C) (D) (E)	45. (A) (B) (C) (D) (E)
6. (A) (B) (C) (D) (E)	26. (A) (B) (C) (D) (E)	46. (A) (B) (C) (D) (E)
7. (A) (B) (C) (D) (E)	27. (A) (B) (C) (D) (E)	47. (A) (B) (C) (D) (E)
8. (A) (B) (C) (D) (E)	28. (A) (B) (C) (D) (E)	48. (A) (B) (C) (D) (E)
9. (A) (B) (C) (D) (E)	29. (A) (B) (C) (D) (E)	49. (A) (B) (C) (D) (E)
10. (A) (B) (C) (D) (E)	30. (A) (B) (C) (D) (E)	50. (A) (B) (C) (D) (E)
11. (A) (B) (C) (D) (E)	31. (A) (B) (C) (D) (E)	
12. (A) (B) (C) (D) (E)	32. (A) (B) (C) (D) (E)	
13. (A) (B) (C) (D) (E)	33. (A) (B) (C) (D) (E)	
14. (A) (B) (C) (D) (E)	34. (A) (B) (C) (D) (E)	
15. (A) (B) (C) (D) (E)	35. (A) (B) (C) (D) (E)	
16. (A) (B) (C) (D) (E)	36. (A) (B) (C) (D) (E)	
17. (A) (B) (C) (D) (E)	37. (A) (B) (C) (D) (E)	
18. (A) (B) (C) (D) (E)	38. (A) (B) (C) (D) (E)	
19. (A) (B) (C) (D) (E)	39. (A) (B) (C) (D) (E)	
20. (A) (B) (C) (D) (E)	40. (A) (B) (C) (D) (E)	

PRACTICE TEST 6

Time: 60 minutes

Directions: Select the BEST answer for each of the 50 multiple-choice questions. If the exact solution is not one of the five choices, select the answer that is the best approximation. Then, fill in the appropriate oval on the answer sheet.

Notes:

1. A calculator will be needed to answer some of the questions on the test. Scientific, programmable, and graphing calculators are permitted. It is up to you to determine when and when not to use your calculator.
2. Angles on the Level 2 test are measured in degrees and radians. You need to decide whether your calculator should be set to degree mode or radian mode for a particular question.
3. Figures are drawn as accurately as possible and are intended to help solve some of the test problems. If a figure is not drawn to scale, this will be stated in the problem. All figures lie in a plane unless the problem indicates otherwise.
4. Unless otherwise stated, the domain of a function f is assumed to be the set of real numbers x for which the value of the function, $f(x)$, is a real number.
5. Reference information that may be useful in answering some of the test questions can be found below.

Reference Information	
Right circular cone with radius r and height h:	Volume $= \dfrac{1}{3}\pi r^2 h$
Right circular cone with circumference of base c and slant height ℓ:	Lateral Area $= \dfrac{1}{2}c\ell$
Sphere with radius r:	Volume $= \dfrac{4}{3}\pi r^3$ Surface Area $= 4\pi r^2$
Pyramid with base area B and height h:	Volume $= \dfrac{1}{3}Bh$

PRACTICE TEST 6 QUESTIONS

1. If $\dfrac{2a + 2b}{\dfrac{1}{2}} = 9,$ then $\dfrac{1}{a + b} =$

   (A) $\dfrac{1}{9}$

   (B) $\dfrac{4}{9}$

   (C) $\dfrac{2}{3}$

   (D) $\dfrac{9}{4}$

   (E) 9

2. If $f(x) = e^{2x}$, then $f(\ln 2) =$

   (A) 2
   (B) e^2
   (C) 4
   (D) e^4
   (E) $\ln 4$

3. If $2^3(2^{3n})(2) = \dfrac{1}{4},$ then $n =$

   (A) $-\dfrac{5}{3}$

   (B) -2

   (C) $-\dfrac{2}{9}$

   (D) $-\dfrac{2}{3}$

   (E) $-\dfrac{1}{3}$

4. If $x = 4 - y$ and $x \neq \pm y,$ $\dfrac{y - x}{x^2 - y^2} =$

   (A) -4

   (B) $-\dfrac{1}{2}$

   (C) $-\dfrac{1}{4}$

   (D) $\dfrac{1}{2}$

   (E) $\dfrac{1}{4}$

GO ON TO THE NEXT PAGE

5. What is the reciprocal of $8 - 3i$?

    (A) $\dfrac{1}{8}$

    (B) $\dfrac{8 + 3i}{55}$

    (C) $\dfrac{8 - 3i}{55}$

    (D) $\dfrac{8 + 3i}{73}$

    (E) $\dfrac{1}{11}$

USE THIS SPACE AS SCRATCH PAPER

6. What is the solution set to $|x| + |x - 4| > 4$?

    (A) $\{x: 0 < x < 4\}$
    (B) $\{x: x > 4\}$
    (C) $\{x: x < 0\}$
    (D) $\{x: x < 0 \text{ or } x > 4\}$
    (E) $\{x: x < -4 \text{ or } x > 0\}$

7. An equation of the line parallel to $8x - 2y = 5$ and containing the point $(-2, 2)$ is

    (A) $y - 2 = 4(x - 2)$

    (B) $y = 4x + \dfrac{5}{2}$

    (C) $y = 4x - \dfrac{5}{2}$

    (D) $y + 2 = 4(x - 2)$
    (E) $y = 4x + 10$

8. If $\dfrac{x + 3}{x - 7} \leq 0$, then which of the following describes x?

    (A) $-3 \leq x < 7$
    (B) $x < 7$
    (C) $x \leq -3 \text{ or } x \geq 7$
    (D) $-3 \leq x \leq 7$
    (E) $x \leq -3 \text{ or } x > 7$

9. Which of the following expressions represents the statement "x is proportional to h and inversely proportional to the square of r"?

    (A) $x = khr^2$
    (B) $x = kh(-r^2)$

    (C) $x = \dfrac{kh}{r^2}$

    (D) $x = kh\sqrt{r}$

    (E) $x = \dfrac{k}{hr^2}$

GO ON TO THE NEXT PAGE

10. What is the vertex of the parabola given by $f(x) = 4x^2 - 6x + 9$?

(A) $\left(\dfrac{3}{4}, \dfrac{135}{16}\right)$

(B) $\left(\dfrac{3}{2}, 9\right)$

(C) $\left(-\dfrac{3}{4}, -\dfrac{27}{4}\right)$

(D) $\left(\dfrac{1}{2}, 7\right)$

(E) $\left(\dfrac{3}{4}, \dfrac{27}{4}\right)$

11. If $270 \le \theta \le 360°$ and $\cos \theta = 0.43$, then $\csc \theta =$

(A) -1.11

(B) -0.90

(C) 0.90

(D) 1.11

(E) 2.33

12. What are the zeroes of $f(x) = 6x^3 - 5x^2 - 25x$?

(A) $\left\{-\dfrac{5}{2}, \dfrac{5}{3}\right\}$

(B) $\left\{-\dfrac{5}{3}, \dfrac{5}{2}\right\}$

(C) $\left\{-\dfrac{5}{2}, \dfrac{5}{2}, \dfrac{5}{3}\right\}$

(D) $\left\{-\dfrac{5}{3}, 0, \dfrac{5}{2}\right\}$

(E) $\left\{-\dfrac{5}{2}, 0, \dfrac{5}{3}\right\}$

13. The probability that there will be a lightning storm tomorrow is $\dfrac{1}{8}$ and, independently, the probability that there will be a lightning storm the day after tomorrow is $\dfrac{1}{11}$. What is the probability that there will be a storm tomorrow but *not* the day after tomorrow?

(A) $\dfrac{1}{88}$

(B) $\dfrac{1}{8}$

(C) $\dfrac{5}{44}$

(D) $\dfrac{19}{88}$

(E) $\dfrac{91}{88}$

USE THIS SPACE AS SCRATCH PAPER

GO ON TO THE NEXT PAGE

14. An operation is defined on any three real numbers by
    $a \bullet b \bullet c = a^{c-b}$. If $3 \bullet n \bullet 1 = \dfrac{1}{27}$, then $n =$

    (A) -3
    (B) -2
    (C) 2
    (D) 4
    (E) 5

15. If $(x - 2)^{\frac{3}{2}} = 64$, then $x =$

    (A) 4
    (B) 8
    (C) 14
    (D) 16
    (E) 18

16. If $\sin 2\theta = \dfrac{2}{5}$, then $\dfrac{1}{\sin\theta \, \cos\theta} =$

    (A) $\dfrac{1}{5}$

    (B) $\dfrac{5}{4}$

    (C) $\dfrac{5}{2}$

    (D) 5

    (E) 10

17. What does the angle $480°$ equal in radian measure?

    (A) $\dfrac{2\pi}{3}$

    (B) $\dfrac{4\pi}{3}$

    (C) $\dfrac{8\pi}{3}$

    (D) $\dfrac{16\pi}{3}$

    (E) $\dfrac{5\pi}{2}$

18. If $f(x) = \dfrac{x^2 + 2x - 3}{x^2 - 1}$, what value does the function approach as x approaches 1?

    (A) -4
    (B) -2
    (C) 1
    (D) 2
    (E) 4

USE THIS SPACE AS SCRATCH PAPER

GO ON TO THE NEXT PAGE

19. If $4i$ is a zero of the polynomial $p(x)$, then which of the following must be a factor of $p(x)$?

    (A) $-4i$
    (B) $x^2 + 16$
    (C) $x^2 + 17$
    (D) $x^2 - 16$
    (E) $x^2 - 8ix + 16i^2$

20. If, for all $a \neq b$, $f(a, b) = \dfrac{(a - b)}{(b - a)}$, then

    $f(\sqrt{5}, \sqrt{3}) =$

    (A) -1
    (B) $\sqrt{3} - \sqrt{5}$
    (C) $\dfrac{(-2 - \sqrt{15})}{2}$
    (D) 1
    (E) 2

21. If $f(x) = 2x + 6$ and $g[f(-9)] = -3$, then $g(x)$ could be which of the following?

    (A) $\dfrac{x}{2} - 3$
    (B) $\dfrac{x}{3} + 1$
    (C) $15 - x$
    (D) $-\dfrac{x}{4}$
    (E) $x - 9$

22. Which of the following is an x-intercept of the hyperbola $\dfrac{x^2}{8} - \dfrac{y^2}{9} = 1$?

    (A) $(-2\sqrt{2}, 0)$
    (B) $(2, 0)$
    (C) $(-3, 0)$
    (D) $(4, 0)$
    (E) $(8, 0)$

GO ON TO THE NEXT PAGE

23. What is the length of segment AB in Figure 1?

    (A) 3.6
    (B) 6.4
    (C) 6.7
    (D) 7.5
    (E) 45

USE THIS SPACE AS SCRATCH PAPER

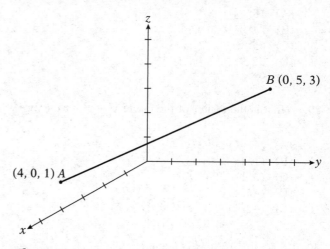

Figure 1

24. For $x \neq -1$ and $x \neq \dfrac{1}{3}$, if $f(x) = 1 - 3x$ and $g(x) = 3x^2 + 2x - 1$, then $\left(\dfrac{f}{g}\right)(x) =$

    (A) $\dfrac{1}{3}x^2 - \dfrac{3}{2}x$

    (B) $\dfrac{-1}{x + 1}$

    (C) $\dfrac{1}{x + 1}$

    (D) $\dfrac{-1}{x - 1}$

    (E) $3x^2 + 5x - 2$

25. If $f(x) = 3^x$ for all real values of x and $f^{-1}(n) = -2$, then $n =$

    (A) -9
    (B) -6
    (C) $\sqrt[3]{2}$
    (D) $\dfrac{1}{9}$
    (E) 9

26. If $\log_b 4 = 16$, then $b =$

    (A) 0.25
    (B) 0.50
    (C) 1.09
    (D) 2
    (E) 4

27. $\cot (\arcsin 0.4) =$

    (A) 0.44
    (B) 0.56
    (C) 0.92
    (D) 2.29
    (E) 2.36

GO ON TO THE NEXT PAGE

28. If $\cos(45 + 2x)° = \sin(3x)°$, then $x =$

    (A) 18°
    (B) 27°
    (C) 45°
    (D) 22.5°
    (E) 9°

29. What is the center of the circle $x^2 + y^2 - 8x + 2y + 8 = 0$?

    (A) $(4, -1)$
    (B) $(1, 4)$
    (C) $(2, 1)$
    (D) $(-4, 1)$
    (E) $(-2, 1)$

30. If $f(x) = \dfrac{3}{2}x + \sqrt{x}$, then $f[f(4)] =$

    (A) $12 + 2\sqrt{2}$
    (B) 20
    (C) $14\sqrt{2}$
    (D) 8
    (E) 16

31. What is the range of the piecewise function

    $f(x)\{|-x + 6| \text{ if } x \le 1$
    $\qquad\{x^2 + 4 \text{ if } x > 1?$

    (A) $y \ge 0$
    (B) $y \ge 5$
    (C) $4 \le y \le 8$
    (D) $y > 4$
    (E) All real numbers.

32. If vector $\vec{v} = (-1, -8)$ and vector $\vec{u} = (2, -4)$, then vector $\vec{u} + \vec{v} =$

    (A) $(-1, -12)$
    (B) $(3, 4)$
    (C) $(-12, -1)$
    (D) $(-3, -4)$
    (E) $(1, -12)$

33. A cube has edges of length 5. If P and Q are points on its surface, what is the maximum straight-line distance from P to Q?

    (A) $5\sqrt{2}$
    (B) $10\sqrt{2}$
    (C) $5\sqrt{3}$
    (D) $3\sqrt{5}$
    (E) 15

GO ON TO THE NEXT PAGE

USE THIS SPACE AS SCRATCH PAPER

34. If $f(x) = 4^{\frac{x}{4}}$, then $f\left(\log_2 \dfrac{1}{256}\right) =$

    (A) $\dfrac{1}{65,536}$

    (B) $\dfrac{1}{64}$

    (C) $\dfrac{1}{16}$

    (D) $3\sqrt{3}$

    (E) 16

35. For $x \neq 0$, if $3^{-2} - 6^{-2} = x^{-2}$, then $x =$

    (A) $3\sqrt{3}$

    (B) $2\sqrt{3}$

    (C) ± 12

    (D) $\pm 2\sqrt{3}$

    (E) ± 6

36. If $f(x) = |x|$ and $h(x)$ is obtained by shifting $f(x)$ down 5 units, right 1 unit, and reflecting it over the line $y = -5$, then $h(3) =$

    (A) -9
    (B) -7
    (C) -5
    (D) -3
    (E) 3

37. If the lines $y_1 = (n + 1)x + 12$ and $y_2 = (2n - 3)x + 2$ are parallel, then n could equal which of the following?

    (A) -4
    (B) -0.78
    (C) 0.67
    (D) 1.28
    (E) 4

38. If $f(x) = x^2 + 6$ for all $x \geq 0$, then the graph of $f^{-1}(x)$ intersects the x-axis at

    (A) zero points.
    (B) exactly one point.
    (C) exactly two points.
    (D) exactly three points.
    (E) f^{-1} is undefined.

GO ON TO THE NEXT PAGE

39. Thirteen students receive the following grades on a math test:

    60, 78, 90, 67, 88, 92, 81, 100, 95, 83, 83, 86, 74.

    What is the interquartile range of the test scores?

    (A) 14
    (B) 83
    (C) 15
    (D) 16
    (E) 40

USE THIS SPACE AS SCRATCH PAPER

40. What is the value of n if the determinant of matrix X is given as:

    $$\det X = \begin{vmatrix} 9 & -3 \\ 4 & n \end{vmatrix} = 0?$$

    (A) -12
    (B) $-\dfrac{4}{3}$
    (C) $-\dfrac{3}{4}$
    (D) $\dfrac{3}{4}$
    (E) $\dfrac{4}{3}$

41. In Figure 2, which of the following must be true?

    I. $\cot x = \dfrac{3}{4}$
    II. $\cos x = \sin y$
    III. $\tan x = \tan y$

        (A) I only
        (B) II only
        (C) II and III only
        (D) I and II only
        (E) I, II, and III

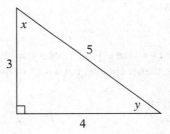

Figure 2

42. Which of the following statements does *not* describe a positive correlation?

    (A) A person's height and weight
    (B) The percentage of registered voters and the percentage of actual voters
    (C) The number of DVD owners and total DVD sales
    (D) The value of a car and its age
    (E) A student's GPA and SAT scores

43. The graph of which of the following is symmetric with respect to the origin?

    (A) $y = x^2 - 1$
    (B) $y = x^3 - 2x$
    (C) $y^2 = x + 8$
    (D) $y = -|x + 1|$
    (E) $y = (x + 3)^2$

GO ON TO THE NEXT PAGE

44. The graph of $y = -4x + 10$ can be expressed as a set of parametric equations. If $x = 3 + t$ and $y = f(t)$, then what does $f(t)$ equal?

    (A) $-4t - 2$
    (B) $-4t - 22$
    (C) $4t - 2$
    (D) $\dfrac{1}{4}t + 7$
    (E) $-4t - 12$

45. If $x_0 = 2$ and $x_{n+1} = \sqrt[3]{-4x_n}$, then $x_4 =$

    (A) -8
    (B) -2
    (C) 2
    (D) 4
    (E) 8

46. In a group of 40 of Ms Jones's students, students are either sophomores or juniors (but not both) and study either geometry or algebra 2 but not both. If 18 sophomores study geometry, 16 students are juniors, and 13 students study algebra 2, how many juniors study algebra 2?

    (A) 6
    (B) 7
    (C) 8
    (D) 9
    (E) 10

47. How long is the base of an isosceles triangle if the other two sides measure 8 cm, and each base angle measures 41°?

    (A) 5.3
    (B) 7.9
    (C) 13.9
    (D) 11.3
    (E) 12.1

48. A committee of 3 people is to be selected from a group of 6 women and 4 men. Assuming the selection is made randomly, what is the probability that the committee consists of 2 women and 1 man?

    (A) $\dfrac{1}{30}$
    (B) $\dfrac{1}{8}$
    (C) $\dfrac{1}{4}$
    (D) $\dfrac{1}{3}$
    (E) $\dfrac{1}{2}$

GO ON TO THE NEXT PAGE

49. A portion of the graph of $y = e^x$ is shown in Figure 3. What is the sum of the areas of the three inscribed rectangles?

    (A) 124
    (B) 126
    (C) 465
    (D) 809
    (E) 931

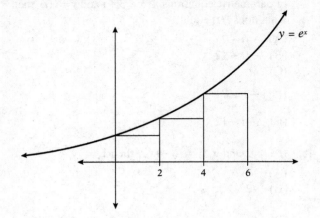

Figure 3

50. What is the lateral area of the right circular cone shown in Figure 4?

    (A) 50π
    (B) 75π

    (C) $125\sqrt{\dfrac{3}{3}}\pi$

    (D) $25\sqrt{3}\pi$
    (E) 100π

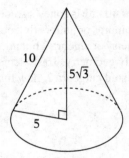

Figure 4

S T O P

IF YOU FINISH BEFORE TIME IS CALLED, YOU MAY CHECK YOUR WORK ON THIS TEST ONLY.
DO NOT TURN TO ANY OTHER TEST IN THIS BOOK.

ANSWER KEY

1. B	11. A	21. B	31. B	41. D
2. C	12. D	22. A	32. E	42. D
3. B	13. C	23. C	33. C	43. B
4. C	14. D	24. B	34. C	44. A
5. D	15. E	25. D	35. D	45. C
6. D	16. D	26. C	36. B	46. B
7. E	17. C	27. D	37. E	47. E
8. A	18. D	28. E	38. B	48. E
9. C	19. B	29. A	39. C	49. B
10. E	20. A	30. A	40. B	50. A

ANSWERS AND SOLUTIONS

1. B

$$\frac{2a + 2b}{\frac{1}{2}} = 9.$$

$$2(2a + 2b) = 9.$$

$$4(a + b) = 9a + b = \frac{\frac{9}{4}}{a+b} = \frac{1}{\frac{9}{4}} = \frac{4}{9}.$$

2. C

$$f(\ln\ 2) = e^{2\ln\ 2} = e^{\ln\ 4} = 4.$$

If you don't recognize that $e^{\ln 4} = 4$, use the e^x function on your calculator for this problem.

3. B

$$2^3(2^{3n})(2) = \frac{1}{4}.$$

$$2^{3+3n+1} = 2^{-2}.$$

$$3n + 4 = -2.$$

$$3n = -6.$$

$$n = -2.$$

4. C

$$\frac{y - x}{x^2 - y^2} = \frac{-(x - y)}{(x - y)(x + y)}.$$ Because $x \neq y$, you can simplify this to:

$$\frac{-1}{x + y}.$$ Substitute $x = 4 - y$ to get:

$$\frac{-1}{x + y} = \frac{-1}{4 - y + y} = -\frac{1}{4}.$$

5. D The complex conjugate of $8 - 3i$ is $8 + 3i$. To simplify the fraction, multiply the numerator and the denominator by the complex conjugate. Recall that $i^2 = -1$.

$$\frac{1}{8 - 3i} = \frac{1}{8 - 3i} \times \frac{8 + 3i}{8 + 3i}$$

$$= \frac{8 + 3i}{(8 - 3i)(8 + 3i)} = \frac{8 + 3i}{64 - 9i^2}$$

$$= \frac{8 + 3i}{64 - (-9)} = \frac{8 + 3i}{73}.$$

6. **D** The critical points of the inequality are $x = 0$ and $x = 4$. Evaluate the three intervals created by 0 and 4 by choosing values of x in each interval:

Let $x = 5$, $|5| + |5 - 4| > 4$.

Let $x = 2$, $|2| + |2 - 4| = 4$.

Let $x = -1$, $|-1| + |-1 - 4| > 4$.

The solution is, therefore, $x < 0$ or $x > 4$.

7. **E** Write the equation of the line $8x - 2y = 5$ in slope-intercept form to determine its slope.

$$-2y = -8x + 5.$$

$$y = 4x - \frac{5}{2}.$$

$$m = 4.$$

The equation of the line parallel to it and passing through the point $(-2, 2)$ is:

$$y - 2 = 4(x - -2).$$

$$y - 2 = 4x + 8.$$

$$y = 4x + 10.$$

8. **A** Find the critical points where the numerator and denominator of the rational expression equal zero. Then, determine which intervals satisfy the inequality

$$\frac{x + 3}{x - 7} \le 0.$$

Critical points: $x = -3$ and $x = 7$.

Note that $x \ne 7$ because the denominator cannot equal zero.

Test when $x = 0$. $\frac{3}{-7} \le 0$ is a true statement, so the interval between -3 and 7 is part of the solution. The solution is the interval $-3 \le x < 7$.

9. **C** Because x is *inversely* proportional to the square of r, r^2 should be in the denominator.

"X is proportional to h and inversely proportional to the square of r" is equivalent to $x = \dfrac{kh}{r^2}$.

10. **E** Complete the square to write the equation of the parabola in standard form.

$$f(x) = 4x^2 - 6x + 9.$$

$$y = 4x^2 - 6x + 9.$$

$$y - 9 = 4\left(x^2 - \frac{3}{2}x \right).$$

$$y - 9 + 4\left(\frac{9}{16} \right) = 4\left(x^2 - \frac{3}{2}x + \frac{9}{16} \right).$$

$$y - \frac{27}{4} = 4\left(x - \frac{3}{4} \right)^2.$$

The vertex is $\left(\dfrac{3}{4}, \dfrac{27}{4} \right)$. You can verify this answer by by graphing the function on your graphing calculator.

11. **A**

Because $\cos \theta = 0.43$,

$$\cos^{-1}(0.43) \approx 64.53°$$

$$\csc \theta = \frac{1}{\sin 64.53°} = \sin(64.53)^{-1} \approx 1.1076.$$

Remember that $270 \le \theta \le 360°$, so θ lies in quadrant IV. The sine must, therefore, be negative. -1.11 is the correct answer choice.

12. **D** Set the polynomial equal to zero and factor.

$$6x^3 - 5x^2 - 25x = 0.$$

$$x(6x^2 - 5x - 25) = 0.$$

$$x(3x + 5)(2x - 5) = 0.$$

$$x = 0 \text{ or } x = -\frac{5}{3} \text{ or } x = \frac{5}{2}.$$

13. **C** Because the events are independent find the product of their probabilities.

The probability that there will NOT be a storm the day after tomorrow is:

$$1 - \frac{1}{11} = \frac{10}{11}.$$

The probability that there will be a storm tomorrow but *not* the day after tomorrow is:

$$\frac{1}{8} \times \frac{10}{11} = \frac{10}{88} = \frac{5}{44}.$$

14. **D**

$$a \blacksquare b \blacksquare c = a^{c-b}$$

$$3 \blacksquare n \blacksquare 1 = \frac{1}{27}.$$

$$3^{1-n} = 3^{-3}.$$

$$1 - n = -3$$

$$4 = n.$$

15. **E** Raise each side of the equation to the $\frac{2}{3}$ power to solve for x:

$$(x - 2)^{\frac{3}{2}} = 64.$$

$$[(x - 2)^{\frac{3}{2}}]^{\frac{2}{3}} = 64^{\frac{2}{3}}.$$

$$x - 2 = 64^{\frac{2}{3}} = (4^3)^{\frac{2}{3}} = 4^2.$$

$$x = 16 + 2 = 18.$$

16. **D** The double angle formula for sine is:

$$\sin 2\theta = 2 \sin \theta \cos \theta.$$

Because $\sin 2\theta = \frac{2}{5}$, $2 \sin \theta \cos \theta$ also equals $\frac{2}{5}$.

$$\frac{1}{\sin \theta \cos \theta} = 2\left(\frac{1}{\frac{2}{5}}\right) = 5.$$

17. **C** Recall that π radians = 180°. To convert the given angle to degrees, multiply it by $\frac{\pi}{180}$.

$$480 \times \frac{\pi}{180} = \frac{480\pi}{180} = \frac{8\pi}{3}.$$

18. **D** Factor the numerator and denominator. Then, simplify the expression and evaluate it when $x = 1$.

$$f(x) = \frac{x^2 + 2x - 3}{x^2 - 1} = \frac{(x-1)(x+3)}{(x-1)(x+1)} = \frac{x+3}{x+1}.$$

When $x = 1$, $\frac{1+3}{1+1} = \frac{4}{2} = 2.$

19. **B** Recall that complex zeroes occur in conjugate pairs. If $4i$ is a zero of the polynomial $p(x)$, then $-4i$ is also a zero. One factor of the polynomial is $(x - 4i)$ $(x + 4i)$.

$$(x - 4i)(x + 4i) = x^2 + 4ix - 4ix - 16i^2$$

$$= x^2 - 16i^2 = x^2 - (-16) = x^2 + 16.$$

20. **A** Save time on this problem by recognizing that $b - a = -(a - b)$.

$$f(a, b) = \frac{a - b}{b - a} = -1.$$

The function $f(a, b)$ equals -1 for all values of a and b except $a \neq b$, so $f(\sqrt{5}, \sqrt{3}) = -1$.

21. **B**

$$f(-9) = 2(-9) + 6 = -12.$$

For $g[f(-9)]$ to equal -3, $g(-12)$ must equal -3. There are many possible functions that would have an output of -3 when -12 is the input. Of the possible answers, Answer B is the only one that works.

$$g(-12) = -\frac{12}{3} + 1 = -4 + 1 = -3.$$

22. **A** One way to determine the x-intercept is to set y equal to zero and solve for x.

$$\frac{x^2}{8} - \frac{y^2}{9} = 1.$$

$$\frac{x^2}{8} = 1.$$

$$x^2 = 8.$$

$$x = \pm 2\sqrt{2}.$$

$(-2\sqrt{2}, 0)$ is one possible answer.

23. **C**

$$\text{Distance} = \sqrt{(x_2 - x_1)^2 + (y_2 - y_1)^2 + (z_2 - z_1)^2}$$

$$= \sqrt{(0 - 4)^2 + (5 - 0)^2 + (3 - 1)^2}$$

$$= \sqrt{(-4)^2 + 5^2 + 2^2}$$

$$= \sqrt{16 + 25 + 4}$$

$$= \sqrt{45} \approx 6.7.$$

24. **B**

$$\left(\frac{f}{g}\right)(x) = \frac{f(x)}{g(x)} =$$

$$\frac{1 - 3x}{3x^2 + 2x - 1} =$$

$$\frac{-(3x - 1)}{(x + 1)(3x - 1)} =$$

$$\frac{-1}{x + 1}.$$

25. **D** The inverse of the exponential function $f(x) = 3^x$ is the logarithmic function $f^{-1}(x) = \log_3 x$.

$$f^{-1}(n) = \log_3 n = -2.$$

$$3^{-2} = \frac{1}{9}.$$

26. **C** If $\log_b 4 = 16$, then $b^{16} = 4$. Take the 16th root of each side of the equation.

$$(b^{16})^{\frac{1}{16}} = 4^{\frac{1}{16}}.$$

$$b = 4^{\frac{1}{16}} \approx 1.09.$$

27. **D** First, find the angle whose sine is 0.4.

$$\sin^{-1}(0.4) = 23.58°$$

Then, determine the cotangent of the angle.

$$(\tan 23.58°)^{-1} \approx 2.29.$$

28. **E** Because $\cos x = \sin(90 - x)$, you know:

$$\cos(45 + 2x) = \sin[90 - (45 + 2x)].$$

$$90 - (45 + 2x) = 3x.$$

$$45 - 2x = 3x.$$

$$45 = 5x.$$

$$x = 9°.$$

29. **A** Complete the square to get the standard form of the equation of the circle.

$$x^2 + y^2 - 8x + 2y + 8 = 0.$$

$$(x^2 - 8x) + (y^2 + 2y) = -8.$$

$$(x^2 - 8x + 16) + (y^2 + 2y + 1) = -8 + 16 + 1.$$

$$(x^2 - 4)^2 + (y + 1)^2 = 9.$$

The circle's center is $(4, -1)$.

30. **A**

Because $f(x) = \dfrac{3}{2}x + \sqrt{x}$,

$$f(4) = \frac{3}{2}(4) + \sqrt{4} = 6 + 2 = 8.$$

$$f[f(4)] = f(8) = \frac{3}{2}(8) + \sqrt{8} = 12 + 2\sqrt{2}.$$

31. **B** The graph is part of the "v-shaped" absolute value graph when $x \le 1$. Because the function only consists of the ray formed when $x \le 1$, it begins at $(1, 5)$ and extends diagonally upward in the negative direction of x. When $x > 1$, the graph is a parabola whose vertex is $(0, 4)$. All y values greater than or equal to 5 satisfy the range.

32. **E**

Vector $\vec{v} = (-1, -8)$ and vector $\vec{u} = (2, -4)$.

$$\vec{u} + \vec{v} = (-1 + 2, -8 + -4).$$

$$\vec{u} + \vec{v} = (1, -12).$$

33. **C** The maximum straight-line distance is the distance between opposite vertices of the cube. Recall that distance between opposite vertices of any rectangular prism is:

$$\text{Distance} = \sqrt{\ell^2 + w^2 + h^2}$$

$$= \sqrt{5^2 + 5^2 + 5^2}$$

$$= \sqrt{75} = 5\sqrt{3}.$$

34. **C**

First, evaluate $\log_2 \dfrac{1}{256}$:

$$\text{Log}_2 \frac{1}{256} = -8 \text{ because } 2^{-8} = \frac{1}{256}.$$

If $f(x) = 4^{\frac{x}{4}}$, then $f(-8) = 4^{-2} = \dfrac{1}{16}$.

35. **D**

$$3^{-2} - 6^{-2} = x^{-2}.$$

$$\frac{1}{3^2} - \frac{1}{6^2} = \frac{1}{x^2}.$$

$$\frac{1}{9} - \frac{1}{36} = \frac{1}{x^2}.$$

Multiply both sides of the equation by the LCD, $36x^2$.

$$4x^2 - x^2 = 36.$$

$$3x^2 = 36.$$

$$x^2 = 12.$$

$$x = \pm\sqrt{12} = \pm 2\sqrt{3}.$$

36. **B** Shifting $f(x)$ down 5 units results in:

$$h(x) = f(x) - 5.$$

$$h(x) = |x| - 5.$$

Then, shifting the function right 1 unit results in:

$$h(x) = |x - 1| - 5.$$

Finally, reflecting it over the line $y = -5$ results in:

$$h(x) = -|x - 1| - 5.$$

$$h(3) = -|3 - 1| - 5 = -2 - 5 = -7.$$

37. **E** The slopes of parallel lines are equal.

$$n + 1 = 2n - 3.$$

$$4 = n.$$

38. **B**

$$f^{-1}(x) = \sqrt{x - 6}.$$

The graph of f^{-1} is defined for all $x \geq 0$. It intersects the x-axis at the point $(6, 0)$, so Answer B is the correct answer choice.

39. **C** Start by arranging the test scores in order of lowest to highest:

60, 67, 74, 78, 81, 83, 83, 86, 88, 90, 92, 95, 100

The median of the data is 83. To find the interquartile range, find the lower quartile by determining the median of the data to the left of the median, 83. Then, find the upper quartile by determining the median of the data to the right of the median, 83.

$$\text{Lower quartile} = \frac{74 + 78}{2} = 76.$$

$$\text{Upper quartile} = \frac{90 + 92}{2} = 91.$$

The interquartile range is $91 - 76 = 15$.

40. **B**

$$\det X = 9n - (-3)(4) = 0.$$

$$9n + 12 = 0.$$

$$9n = -12.$$

$$n = -\frac{12}{9} = -\frac{4}{3}.$$

41. **D** The first statement is true because

$$\cot x = \frac{\text{adjacent}}{\text{opposite}} = \frac{3}{4}.$$

The second statement is also true because $\cos x = \frac{3}{5}$, and $\sin y = \frac{3}{5}$.

The third statement is not true because $\tan x = \frac{4}{3}$, and $\tan y = \frac{3}{4}$. Answer D is the correct choice.

42. **D** If two variables have a high positive correlation, as one variable increases the other variable also increases. Answer D, "The value of a car and its age," does not represent a positive correlation. In general, as a car ages, its value decreases.

43. **B** If the graph is symmetric with respect to the origin the points (x, y) and $(-x, -y)$ satisfy the equation. Replace x with $-x$ and y with $-y$ to determine if the resulting equation is equivalent to the given one.

For the equation in Answer B:

$$-y = (-x)^3 - 2(-x).$$

$$-y = -x^3 + 2x.$$

$$y = x^3 - 2x.$$

The resulting equation is equivalent to the original, $y = x^3 - 2x$, so the graph is symmetric with respect to the origin.

44. **A** Substitute $x = 3 + t$ into the equation for y to solve for y in terms of t.

$$y = f(t) = -4(3 + t) + 10.$$

$$y = -12 + -4t + 10.$$

$$y = -4t - 2.$$

45. **C** The function $x_{n+1} = \sqrt[3]{-4x_n}$ is recursive. Because you are given the first term of the sequence, you can define the other terms using it.

$$x_0 = 2.$$

$$x_1 = \sqrt[3]{-4(-2)} = -2.$$

$$x_2 = \sqrt[3]{-4 - 2} = 2.$$

$$x_3 = \sqrt[3]{-4 - 2} = -2.$$

$$x_4 = \sqrt[3]{-4 - 2} = 2.$$

46. **B** Use either a Venn Diagram or a table to organize the given information in this problem. Because 16 students are juniors, there are 40 – 16 = 24 sophomores in the group. 18 sophomores study geometry, so 24 – 18 = 6 study algebra 2.

	Sophomores	Juniors
Geometry	18	x
Algebra 2	6	$16 - x$

13 total students study algebra 2.

$6 + 16 - x = 13.$

$22 - x = 13.$

$x = 9.$

The problem asks for the number of juniors studying algebra 2, however. 16 – 9 = 7.

47. **E** If each base angle measures 41°, the vertex angle of the isosceles triangle measures 180 – 2(41) = 98°. Let x = the length of the base. By the Law of Sines:

$$\frac{\sin 41°}{8} = \frac{\sin 98°}{x}.$$

$x \sin 41° = 8 \sin 98°$

$x = 12.1$ cm.

48. **E** First, determine the number of possible ways to choose 3 people from a group of 10.

$$_{10}C_3 = \frac{10!}{3!7!} = 120.$$

Then, determine how many possible ways to choose 2 women from 6 and 1 man from 4.

$$_6C_2 = \frac{6!}{2!4!} = 15.$$

$$_4C_1 = \frac{4!}{1!3!} = 4.$$

The probability that the committee consists of 2 women and 1 man is, therefore, $\frac{15(4)}{120} = \frac{60}{120} = \frac{1}{2}.$

49. **B** The base of each rectangle measures 2 units, and the height of each can be determined by evaluating $y = e^x$ when x equals the smallest value possible in each rectangle. The areas of the three rectangles are:

$A_1 = 2(e^0) = 2.$

$A_2 = 2(e^2) \approx 14.78.$

$A_3 = 2(e^4) \approx 109.20.$

The sum of the three areas is approximately 126 square units.

50. **A**

The lateral area of a cone equals $\frac{1}{2}c\ell$, where c = the circumference of the base and ℓ = the slant height.

For the given cone:

$$L = \frac{1}{2}c\ell = \frac{1}{2}(2\pi)(5)(10)$$

$$= \frac{1}{2}(100\pi) = 50\pi.$$

▰▰▰ DIAGNOSE YOUR STRENGTHS AND WEAKNESSES

Check the number of each question answered correctly and "X" the number of each question answered incorrectly.

Algebra	1	3	4	6	8	9	15	35	Total Number Correct
8 questions									

Solid Geometry	23	33	50	Total Number Correct
3 questions				

Coordinate Geometry	7	10	22	29	36	37	43	Total Number Correct
7 questions								

Trigonometry	11	16	17	27	28	41	47	Total Number Correct
7 questions								

Functions	2	12	18	19	20	21	24	25	26	30	31	34	38	44	45	Total Number Correct
15 questions																

Data Analysis, Statistics, and Probability	13	39	42	48	Total Number Correct
4 questions					

Numbers and Operations	5	14	32	40	46	49	Total Number Correct
6 questions							

Number of correct answers $- \frac{1}{4}$ **(Number of incorrect answers) = Your raw score**

_____ $- \frac{1}{4}$ (_____) = _____

Compare your raw score with the approximate SAT Subject Test score below:

	Raw Score	SAT Subject Test Approximate Score
Excellent	43–50	770–800
Very Good	33–43	670–770
Good	27–33	620–670
Above Average	21–27	570–620
Average	11–21	500–570
Below Average	< 11	< 500

PRACTICE TEST 7

Treat this practice test as the actual test and complete it in one 60-minute sitting. Use the following answer sheet to fill in your multiple-choice answers. Once you have completed the practice test:

1. Check your answers using the Answer Key.
2. Review the Answers and Solutions.
3. Fill in the "Diagnose Your Strengths and Weaknesses" sheet and determine areas that require further preparation.

PRACTICE TEST 7

MATH LEVEL 2

■ ANSWER SHEET

Tear out this answer sheet and use it to complete the practice test. Determine the BEST answer for each question. Then, fill in the appropriate oval using a No. 2 pencil.

1. Ⓐ Ⓑ Ⓒ Ⓓ Ⓔ	21. Ⓐ Ⓑ Ⓒ Ⓓ Ⓔ	41. Ⓐ Ⓑ Ⓒ Ⓓ Ⓔ
2. Ⓐ Ⓑ Ⓒ Ⓓ Ⓔ	22. Ⓐ Ⓑ Ⓒ Ⓓ Ⓔ	42. Ⓐ Ⓑ Ⓒ Ⓓ Ⓔ
3. Ⓐ Ⓑ Ⓒ Ⓓ Ⓔ	23. Ⓐ Ⓑ Ⓒ Ⓓ Ⓔ	43. Ⓐ Ⓑ Ⓒ Ⓓ Ⓔ
4. Ⓐ Ⓑ Ⓒ Ⓓ Ⓔ	24. Ⓐ Ⓑ Ⓒ Ⓓ Ⓔ	44. Ⓐ Ⓑ Ⓒ Ⓓ Ⓔ
5. Ⓐ Ⓑ Ⓒ Ⓓ Ⓔ	25. Ⓐ Ⓑ Ⓒ Ⓓ Ⓔ	45. Ⓐ Ⓑ Ⓒ Ⓓ Ⓔ
6. Ⓐ Ⓑ Ⓒ Ⓓ Ⓔ	26. Ⓐ Ⓑ Ⓒ Ⓓ Ⓔ	46. Ⓐ Ⓑ Ⓒ Ⓓ Ⓔ
7. Ⓐ Ⓑ Ⓒ Ⓓ Ⓔ	27. Ⓐ Ⓑ Ⓒ Ⓓ Ⓔ	47. Ⓐ Ⓑ Ⓒ Ⓓ Ⓔ
8. Ⓐ Ⓑ Ⓒ Ⓓ Ⓔ	28. Ⓐ Ⓑ Ⓒ Ⓓ Ⓔ	48. Ⓐ Ⓑ Ⓒ Ⓓ Ⓔ
9. Ⓐ Ⓑ Ⓒ Ⓓ Ⓔ	29. Ⓐ Ⓑ Ⓒ Ⓓ Ⓔ	49. Ⓐ Ⓑ Ⓒ Ⓓ Ⓔ
10. Ⓐ Ⓑ Ⓒ Ⓓ Ⓔ	30. Ⓐ Ⓑ Ⓒ Ⓓ Ⓔ	50. Ⓐ Ⓑ Ⓒ Ⓓ Ⓔ
11. Ⓐ Ⓑ Ⓒ Ⓓ Ⓔ	31. Ⓐ Ⓑ Ⓒ Ⓓ Ⓔ	
12. Ⓐ Ⓑ Ⓒ Ⓓ Ⓔ	32. Ⓐ Ⓑ Ⓒ Ⓓ Ⓔ	
13. Ⓐ Ⓑ Ⓒ Ⓓ Ⓔ	33. Ⓐ Ⓑ Ⓒ Ⓓ Ⓔ	
14. Ⓐ Ⓑ Ⓒ Ⓓ Ⓔ	34. Ⓐ Ⓑ Ⓒ Ⓓ Ⓔ	
15. Ⓐ Ⓑ Ⓒ Ⓓ Ⓔ	35. Ⓐ Ⓑ Ⓒ Ⓓ Ⓔ	
16. Ⓐ Ⓑ Ⓒ Ⓓ Ⓔ	36. Ⓐ Ⓑ Ⓒ Ⓓ Ⓔ	
17. Ⓐ Ⓑ Ⓒ Ⓓ Ⓔ	37. Ⓐ Ⓑ Ⓒ Ⓓ Ⓔ	
18. Ⓐ Ⓑ Ⓒ Ⓓ Ⓔ	38. Ⓐ Ⓑ Ⓒ Ⓓ Ⓔ	
19. Ⓐ Ⓑ Ⓒ Ⓓ Ⓔ	39. Ⓐ Ⓑ Ⓒ Ⓓ Ⓔ	
20. Ⓐ Ⓑ Ⓒ Ⓓ Ⓔ	40. Ⓐ Ⓑ Ⓒ Ⓓ Ⓔ	

PRACTICE TEST 7

Time: 60 minutes

Directions: Select the BEST answer for each of the 50 multiple-choice questions. If the exact solution is not one of the five choices, select the answer that is the best approximation. Then, fill in the appropriate oval on the answer sheet.

Notes:

1. A calculator will be needed to answer some of the questions on the test. Scientific, programmable, and graphing calculators are permitted. It is up to you to determine when and when not to use your calculator.
2. Angles on the Level 2 test are measured in degrees and radians. You need to decide whether your calculator should be set to degree mode or radian mode for a particular question.
3. Figures are drawn as accurately as possible and are intended to help solve some of the test problems. If a figure is not drawn to scale, this will be stated in the problem. All figures lie in a plane unless the problem indicates otherwise.
4. Unless otherwise stated, the domain of a function f is assumed to be the set of real numbers x for which the value of the function, $f(x)$, is a real number.
5. Reference information that may be useful in answering some of the test questions can be found below.

Reference Information	
Right circular cone with radius r and height h:	Volume $= \frac{1}{3}\pi r^2 h$
Right circular cone with circumference of base c and slant height ℓ:	Lateral Area $= \frac{1}{2}c\ell$
Sphere with radius r:	Volume $= \frac{4}{3}\pi r^3$
	Surface Area $= 4\pi r^2$
Pyramid with base area B and height h:	Volume $= \frac{1}{3}Bh$

▰ PRACTICE TEST 7 QUESTIONS

USE THIS SPACE AS SCRATCH PAPER

1. If $3^x = 18$, $18^x =$
   (A) 2.6
   (B) 3
   (C) 108
   (D) 2,007
   (E) 34,012,224

2. A number k is increased by 12. If the cube root of that result equals -3, $k =$
   (A) -39
   (B) -27
   (C) -15
   (D) 15
   (E) 39

3. $\dfrac{(n!)^2}{(n-1)!^2} =$
   (A) n
   (B) $2n$
   (C) n^2
   (D) $(n-1)^2$
   (E) n^4

4. A point Q is in the second quadrant at a distance of $\sqrt{41}$ from the origin. Which of the following could be the coordinates of Q?
   (A) $(-1, 41)$
   (B) $(-4, 5)$
   (C) $(-8, \sqrt{23})$
   (D) $(5, -4)$
   (E) $(-6, 5)$

5. $\tan \theta (\sin \theta) + \cos \theta =$
   (A) $2 \cos \theta$
   (B) $\cos \theta + \sec \theta$
   (C) $\csc \theta$
   (D) $\sec \theta$
   (E) 1

GO ON TO THE NEXT PAGE

6. What is the domain of $f(x) = \sqrt{2 - x^2}$?

    (A) $x \le \sqrt{2}$

    (B) $x \ge -\sqrt{2}$

    (C) $-\sqrt{2} \le x \le \sqrt{2}$

    (D) $x \le -\sqrt{2}$ or $x \ge \sqrt{2}$

    (E) All real numbers

7. If $6n^3 = 48n^2$, then which of the following is the solution set for n?

    (A) $\{0\}$
    (B) $\{8\}$
    (C) $\{-8, 0, 8\}$
    (D) $\{0, 8\}$
    (E) $\{-8, 8\}$

8. If $f(x) = \sqrt{x}$ and $f[g(x)] = 2\sqrt{x}$, then $g(x) =$
    (A) $4x$
    (B) $2x$
    (C) $2x^2$

    (D) $\dfrac{x}{2}$

    (E) x^3

9. How many 3-person committees can be formed from a group of 10?

    (A) 6
    (B) 60
    (C) 120
    (D) 240
    (E) 720

10. What is the magnitude of vector $\vec{v}$ with initial point $(4, -1)$ and terminal point $(0, 2)$?

    (A) 3
    (B) 4
    (C) 5

    (D) $\sqrt{7}$
    (E) 25

GO ON TO THE NEXT PAGE

11. $p \square q$ is defined as $\dfrac{p^q}{pq}$ for all positive real numbers. Which of the following is equivalent to $\dfrac{p}{2}$?

   (A) $p \square 1$
   (B) $p \square p$
   (C) $p \square \dfrac{1}{2}$
   (D) $1 \square q$
   (E) $p \square 2$

12. If the graph of the equation $y = mx + 5$ has points in the 3rd quadrant, then which of the following must be true for m?

   (A) $m = 0$
   (B) $m < 0$
   (C) $0 < m < 1$
   (D) $m > 0$
   (E) $m = 5$

13. If a is an even integer, and b is an odd integer, then which of the following must be odd?

   (A) ab
   (B) a^b
   (C) $a + b + 1$
   (D) $2b + 1$
   (E) $a - 2b$

14. What is the sum of the coefficients in the expansion of $(1 - 2x)^3$?

   (A) -7
   (B) -1
   (C) 9
   (D) 18
   (E) 27

15. If $25x^2 - 20x + k = 0$ has $\dfrac{2}{5}$ as a double root, $k =$

   (A) 4
   (B) $\dfrac{4}{25}$
   (C) 5
   (D) -5
   (E) 1

GO ON TO THE NEXT PAGE

16. A triangle has sides measuring 3, 5, and 7 inches. What is the measure of its largest angle?

    (A) 135°
    (B) 60°
    (C) 120°
    (D) 150°
    (E) 153°

17. Which of the following is the equation of the circle with x-intercept $(-3, 0)$ and y-intercept $(0, 3)$ whose center is in the 2nd quadrant?

    (A) $(x - 3)^2 + (y - 3)^2 = 9$
    (B) $(x - 3)^2 + (y + 3)^2 = 9$
    (C) $(x + 3)^2 + (y - 3)^2 = 3$
    (D) $(x - 3)^2 + (y + 3)^2 = 3$
    (E) $(x + 3)^2 + (y - 3)^2 = 9$

18. Cost is a function of the number of units produced as given by: $C(n) = 0.02n^2 - 42n + 5,000$. How many units, n, produce a minimum cost C?

    (A) 525
    (B) 1,050
    (C) 2,100
    (D) 17,050
    (E) 125,000

19. Some number n is added to the three numbers $-2, 10,$ and 94 to create the first three terms of a geometric sequence. What is the value of n?

    (A) 1
    (B) 2
    (C) 3
    (D) 4
    (E) 5

20. A right circular cylinder has a height of 15 and a radius of 4. If A and B are two points on the surface of the cylinder, what is the maximum possible length of AB?

    (A) 15.1
    (B) 15.5
    (C) 17
    (D) 21.2
    (E) 26

USE THIS SPACE AS SCRATCH PAPER

GO ON TO THE NEXT PAGE

21. Five integers are arranged from least to greatest. If the median is 12 and the only mode is 5, what is the least possible range for the 5 numbers?

    (A) 5
    (B) 7
    (C) 8
    (D) 9
    (E) 14

22. Which of the following equations only has roots of 4 and $-\dfrac{1}{2}$?

    (A) $2x^3 + x^2 - 32x - 16 = 0$
    (B) $2x^2 + 7x - 4 = 0$
    (C) $2x^2 - 9x - 4 = 0$
    (D) $2x^2 - 7x - 4 = 0$
    (E) $4(2x + 1) = 0$

23. What is the maximum value of $f(x) = 7 - (x - 6)^2$?

    (A) -7
    (B) -6
    (C) 1
    (D) 6
    (E) 7

24. If $\sec \theta < 0$ and $\cot \theta > 0$, then in which quadrant does θ lie?

    (A) I
    (B) II
    (C) III
    (D) IV
    (E) II or III

25. What is the sum of the integers from 1 to 100?

    (A) 4,950
    (B) 5,000
    (C) 5,050
    (D) 9,900
    (E) 10,100

GO ON TO THE NEXT PAGE

26. The ellipse given by the equation $9x^2 + 4y^2 - 36x - 12y + 18 = 0$ is centered at

    (A) $\left(2, \dfrac{3}{2}\right)$

    (B) $\left(4, \dfrac{9}{4}\right)$

    (C) $\left(\dfrac{3}{2}, 2\right)$

    (D) $\left(-2, -\dfrac{3}{2}\right)$

    (E) $(-2, -3)$

27. Which of the following lines are asymptotes of the graph of $f(x) = \dfrac{2(x-4)}{x^2 - 1}$?

    I. $x = 4$
    II. $x = \pm 1$
    III. $y = 0$

    (A) I only
    (B) II only
    (C) I and II only
    (D) II and III only
    (E) I, II, and III

28. On a construction job, there is a 0.08 probability a certain tool is in error of 2% or more. If 4 tools are used, what is the probability that all of them are in error of 2% or more?

    (A) 0.00004
    (B) 0.0005
    (C) 0.02
    (D) 0.40
    (E) 0.32

29. If $\cos 2\theta = \dfrac{2}{7}$, then $\dfrac{1}{\cos^2 \theta - \sin^2 \theta} =$

    (A) -1

    (B) $\dfrac{7}{2}$

    (C) $\dfrac{2}{7}$

    (D) $\dfrac{49}{4}$

    (E) $\dfrac{1}{7}$

USE THIS SPACE AS SCRATCH PAPER

GO ON TO THE NEXT PAGE

30. If $8 \sin^2 \theta + 2 \sin \theta - 1 = 0$, then what is the smallest positive value of θ?

    (A) $7.3°$
    (B) $14.5°$
    (C) $30°$
    (D) $60°$
    (E) $75.5°$

31. What value does $f(x) = \dfrac{3x - 16}{x + 7}$ approach as x gets infinitely large?

    (A) $\dfrac{1}{3}$
    (B) $\dfrac{1}{2}$
    (C) 1
    (D) 2
    (E) 3

32. If $8.1^a = 3.6^b$, then $\dfrac{a}{b} =$

    (A) -0.35
    (B) 0.61
    (C) 0.67
    (D) 1.63
    (E) 1.5

33. A point has rectangular coordinates $(2, 5)$. If the polar coordinates are (r, θ), then $\theta =$

    (A) $21.8°$
    (B) $23.6°$
    (C) $66.4°$
    (D) $68.2°$
    (E) $80.2°$

34. The graph of $f(x) = x^2$ is translated 2 units down and 4 units left. If the resulting graph represents $g(x)$, then $g(-5) =$

    (A) -1
    (B) 3
    (C) 45
    (D) 79
    (E) 81

35. $(12 \sin x)(2 \sin x) - (8 \cos x)(-3 \cos x) =$

    (A) 1
    (B) -1
    (C) 24
    (D) $48 \sin^2 x$
    (E) $24 \sin^2 x - 24 \cos^2 x$

USE THIS SPACE AS SCRATCH PAPER

GO ON TO THE NEXT PAGE

36. If a two dice are rolled, what is the probability the sum of the numbers is 4 or 5?

    (A) $\dfrac{1}{12}$

    (B) $\dfrac{1}{9}$

    (C) $\dfrac{5}{36}$

    (D) $\dfrac{1}{6}$

    (E) $\dfrac{7}{36}$

37. If $f(x) = \dfrac{12}{x}$, then $f^{-1}(-8) =$

    (A) -96
    (B) -1.5
    (C) -0.67
    (D) -0.50
    (E) 1.5

38. Which of the following is an even function?
    (A) $f(x) = 2 \sec x$
    (B) $f(x) = x^3$
    (C) $f(x) = -(x + 3)^2$
    (D) $f(x) = \tan x$
    (E) $f(x) = (x + 1)^4$

39. All of the following functions have a period of π except which one?
    (A) $y = \sin 2x + 2$
    (B) $y = 2 \cos 2x$

    (C) $y = \dfrac{1}{2} \cos 2\pi x$

    (D) $y = 4 \tan x$
    (E) $y = 2 \csc 2x$

40. The French Club consists of 10 members and is holding officer elections to select a president, secretary, and treasurer for the club. A member can only be selected for one position. How many possibilities are there for selecting the three officers?
    (A) 30
    (B) 27
    (C) 72
    (D) 720
    (E) 90

GO ON TO THE NEXT PAGE

41. The graph in Figure 1 could be a portion of the graph of which of the following functions?

   I. $f(x) = x^3 + ax^2 + bx^1 + c$
   II. $g(x) = -x^3 + ax^2 + bx^1 + c$
   III. $h(x) = -x^5 + ax^4 + bx^3 + cx^2 + dx + e$

    (A) I only
    (B) II only
    (C) I and II only
    (D) II and III only
    (E) I, II, and III

USE THIS SPACE AS SCRATCH PAPER

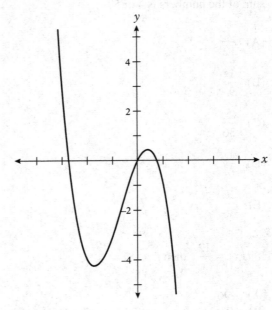

Figure 1

42. If $f(x) = \ln e^{2x}$, then what is the smallest possible integer x such that $f(x) > 10{,}000$?

    (A) 2,501
    (B) 4,999
    (C) 5,000
    (D) 5,001
    (E) 10,001

43. If $\log_2 (x - 1) = \log_4 (x - 9)$, then $x =$

    (A) −2
    (B) 2
    (C) 5
    (D) −2 or 5
    (E) No solution

44. If $[n]$ represents the greatest integer less than or equal to n, then which of the following is the solution to $2[n] - 16 = 6$?

    (A) $n = 11$
    (B) $11 \le n < 12$
    (C) $n = 12$
    (D) $11 < n < 12$
    (E) $11 < n \le 12$

45. If a rectangular prism has faces with areas of 10, 12 and 30 units², then what is its volume?

    (A) 30
    (B) 60
    (C) 90
    (D) 120
    (E) 150

GO ON TO THE NEXT PAGE

46. Given θ is in the first quadrant, if sec θ = 3, what is the value of sin 2θ?

    (A) 0.63
    (B) 0.31
    (C) 0.33
    (D) 0.67
    (E) 0.94

47. What are the intercepts of the circle given by the equation $(x + 4)^2 + (y - 4)^2 = 2$?

    (A) (−4, 0), (0, 4)
    (B) (4, 0), (0, −4)
    (C) (0, ±4), (±4, 0)
    (D) (0, −4), (−4, 0)
    (E) There are no intercepts.

48. The mean score on a math test is 85%. If the teacher decides to scale the grades by increasing each score by 5 percentage points, what is the new mean of the data?

    (A) 85%
    (B) 86%
    (C) 87.5%
    (D) 88%
    (E) 90%

49. If $0 \le x \le \dfrac{\pi}{2}$, $f(x) = \sin(\arctan x)$ and $g(x) = \tan(\arcsin x)$, then $f\left(g\left(\dfrac{1}{4}\right)\right) =$

    (A) 0.26
    (B) 0.75
    (C) 0.25
    (D) 1.25
    (E) 0.24

50. $|6 - 3i| =$

    (A) 3
    (B) $3\sqrt{5}$
    (C) 9
    (D) $3\sqrt{3}$
    (E) 45

S T O P

IF YOU FINISH BEFORE TIME IS CALLED, YOU MAY CHECK YOUR WORK ON THIS TEST ONLY.
DO NOT TURN TO ANY OTHER TEST IN THIS BOOK.

USE THIS SPACE AS SCRATCH PAPER

ANSWER KEY

1. D	11. E	21. D	31. E	41. D
2. A	12. D	22. D	32. B	42. D
3. C	13. D	23. E	33. D	43. E
4. B	14. B	24. C	34. A	44. B
5. D	15. A	25. C	35. C	45. B
6. C	16. C	26. A	36. E	46. A
7. D	17. E	27. D	37. B	47. E
8. A	18. B	28. A	38. A	48. E
9. C	19. D	29. B	39. C	49. C
10. C	20. C	30. B	40. D	50. B

ANSWERS AND SOLUTIONS

1. **D** Take either the log or natural log of both sides of the equation to solve for x.

$$3^x = 18.$$
$$\log 3^x = \log 18.$$
$$x \log 8 = \log 18.$$
$$x = \frac{\log 18}{\log 3} \approx 2.6309.$$
$$18^x = 18^{2.309} \approx 2,007.$$

2. **A**

$$(k + 12)^{\frac{1}{3}} = -3.$$

Cube each side of the equation to solve for k.

$$\left[(k + 12)^{\frac{1}{3}}\right]^3 = (-3)^3.$$
$$k + 12 = -27.$$
$$k = -39.$$

3. **C**

$$\frac{(n!)^2}{(n-1)!^2}$$
$$= \left[\frac{n!}{(n-1)!}\right]^2$$
$$= n^2.$$

4. **B** $(-4, 5)$ is the only given point that is both in the second quadrant and at a distance of $\sqrt{41}$ from the origin.

$$\sqrt{(-4 - 0)^2 + (5 - 0)^2} =$$
$$\sqrt{4^2 + 5^2} =$$
$$\sqrt{16 + 25} =$$
$$\sqrt{41}.$$

5. **D**

$$\tan \theta(\sin \theta) + \cos \theta =$$

$$\frac{\sin \theta}{\cos \theta}(\sin \theta) + \cos \theta =$$

$$\frac{\sin^2 \theta}{\cos \theta} + \frac{\cos^2 \theta}{\cos \theta} =$$

$$\frac{\sin^2 \theta + \cos^2 \theta}{\cos \theta} =$$

$$\frac{1}{\cos \theta} = \sec \theta.$$

6. **C** The radicand must be greater than or equal to zero.

$$2 - x^2 \geq 0.$$

$$2 \geq x^2.$$

$$x \leq -\sqrt{2} \text{ or } x \geq \sqrt{2}.$$

7. **D**

$$6n^3 = 48n^2.$$

$$6n^3 - 48n^2 = 0.$$

$$6n^2(n - 8) = 0n = 0 \text{ or } 8.$$

8. **A** Because you know the composition of f and g results in $2\sqrt{x}$, you need to determine what input value of f will result in $2\sqrt{x}$.

$$\sqrt{4x} = 2\sqrt{x}.$$

Therefore, $g(x) = 4x$. Test your answer by checking the composition.

$$g(x) = 4x, \text{ so } f(g(x)) = f(4x) = \sqrt{4x} = 2\sqrt{x}.$$

9. **C**

$$\frac{10!}{3!(10 - 3)!} = \frac{10!}{3!7!}.$$

$$= \frac{8 \times 9 \times 10}{1 \times 2 \times 3}.$$

$$= 120.$$

10. **C** The components of v are given by $(4 - 0, -1 - 2)$, or $(4, -3)$. The magnitude is the length of v.

$$\|v\| = \sqrt{4^2 + (-3)^2}.$$

$$\|v\| = \sqrt{25}.$$

$$\|v\| = 5.$$

11. **E**

$$p \square 2 = \frac{p^2}{p(2)}.$$

$$= \frac{p}{2}.$$

12. **D** Because the y-intercept of the line $y = mx + 5$ is positive, then the slope of the line must be positive in order for part of the line to fall in the 3rd quadrant. $m > 0$ is the correct answer choice.

13. **D** Because b is odd, multiplying b by two will always result in an even number. Adding one to an even product will always result in an odd number, so Answer D is the correct choice. If you're not sure about number theory, try substituting values for a and b. Let $a = 4$ and $b = 3$.

$$ab = 4(3) = 12.$$

$$a^b = 4^3 = 64.$$

$$a + b + 1 = 4 + 3 + 1 + 8.$$

$$2b + 1 = 2(3) + 1 = 7.$$

$$a - 2b = 4 - 2(3) = 4 - 6 = -2.$$

7 is the only odd result.

14. **B** The binomial expansion of $(1 - 2x)^3$ is:

$$1 - 6x + 12x^2 - 8x^3.$$

The sum of the coefficients is therefore: $1 + (-6) + 12 + (-8) = -1$.

15. **A** Because $\frac{2}{5}$ is a double root, $\left(x - \frac{2}{5}\right)$ is a factor of the quadratic equation two times.

$$\left(x - \frac{2}{5}\right)\left(x - \frac{2}{5}\right) = 0.$$

$$(5x - 2)(5x - 2) = 0.$$

$$25x^2 - 10x + 4 = 0.$$

$$k = 4.$$

16. **C** The largest angle of a triangle is opposite its longest side. Let θ = the largest angle of the triangle. θ is opposite the side measuring 7 inches. Using the Law of Cosines:

$$7^2 = 3^2 + 5^2 - 2(3)(5) \cos \theta.$$

$$49 = 9 + 25 - 30 \cos \theta.$$

$$15 = -30 \cos \theta.$$

$$\cos \theta = -\frac{1}{2}.$$

$$\theta = \cos^{-1} -\frac{1}{2} \approx 120°.$$

17. **E** Because the center of the circle must lie in the 2nd quadrant, its coordinates are $(-3, 3)$. The radius of the circle is $3^2 = 9$.

Therefore, the standard form of the equation of the circle is $(x + 3)^2 + (y - 3)^2 = 9$.

18. **B** The minimum value of a quadratic equation $ax^2 + bx + c$ occurs when $x = -\frac{b}{2a}$. When graphed the minimum occurs at the vertex of a parabola that is concave up.

$$C(n) = 0.02n^2 - 42n + 5,000.$$

$$n = -\frac{b}{2a} = -\frac{(-42)}{2(0.02)} = 1,050 \text{ units.}$$

19. **D** For the three terms to be part of a geometric sequence there must be a common ratio between consecutive terms. Add n to each of the three terms to get the progression $-2 + n$, $10 + n$, $94 + n$. Now, set the common ratios equal to each other and solve for n.

$$\frac{10 + n}{-2 + n} = \frac{94 + n}{10 + n}$$

$$(10 + n)(10 + n) = (-2 + n)(94 + n).$$

$$100 + 20n + n^2 = -188 + 92n + n^2.$$

$$288 = 72n.$$

$$n = 4.$$

20. **C** Think of A and B as vertices of a right triangle with one leg measuring 8 units (the diameter of the cylinder's base) and one leg measuring 15 units (the height).

$$AB = \sqrt{8^2 + 15^2}.$$

$$AB = \sqrt{64 + 225}.$$

$$AB = \sqrt{289} = 17.$$

21. **D** Because the median is 12, the 3rd term when arranged from least to greatest is 12. The mode is 5, so the 2 integers less than 12 equal 5. Note that 5 is the *only* mode. Because the problem asks for the *least* possible range, assume the five integers are:

5, 5, 12, 13, 14

The range equals $14 - 5$, or 9.

22. **D** An equation with roots of 4 and $-\frac{1}{2}$ has factors $x - 4$ and $x + \frac{1}{2}$.

$$(x - 4)\left(x + \frac{1}{2}\right) = 0.$$

$$(x - 4)(2x + 1) = 0.$$

$$2x^2 + x - 8x - 4 = 0.$$

$$2x^2 - 7x - 4 = 0.$$

23. **E** The maximum value of $f(x) = 7 - (x - 6)^2$ is the y-coordinate of its vertex.

$$f(x) = 7 - (x - 6)^2$$

$$y - 7 = -(x - 6)^2$$

The vertex is $(6, 7)$, so the maximum value is 7.

24. **C**

If $\sec \theta < 0$, then $\cos \theta < 0$.

If $\cot \theta > 0$, then $\tan \theta > 0$.

The cosine is negative in both quadrants II and III. For the tangent to be positive, however, $\sin \theta$ must also be a negative value. This occurs in quadrant III only.

25. **C** The integers from 1 to 100 form an arithmetic sequence having 100 terms. $n = 100$, $a_1 = 1$, and $a_n = 100$. Substitute these values into the formula for the sum of a finite arithmetic sequence to get:

$$S_n = 1 + 2 + 3 + 4 + 5 + \cdots + 100.$$

$$S_n = \frac{n}{2}(a_1 + a_n).$$

$$S_n = \frac{100}{2}(1 + 100).$$

$$S_n = 50(101) = 5,050.$$

26. **A** Complete the square to write the equation of the ellipse in standard form.

$$9x^2 + 4y^2 - 36x - 12y + 18 = 0.$$

$$(9x^2 - 36x) + (4y^2 - 12y) = -18.$$

$$9(x^2 - 4x + 4) + 4\left(y^2 - 3y + \frac{9}{4}\right) = -18 + 36 + 9.$$

$$9(x - 2)^2 + \left(y - \frac{3}{2}\right)^2 = 27.$$

$$\frac{(x - 2)^2}{3} + \frac{\left(y - \left(\frac{3}{2}\right)\right)^2}{\left(\frac{27}{4}\right)} = 1.$$

The center of the ellipse is $\left(2, \frac{3}{2}\right)$.

27. **D** The function $f(x) = \dfrac{2(x - 4)}{x^2 - 1}$ has vertical asymptotes at the zeroes of the denominator.

$$x^2 - 1 = 0.$$

$$x = \pm 1.$$

Because the degree of the numerator is less than the degree of the denominator, a horizontal asymptote exists at $y = 0$.

Statements II and III are, therefore, true.

28. **A** The probability that all 4 tools are in error of 2% or more is:

$$0.08(0.08)(0.08)(0.08) \approx 04.10 \times 10^{-5}.$$

29. **B** The double angle formula for cosine is:

$$\cos 2\theta = \cos^2 \theta - \sin^2 \theta.$$

Since $\cos 2\theta = \dfrac{2}{7}$, $\cos^2 \theta - \sin^2 \theta$ also equals $\dfrac{2}{7}$.

$$\frac{1}{\cos^2 \theta - \sin^2 \theta} = \frac{1}{\frac{2}{7}} = \frac{7}{2}.$$

30. **B** Factor the equation and solve for θ.

$$8 \sin^2 \theta + 2 \sin \theta - 1 = 0.$$

$$(4 \sin \theta - 1)(2 \sin \theta + 1) = 0.$$

$$\sin \theta = -\frac{1}{2} \text{ or } \sin \theta = \frac{1}{4}.$$

$$\theta \approx -30° \text{ or } 14.5°.$$

14.5° is the smallest positive value of θ.

31. **E** Graph the function to see that it has a horizontal asymptote at $y = 3$. (Because the degree of the numerator equals the degree of the denominator, a horizontal asymptote occurs at $\dfrac{3}{1}$, the ratio of the coefficients of the x terms.)

Alternately, you can evaluate the function at a large value of x. For example, let $x = 10,000$:

$$f(10,000) = \frac{3(10,000) - 16}{10,000 + 7}$$

$$= 2.9963.$$

The function approaches 3 as x gets infinitely large.

32. **B** Take the logarithm of both sides of the equation to solve for $\dfrac{a}{b}$.

$$8.1^a = 3.6^b.$$

$$a \log 8.1 = b \log 3.6.$$

$$\frac{a}{b} = \frac{\log 3.6}{\log 8.1}.$$

$$\frac{a}{b} \approx 0.61.$$

33. **D** Because the rectangular coordinates (x, y) are (2, 5):

$$\tan \theta = \frac{y}{x} = \frac{5}{2}.$$

$$\tan^{-1}\left(\frac{5}{2}\right) \approx 68.2°.$$

34. **A** Translating the graph of $f(x) = x^2$ 2 units down and 4 units left results in:

$$g(x) = (x + 4)^2 - 2$$

Now, evaluate the function for $x = -5$.

$$g(-5) = (-5 + 4)^2 - 2 = 1 - 2 = -1.$$

35. **C**

$$(12 \sin x)(2 \sin x) - (8 \cos x)(-3 \cos x) =$$

$$24 \sin^2 x + 24 \cos^2 x =$$

$$24(\sin^2 x + \cos^2 x) =$$

$$24(1) = 24.$$

36. **E** There are 36 possible outcomes when two dice are rolled. The following rolls result in a sum of 4 or 5:

$$\{(2,2), (3,1), (1,3), (4,1), (1,4), (2,3), (3,2)\}$$

Seven out of the 36 have a sum of 4 or 5, so the probability is $\frac{7}{36}$.

37. **B** Reflecting the graph of $f(x) = \frac{12}{x}$ over the line $y = x$ results in the original function. The inverse function of $f(x) = \frac{12}{x}$ is, therefore, $f^{-1}(x) = \frac{12}{x}$.

$$f^{-1}(-8) = \frac{12}{-8} = -1.5.$$

38. **A** Recall that a function is even if it is symmetric with respect to the y-axis and $f(-x) = f(x)$.

Because the cosine function is an even function, its reciprocal function, the secant function, is also even. Answer A is the correct answer choice.

39. **C** All of the functions have a period of $\frac{2\pi}{2}$ or π with the exception of $y = \frac{1}{2} \cos 2\pi x$. It has a period of $\frac{2\pi}{2\pi} = 1$. Answer C is the correct answer choice.

40. **D** There are 10 possible people that could serve as president. Once the president is chosen, there are 9 possible people that could serve as secretary, and once that person is chosen, there are 8 remaining people that could serve as treasurer. The total number of ways of selecting the three officers is:

$$10 \times 9 \times 8 = 720.$$

41. **D** The graph has three zeroes. Because it rises to the left and falls to the right, it represents an odd-degree polynomial with a negative leading coefficient. Either statement II or III are possible answers.

42. **D** Because $f(x) = \ln e^{2x}$ must be greater than 10,000:

$$2x > 10,000$$

$$x > 5,000$$

The smallest possible integer greater than 5,000 is 5,001.

43. **E** Use the change of base formula to rewrite the right side of the equation.

$$\log_2(x - 1) = \log_4(x - 9).$$

$$\log_2(x - 1) = \frac{\log_2(x - 9)}{\log_2 4}.$$

$$\log_2(x - 1) = \frac{\log_2(x - 9)}{2}.$$

Now, solve for x.

$$2 \log_2(x - 1) = \log_4(x - 9).$$

$$(x - 1)^2 = x - 9.$$

$$x^2 - 2x + 1 = x - 9.$$

$$x^2 - 3x + 10 = 0.$$

Solving for x using the quadratic formula results in no real solution.

44. **B**

$$2[n] - 16 = 6.$$

$$2[n] = 22.$$

$$[n] = 11.$$

11 is the greatest integer less than or equal to n, so n must be on the interval $11 \leq n < 12$.

45. **B** Let w = the width, l = the length, and h = the height of the prism. Using the three given areas:

$$wh = 10.$$

$$wl = 30.$$

$$lh = 12.$$

Use substitution to solve for the variables and determine $w = 5$, $l = 6$, and $h = 2$.

The volume is, therefore, $6 \times 5 \times 2 = 60$ units³.

46. **A** If $\sec \theta = 3$, then $\cos \theta = \dfrac{1}{3}$. Picture a right triangle in quadrant I to determine that the value of $\sin \theta = \dfrac{2\sqrt{2}}{3}$.

Recall the double angle formula for sine:

$$\sin 2\theta = 2 \sin \theta \cos \theta.$$

$$\sin 2\theta = 2\left(\frac{2\sqrt{2}}{3}\right)\left(\frac{1}{3}\right) = \frac{4\sqrt{2}}{9} \approx 0.63.$$

47. **E** The circle given by the equation $(x + 4)^2 + (y - 4)^2 = 2$ is centered at $(-4, 4)$ and has a radius of $\sqrt{2}$. Because the radius is less than 4 units long, there are no x and y intercepts.

48. **E** If each score is increased by 5 percentage points, the mean also increases by 5. The new mean would, therefore, be $85 + 5 = 90\%$.

49. **C**

$$g\left(\frac{1}{4}\right) = \tan\left(\arcsin\frac{1}{4}\right) \approx 0.258.$$

$$f(0.258) = \sin(\arctan 0.258) = 0.25.$$

50. **B** Recall that the absolute value of a complex number is given by: $|a + bi| = \sqrt{a^2 + b^2}$.

$$|6 - 3i| = \sqrt{6^2 + (-3)^2} = \sqrt{45} = 3\sqrt{5}$$

▨ DIAGNOSE YOUR STRENGTHS AND WEAKNESSES

Check the number of each question answered correctly and "X" the number of each question answered incorrectly.

Algebra	1	2	3	7	14	32	43	44	Total Number Correct
8 questions									

Solid Geometry	20	45	Total Number Correct
2 questions			

Coordinate Geometry	4	12	17	26	33	34	47	Total Number Correct
7 questions								

Trigonometry	5	16	24	29	30	35	46	49	Total Number Correct
8 questions									

Functions	6	8	15	18	22	23	27	37	38	39	41	42	Total Number Correct
12 questions													

Data Analysis, Statistics, and Probability	21	28	36	48	Total Number Correct
4 questions					

Numbers and Operations	9	10	11	13	19	25	31	40	50	Total Number Correct
9 questions										

Number of correct answers − $\frac{1}{4}$ (Number of incorrect answers) = Your raw score

_____ − $\frac{1}{4}$ (_____) = _____

Compare your raw score with the approximate SAT Subject Test score below:

	Raw Score	SAT Subject Test Approximate Score
Excellent	43–50	770–800
Very Good	33–43	670–770
Good	27–33	620–670
Above Average	21–27	570–620
Average	11–21	500–570
Below Average	< 11	< 500

PRACTICE TEST 8

Treat this practice test as the actual test and complete it in one 60-minute sitting. Use the following answer sheet to fill in your multiple-choice answers. Once you have completed the practice test:

1. Check your answers using the Answer Key.
2. Review the Answers and Solutions.
3. Fill in the "Diagnose Your Strengths and Weaknesses" sheet and determine areas that require further preparation.

PRACTICE TEST 8

MATH LEVEL 2

ANSWER SHEET

Tear out this answer sheet and use it to complete the practice test. Determine the BEST answer for each question. Then, fill in the appropriate oval using a No. 2 pencil.

1. Ⓐ Ⓑ Ⓒ Ⓓ Ⓔ	21. Ⓐ Ⓑ Ⓒ Ⓓ Ⓔ	41. Ⓐ Ⓑ Ⓒ Ⓓ Ⓔ
2. Ⓐ Ⓑ Ⓒ Ⓓ Ⓔ	22. Ⓐ Ⓑ Ⓒ Ⓓ Ⓔ	42. Ⓐ Ⓑ Ⓒ Ⓓ Ⓔ
3. Ⓐ Ⓑ Ⓒ Ⓓ Ⓔ	23. Ⓐ Ⓑ Ⓒ Ⓓ Ⓔ	43. Ⓐ Ⓑ Ⓒ Ⓓ Ⓔ
4. Ⓐ Ⓑ Ⓒ Ⓓ Ⓔ	24. Ⓐ Ⓑ Ⓒ Ⓓ Ⓔ	44. Ⓐ Ⓑ Ⓒ Ⓓ Ⓔ
5. Ⓐ Ⓑ Ⓒ Ⓓ Ⓔ	25. Ⓐ Ⓑ Ⓒ Ⓓ Ⓔ	45. Ⓐ Ⓑ Ⓒ Ⓓ Ⓔ
6. Ⓐ Ⓑ Ⓒ Ⓓ Ⓔ	26. Ⓐ Ⓑ Ⓒ Ⓓ Ⓔ	46. Ⓐ Ⓑ Ⓒ Ⓓ Ⓔ
7. Ⓐ Ⓑ Ⓒ Ⓓ Ⓔ	27. Ⓐ Ⓑ Ⓒ Ⓓ Ⓔ	47. Ⓐ Ⓑ Ⓒ Ⓓ Ⓔ
8. Ⓐ Ⓑ Ⓒ Ⓓ Ⓔ	28. Ⓐ Ⓑ Ⓒ Ⓓ Ⓔ	48. Ⓐ Ⓑ Ⓒ Ⓓ Ⓔ
9. Ⓐ Ⓑ Ⓒ Ⓓ Ⓔ	29. Ⓐ Ⓑ Ⓒ Ⓓ Ⓔ	49. Ⓐ Ⓑ Ⓒ Ⓓ Ⓔ
10. Ⓐ Ⓑ Ⓒ Ⓓ Ⓔ	30. Ⓐ Ⓑ Ⓒ Ⓓ Ⓔ	50. Ⓐ Ⓑ Ⓒ Ⓓ Ⓔ
11. Ⓐ Ⓑ Ⓒ Ⓓ Ⓔ	31. Ⓐ Ⓑ Ⓒ Ⓓ Ⓔ	
12. Ⓐ Ⓑ Ⓒ Ⓓ Ⓔ	32. Ⓐ Ⓑ Ⓒ Ⓓ Ⓔ	
13. Ⓐ Ⓑ Ⓒ Ⓓ Ⓔ	33. Ⓐ Ⓑ Ⓒ Ⓓ Ⓔ	
14. Ⓐ Ⓑ Ⓒ Ⓓ Ⓔ	34. Ⓐ Ⓑ Ⓒ Ⓓ Ⓔ	
15. Ⓐ Ⓑ Ⓒ Ⓓ Ⓔ	35. Ⓐ Ⓑ Ⓒ Ⓓ Ⓔ	
16. Ⓐ Ⓑ Ⓒ Ⓓ Ⓔ	36. Ⓐ Ⓑ Ⓒ Ⓓ Ⓔ	
17. Ⓐ Ⓑ Ⓒ Ⓓ Ⓔ	37. Ⓐ Ⓑ Ⓒ Ⓓ Ⓔ	
18. Ⓐ Ⓑ Ⓒ Ⓓ Ⓔ	38. Ⓐ Ⓑ Ⓒ Ⓓ Ⓔ	
19. Ⓐ Ⓑ Ⓒ Ⓓ Ⓔ	39. Ⓐ Ⓑ Ⓒ Ⓓ Ⓔ	
20. Ⓐ Ⓑ Ⓒ Ⓓ Ⓔ	40. Ⓐ Ⓑ Ⓒ Ⓓ Ⓔ	

PRACTICE TEST 8

Time: 60 minutes

Directions: Select the BEST answer for each of the 50 multiple-choice questions. If the exact solution is not one of the five choices, select the answer that is the best approximation. Then, fill in the appropriate oval on the answer sheet.

Notes:

1. A calculator will be needed to answer some of the questions on the test. Scientific, programmable, and graphing calculators are permitted. It is up to you to determine when and when not to use your calculator.
2. Angles on the Level 2 test are measured in degrees and radians. You need to decide whether your calculator should be set to degree mode or radian mode for a particular question.
3. Figures are drawn as accurately as possible and are intended to help solve some of the test problems. If a figure is not drawn to scale, this will be stated in the problem. All figures lie in a plane unless the problem indicates otherwise.
4. Unless otherwise stated, the domain of a function f is assumed to be the set of real numbers x for which the value of the function, $f(x)$, is a real number.
5. Reference information that may be useful in answering some of the test questions can be found below.

Reference Information	
Right circular cone with radius r and height h:	Volume $= \dfrac{1}{3}\pi r^2 h$
Right circular cone with circumference of base c and slant height ℓ:	Lateral Area $= \dfrac{1}{2}c\ell$
Sphere with radius r:	Volume $= \dfrac{4}{3}\pi r^3$ Surface Area $= 4\pi r^2$
Pyramid with base area B and height h:	Volume $= \dfrac{1}{3}Bh$

▮ PRACTICE TEST 8 QUESTIONS

1. If $i = \sqrt{-1}$, then $(6 - i)(6 + i) =$

   (A) 35
   (B) $36 - i$
   (C) 37
   (D) $35 + 12i$
   (E) 36

2. If $f(x) = x^2 - 8x$, then $2f(2x) =$

   (A) $2x^2 - 16x$
   (B) $4x^2 - 16x$
   (C) $8x^2 - 16x$
   (D) $8x^2 - 32x$
   (E) $4x^2 - 32x$

3. If a function f is an odd function and (x, y) is a point on its graph, then which of the following will also be a point on its graph?

   (A) (y, x)
   (B) $(-x, -y)$
   (C) $(-y, -x)$
   (D) $(x, -y)$
   (E) $(-x, y)$

4. What real values of a and b satisfy the equation $a + b + 14i = 4 + (3a - b)i$?

   (A) $a = 5, b = 1$
   (B) $a = \dfrac{9}{2}, b = \dfrac{1}{2}$
   (C) $a = 5, b = -1$
   (D) $a = 3, b = 1$
   (E) $a = \dfrac{9}{2}, b = -\dfrac{1}{2}$

5. Standing 25 feet away from a tree, the angle of elevation of the top of the tree is 26°. Assuming the tree grows perpendicular to the ground, what is its height?

   (A) 12.2 ft
   (B) 16.2 ft
   (C) 19.1 ft
   (D) 21.2 ft
   (E) 29.5 ft

GO ON TO THE NEXT PAGE ▶

6. If $\sin \theta = -\dfrac{9}{41}$ and $\pi < \theta < \dfrac{3\pi}{2}$, then $\cos \theta =$

   (A) $-\dfrac{40}{41}$

   (B) $-\dfrac{9}{40}$

   (C) $-\dfrac{32}{41}$

   (D) $\dfrac{9}{40}$

   (E) $\dfrac{40}{41}$

7. Which of the following is an equation of the line with x-intercept of 5 and y-intercept of -1?

   (A) $\dfrac{1}{5}x - y = -1$

   (B) $\dfrac{1}{5}x + y = 1$

   (C) $x - 5y = 5$

   (D) $x + 5y = -5$

   (E) $x - 5y = -5$

8. The product of the roots of a quadratic equation is -5 and their sum is -4. Which of the following could be the quadratic equation?

   (A) $x^2 - 4x + 5 = 0$
   (B) $x^2 - 4x - 5 = 0$
   (C) $x^2 + 4x - 5 = 0$
   (D) $x^2 + 5x - 4 = 0$
   (E) $x^2 - 5x - 4 = 0$

9. If $f(n) = 9^{-n}$, then $f\left(-\dfrac{1}{4}\right) =$

   (A) $9^{-\frac{1}{4}}$
   (B) 3
   (C) $\sqrt{3}$
   (D) $\dfrac{1}{9}$
   (E) 9

10. If $\log_4 x + 3 \log_4 x = 9$, then $x =$

   (A) 1.86
   (B) 2.25
   (C) 9
   (D) 22.6
   (E) 256

GO ON TO THE NEXT PAGE

11. If $f(x) = |x^2 - 5|$ for $-1 \leq x \leq 4$, then what is the range of f?

    (A) $y \geq 0$
    (B) $y \leq 11$
    (C) $4 \leq y \leq 11$
    (D) $0 \leq y \leq 11$
    (E) $0 \leq y \leq 4$

12. $(1 + \sin \theta)(1 - \sin \theta) =$

    (A) $1 - \sin \theta$
    (B) $\cos^2 \theta$
    (C) $1 - 2\sin \theta + \sin^2 \theta$
    (D) $\cos \theta$
    (E) 1

13. What is the minimum value of $f(x) = (x - 1)^2 + 18$?

    (A) -18
    (B) -1
    (C) 19
    (D) 1
    (E) 18

14. Carolyn has 6 magazines. If she wishes to bring 3 of them with her on vacation, how many different combinations of 3 magazines are possible?

    (A) 10
    (B) 18
    (C) 20
    (D) 60
    (E) 80

15. The number of tails showing when a pair of coins was tossed fourteen times was {0, 2, 2, 1, 0, 2, 2, 0, 1, 0, 2, 0, 0, 2}. What is the mean of the data?

    (A) 0
    (B) 0.5
    (C) 1
    (D) 1.5
    (E) 2

16. What is the greatest possible number of points of intersection between a hyperbola and a circle?

    (A) 2
    (B) 3
    (C) 4
    (D) 5
    (E) 6

GO ON TO THE NEXT PAGE

USE THIS SPACE AS SCRATCH PAPER

17. Figure 1 shows one cycle of the graph of $y = -2\cos\left(x + \dfrac{\pi}{4}\right)$. What are the coordinates of the point where the maximum value of the function occurs on the interval shown?

(A) $\left(\dfrac{3\pi}{4}, 2\right)$

(B) $\left(\dfrac{5}{2}, 2\right)$

(C) $(\pi, 2)$

(D) $\left(\dfrac{5\pi}{4}, 2\right)$

(E) $\left(\dfrac{\pi}{2}, 2\right)$

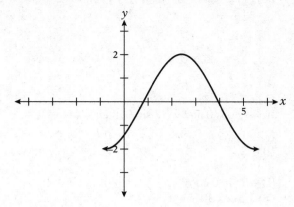

Figure 1

18. Matt's average score on the first four tests of the term is 84%. If he earns a 94% on the fifth test, what will his new average be?

(A) 85%
(B) 86%
(C) 87%
(D) 88%
(E) 89%

19. If a circle has a radius of 4 cm, then what is the length of the arc intercepted by a central angle of 80°?

(A) $\dfrac{\pi}{9}$

(B) $\dfrac{2\pi}{9}$

(C) $\dfrac{4\pi}{9}$

(D) $\dfrac{8\pi}{9}$

(E) $\dfrac{16\pi}{9}$

20. What is the domain of $f(x) = \dfrac{1}{x^2 + 2}$?

(A) $x \neq \pm 2$

(B) $x \neq \pm\sqrt{2}$

(C) $-2 \leq x \leq 2$

(D) $-\sqrt{2} \leq x \leq \sqrt{2}$

(E) All real numbers

GO ON TO THE NEXT PAGE

21. If $f(x) = \sqrt[3]{8x - 1}$, then $f[f^{-1}(2)] =$

    (A) −2

    (B) −1

    (C) 2

    (D) 2.5

    (E) 225

22. If $x = 2 \cos \theta$ and $y = 2 \sin \theta$, then $\sqrt{x^2 + y^2} =$

    (A) 1

    (B) 2

    (C) 4

    (D) $2 \sin \theta \cos \theta$

    (E) $2(\cos \theta + \sin \theta)$

23. Which of the following quadratic equations has roots $7 + i$ and $7 - i$?

    (A) $x^2 - 14x + 49 = 0$

    (B) $x^2 + 14x - 48 = 0$

    (C) $x^2 - 14x + 48 = 0$

    (D) $x^2 - 14x + 50 = 0$

    (E) $x^2 + 14x + 50 = 0$

24. If P is a point on the unit circle in Figure 2, then what are the coordinates of P?

    (A) $(\sin 45°, \cos 45°)$

    (B) $\left(\dfrac{\sqrt{2}}{2}, \dfrac{\sqrt{2}}{2} \right)$

    (C) $(1, 1)$

    (D) $\left(\dfrac{1}{2}, \dfrac{1}{2} \right)$

    (E) $\left(\sqrt{\dfrac{3}{2}}, \dfrac{1}{2} \right)$

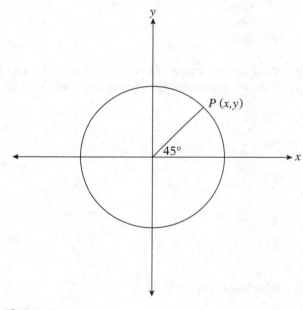

Figure 2

25. What is the remainder when the polynomial $x^4 - 2x^3 - 8x + 5$ is divided by $x - 3$?

    (A) −2

    (B) 2

    (C) 3

    (D) 8

    (E) 164

GO ON TO THE NEXT PAGE

26. In $\triangle ABC$ in Figure 3, $\dfrac{(\sin A \ \tan B)}{\sec A} =$

    (A) $\dfrac{b^2}{c^2}$

    (B) $\dfrac{b}{c}$

    (C) 1

    (D) $\dfrac{ab}{c^2}$

    (E) -1

27. A ball is dropped from a height of 8 feet. If it always rebounds $\dfrac{2}{3}$ the distance it has fallen, how high will it reach after it hits the ground for the third time?

    (A) 5.33
    (B) 3.56
    (C) 2.37
    (D) 1.58
    (E) 2.73

28. The solution set of $7x - 2y < 0$ lies in which quadrants?

    (A) I only
    (B) I and II
    (C) I, II, and III
    (D) I, II, and IV
    (E) I, III, and IV

29. If θ is an acute angle and $\cot \theta = 5$, then $\sin \theta =$

    (A) $5\sqrt{\dfrac{26}{26}}$

    (B) $\dfrac{1}{5}$

    (C) $\sqrt{26}$

    (D) $\sqrt{\dfrac{26}{5}}$

    (E) $\dfrac{\sqrt{26}}{26}$

30. The linear regression model $G = 0.03m + 0.2$ relates grade point average (G) to the number of daily minutes a person spends studying (m). When a person studies for an hour and forty minutes each day, the predicted GPA is

    (A) 2.8
    (B) 3.0
    (C) 3.2
    (D) 3.8
    (E) 4.4

USE THIS SPACE AS SCRATCH PAPER

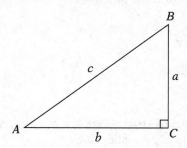

Figure 3

GO ON TO THE NEXT PAGE

31.　If $\dfrac{n!}{2} = (n-1)!$　then $n =$

(A)　1
(B)　2
(C)　3
(D)　4
(E)　8

32.　The sides of a triangle are 4, 5, and 8 cm. What is the measure of its smallest angle?

(A)　42.1°
(B)　70.5°
(C)　59.4°
(D)　24.1°
(E)　30.0°

33.　What is the length of the major axis of the ellipse $\dfrac{4(x+8)^2}{9} + \dfrac{(y-1)^2}{9} = 1$?

(A)　$\dfrac{3}{2}$

(B)　3
(C)　6
(D)　9
(E)　81

34.　If $4^k = 5^{k+3}$, then $k =$

(A)　−21.6
(B)　−15
(C)　−2.5
(D)　0.86
(E)　3.5

35.　If $\sqrt[3]{n} = 7.128$, then $\sqrt[3]{17n} =$

(A)　2.6
(B)　4.1
(C)　121.1
(D)　18.3
(E)　29.4

36.　A cone-shaped cup has a height of 10 units and a radius of 3 units. The cup is filled with water and the height of the water is 6 units. What is the radius of the surface of the water?

(A)　1.5 units
(B)　1.8 units
(C)　2 units
(D)　3 units
(E)　5 units

37. If $x(x-4)(x-2) > 0$, then which of the following is the solution set?

    (A) $0 < x < 2$

    (B) $x < 0$ or $2 < x < 4$

    (C) $x > 0$

    (D) $x < 0$ or $x > 4$

    (E) $0 < x < 2$ or $x > 4$

USE THIS SPACE AS SCRATCH PAPER

38. Assuming each dimension must be an integer, how many different rectangular prisms with a volume of 18 cm³ are there?

    (A) 2

    (B) 3

    (C) 4

    (D) 5

    (E) 6

39. If $2,200 in invested at a rate of 6% compounded quarterly, how much will the investment be worth in 4 years?

    (A) 2,538

    (B) 2,620

    (C) 2,777

    (D) 2,792

    (E) 5,589

40. Assuming $a > 1$, which of the following expressions represents the greatest value?

    (A) $\dfrac{a+1}{a+1}$

    (B) $\dfrac{a}{a+1}$

    (C) $\dfrac{a}{a-1}$

    (D) $\dfrac{a-1}{a-2}$

    (E) $\dfrac{a+1}{a-1}$

41. If $4n + 1$, $6n$, and $7n + 2$ are the first three terms of an arithmetic sequence, what is the sum of the first 20 terms of the sequence?

    (A) 108

    (B) 605

    (C) 830

    (D) 1,210

    (E) 2,420

GO ON TO THE NEXT PAGE

42. Which are the real zeroes of $f(x) = x^3 - 2x^2 - 8x$?

    (A) $x = 0, x = 4$
    (B) $x = 0, x = 4$ and $x = -2$
    (C) $x = 1, x = 4$ and $x = 3$
    (D) $x = 4, x = 5, x = 2$
    (E) $x = 1, x = 4, x = 2$

43. What is the range of $f(x) = -3 \sin(4x + \pi) + 1$?

    (A) $-2 \le y \le 4$
    (B) $-3 \le y \le 3$
    (C) $-\dfrac{1}{2} \le y \le \dfrac{5}{2}$
    (D) $0 \le y \le 2\pi$
    (E) All real numbers

44. If $f(x) = \dfrac{x^2 + 7x + 10}{2x^2 + 3x - 2}$, what value does the function approach as x approaches -2?

    (A) $\dfrac{3}{5}$
    (B) $\dfrac{7}{3}$
    (C) $-\dfrac{5}{3}$
    (D) -2
    (E) $-\dfrac{3}{5}$

45. Figure 4 shows a portion of the graph of which of the following functions?

    (A) $y = \tan(2x) - 2$
    (B) $y = \tan\left(\dfrac{x}{2}\right) - 2$
    (C) $y = \cot\left(\dfrac{x}{2}\right) - 2$
    (D) $y = \cot\left(\dfrac{x}{2} - 2\right)$
    (E) $y = \tan x - 2$

USE THIS SPACE AS SCRATCH PAPER

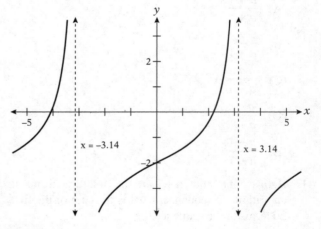

Figure 4

GO ON TO THE NEXT PAGE

USE THIS SPACE AS SCRATCH PAPER

46. $\displaystyle\sum_{k=0}^{7}(-2)^k =$

   (A) −85
   (B) 43
   (C) 128
   (D) 171
   (E) 255

47. A line has parametric equations $x = t - 12$ and $y = 4t - 1$. Given t is the parameter, what is the y-intercept of the line?

   (A) −4
   (B) 12
   (C) 47
   (D) 49
   (E) 4

48. What is the area of the triangle in Figure 5?

   (A) 5.2
   (B) 6.5
   (C) 6.9
   (D) 13.8
   (E) 16.8

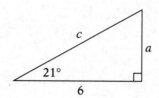

Figure 5

49. In how many ways can the letters of the word SICILY be arranged using all of the letters?

   (A) 60
   (B) 120
   (C) 240
   (D) 360
   (E) 720

50. If students are randomly chosen from a group of 11 boys and 9 girls, what is the probability of choosing 2 boys and 2 girls?

   (A) $\dfrac{11}{969}$

   (B) $\dfrac{132}{323}$

   (C) $\dfrac{30}{1,615}$

   (D) $\dfrac{22}{323}$

   (E) $\dfrac{1}{4,845}$

S T O P

IF YOU FINISH BEFORE TIME IS CALLED, YOU MAY CHECK YOUR WORK ON THIS TEST ONLY.
DO NOT TURN TO ANY OTHER TEST IN THIS BOOK.

ANSWER KEY

1. C	11. D	21. C	31. B	41. D
2. D	12. B	22. B	32. D	42. B
3. B	13. E	23. D	33. C	43. A
4. E	14. C	24. B	34. A	44. E
5. A	15. C	25. D	35. D	45. B
6. A	16. C	26. A	36. B	46. A
7. C	17. A	27. C	37. E	47. C
8. C	18. B	28. C	38. C	48. C
9. C	19. E	29. E	39. D	49. D
10. D	20. E	30. C	40. E	50. B

ANSWERS AND SOLUTIONS

1. **C**

Because $i = \sqrt{-1}$, $i^2 = \sqrt{-1}(\sqrt{-1}) = -1$.

$(6 - i)(6 + i) =$

$36 + 6i - 6i - i^2 =$

$36 - i^2 =$

$36 - (-1) = 37.$

2. **D** Given $f(x) = x^2 - 8x$,

$2f(2x) = 2[(2x)^2 - 8(2x)]$

$= 2(4x^2 - 16x)$

$= 8x^2 - 32x.$

3. **B** An odd function is symmetric with respect to the origin. If (x, y) is a point on f, then $(-x, -y)$, the reflection of the point about the origin, is also on the graph.

4. **E** Because $a + b + 14i = 4 + (3a - b)i$, $a + b = 4$ and $3a - b = 14$. Set up a system and use the linear combination method to solve for a and b.

$a + b = 4$

$\underline{+ \; 3a - b = 14}$

$4a + 0b = 18$

$a = \dfrac{9}{2}$

$\dfrac{9}{2} + b = 4$, so $b = -\dfrac{1}{2}$.

5. **A** Let h = the height of the tree.

$\tan 26° = \dfrac{h}{25}.$

$h = 25(\tan 26°) \approx 12.2$ feet.

6. **A** Think of sine either in terms of the opposite leg and hypotenuse of a right triangle or in terms of the point (x, y) and r of a unit circle. Because $\pi < \theta < \dfrac{3\pi}{2}$, θ lies in quadrant III and its cosine is negative.

$$\sin \theta = -\frac{9}{41} = -\frac{y}{r}.$$

Because $r = \sqrt{x^2 + y^2}$, $41 = \sqrt{x^2 + (-9)^2}$.

$$x = 40.$$

$$\cos \theta = -\frac{x}{r} = -\frac{40}{41}$$

7. **C** The line passes through the points $(5, 0)$ and $(0, -1)$. The slope of the line is $m = \dfrac{1}{5}$.

Because the y-intercept is given, you can easily write the equation in slope-intercept form.

$$y = \frac{1}{5}x - 1.$$

$$x - 5y = 5.$$

8. **C** Recall that a quadratic equation can be thought of as: $a[x^2 - (\text{sum of the roots})x + (\text{product of the roots})] = 0$. Substitute the sum $= -4$, and the product $= -5$ to get:

$$a(x^2 - -4x + -5) = 0.$$

$$a(x^2 + 4x - 5) = 0.$$

When $a = 1$, the result is the equation given in Answer C: $x^2 + 4x - 5 = 0$.

9. **C**

$$f\left(-\frac{1}{4}\right) = 9^{-\left(\frac{-1}{4}\right)} = 9^{\frac{1}{4}}$$

$$= (3^2)^{\frac{1}{4}} = 3^{\frac{2}{4}} = 3^{\frac{1}{2}}$$

$$= \sqrt{3}.$$

10. **D**

$$\log_4 x + 3\log_4 x = 9$$

$$4\log_4 x = 9$$

$$\log_4 x = \frac{9}{4}$$

$$4^{\frac{9}{4}} = x$$

$$x = 22.6.$$

11. **D** Graph $f(x) = |x^2 - 5|$ to determine its range on the specified interval. Because the domain is specified as $-1 \le x \le 4$, the curve has a beginning and an ending point.

When $x = -1$, $y = 4$, and when $x = 4$, $y = 11$. The range is the set of all possible y values, so realize that the y values decrease between 4 and 11. The range is $0 \le y \le 11$.

12. **B** Recall that $\sin^2 \theta + \cos^2 \theta = 1$, so $\cos^2 \theta = 1 - \sin^2 \theta$.

$$(1 + \sin \theta)(1 - \sin \theta) =$$

$$1 + \sin \theta + \sin \theta - \sin^2 \theta =$$

$$1 - \sin^2 \theta =$$

$$\cos^2 \theta.$$

13. **E** The minimum value of the function is the y-coordinate of the parabola's vertex. For the function $f(x) = (x - 1)^2 + 18$, the vertex is $(1, 18)$. (You can check this by graphing the parabola on your graphing calculator.) The minimum value is, therefore, 18.

14. **C**

$$_6C_3 = \frac{6!}{3!(6 - 3)!}$$

$$= \frac{4 \times 5 \times 6}{1 \times 2 \times 3}$$

$$= 20.$$

15. **C** The mean is the sum of the data divided by the number of terms.

$$\frac{(0 + 2 + 2 + 1 + 0 + 2 + 2 + 0 + 1 + 0 + 2 + 0 + 0 + 2)}{14} =$$

$$\frac{14}{14} = 1$$

16. **C** There are 4 possible points of intersection as shown:

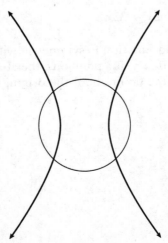

17. **A** The graph of $y = -2\cos\left(x + \dfrac{\pi}{4}\right)$ is the graph of $y = \cos x$ with a phase shift of $\dfrac{\pi}{4}$ units left, an amplitude of 2, and reflected over the x-axis. The maximum value occurs at the point where $x = \pi - \dfrac{\pi}{4} = \dfrac{3\pi}{4}$. The y-coordinate at that point is 2.

18. **B** Let $s =$ the sum of the scores of Matt's first four tests.

$$\dfrac{s}{4} = 84.$$

$$s = 336.$$

Matt's new average is $\dfrac{336 + 94}{5} = 86\%$.

19. **E** Use the formula $s = r\,\theta$, where $s =$ the arc length and $r =$ the radius of the circle. Convert 80° to radian measure first.

$$80\left(\dfrac{\pi}{180}\right) = \dfrac{4\pi}{9} \text{ radians.}$$

Now, solve for the arc length:

$$s = 4\left(\dfrac{4\pi}{9}\right) = \dfrac{16\pi}{9} \text{ cm.}$$

20. **E** The denominator cannot equal zero.

$$x^2 + 2 \neq 0$$

$$x^2 \neq -2.$$

Recall that on the SAT Subject Test, unless otherwise stated, the domain of a function f is assumed to be the set of real numbers x for which $f(x)$ is a real number. Because x is a squared term, it will, therefore, never equal a negative number. The domain is the set of all real numbers.

21. **C** This problem can be done quickly and with little work if you recall that the composition of a function and its inverse function, $f^{-1}[f(x)]$ and $f[f^{-1}(x)]$, equal x.

$$f^{-1}[f(2)] = 2.$$

22. **B**

$$\sqrt{(x^2 + y^2)} = \sqrt{(2\cos\theta)^2 + (2\sin\theta)^2}$$
$$= \sqrt{[4(\cos^2\theta + \sin^2\theta)]}.$$

Recognize that you can use one of the Pythagorean Identities, $\cos^2\theta + \sin^2\theta = 1$, to simplify the expression.

$$= \sqrt{[4(\cos^2\theta + \sin^2\theta)]} = \sqrt{4(1)} = 2.$$

23. **D** The sum of the roots is: $7 + i + 7 - i = 14$.

The product of the roots is: $(7 + i)(7 - i) = 49 - i^2 = 50$.

The quadratic equation is, therefore, given by the equation:

$$a\begin{bmatrix} x^2 - (\text{sum of the roots})x \\ + (\text{product of the roots}) \end{bmatrix} = 0.$$

$$a(x^2 - 14x + 50) = 0.$$

Setting a equal to 1 results in one possible answer:

$$x^2 - 14x + 50 = 0.$$

24. **B** Because the circle is a unit circle, the coordinates of P are $(\cos 45°, \sin 45°)$. This can be simplified to $\left(\dfrac{\sqrt{2}}{2}, \dfrac{\sqrt{2}}{2}\right)$.

If you don't know what the cosine and sine of 45° equal, let (x, y) be the coordinates of P, and draw a right triangle with legs of length x and y. The triangle is a 45°–45°–90° triangle, so use the ratios of the sides of this special right triangle to determine that the coordinates of point P are $\left(\dfrac{\sqrt{2}}{2}, \dfrac{\sqrt{2}}{2}\right)$.

25. **D** Use either synthetic or long division to divide $x^4 - 2x^3 - 8x + 5$ by $x - 3$. Remember to include a zero placeholder for the x^2 term.

$$3\,\underline{|\,1\ -2\ \ 0\ \ -8\ \ 5}$$
$$\ \ \ \ 3\ \ \ 3\ \ \ 9\ \ \ 3$$

The remainder is 8.

26. **A** Use right triangle trigonometry to determine values for the three trigonometric functions.

$$\sin A = \frac{\text{opposite}}{\text{hypotenuse}} = \frac{a}{c}.$$

$$\tan B = \frac{\text{opposite}}{\text{adjacent}} = \frac{b}{a}.$$

$$\sec A = \frac{1}{\cos A} = \frac{\text{hypotenuse}}{\text{adjacent}} = \frac{c}{b}.$$

$$\frac{\sin A \tan B}{\sec A} = \frac{\frac{a}{c}\left(\frac{b}{a}\right)}{\frac{c}{b}}.$$

$$= \frac{\frac{b}{c}}{\frac{c}{b}} = \frac{b^2}{c^2}.$$

27. **C** Recognize that the heights of the bouncing ball form a geometric sequence with a common ratio of $\frac{2}{3}$ and an initial term of 8. After hitting the ground for the first time, the ball will reach a height of $(8)\left(\frac{2}{3}\right) = 5.33$. After the second bounce, the ball will reach a height of $(8)\left(\frac{2}{3}\right)^2 = 3.56$. After the third bounce, the ball will reach a height of $(8)\left(\frac{2}{3}\right)^3 = 2.37$ feet.

28. **C** Solve the inequality for y to get $y > \frac{7}{2}x$. Then, graph the linear equation $y = \frac{5}{2}x$. The solution to the inequality is the shaded area above the line, and that region falls in quadrants I, II, and III.

29. **E** Because θ is an acute angle, think of the right triangle that contains one angle of measure θ.

$$\cot \theta = 5 = \frac{\text{adjacent}}{\text{opposite}}.$$

Solve for the hypotenuse: $x = \sqrt{(5^2 + 1^2)} = \sqrt{26}$.

$$\sin \theta = \frac{\text{opposite}}{\text{hypotenuse}} = \frac{1}{\sqrt{26}} = \frac{\sqrt{26}}{26}.$$

30. **C**

$$G = 0.03m + 0.2.$$

$$G = 0.03(100) + 0.2.$$

$$G = 3.2.$$

31. **B**

$$\frac{n!}{2} = (n - 1)!$$

$$\frac{n!}{(n - 1)!} = 2.$$

$$n = 2.$$

32. **D** The Law of Cosines states: $c^2 = a^2 + b^2 - 2ab \cos \angle C$.

$4^2 = 5^2 + 8^2 - 2(5)(8) \cos \angle C$, where C is the angle opposite the shortest side.

$$16 = 89 - 80 \cos \angle C.$$

$$-73 = -80 \cos \angle C.$$

$$\cos^{-1}\left(\frac{73}{80}\right) = 24.1°$$

33. **C** The length of the major axis equals $2a$. In this problem, $a = \sqrt{9}$.

$$2a = 6.$$

34. **A** Take the log of both sides of the equation to solve for k.

$$\log(4^k) = \log(5^{k+3}).$$

$$k \log 4 = (k + 3)\log 5.$$

$$k\left(\frac{\log 4}{\log 5}\right) = k + 3.$$

$$k(0.86135) = k + 3.$$

$$k = -21.6.$$

35. **D**

$$\sqrt[3]{17n} = (\sqrt[3]{17})(\sqrt[3]{n}) = (\sqrt[3]{17})(7.128)$$

$$= 18.3.$$

36. **B** Filling the cone-shaped cup with water creates a cone similar to the cup itself. The radii and heights of the two cones are proportional. Let r = the radius of the surface of the water.

$$\frac{6}{10} = \frac{r}{3}.$$

$$18 = 10r.$$

$$1.8 = r.$$

37. **E** The critical points of the inequality $x(x - 4)$ $(x - 2) > 0$ are $x = 0, 4$, and 2. Evaluate the 4 intervals created by these points by determining if the inequality is satisfied on each interval. $0 < x < 2$ or $x > 4$ is the correct answer choice.

38. **C** The volume a rectangular prism is given by the formula $V = \ell \times w \times h$, so you need to find three integers whose product is 18. There are four possibilities:

$1 \times 1 \times 18$

$1 \times 2 \times 9$

$1 \times 3 \times 6$

$2 \times 3 \times 3$

39. **D** $A = P\left(1 + \dfrac{r}{n}\right)^{nt}$ where n is the number of times the investment is compounded per year.

$A = 2,200\left(1 + \dfrac{0.06}{4}\right)^{4(4)}$.

$A = 2,200(1.015)^{16}$.

$A \approx 2,792$.

40. **E** Answer A equals one and Answer B is less than one, so both can be eliminated. Because C and E have the same denominator, and $a < a + 1$, C will always be less than E. It can also be eliminated as a possible answer choice. Substitute a few values of a into answers D and E to compare the expressions.

If $a = 7$, $\dfrac{6}{5} < \dfrac{8}{6}$.

If $a = 10$, $\dfrac{9}{8} < \dfrac{11}{9}$.

Answer E will always result in a greater value.

41. **D** Because the expressions represent the terms of an arithmetic sequence, there must be a common difference between consecutive terms.

$6n - (4n + 1) = 7n + 2 - 6n$.

$2n - 1 = n + 2$.

$n = 3$.

The first three terms are, therefore, 13, 18, and 23, making the common difference between terms, d, equal 5. The first term of the sequence is $a_1 = 13$, and the 20th term is $a_{20} = a_1 + (n - 1)d = 13 + (20 - 1)(5) = 108$.

The sum of a finite arithmetic sequence is:

$S_n = \dfrac{n}{2}(a_1 + a_n)$, where n = the number of terms.

$S_n = \dfrac{20}{2}(13 + 108) = 1,210$.

42. **B** Because $f(x)$ is a third-degree function, it can have, at most, three zeroes.

$$x^3 - 2x^2 - 8x = 0.$$
$$x(x^2 - 2x - 8) = 0.$$
$$x(x - 4)(x + 2) = 0.$$
$$x = 0, x = 4, \text{ and } x = -2.$$

43. **A** The function $f(x) = -3 \sin(4x + \pi) + 1$ has an amplitude of $|a| = |-3| = 3$ and a vertical shift of 1 unit up. The range spans from $y = 1 - 3 = -2$ to $y = 1 + 3 = 4$, so $-2 \leq y \leq 6$ is the correct answer choice.

44. **E** Factor the numerator and denominator. Then, simplify the expression and evaluate it when $x = -2$.

$$f(x) = \dfrac{x^2 + 7x + 10}{2x^2 + 3x - 2} = \dfrac{(x + 5)(x + 2)}{(2x - 1)(x + 2)}$$

$$= \dfrac{(x + 5)}{(2x - 1)}$$

When $x = -2$, $\dfrac{(x + 5)}{(2x - 1)} = -\dfrac{3}{5}$.

45. **B** The figure shows the graph of $y = \tan x$ shifted 2 units down with a period of 2π. The correct equation is $y = \tan\left(\dfrac{x}{2}\right) - 2$.

46. **A** Substitute $k = 0, 1, 2, \ldots 7$ into the summation to get:

$1 - 2 + 4 - 8 + 16 - 32 + 64 - 128 = -85$.

47. **C** Because $x = t - 12$, $t = x + 12$. Substitute this value into the second equation to get:

$y = 4(x + 12) - 1$.

$y = 4x + 48 - 1$.

$y = 4x + 47$.

The y-intercept of the resulting line is $(0, 47)$.

48. **C**

$$\text{Area} = \frac{1}{2}(\text{base} \times \text{height})$$

$$A = \frac{1}{2}(6a).$$

Use trigonometry to determine a:

$$\tan 21° = \frac{a}{6}.$$

$$a \approx 2.303.$$

$$A = \frac{1}{2}(6)(2.303) \approx 6.9.$$

49. **D** Find the number of permutations of six letters taken six at a time, 2 of which are repeated.

$$\frac{6!}{2!} = \frac{6 \times 5 \times 4 \times 3 \times 2 \times 1}{2 \times 1} = 360.$$

50. **B**

$$\frac{{}_9C_2({}_{11}C_2)}{{}_{20}C_4} =$$

$$\frac{\left(\dfrac{9!}{2!7!}\right)\left(\dfrac{11!}{2!9!}\right)}{\left(\dfrac{20!}{4!16!}\right)} =$$

$$\frac{1,980}{4,845} = \frac{132}{323}.$$

▬▬ DIAGNOSE YOUR STRENGTHS AND WEAKNESSES

Check the number of each question answered correctly and "X" the number of each question answered incorrectly.

Algebra	10	31	34	35	37	39	Total Number Correct
6 questions							

Solid Geometry	36	38	Total Number Correct
2 questions			

Coordinate Geometry	7	16	28	33	Total Number Correct
4 questions					

Trigonometry	5	6	12	19	22	24	26	29	32	48	Total Number Correct
10 questions											

Functions	2	3	8	9	11	13	17	20	21	23	25	43	45	47	Total Number Correct
14 questions															

Data Analysis, Statistics, and Probability	15	18	30	50	Total Number Correct
4 questions					

Numbers and Operations	1	4	14	27	40	41	42	44	46	49	Total Number Correct
10 questions											

Number of correct answers $-\frac{1}{4}$ (Number of incorrect answers) = Your raw score

_____ $-\frac{1}{4}$ (_____) = _____

Compare your raw score with the approximate SAT Subject Test score below:

	Raw Score	SAT Subject Test Approximate Score
Excellent	43–50	770–800
Very Good	33–43	670–770
Good	27–33	620–670
Above Average	21–27	570–620
Average	11–21	500–570
Below Average	< 11	< 500